SIXTH EDITION

PSYCHOLOGY AND PERSONAL GROWTH

Nelson Goud

Abe Arkoff

Boston   New York   San Francisco
Mexico City   Montreal   Toronto   London   Madrid   Munich   Paris
Hong Kong   Singapore   Tokyo   Cape Town   Sydney

Executive Editor: Carolyn Merrill
Series Editorial Assistant: Jonathan Bender
Senior Marketing Manager: Wendy Gordon
Editorial-Production Service: Omegatype Typography, Inc.
Composition and Prepress Buyer: Linda Cox
Manufacturing Buyer: Joanne Sweeney
Cover Administrator: Kristina Mose-Libon
Electronic Composition: Omegatype Typography, Inc.

For related titles and support material, visit our online catalog at www.ablongman.com.

Between the time Website information is gathered and then published, it is not unusual for some sites to have closed. Also, the transcription of URLs can result in unintended typographical errors. The publisher would appreciate notification where these occur so that they may be corrected in subsequent editions. Thank you.

Library of Congress Cataloging-in-Publication Data

CIP data not available at the time of publication.

ISBN 0-205-33501-2

Printed in the United States of America

10 9 8 7 6 5 4 3 2   07 06 05 04 03

To my children David and Debbie,
and for Bonnie.

—Nelson Goud

For my fellow growers
Susan, Amy, and Ty.

—Abe Arkoff

CONTENTS

SECTION TWO   HUMAN COMMUNICATION   **73**

PREFACE

In 1845, when he was 28 years old, Henry Thoreau began his experiment in living at Walden Pond. He wrote that he went to the woods because "I wished to live deliberately, to front only the essential facts of life, and see if I could not learn what it had to teach, and not, when I came to die, discover that I had not lived" (Thoreau, 1854/1962, p. 172).*

One essential fact of life is how to choose and create an authentic life, a life that is truly lived. Knowing who you are and want to be—your being and becoming—does not require a two-year visit to Walden Pond. You can explore your essence right where you are, right now. This book offers one way to begin this quest of knowing yourself and the life paths you are pursuing. Over eighty readings and thirty-two applied activities are offered that apply psychology to personal growth. These selections focus on six themes: identity, human communication, growth dynamics, human relationships, emotions and feelings, and a quality life.

Some of the selections will have immediate relevance and application. Others may take some thought, discussion, or writing to fully comprehend their message. Each article has a Follow-Up section that provides guidance in interpreting the ideas. You are strongly urged to answer at least one of these questions for each assigned article.

Applied Activities are offered at the end of each of the six sections. These exercises apply and extend the main ideas of the section. Completing these activities will aid in integrating what you've learned into your life.

To Instructors

This book is designed so that most of the articles can be read within a semester. Depending on your teaching style, the articles can be used for small and large group discussion, student journal assignments, or as launching pads for related topics. Some articles are supplemented by short features entitled "Along These Lines," which amplify and expand the points made in the articles and give the reader more to think about. Some students need little or no guidance and others need a great deal of structure in interpreting a reading.

*Thoreau, H. (1854/1962). *Thoreau: Walden and and other writings,* J. W. Krutch, Ed. New York: Bantam Books, Inc.

I have found it helpful to have students complete at least one of the Follow-Up items for every assigned article. I would also recommend that at least one Applied Activity be assigned per section. If you use small groups as part of your instruction, it is suggested that students read Section 2 (Human Communication) prior to any group interaction. Additional teaching suggestions are offered in the supplemental Instructor's Manual and Test Bank.

An Invitation
Students and instructors are invited to share their comments, reading suggestions, or other ideas with me at the address below:

Nelson Goud, Ph.D.
School of Education
Indiana University–Purdue University at Indianapolis
902 W. New York Street
Indianapolis, IN 46202

THANKS

A note of thanks to those who made it possible to complete this book.

Section One   Identity

Carl Rogers. "The Search for Identity." From *Freedom To Learn,* Third edition, by Carl Rogers & H. Jerome Freiberg. Copyright © 1994. Reprinted by permission of Prentice-Hall, Inc., Upper Saddle River, NJ.

Jon Kabat-Zinn. From *Wherever You Go, There You Are.* Copyright © 1994. Hyperion.

Richard Cohen. "Suddenly I'm the Adult?" Reprinted by permission of the author.

Sydney Lewis. "One Foot Out the Door." Copyright © 1996 *A Totally Alien Life-Form: Teenagers* by Sydney Lewis. Reprinted by permission of The New Press.

Len Smith. "The Monster." Printed by permission of the author.

Aaron R. Kipnis and Elizabeth Herron. "Ending the Battle between the Sexes." Reprinted by permission of the authors.

Sam Keen. "On Being A Man." From *Fire In the Belly: On Being a Man.* Copyright © 1991. New York: Bantam Books.

Lillian Rubin. "From Both Sides." From *Intimate Strangers: Men and Women Together.* Copyright © 1983. New York: Harper and Row.

Lisen Stromberg. "Boy in Blue Tutu." From *Mothering,* March/April 1999. Reprinted by permission of the author.

Lois Gould. "X: A Fabulous Child's Story." From the same-titled book published by Daughters Publishing Company, Inc. Copyright © 1972 by Lois Gould. Reprinted by permission of Daughters Publishing Company, Inc.

Christopher A. Schaefer. "Occupational Exploration." Reprinted by permission of the author.

Craig Mosher. "Woodworker." From *The Humanist,* January/February 1975. Reprinted by permission of the author.

"Thoreau on Work." A collection of quotations from *Thoreau: Walden and Other Writings.* Edited by Joseph Wood Krutch. Copyright © 1962. New York: Bantam Books.

Denise Karuth. "If I Were a Car, I'd Be a Lemon." From *Ordinary Moments: The Disabled Experience,* 1984, Ed. Alan J. Brightman, by University Park Press. Reprinted by permission of Alan J. Brightman.

"Think People First" was developed by Ohio Public Images/Public Images Network.

Section Two Human Communication

Warner Burke. "Interpersonal Communication." Reprinted with permission from NTL Institute. From the Selected Series Reading Nine, *Behavioral Science and the Manager's Role*, pp. 78–84, edited by Warner Burke. Copyright © 1969.

Carl Rogers. "To Hear and to Be Heard." From *Freedom To Learn* by Carl Rogers. Copyright © 1969. Reprinted by permission of Prentice-Hall, Inc., Upper Saddle River, NJ.

"John Steinbeck on Listening." From *Log from the Sea of Cortez.* Copyright © 1976. New York: Penguin Books.

Deborah Tannen. "You Just Don't Understand." From *You Just Don't Understand* by Deborah Tannen. Copyright © 1990. Reprinted by permission of HarperCollins Publishers.

Frances Vaughan. "Awakening Intuition." From *Awakening Intuition* by Frances E. Vaughan, Copyright © 1979 by Frances E. Vaughan. Used by permission of Doubleday, a division of Random House, Inc.

Ernest Hartmann, M.D. "Nature and Uses of Dreaming." From *USA Today Magazine*, March 1999.

Lou Beeker Schultz. "Personal Journaling as a Life Companion." Reprinted by permission of the dedicated journaler and "comma writer," Lou Beeker Schultz.

Arthur J. Lange and Patricia Jakubowski. "Assertive, Nonassertive, and Aggressive Behavior." Adapted from *Responsible Assertive Behavior.* Copyright © 1976 by Research Press. Used by permission of Research Press, Champaign, IL.

"Intuitive Problem-Solving through Guided Imagery" activity. Adapted from *Awakening Intuition* by Frances E. Vaughan. Used by permission.

Section Three Growth Dynamics

Abraham Maslow. "Self-Actualizing and Beyond." From *Challenges of Humanistic Psychology,* James Bugental (ed.), 1967, McGraw-Hill. Used by kind permission of James Bugental.

Tom Keating. "Herbie." From *Indiana Faces and Other Places* by Tom Keating. Published by Indiana Only Press in arrangement with Central Newspapers, Inc. and *The Indianapolis Star.* Copyright © 1982. Reprinted by permission of Frank Caperton, Indianapolis Newspapers, Inc.

Harold Bloomfield and Robert B. Kory. "Getting Unstuck: Joyfully Recreating Your Life." From *Inner Joy.* Used by permission of Harold H. Bloomfield. Copyright © 1980 by Harold H. Bloomfield, M.D., and Robert B. Kory.

Poe Ballantine. "Advice to William Somebody." From *The Sun,* June 2000. Used by permission of Poe Ballantine.

Jenny Montgomery. "Left Behind." Originally titled "Suicide Leaves Friends Bewildered." From *The IUPUI Sagamore,* Sept. 19, 2000. Used by permission of Jennifer Montgomery.

Steve Regan. "Think Nanny." Reprinted by kind permission of the ol' Iowan, Dr. Steve Regan.

"Love Maps" activity. Adapted from *The Seven Principles for Making Marriage Work*, by John Gottman and Nan Silver. Copyright © 1999. Three Rivers Press. Used by permission.

Section Five   Emotions and Feelings

Daniel Goleman. "What's Your Emotional IQ?" From *Emotional Intelligence* by Daniel Goleman, Copyright © 1995 by Daniel Goleman. Used by permission of Bantam Books, a division of Random House, Inc.

Wayne Dyer. "Worry." From *Your Erroneous Zones.* © 1976 by Wayne W. Dyer. Reprinted by permission of HarperCollins Publisher, Inc.

Daniel A. Sugarman and Lucy Freeman. "The Positive Face of Anxiety." From *The Search for Serenity,* Macmillan. Copyright © 1970 by Daniel Sugarman and Lucy Freeman. Reprinted by kind permission of Daniel Sugarman.

William A. Sadler, Jr. "The Causes of Loneliness." From *Science Digest,* July 1975. Used by permission of the author.

Wayne Dyer. "Anger." From *Your Erroneous Zones.* © 1976 by Wayne W. Dyer. Reprinted by permission of HarperCollins Publisher, Inc.

Jon Queijo. "Jealousy and Envy: The Demons within Us." From *Bostonia Magazine,* May/June 1988. Reprinted by kind permission of Jon Queijo.

Tom Peyton. "My Tyrant." Originally titled "In Solitude, the True Self Is Revealed." From *The Indianapolis Star,* July 12, 1995. Reprinted by permission of Frank Caperton, Indianapolis Newspapers, Inc.

Sanford Colley. "On the Death of a Father." From the *Journal of Humanistic Education and Development,* 32(2), 89–91. Copyright © 1993 by the American Counseling Association. Reprinted by permission. No further reproduction authorized without written permission of the American Counseling Association.

Judith Viorst. "Loss and Mourning." Reprinted by permission of Simon & Schuster from *Necessary Losses* by Judith Viorst. Copyright © 1986 by Judith Viorst.

Section Six   A Quality Life

Carin Rubenstein and Phillip Shaver. "Active Solitude." From *In Search of Intimacy* by Carin Rubenstein and Phillip Shaver. Copyright © 1982 by Carin Rubenstein and Phillip Shaver. Used by permission of Dell Books, a division of Random House, Inc.

Robert Sullivan. "Personality and Money Orientations." Adapted from "Americans and Their Money," *Worth,* June 1994. © 1994 *Worth* magazine. Reprinted by permission.

O. Henry. "The Last Leaf." Reprinted by permission from *The Best of O. Henry* by O. Henry. Copyright © 1992 by Running Press Book Publishers, published by Courage Books, an imprint of Running Press, Philadelphia and London.

J. William Worden and William Proctor. "Personal Death Awareness (PDA)." From *PDA: Personal Death Awareness* (New York: Prentice-

AND MORE THANKS

There are several pieces in this book which have unnamed authors. These contributions are from students in the senior author's Developing Human Potential course. They wish to remain anonymous but are willing to share their thoughts. I applaud their articulate and caring excerpts, all of which provide a personalized perspective of the book's themes.

All of the illustrations were drawn by Tom McCain, a professional cartoonist, illustrator, and old friend. Copyright © 1996 by tom mcCain and reprinted with permission. Thanks "½" for the usual outstanding work. All photos and captions by Nelson Goud, copyright © 2001.

Great appreciation is extended to those assisting in the preparation and research of the manuscript: Bonnie Beaumont, Emily Runion, Carol Dillon, and Rae Kornbroke. Executive editor Carolyn Merrill and editorial assistant Lara Zeises were valuable guides in the many steps required to complete a manuscript, and my appreciation also extends to Anne Rogers and the crew at Omegatype Typography, Inc., for their usual excellent work.

IDENTITY

What am I? Where am I? Who am I?
No one can answer these questions—
Why have I been so afraid to try?
I know if I look it's all there to see;
So I opened one small door to look inside,
And from out of that door a small voice cried,
"Have you come to set me free?"
It scared me a bit—Should I close the door?
No, I had to find out whose voice had cried,
Should I step inside and ask the voice to say more?
Perhaps if I took just one small glance inside—
So I peered through the door, but all was dim;
Could I summon the courage to step within—
And find the voice before its echo died?

—Anonymous

Who am I? This is the essential question of identity. It is rarely asked in public (thankfully), but is almost always raised during times of personal change. Throughout our lifetime we will be redefining who we think we are. Our identity, or sometimes called our self-concept, is crucial for positioning ourselves in life. It is the center of how we view others and the world. For a brief check of the current status of

1

your identity, provide 10 answers to this question "Who are you?" Just list your answers as quickly as you can.

_____	_____
_____	_____
_____	_____
_____	_____
_____	_____

Your answers may offer some helpful clues about your identity. You may define yourself primarily by *roles* such as age, gender, race, major or occupation, marital status, organizational membership, and so on. You may define yourself by *individual* qualities such as how you think, believe, or feel. Imagine yourself ten years ago looking at the list you just wrote. You probably would have wondered—Who is this person? Our identity both initiates and reflects our development as a person.

The confidence you have in your identity will vary. Sometimes there will be a strong sense of who you are and where you are going in life. Then there are times of questioning and doubt about who this person is inside your skin. Identity changes can occur rapidly or gradually. Some identity changes are forced upon a person, others are natural developmental shifts, and even others are the product of deliberate effort. Most identity change does not occur in the manner hoped for by this undergraduate student:

I am very confused. I am glad I decided to go to a therapist so I can know who I am and where I should be going career-wise. I am glad there is a break before next semester so I can spend time with God and discover who I am and where I am going. I hope I will know before next semester starts.

Perhaps this student found her identity during the holiday break—it *could* happen—but it's unlikely. This student, however, stated what most of us want when confronted with an identity crisis—a quick solution because it is so unsettling.

This section focuses on major issues in identity formation. The articles selected examine identity from several perspectives.

- In "The Search for Identity," Carl Rogers, a major theorist and therapist, discusses how the struggle to discover an identity is a modern problem. He explains how finding and creating an identity is a lifetime journey. His account of how artist Georgia O'Keeffe discovered her artistic identity has relevance for us all.

- In "The Basic Relationship," Abe Arkoff suggests that the way we come to see and regard ourselves is our most fundamental relationship. Included in this piece are explanations of the various forms of self-image and multiple subpersonalities.
- Nelson Goud elaborates on a little known concept of the pioneering psychologist Abraham Maslow called "Rubricizing." He discusses how we place people, including ourselves, into identity categories, and how rubricizing helps or hinders.
- Being aware of what we are experiencing now is the focus of "Mindfulness" by Jon Kabat-Zinn.
- In "Suddenly I'm the Adult?" Richard Cohen provides a personalized history of his identity milestones. Of particular emphasis is how he became an adult. Most of us will quickly spot parallels in our own lives.
- The struggle to become a young adult is the theme of "One Foot Out the Door" by Sydney Lewis.
- Len Smith tells a story of a night facing fears and revitalizing a love life in "The Monster."
- The differing, and sometimes baffling or hostile interactions between men and women are explored by Aaron R. Kipnis and Elizabeth Herron in "Ending the Battle between the Sexes."
- Psychologist/philosopher Sam Keen summarizes some of the dilemmas of the male role in "On Being a Man."
- Lillian Rubin discusses gender differences in expressing feelings in "From Both Sides."
- In "Boy in Blue Tutu," Lisen Stromberg discusses the issues she faces when her son chooses, at times, traditionally feminine activities.
- What would it be like if a person's gender was not known? This topic is elaborated by Lois Gould in "X: A Fabulous Child's Story."
- The world of work is the theme of four short pieces: "Occupational Exploration," by Christopher A. Schaefer; "Woodworker," by Craig Mosher; "Don't Look Too Closely," by Nels Goud; and "Thoreau on Work," quotes from Henry Thoreau.
- Sometimes a major part of one's identity is forced on a person. Such is the case with Denise Karuth. In "If I Were a Car, I'd Be a Lemon," she discusses how she views her world and herself as a person with a physical disability. Karuth reveals how her

life has been drastically affected, but also shows how her personhood is essentially no different from yours or mine.

- Body image, as it relates to one's identity, is explored in Abe Arkoff's "To a Body, with Love." In this piece he demonstrates a unique way of communicating with your body.

You are urged to attempt one or all of the Follow-Up questions at the end of each article. They are designed to personalize the ideas mentioned in the articles. At the end of the section are Applied Activities that extend and apply the concepts presented.

The Search for Identity: A Modern Problem

Carl Rogers

We are, perhaps all of us, engaged in a struggle to discover our identity, the person we are and choose to be. This is a very pervasive search; it involves our clothes, our hair, our appearance. At a more significant level, it involves our choice of values, our stance in relation to parents and others, the relationship we choose to have to society, our whole philosophy of life. It is, in these days, a most perplexing search. As one college woman says:

I'm confused. Just when I think I'm getting my head together, I talk with some fellow who's sure he knows what life is all about. And because I'm uncertain, I'm really impressed. And then when I get away I realize that's his answer. It can't be the answer for me. I've got to find my own. But it's hard when everything is so loose and unsure.

I see this search for one's real self, for identity, as much more of a problem today than it was in the historical past. During most of history, it made little difference whether the individual discovered himself. Perhaps he lived a more comfortable life if he did not because the identity he lived was defined for him. It is interesting to imagine ourselves back in feudal times. The serf was expected to be a serf throughout his life, as were his children after him. In return he was permitted to eke out a meager living, most of his work going to support the lord of the manor, who in turn protected him. The nobleman was, in a more luxurious way, also constricted. He was the lord, responsible for his followers, and his children would continue the role of the nobleman. In our own country, during one dark period of our history, the slave was always the slave and the master always the master. The difficulties of abandoning these role identities are still painfully with us. While the rigidity of the defined role seems incredibly restrictive to us now, it should not blind us to the fact that such rigidity made life simpler in many ways. The cobbler knew that he and his sons would always be cobblers; his wife knew that she and her daughters would always be primarily servants of their husbands. There were almost no options, and peculiarly enough this gave people a type of security that we have left behind. Perhaps one of the few analogies that are comprehensible to us is the peacetime army. Many men and women have come to accept army life with more satisfaction than they had supposed possible. There are almost no decisions: they are told what to wear, how to behave, where to live, and what to do. They can gripe as freely as they wish, without any responsibility for their lives. They are given an identity, told who they are; and the agonizing personal search that most of us must go through is at least temporarily abrogated.

It is for reasons of this sort that I say the search for one's real self is a peculiarly modern problem. The individual's life is no longer defined (though it may be influenced) by one's family, social class, color, church, or nation. We carry the burden ourselves of discovering our identity. I believe the only person today who does not suffer this painful search for self is the person who voluntarily surrenders his or her individual identity to some organization or institution that defines the purposes, the values, the philosophy to be followed. Examples include people who completely commit themselves to some strict religious sect that is sure of all the answers; those who commit themselves to a rigorous ideology (whether revolutionary or reactionary) that defines their philosophy, their life-style, and their actions; those who give themselves completely to science or industry or traditional education (though there are large cracks in the certainties of all these institutions); or, as I mentioned, those who give their lives to the military. I can thoroughly understand the satisfactions and securities that cause individuals to make such commitments, one of which is to gain a certain comfort.

The transition from conformity to freedom creates a strong sense of disequilibrium and discomfort. Yet I suspect that the majority of young people prefer the more painful burden of choosing the uniqueness that is involved in discovering the real self. I know that is my choice. Still, one of the most common fears of people trying to discover who they really are inside is that this undiscovered "me" will turn out to be a worthless, bizarre, evil, or horrible creature. Something of this fear is expressed by a searching student:

I feel my mind is open, kind of like a funnel, and on top there are sparks and exciting things, but down deeper in the funnel it's dark, and I'm afraid to go down in there because I'm scared of what I might find. I'm not going to do it just now.

This attitude is a very common one indeed. There are a number of ways in which individuals pursue this goal of becoming themselves. Some lives have been badly distorted or warped by early childhood. For them, the search for solidity in themselves, for their own real self, may be a long or painful one. Others more fortunate are already in the process of discovery and have an easier time. Some are sufficiently frightened by the risks involved in the search that they endeavor to freeze themselves as they are, fearful of any road that would lead into unknown territory. I

will briefly describe several of the ways in which people venture, as they search for the real self.

THE LIFETIME JOURNEY OF SELF-DISCOVERY

This process of self-discovery, self-acceptance, and self-expression is not something that goes on only in therapy or in groups. Many people have neither of these experiences. For those who do, the therapy or the group exists for only a limited time. But for all of us, the search to become the person we most uniquely are is a lifetime process. I believe this is one reason why biography holds a fascination for so many readers. We like to follow the struggle of individuals to become what they are capable of becoming. For me, this is illustrated by the book I have just finished reading: the life story of artist Georgia O'Keeffe [*Portrait of An Artist: A Biography of Georgia O'Keeffe*, by L. Lisle (1980)]. There are many steps in her development. At fourteen, the inwardly independent but outwardly conforming girl won a gold medal for her ladylike deportment at a strict Catholic school. But by the age of sixteen, she was beginning to dress in a "tailored, midwestern corsetless style" (in 1903!), which was to be a characteristic throughout her many years. And at age twenty-nine she locked herself into her studio and analyzed all her work up to that point with "ruthless detachment." She could tell which paintings had been done to please one professor and which to please another. She could tell which had been influenced by well-known artists of the day.

> Then an idea dawned on her. There were abstract shapes in her mind integral to her imagination, unlike anything she had been taught. 'This thing that is your own is so close to you, often you never realize it's there,' she later explained. . . . 'I could think of a whole string of things I'd like to put down but I'd never thought of doing it because I'd never seen anything like it.' . . . She had made up her mind. This was what she would paint. (p. 81)

As you can imagine, this decision was the initial step toward becoming the great artist of her mature years. Even in her nineties, she relentlessly pursued that goal of painting her own unique perceptions of the desert, of bleached bones, of huge and gorgeous flowers—to the point that one has only to look at one of her paintings to realize "That's an O'Keeffe."

Like Georgia O'Keeffe, each of us is the artist or the architect of his or her own life. We can copy others, we can live to please others, or we can discover what is unique and precious to us and paint that, become that. It is a task that takes a lifetime.

YOU CAN BE YOURSELF

Let me try to summarize what it means to me to find one's real self. In the first place it is a process, a direction, not some static achievement. In my estimation no one is ever completely successful in finding all her real (and ever-changing) self. But there are certain characteristics of this process. Persons move away from hiding behind facades and pretenses, whether these have been held consciously or unconsciously. They move toward a greater closeness to and awareness of their inward experiences. They find this development exceedingly complex and varied, ranging from wild and crazy feelings to solid, socially approved ones. They move toward accepting all of these experiences as their own; they discover that they are people with an enormous variety of reactions. The more they own and accept their inner reactions—and are unafraid of them—the more they can sense the meanings those reactions have. The more all this inner richness belongs to them, the more they can appropriately *be* their own experiences. An individual may become aware of a childish need to depend on someone, to be cared for and protected. In appropriate situations she can let herself be that childish, dependent self. She may discover that certain situations anger her.

"The Right Track"

When you are very young, life, like these railroad tracks, appears to go on forever. We wonder and dream about what awaits us down the way. If there is an end, it is too distant to even think about. Sometimes our lifetrack feels just right. Other times we may have doubts about our lifetrack. Something isn't right, something is missing in our travels. Bernard Malamud's words begin to make sense—"If your train's on the wrong track, every station you come to is the wrong station." If this happens, it is often wise to choose another lifetrack. But just switching tracks is not sufficient because, as Will Rogers warned, "Even if you're on the right track, you'll get run over if you just sit there."

She can more easily express that anger as it arises in the situation that arouses it, rather than suppress it until it pours out explosively onto some innocent victim. A man can discover soft, tender, loving feelings (which are especially difficult for men to own) and can express them with satisfaction, not shame. These people are becoming involved in the wider range of their feelings, attitudes, and potential. They are building a good relationship with what is going on within themselves. They are beginning to appreciate and like, rather than hate and mistrust, all their experiences. Thus, they are coming closer to finding and being all of themselves in the moment. To me this is the way that the person moves toward answering the question, "Who am I?"

Follow-Up

1. *Rogers quotes a college woman who is easily impressed with someone who knows for sure about life and his identity. Then she realizes that this is his answer, not hers. But she is confused on how to find her answers. When you are not sure of who you are, are you also easily influenced by confident and seemingly authoritative persons? Provide an example, if possible. Have you, like the above student, chosen to find your way and answers, even though this approach is loaded with doubts and uncertainties? If yes, try to give a real life example.*

2. *Rogers discusses how even some modern day groups offer ready-made identities in which few decisions have to be made. He mentions the military as well as political and religious sects. Do these kinds of identity solutions appeal to you? Why or why not? For further reading on this topic try the classic small book,* **True Believers,** *by the longshoreman philosopher Eric Hoffer.*

3. *Rogers explains how the artist Georgia O'Keeffe found her artistic voice. She said that she locked herself in her studio and looked at her work with "ruthless detachment." She then realized that she had not been painting the images that seemed to exist only in her mind. These images became her artistic identity. She concluded that "this thing that is your own is so close to you, often you never realize it's there."*

   Try looking at your own life with "ruthless detachment" to discover which parts are direct results of others' influence and which parts are uniquely yours. How can you blend the most significant of each into your own voice?

4. *Rogers mentions that biography appeals to many because it provides some hints on how others struggle with identity issues. Have you experienced this effect? Consider reading a biography of someone you admire.*

5. *In the last paragraph of his article, Rogers talks about several characteristics of the process of becoming one's real self. One characteristic is moving away from facades and pretenses. Have you found that you become truer to your identity when you drop false fronts? Consider trying out some of the ideas in this paragraph. If you're interested in a fuller discussion of these characteristics, you will find them in* **On Becoming a Person** *by Carl Rogers.*

The Basic Relationship

Abe Arkoff

John Vasconcellos is a highly esteemed member of the California legislature, but he speaks candidly about his own early failure to value himself and of many later years of therapy to develop his self-esteem and personhood. Recently, recalling his own long trek to a better sense of self, he wrote,

> In school, I was a high-achiever, receiving awards and excellent grades. In adulthood, I became a prominent lawyer in a prestigious firm. My first campaign for a seat in the state legislature in 1966 was successful, and I have now been reelected eleven times.
>
> Yet, through it all, I had almost no sense of my self, no self-esteem. I worked for my successes only in a constant attempt to please others. My intellect functioned superbly, but the rest of my self barely functioned at all. I had been conditioned to know myself basically as a sinner, guilt-ridden and ashamed, constantly beating my breast and professing my unworthiness. I had so little self-esteem that I lost my first election (running for eighth-grade president) by one vote—my own (Vasconcellos, 1989, pp. xiv–xv).

Vasconcellos notes that personal experience has taught him the importance of valuing oneself. He has increasingly focused on the issue of self-esteem both to help himself and others develop "a strong sense of self." He is the author of legislation creating the California Task Force to Promote Self-Esteem and Personal and Social Responsibility whose aim is to promote the well-being of the individual and society as a way of preventing rather than just reacting to serious social ills.

As a clinical psychologist, I have worked with many people who have come to me for help. Some were deeply troubled. Of these, I cannot recall a single one who had a good relationship with herself or himself. Not one was her or his own best friend. When they began to like themselves and trust themselves, I knew they were getting better. When they began to take some pride in themselves, I knew they were getting well.

Not long ago I heard a comedienne ask a group this question: "How many of you know how it feels to be the only person in a relationship?" This got a laugh, but thinking back on my clinical experience with human beings, it seems clear to me that the most important relationship we each have is the one with ourselves. How strange that most of us do not think of this as a relationship at all. How strange that this is the relationship in which we sometimes appear least humane, treating ourselves in a way we would never treat somebody else.

Think about this with reference to your own self. You are always in your own presence, and just as you are aware of the world around you, you are aware of yourself. You think, you feel, you act. You also observe yourself thinking and feeling and acting. You reflect on yourself and come to know yourself. You have *reflective awareness*—the ability to consider your behavior as you observe it.

Because you have the power of reflective awareness, you are both actor and audience in your life. You perform and at the same time watch yourself perform. But you are not a passive audience. You, the audience, attend and consider. You weigh and evaluate. Sometimes you applaud, sometimes you hiss or jeer, sometimes rise and command. You (the actor) are influenced by you (the audience) just as you (the audience) are influenced by you (the actor).

Of course, there are other people in the audience too. In their response to you, they tell you who they think you are and what you can and can't do and should and shouldn't do. You observe these others and observe them observe you and observe yourself. Out of all these observations you shape and reshape the idea of who you are, and you shape and reshape your relationship to yourself. Your relationship to yourself could be called "the basic relationship" because how you come to see and regard yourself becomes such a fundamental force in your life.

THE DYNAMIC SELF-IMAGE

Our self-image is influenced by all that is happening in our life, and at the same time it is involved in making things happen—in guiding and controlling our behavior. It is dynamic, that is, active, changing, forceful (Markus & Wurf, 1987). Among its powers are those affecting the way we see our world, how we function in it, and how we relate to those with whom we come in contact.

The Self-Image and Perception

The way we perceive or view ourselves affects the way we view our world. We are the center of our universe. Perceptual psychologists Combs, Avila, and Purkey (1978) note that the self is the yardstick used to make judgments. They write, "Others are regarded as taller, shorter, smarter, more unscrupulous, older, or younger than ourself. As the self changes, the yardstick changes, and what we believe to be true changes with it. What is considered 'old' is likely to be quite differently defined at ages six, sixteen, thirty-six, or sixty" (p. 19).

In any situation the things possible for us to perceive are almost limitless. What we select to perceive and the meaning we attach to these perceptions relate closely to the picture we have of ourselves. By way of example, Don Hamachek (1978) writes, "Depending on one's concept of self, an exam is perceived as either something to avoid failing or something to pass with as high a grade as possible; a class discussion is viewed as either something to actively engage in or something to sit quietly through for fear of saying the wrong thing; front seats of classrooms are seen as either vantage points for better seeing or potentially dangerous spots where one could be more easily seen and, heaven forbid, called on!" (pp. 44–45).

The Self-Image and Behavior

Because of its influence on our perceptions, our self-image influences our behavior in many ways. Some psychologists believe that the basic human force is the striving to maintain and enhance our conception of ourselves (Combs, Richards, & Richards, 1976). We present ourselves to others in ways calculated to enhance our image in their eyes and in our own. We defend our image from attack, whether this be assault from without or doubts arising from within.

Our self-image serves us as a basic frame of reference—as a foundation or guide for our actions. We would be lost without it, and therefore we defend it against change. Some of us seem to be resistant to growth or positive movement in our lives, but this may be our way of being true to our picture of ourselves (Rosenberg, 1979).

Psychologists have suggested that when a person believes something to be so, he or she tends to behave in a way that makes it so; this is called a "self-fulfilling prophecy." If we see ourselves in a positive light, we are apt to try harder because we think our efforts will pay off, and we are more likely to succeed or define the outcome as successful. If we have a low opinion of ourselves, we may avoid a situation or approach it halfheartedly, and we are more likely to fail or to interpret the results as failure (Langer & Dweck, 1973).

The Self-Image and Relationships with Others

Our self-image influences our perceptions of others and our relationships with them. There is considerable evidence that we tend to see others as we see ourselves. Emerson wrote, "What we are, that only can we see." Hamachek (1978) adds, "When we think we are looking out a window, it could be that we are merely gazing into a looking-glass" (p. 47). He suggested that a good way to find out what a person is really like is to find out what this person thinks others are like. He writes, "The man who tells us that people are basically trustworthy and kind—ignoring the plain fact that they can also be devious and cruel—may be saying more about himself than about the world" (p. 47).

People who like and accept themselves tend to accept others (Berger, 1952; Pirot, 1986). Research shows that individuals who hold themselves in high esteem tend to take a favorable view of others and also expect more acceptance and less rejection (Baron, 1974; Walster, 1965). And, of course, when others are approached in this light, they are more likely to respond favorably.

If we dislike or reject ourselves, we are more likely to view and treat others in the same way, and consequently our relations with others will suffer. Oscar Wilde observed that "all criticism is a form of autobiography." Hamachek suggests some personal research that one can do on this point. He writes, "Pay particular attention to your feelings about yourself for the next three or four days and note how they influence your behavior toward others. It may be that it is not our friend or our loved one or our children we are mad at; it is ourselves. What we feel toward ourselves gets aimed at others, and we sometimes treat others not as persons, but as targets" (p. 46).

We tend to form relationships with persons who are similar to us, who see us as we see ourselves and who confirm our own positive self-impressions (Swan, 1984; Taylor & Brown, 1988). It's hard for us to rest easy in the company of those who don't see us as we wish to be seen (Lang, Phillipson, & Lee, 1966). Joseph Joubert understood this prime requisite of friendship when he wrote, "When my friends are one-eyed, I look at their profile."

THE MULTIPLE SELF

One of Shakespeare's most famous lines (part of the counsel that Polonius gives his son Laertes in *Hamlet*) reads, "This above all: to thine own self be true." Kenneth Gergen (1972), a psychologist who has made an extensive study of the self-concept, calls this advice "poor psychology." He believes we are unlikely to find a single self to be true to.

Gergen's research suggests that we are considerably affected by the situations in which we find ourselves—the self we are in one situation may be very different from the self we are in another. Different environments may prompt different thoughts and feelings about ourselves and therefore different behaviors. When we are talking to someone who is in a superior position, our self-relevant thoughts and feelings may be quite different from when we are with a subordinate. When we are standing up to a group, we may see ourselves differently from when we have reluctantly decided to go along with it (Markus & Kunda, 1986).

Gergen questions the assumption that many psychologists and laypersons make that it is good—or even normal—to have a firm and coherent sense of self. In fact, he suggests that we should become concerned when we become too comfortable with a self or set in a particular identity. This may simply mean we have settled into a routine of the same situations ("a rut") that calls forth the same old responses.

Gergen concludes that "we are made of soft plastic and molded by social circumstances," but other research suggests that the self-concept is not all that malleable. Taken together, the evidence supports the conclusion that the self-concept is *both* stable and malleable. We have a certain core of ideas about ourselves, and we resist information that challenges this core. At the same time, we are influenced by the situations in which we find ourselves. How we see ourselves in a particular situation results from the reconciliation of self-conceptions prompted by this core and those called forth by that situation (Markus & Kunda, 1986). It can be trying when a core conception is challenged—for example, when we pride ourselves on our honesty but also see we are sorely tempted to lie or cheat to gain an important end.

Subpersonalities

Another psychologist, John Vargiu (1977), also believes that we may not be a single self, but he doesn't agree with Gergen that we shouldn't be. Where Gergen attributes our variability to the varying situations in which we find ourselves, Vargiu attributes it to a number of *subpersonalities*—semi-autonomous personages within us all striving for expression. He holds that we need to understand these subpersonalities better and bring them into harmony with each other; doing so, we become a single harmonized self.

St. Augustine eloquently described the struggle between two of his subpersonalities —the "animal man" and the "spiritual man." Recalling this struggle in his *Confessions,* he wrote, "My inner self was a house divided against itself." Ted Kennedy was described in a 1991 *Time* magazine profile as seemingly a person of several sets of selves. One set: statesman, serious lawmaker, family patriarch. The other set: over-age, drunken frat-house boor, and party animal. The profiler suggested, "A man with Kennedy's temperament and past

may need a sort of unofficial self that he can plunge back into now and then—a rowdy, loutish oblivion where he feels easy, where he takes a woozy vacation from being a Kennedy" (Morrow, 1991, p. 27).

You may recall seeing an acquaintance behave in a quite uncharacteristic way. You wonder, what's got into him? Or you think, she's not herself today. Of course, she *is* herself—but a different one of her selves or subselves or subpersonalities.

Consider the inconsistencies or subpersonalities that may exist within yourself. Have you noted that you sometimes seem to get caught up in a particular way of being and behaving? You recognize it and could even give it a label since it is so salient and you have been caught up in it before. When you are under its spell, you see yourself and your world differently and behave differently, perhaps in a way you like or don't like. You may be able to identify a number of these subpersonalities in yourself, some in harmony and some in conflict with each other.

It may be useful to identify and study the subpersonalities in yourself. When I did so recently, these subselves were most salient: The Creative but Tiring Soul (a subself that enjoyed creating something new or different and watching it develop—for a while), Dad (a caring, helpful subself), The Relentless Searcher (a subself that was always looking for something better but never quite finding it), and The Wise Old Man (an emerging subself, one with the ability to understand, accept, and enjoy things as they are). I was pleased to note that The Examiner (a subself that was constantly scrutinizing things to see if they measured up) had been largely decommissioned.

It is important not to confuse the concept of "subpersonalities," which applies to normal behavior, with that of "multiple personality," which is a serious and disabling disorder (Rowan, 1990). This latter condition is quite rare and better known to Hollywood and television script writers than to psychiatrists or psychologists. The added personalities in multiple personality disorder are quite autonomous, even with differences in handedness (left or right dominance) and in patterns of handwriting and brain waves (Putnam, 1984) and usually operate without the awareness of the original personality.

Possible Selves

Markus and her colleagues (Markus & Kunda, 1986; Markus & Nurius, 1986) have been interested in the concept of *possible selves*—the images we have concerning the persons we might be in the future. These include the selves we expect to be, the selves we hope to be, and also those we fear we might become. These images function as incentives and serve to guide us toward certain kinds of behaviors and away from others.

Markus (Markus & Nurius, 1986) points out that our possible selves are influenced by our individual histories and also by developments in society. Social advances such as increased opportunities for women and blacks create new hoped-for possible selves among these groups. New or exacerbated social problems create new dreaded possible selves such as the AIDS-afflicted self, the drug-dependent self, the bag lady, and the street person.

The most striking finding of a study that compared possible selves in delinquent and nondelinquent boys (Oyserman & Markus, 1986) was the intensely negative set of feared selves among the delinquents (for example, being alone, poor, depressed, flunking out of school, junkie, drug pusher, criminal). Unwanted possible selves are not necessarily a negative influence because they can motivate the person to avoid them or to prepare to cope with them. However, for this process to be fully effective, the negative possible self must be countered by a positive possible self or direction that suggests what might be done. Not surprisingly, delinquent boys proved to have fewer matched pairs of negative and positive selves.

Approaches to Self-Knowledge

A useful way to gain more self-knowledge is to make ourselves the object of study just as though we were a course in which we had enrolled. During one period of his life, Sigmund Freud spent the last half-hour of each working day analyzing himself. In one of my workshops, I share some things I have learned about myself from living with myself all these years and then ask my students to write a list of things they have learned about themselves. Some are a bit dumbfounded, but once they have set themselves to the task, most find they have quite a lot to write down.

One master at the art of self-reflection is Hugh Prather. In his notebooks, he carefully observes himself and candidly shares these observations with his readers. The following brief example from his book *Notes to Myself* shows him in his watchful but positive, nurturant pursuit of self-knowledge:

> One kind of lie that I tell pops out in conversation and takes me by surprise. Sometimes I like to correct these lies right on the spot, and when I do I find that most people don't think less of me. This kind of lie, when I notice it, usually helps me see where I feel inadequate—the areas where I could be more acceptant of myself.

Wilson Van Dusen (1972), a pioneer of inner space, notes that we are constantly generating fantasies, images, and feelings that tell us who we are. He writes that "we are almost overburdened with clues to our own nature" (p. 4). But he concludes that we scarcely make use of these clues and, therefore, remain strangers to ourselves.

Van Dusen pictures our inner life as a "mind-castle," but one that is lamentably underesteemed and unexamined. He writes, "If one were locked up in an ancient castle for one's whole life—a castle full of artifacts, dungeons, endless rooms, art, and books—one would spend much time exploring and recreating the lives of the inhabitants" (p. 1). Van Dusen maintains that indeed we are ensconced in such a mind-castle, but we don't avail ourself of the opportunity to explore. He continues, "Many know little more than a sitting room in the east wing and assume this is the whole. The size of the mind-castle is little appreciated. It includes all you have experienced, will experience, and in the remote corners, all you can experience" (p. 1).

Van Dusen recommends cultivation of the "lost art" of self-reflection, which he describes as "a gazing at one's life and circumstances as though it were a painting to be examined, felt, appreciated" (p. 49). To do this, he says, requires (1) some minutes of peaceful leisure, (2) the experiencing of what is, and (3) mulling this over or reflecting upon it. He also recommends that one does this regularly and writes it down afterward in a personal journal.

Accepting Ourselves

Some of the dictionary's definitions of the word *accept* are "to be favorably disposed toward," "to believe in," and "to receive as adequate or satisfactory." If we accept ourselves or show *self-acceptance*, we are favorably disposed toward ourselves and believe we are okay. That doesn't mean we don't want to be better, but it does mean whatever we are right now, it's all right to be. If we reject ourselves or show *self-rejection*, we don't like or believe in ourselves, and we feel inadequate.

Before considering self-acceptance more fully, it may be helpful to look at self-rejection—all the things self-acceptance is not. Following is a checklist of behaviors seen in those who find themselves personally unacceptable, which is adapted from larger listings by Wayne Dyer (1976) and by Bloomfield and Kory (1980). The list is presented here just to get you thinking about yourself—it's not a deep and definitive device. As you think, answer each item "yes" or "no."

_____ 1. Do you feel embarrassed by your abilities or accomplishments?

_____ 2. Do you give credit to others when you really deserve it yourself?

_____ 3. Do you put others above you when you are really their equal or superior?

_____ 4. Do you fail to stand up for the things you really believe in?

_____ 5. Do you put yourself down when you have made a mistake?

_____ 6. Do you let others put you down?

_____ 7. Do you have a cute name for yourself that reduces you in some way?

_____ 8. Do you depend on others to bolster your opinions?

_____ 9. Do you believe that others cannot possibly find you attractive?

_____ 10. Do you believe that others are being kind out of charity or some ulterior motive?

_____ 11. Do you find it hard to say no to a request because of what the person might think of you?

_____ 12. Do you find it hard to complain about poor treatment because you are afraid of making a fuss?

Because the items in the preceding list reflect self-rejection, each item that you answered "yes" suggests an area for you to work on to change the "yes" to "no." But don't put yourself down for your "yeses"—that would be another bit of self-rejecting behavior.

Showing one's "true face" even to oneself can be a difficult task when it is a face one has somehow come to think is wrong or even evil. Some lesbians and gays have written of their confusion or consternation at discovering their sexual orientation and of their struggle to "come out of the closet" and be who they truly were. In one study (Jay & Young, 1979), a woman reported that she didn't realize she was a lesbian until she was 20, and her coming out was traumatic. "I used to look at myself in the mirror and cry. I couldn't believe what I was. How could a good girl like me be something as wicked as a lesbian? Once I found the gay bars and gay community I found that there were many 'good girl' lesbians" (pp. 55–56). She noted that since then, her self-image had improved each year, and now she wouldn't want to be anyone other than who she is.

We must constantly seek to understand ourselves if we are to become ourselves; but the understanding does not come once and for all. It comes little by little as we observe ourselves in every new situation. In every situation, we can learn to tell whether we are being genuine and true to ourselves, or phony and unauthentic (Friedman, 1958).

For ten years, I was a volunteer working with hospice patients and those with life-threatening illness. Being with a number of persons as they faced death, I've come to believe that dying has been hardest for those who never really lived their lives—those who were losing both life and their last chance to become themselves. I am reminded of the story told about Rabbi Zusya as he approached death. Rabbi Zusya said that when he met the Holy One, he would not be asked, "Why were you not like Moses?" No, he would be asked, "Why were you not like Zusya?" Zusya added, "It is for this reason that I tremble."

References

Baron, P. (1974). Self-esteem, ingratiation, and evaluation of unknown others. *Journal of Personality and Social Psychology, 30,* 104–109.

Berger, E. (1952). The relation between expressed acceptance of self and expressed acceptance of others. *Journal of Abnormal and Social Psychology, 47,* 778–782.

Bloomfield, H. H., & Kory, R. B. (1980). *Inner joy: New strategies to put more pleasure and satisfaction in your life.* New York: Wyden.

Combs, A. W., Avila, D. L., & Purkey, W. W. (1978). *Helping relationships: Basic concepts for the helping professions* (2nd ed.). Boston: Allyn and Bacon.

Combs, A. W., Richards, A. C., & Richards, F. (1976). *Perceptual psychology: A humanistic approach to the study of persons.* New York: Harper & Row.

Dyer, W. W. (1976). *Your erroneous zones.* New York: Funk & Wagnalls.

Friedman, M. (1958). *To deny our nothingness: Contemporary images of man.* London: Macmillan.

Gergen, K. J. (1972, May). The healthy, happy human wears many masks. *Psychology Today,* 31–35, 64, 66.

Hamachek, D. E. (1978). *Encounters with the self* (2nd ed.). New York: Holt, Rinehart and Winston.

Jay, K., & Young, A. (1979). *The gay report.* New York: Summit Books.

Lang, R. D., Phillipson, H., & Lee, A. R. (1966). *Interpersonal perception: A theory and method of research.* New York: Springer.

Langer, E. J., & Dweck, C. S. (1973). *Personal politics: The psychology of making it.* Englewood Cliffs, NJ: Prentice-Hall.

Markus, H., & Kunda, Z. (1986). Stability and malleability of the self-concept. *Journal of Personality and Social Psychology, 51*(4), 858–866.

Markus, H., & Nurius, P. (1986). Possible selves. *American Psychologist, 41*(9), 954–969.

Markus, H., & Wurf, E. (1987). The dynamic self-concept: A social psychological perspective. *Annual Review of Psychology, 38*, 299–337.

Morrow, L. (1991, April 29). The trouble with Teddy. *Time*, 24–27.

Oyserman, D., & Markus, H. (1986). *Possible selves, motivation, and delinquency*. Unpublished manuscript, University of Michigan.

Pirot, M. (1986). The pathological thought and dynamics of the perfectionist. *Journal of Individual Psychology, 42*(1), 51–58.

Prather, H. (1970). *Notes to myself*. Moab, UT: Real People Press.

Putnam, F. W. (1984). The psychophysiologic investigation of multiple personality disorder: A review. *Psychiatric Clinics of North America, 7*(1), 31–39.

Rosenberg, M. (1979). *Conceiving the self*. New York: Basic Books.

Rowan, J. (1990). *Subpersonalities: The people inside us*. New York: Routledge.

Swan, W. B., Jr. (1984). Quest for accuracy in person perception: A matter of pragmatics. *Psychological Review, 91*, 457–477.

Taylor, S. E., & Brown, J. D. (1988). Illusion and well-being: A social psychological perspective on mental health. *Psychological Bulletin, 103*(2), 193–210.

Van Dusen, W. (1972). *The natural depth in man*. New York: Harper & Row.

Vargiu, J. G. (1977). Subpersonalities. In A. Arkoff (Ed.), *Psychology and personal growth* (3rd ed., pp. 22–27). Boston: Allyn & Bacon.

Vasconcellos, J. (1989). Preface. In A. M. Mecca, N. J. Smelser, & J. Vasconcellos (Eds.), *The social importance of self-esteem* (pp. xi–xxi). Berkeley: University of California Press.

Walster, E. (1965). The effect of self-esteem on romantic liking. *Journal of Experimental Social Psychology, 1*, 184–197.

Follow-Up

1. *Do you have a good relationship with yourself? Describe this relationship as it seems to you.*
2. *What subpersonalities can you detect in yourself? Name and describe each one and its influence on you.*
3. *How much insight into yourself do you have? How much of a puzzle are you? Discuss an important aspect of yourself that remains a mystery to you.*
4. *Is your life right for you? Are you on the way to becoming yourself? Give your evidence.*

Rubricizing

Nelson Goud

She was standing in line waiting to board the Denver to Seattle flight. In her 70's, she had gray-blue hair, a red dress, and a satchel clutched under her right arm. What she did not have was a left arm. I became immediately sympathetic as the old lady negotiated the movements necessary to board the plane. On the plane she was two seats away in the same row. About 30 minutes into the flight she pulled out a paperback novel, opened to a marked page, and held the book in her only hand. I snuck a look—readers cannot seem to help but check out what other readers read—and saw *Lake Wobegon Days* on the cover. I had read it a couple of months ago and could not resist the urge to ask how she liked it. Besides, this one-armed old lady just had to be lonely and probably experienced life on the fringe, a human satellite. "How's it going in Lake Wobegon lately?" I asked while eating lunch. She talked about the book a bit and seemed quite friendly. We kept chatting and somewhere in there music was mentioned. We discovered we were big band fans. I droned on about my favorites and how I played the trumpet. She was politely attentive and when I finally took a breath she said, "I played in a big band once." This surprised me. "What did you play?" I asked. "Sax," she said. I asked if this was in high school. "Oh, no. I was 17 though. I played in an all-female professional big band which toured all the USO places in the U.S. and Europe in WWII." Not only did she know of my favorite big band leaders, but saw and talked with them in their prime. After many minutes of answering my eager questions, I noticed that the one-armed old lady had "disappeared." She had become a different person. I even for-

got about her loss of an arm and asked if she still played the sax. She just smiled and said she hadn't picked it up in a while. We deplaned and she met her daughter and two friends and I knew then I was a better reader of books than people.

At a meeting during a national convention, I found myself seated next to a counselor dressed in the garb of a 1960's throwback—Army fatigues, long hair, beard, and a detached, peaceful gaze.

"I'm having a most fascinating time at this convention," he said during a break.

"Why is that?" I asked.

"Take a look at my nametag," he motioned.

It read "Rev. Bill Smith." He then explained that prior to reading his nametag, conventioneers react to him like they would to a hippie—that is, either ignoring him, staring, or engaging in the hippie lingo.

"The thing is," he continued, "I am not a man of the cloth. When they finally see the nametag they stop talking for a few seconds. You can sense the confusion going on as they try to figure out how to act with a 'hippie preacher.' Most people do not have that category and do not know what to say or do. I need the nametag to get into the workshops so I keep it on. So far I have learned more about people with my nametag than from the workshops."

Peace, brother, love, and that's a far out story, Reverend.

These are examples of "rubricizing" (pronounced roo-bri-sigh-zing), a term coined by Abraham Maslow. He believed that there are two major ways to perceive any experience. One is to observe its unique essence, how the experience is truly different and individualistic. The second, rubricizing, is to respond to an experience as a representative of a category (rubric). Rubricizing perception is similar to the actions of a file clerk who recognizes only what is minimally necessary to place a paper under A, B, Y, etc. When we rubricize people, we quickly scan them for certain characteristics (often subconsciously) and place them into one of our mental file folders. A rubricized person becomes a member of a grouping: waiter, teenager, a Johnson kid, math major, jock, married, female, southerner, sorority type, and so on. Rubrics are literally "categories of the mind."

RUBRICIZING CONTINUUM

Rubrics range from the stereotypic to the highly individualistic. A stereotype is a rubric with a pre-packaged set of meanings. Common stereotype subjects are race, religion, occupation, gender, age, marital status, residence, and geographical locale. At the other end of the rubricizing continuum is the individualistic rubric which has meaning only for the perceiver (or possibly just a few others). For instance, I know a person who can glance at the shoes of a person and then tell you his/her food and clothing tastes, social status, and several personality characteristics. To her, people have an astrology chart on their feet. There are also rubrics which fall between these extremes.

POSITIVE AND NEGATIVE ASPECTS

Rubrics can have negative or positive meanings. It is easy to understand why one dislikes being placed in a negative rubric (e.g., "she comes from _____ and you know they never amount to much"). It is also a burden to be rubricized into a positive rubric. This is common for those who stand out in some valued quality like "outstanding student," "talented musician/dancer/artist," "really good looking." Many of the latter also resist being rubricized. Some find the pressure to uphold this

image too daunting over the long haul. But the major resistance comes from the reason that every person has multiple dimensions to his/her identity which also call for expression and recognition. To always be seen characterized in reference to the outstanding quality becomes a constraining and limiting existence.

Rubricizing can be either an enhancing or hindering form of perception. It enhances one's life whenever one is required only to respond to familiar, repetitive tasks or to quickly recognize a single feature. By having only to exert partial attention to a situation, one is then freed to devote more energy to a more difficult activity (or several low challenge activities at one time). One can, for example, plan other activities during a boring committee meeting without missing a key point if it occurs, or one can watch TV and talk to another on surface topics simultaneously.

Rubricizing is a hindrance whenever a situation calls for attention to uniqueness, complexity, wholeness, and change. Trying to understand another person's life, solving a difficult problem, creating something, self-examination—these are kinds of actions which demand more than a quick, cursory scan. One must be open to the shifting multiple dimensions of what is being presented. Carl Rogers explains that this kind of perception requires an "openness to experience" and provides an example:

One of the most satisfying experiences I know—is just fully to appreciate an individual in the same way that I appreciate a sunset. When I look at a sunset . . . I don't find myself saying, "Soften the orange a little on the right hand corner, and put a bit more purple along the base, and use a little more pink in the cloud color" . . . I don't try to control a sunset. I watch it with awe as it unfolds. It is this receptive, open attitude which is necessary to truly perceive something as it is.

It is important to know that rubricizing is usually our *first* perceptual response. One must therefore be especially vigilant in the situations described previously in which rubricizing is a hindrance. In addition, once something is rubricized it tends to keep this meaning unless a stronger, countering experience changes this perception.

Rubricizing can freeze how a person is perceived, so that if major changes occur, they go unnoticed. You may be a significantly different person compared to earlier years, but upon a visit back home or reuniting with friends, find that they treat you as you were back then. Those very close to us are not immune to rubricizing. We have very strong rubrics about our parents (and they of us). I realize I had rubricized my grandmother. Although we had an affectionate relationship, I noticed at the age of 30 that I was acting toward her the same way as I did at 13. It was ritualistic, she was "Grandma" and I was "Grandson." I happened to ask her about her decision to come to America (she was a Dutch immigrant). Telling her life story as a young girl and woman revealed whole new dimensions of her as a person besides being a grandmother. A rubric has been broken whenever you hear or say, "You surprised me by your interest (or background) in . . ." or "I didn't know you had that in you." Take another look at those close to you to see if some rubricizing is going on.

If you value someone or something, then rubricizing diminishes that which you value. Rubricizing can be accurate or inaccurate, but it is always an *incomplete* form of perception. Everything has multiple facets of which we only perceive a portion. Sometimes we unintentionally slip into a rubricizing mode. I know a physical therapist who was talking to a friend who had to have some surgery to heal a fracture. The physical therapist said to her friend, "I have been learning about patients just like you." Her friend replied, "You have not been learning about patients just like me because there is no one like me. You probably mean that you have been learning about injuries similar to mine." The friend naturally resisted being totally classified by a type of injury.

APPLICATIONS

Here are some guidelines for lessening negative rubricizing:

- Be alert to the *language* signals of rubricizing—"She is the *type* who. . . ," "He's that *kind*," "I can *peg* a person by how. . . ."
- Probably the most frequent rubricizing questions is, "What do you do?" or "What is your major?" If answered, it is very likely that this will be the only dimension of your life that is discussed. It becomes the central identity rubric. Some prefer to be perceived primarily in this rubric. However, there are other choices if you desire to place your occupational identity in a larger context. You can refrain from initially asking a new person, "What do you do?" When introducing or meeting someone for the first time, guide the conversation first to other life activities. You can do the same if asked by someone else. I find it helpful to reply "I do quite a few things. I know you're asking about what I do for a living, but I'd like to talk first about . . . (a new book, jazz, a recent trip, a new idea). . . ." Some of my best conversations started this way; sometimes, though, others persist on finding out my occupational identity (or even shift to another rubric ritual—"What is your sign?").

  During the first weeks of a graduate course I request that students refrain from revealing their occupation or major, age, marital status, religion, and residence. Their ideas and feeling on course topics become the central focus rather than their rubrics. Only later, in the larger context of telling life stories, do the above identity markers emerge.
- Start to observe your system of "rubric triggers"—for example, appearance, occupational/major categories, residence,

mannerisms, clothing, names, family background, social interaction style, language usage, and so on. Stereotypic rubrics are relatively easy to spot. Try also to uncover the individual system of rubrics which exist primarily for you.

- Check the accuracy of initial rubricizing. Through observation and interaction one can find out if the first impressions are erroneous or too restrictive. Rubricizing is counteracted by discovering new facets of a person. Even if it is not realistic to look for new facets (e.g., being served by a waiter), basic human respect is enhanced in just knowing that this person, like you, has many dimensions that are not seen.
- Try to thaw out a frozen rubric you have of someone close to you. This usually means to talk about new topics, or to do different activities than what is customarily done.
- Develop further skills in non-rubricizing, receptive perception. Kazantzakis' Zorba seemed to have the secret—"Like the child, he sees everything for the first time. He is forever astonished and wonders why and wherefore . . . each morning when he opens his eyes he sees trees, sea, stones and birds, and is amazed. 'What is this miracle?' he cries." Unless we are alert, rubricizing can gradually erode experiences which were previously delightful. A pretty flower loses its appeal because we see it several times or find out its name. A favorite song, painting, book, poem are now given a glance instead of the full absorption which made them delightful in the first place.

One simple idea to try is to focus on a common rubricized object you see each day. Maybe a tree on the way to work. Try to discover how it is different from other trees, whether it has lost or grown leaves, how the bark looks different after a rain, and is it a home to a bird or two?

- Have you considered that you can rubricize yourself? It is possible to freeze your own identity so that all is left is repeating familiar patterns. Here are some typical self-rubricizing statements: "I am a methodical and prudent type so it is almost impossible to be spontaneous," "As a teacher I am really not qualified to do anything else but teach children," "People from my (family, school, town, etc.) don't try to do . . . , they'll fail."

All the concepts of rubricizing others also apply to ourselves. Self-rubricizing blunts the adventuring edge so necessary for realizing one's potentialities. Ask yourself. What do *you* do?

Follow-Up

1. *Describe an instance where you:*
   a. *Have been rubricized*
   b. *Rubricized another*
   c. *Rubricized yourself*
2. *Choose two statements from the article that have meaning for you and tell why.*
3. *Attempt one or more of the applications explained in the final section of the article.*

Mindfulness

Jon Kabat-Zinn

Mindfulness means paying attention in a particular way: on purpose, in the present moment, and nonjudgmentally. This kind of attention nurtures greater awareness, clarity, and acceptance of present-moment reality. It wakes up to the fact that our lives unfold only in moments.... The key...is an appreciation for the present moment and the cultivation of an intimate relationship with it through a continual attending to it with care and discernment. It is the direct opposite of taking life for granted....

The best way to capture moments is to pay attention....

You can easily observe the mind's habit of escaping from the present moment for yourself. Just try to keep your attention focused on any object for even a short period of time...you may have to remember over and over again to be awake and aware...to look, to feel, to be....

The impulse frequently arises in me to squeeze another this or another that into this moment. Just this phone call, just stopping off here on my way there.... I've learned to identify this impulse and mistrust it. I work hard at saying no to it. It would have me eat breakfast with my eyes riveted to the cereal box, reading for the hundredth time the dietary contents.... This impulse doesn't care what it feeds on, as long as it's feeding.... I like to practice voluntary simplicity to counter such impulses and make sure nourishment comes at a deep level. It involves intentionally doing only one thing at a time and making sure I am here for it.... Voluntary simplicity means going fewer places in one day rather than more, seeing less so I can see more, doing less so I can do more, acquiring less so I can have more....

A commitment to simplicity in the midst of the world is a delicate balancing act. It is always in need of retuning, further inquiry, attention.... You don't get to control it all. But choosing simplicity whenever possible adds to life an element of deepest freedom which so easily eludes us, and many opportunities to discover that less may actually be more....

Try: Asking yourself in this moment, "Am I awake?," "Where is my mind right now?"

Suddenly I'm the Adult?

Richard Cohen

Several years ago, my family gathered on Cape Cod for a weekend. My parents were there, my sister and her daughter, too, two cousins and, of course, my wife, my son and me. We ate at one of those restaurants where the menu is scrawled on a blackboard held by a chummy waiter and had a wonderful time. With dinner concluded, the waiter set the check down in the middle of the table. That's when it happened. My father did not reach for the check.

In fact, my father did nothing. Conversation continued. Finally, it dawned on me. Me! I was supposed to pick up the check. After all these years, after hundreds of restaurant meals with my parents, after a lifetime of thinking of my father as the one with the bucks, it had all changed. I reached for the check and whipped out my American Express card. My view of myself was suddenly altered. With a stroke of the pen, I was suddenly an adult.

Some people mark off their life in years, others in events. I am one of the latter, and I think of some events as rites of passage. I did not become a young man at a particular year, like 13, but when a kid strolled into the store where I worked and called me "mister." I turned around to see whom he was calling. He repeated it several times—"Mister, mister"—looking straight at me. The realization hit like a punch: Me! He was talking to me. I was suddenly a mister.

There have been other milestones. The cops of my youth always seemed to be big, even huge, and of course they were older than I was. Then one day they were neither. In fact, some of them were kids—short kids at that. Another milestone.

The day comes when you suddenly realize that all the football players in the game you're watching are younger than you. Instead of being big men, they are merely big kids. With that milestone goes the fantasy that someday, maybe, you too could be a player—maybe not a football player but certainly a baseball player. I had a good eye as a kid—not much power, but a keen eye—and I always thought I could play the game. One day I realized that I couldn't. Without having ever reached the hill, I was over it.

For some people, the most momentous milestone is the death of a parent. This happened recently to a friend of mine. With the burial of his father came the realization that he had moved up a notch. Of course, he had known all along that this would happen, but until the funeral, the knowledge seemed theoretical at best. As long as one of your parents is alive, you stay in some way a kid. At the very least, there remains at least one person whose love is unconditional.

For women, a milestone is reached when they can no longer have children. The loss of a life, the inability to create one—they are variations on the same theme. For a childless woman who could control everything in life but the clock, this milestone is cruel one indeed.

I count other, less serious milestones—like being audited by the Internal Revenue Service. As the auditor caught mistake after mistake, I sat there pretending that really knowing about taxes was for adults. I, of course, was still a kid. The auditor was buying none of it. I was a taxpayer, an adult. She all but said, Go to jail.

There have been others. I remember the day when I had a ferocious argument with my son and realized that I could no longer bully him. He was too big and the days when I could just pick him up and take him to his room/isolation cell were over. I needed to persuade, reason. He was suddenly, rapidly, older. The conclusion was inescapable. So was I.

One day you go to your friends' weddings. One day you celebrate the birth of their kids. One day you see one of their kids driving, and one day those kids have kids of their own. One day you meet at parties and then at weddings and then at funerals. It all happens in one day. Take my word for it.

I never thought I would fall asleep in front of the television set as my father did, and as my friends' fathers did, too. I remember my parents and their friends talking about insomnia and they sounded like members of a different species. Not able to sleep? How ridiculous. Once it was all I did. Once it was what I did best.

I never thought that I would eat a food that did not agree with me. Now I meet them all the time. I thought I would never go to the beach and not swim. I spent all of August at the beach and never once went into the ocean. I never thought I would appreciate opera, but now the pathos, the schmaltz and, especially, the combination of voice and music appeal to me. The deaths of Mimi and Tosca move me, and they die in my home as often as I can manage it.

I never thought I would prefer to stay home instead of going to a party, but now I find myself passing parties up. I used to think that people who watched birds were weird, but this summer I found myself watching them, and maybe I'll get a book on the subject. I yearn for a religious conviction I never thought I'd want, exult in my heritage anyway, feel close to ancestors long gone and echo my father in arguments with my son. I still lose.

One day I made a good toast. One day I handled a headwaiter. One day I bought a house. One day—what a day!—I became a father, and not too long after that I picked up the check for my own. I thought then and there it was a rite of passage for me. Not until I got older did I realize that it was one for him, too. Another milestone.

Follow-Up

1. *See the Applied Activity titled "Are You An Adult?" at the end of this readings section.*
2. *In this article, Richard Cohen describes several life events that he called milestones. These milestones caused shifts in how he viewed himself as a person. His identity had added another dimension. We all have these identity milestones, little or great, which tell us that we have changed, that we have entered another phase of life, or that we have shifted some basic way of seeing and being in the world.*

   What have been some of your identity milestones?

   _____ _____ _____

   _____ _____ _____

   _____ _____ _____

3. Complete the statement *"I know I'm getting older when . . ."*?

   Samples
   - *I cannot name or tolerate the top 3 rock groups*
   - *I am referred to as* sir *or* ma'am
   - *I read or watch the news*
   - *Cops are my age or younger*
   - *I hear my parent's voice coming out of my mouth*
   - *I really need consistent sleeping hours*
   - *I have a high school reunion*

   Your turn—what are some other indicators that you're getting older?

One Foot out the Door

Sydney Lewis

I was very successful in my high school. I was always very—not a kissass—but I was interested in my teachers and I cared about the school. I love being protected, but I think there is a natural instinct to move on. That's a really huge part of all these problems that teenagers have with their parents. Like my brother, who's seventeen. My mom says, and I agree, that if we were cavemen he would have his own cave now. My sister just suffers from being the youngest. She's the big rebel, she's the black lipstick and Doc Martens—the punk of the family. She wants to cut and dye her hair. My mom says, "Don't you want long, pretty, curly hair?" [feigns anger] *"I don't want to look like Gretchen, and I don't want a flowered room like Gretchen."* [laughs] So, independence!

But for me, going to college—I didn't want to go. I thought my life was good. I thought, "I have this great trusting relationship with my parents, they're very loose—I have no curfew." I was satisfied with my social life. I was feeling maybe I needed a new start, to get away from all the stereotypes in high school, but it wasn't enough of an urge to overpower the comfortableness with my family and my home.

In high school I was plagued by not having a boyfriend—I really didn't have any serious boyfriends until I got to college. I always had trouble in relationships because I was so outspoken. I had a prom my senior year, and I could've gotten a date, but I was too proud to go with someone that I didn't want to go with. And that will stay with me the rest of my life. I had enough attention, it's that no one ever seemed to want to date me seriously. I felt and still feel every day like I'm not good enough.

When I meet a guy I'll be like, "Oh, he'll never like me 'cause I'm not pretty enough or I'm not smart enough." I'm not worthy. I can say to myself, "Look at your grades, look at where you've come in your life," but it doesn't matter—it's still that rejection.

All my friends had boyfriends, always. I don't look at other girls who don't have boyfriends and say, "There's something wrong with that person." But I always felt people looked at me that way. Not just boys, but everyone. "Gretchen has no boyfriend, it must be because there's something wrong with her." I don't know where it comes from, but I have to believe it's partly the fact that you turn on TV or open a magazine and every girl has a boyfriend, every girl is a hundred and twenty pounds, and beautiful. You should be thin, you should have a boyfriend, and you should be smart too. The culture tells you also, not too smart, not too self-empowered, not too independent. And you shouldn't be too good either, because that's not fun.

I've always been at the top of my class academically and involved in volunteer activities. I was Miss Involved, the perfect college candidate. But at the same time, I was so hugely affected by wanting to fit in. I didn't realize how low my self-esteem was, my self-image. I still have body-image problems, I have eating disorders. I'm a self-empowered woman and a feminist, and I believe I can do all these things, and I see how successful I've been in my life—but at the same time I am so affected by not feeling pretty enough, not feeling thin enough.

I've definitely changed a lot going to college. I go to a small college in Minnesota, it's known for being highly liberal and highly intense. As a general rule they get students that were social outcasts in high school—the majority of them are out to be different, weird. It puts me in the absolute norm, and all of a sudden I come off as being really good-looking. What I realized in college was how damaged I was, like emotionally, by the silliest things . . . Like the fact that I didn't make cheerleading when I was younger, or the fact that I always felt fat, and how that had a huge, huge, huge, huge impact on my life. I don't think there's ever been a time, in the last eight years, when I haven't been on a diet. My perspective is: I am heavier than everybody else. [sighs] I'm not anorexic or bulimic, but I definitely have a bad relationship with food.

I never enjoy food, there's always the guilt. Guilt, guilt, guilt. If I eat too much today, then I won't eat tomorrow at all. I weigh myself every single day without fail, and if I gain a pound it affects my mood the whole day. I tie food to emotions. When I'm upset I have two reactions: binge or starve—eat celery and water for a week, or eat a whole pizza. I just can't seem to ever eat normally. When I'm in public—when I go out for dinner, when I am at the college cafeteria—I eat nothing.

My roommates were the ones that said, "Gretchen, something's wrong—you're totally binging." They made me get help, they begged me for months. They were like, "We're calling your parents if you don't." Finally my roommate made the appointment. I said, "Fine, I'll go once"—and I went three times. But oh my God, to this day I'm still denying the fact that I have an eating disorder. Or I see it as, "Lots of people have eating disorders, mine isn't serious—there are people with much worse problems." So when I talk about this it's not me speaking, it's not my true feeling. It's what I've come to accept, and I'm trying to talk myself into it.

How am I gonna stop the "I'm not worthy" stuff? [sighs] You know what is really pathetic? When my therapist asked me that, I answered, "Lose fifteen pounds." [laughs]

And part of me believes that if I just lose the weight I'll be OK. Isn't that awful? And I know that's wrong—I know life's not easier for beautiful people. But you get cut a break here and there when you're beautiful: you get more attention, you get taken more seriously. It's no joke that as an overweight person it's harder for you, and that success is sometimes tied to physical appearance.

The media says everyone should be thin and pretty, and I think that's a *huge* influence on all teenagers. There's such a high expectation to be something they can't be. I think they're uncomfortable, they feel kind of dumped on, like the expectations of them are too much. It's the loss of innocence. We have teenagers growing up with adult issues, and they're without all the emotional resources to deal with that. You're still a child in so many ways: you don't have the stability, the self-confidence yet, but you're *forced* to deal with things. There's nothing sacred about being a teenager anymore—you grow up so fast. . . .

I love my parents, we're very close. And they've both worked hard, they're not rich, they're middle-class people. [sighs] Gosh, this is such a big source of guilt with me. [distressed] How am I gonna tell my parents, who paid for my college education and worked hard, that they gotta sacrifice for me? I work every summer, I work over Christmas break, I do everything I can to help pay for my college education. And I hope somehow I'll be economically stable enough to help them out when they're older. That's the way it should work—like it used to in the olden days when kids took care of their parents. . . .

I want to make a lot of money, I want a beautiful house, and children, and a castle, and I want to be able to travel and see the world and be able to send my children to excellent schools. I want that, and I think part of me actually believes I'm gonna have that, but reality-speaking-wise, I know too much. I'll probably have to live it debt, and just make ends meet—especially if I want to work in the political field. I'm gonna drive a secondhand car and live in a small apartment, and probably not go out to dinner, and coupon-clip for the rest of my life. A couple years ago I thought, "I can't settle for that." Now I'm kind of like, "There's nothing wrong with that." I've come to realize that having a job you like is probably the most important thing.

I'm going to Washington, D.C., next term, through a program at school. I'm going to be working on the national deficit with an interest group that's Generation X, twenty-something politics. We're doing Social Security reform, the environment, infrastructure, education. I was thinking about what I could do when I come back—like maybe talk to high school classes. Going back and just explaining in simple terms, the debt, the deficit, what it means, how it affects you. I know I was scared off by economic terms in high school, but it's not that hard to understand. I want people to know, that is my whole goal. Because they don't really know. And who's to blame? You don't see it on the news, you don't see it in the kids' papers or magazines. What about *Seventeen* magazine? For all their hair and looks and makeup and fashion, what about something on the deficit? The right things are not in the media. There's such an audience: they watch so much TV, they read so many magazines; it'd be so easy to reach them, yet no one's doing it. That's kind of where my focus is going to be.

I'm thinking if I were to have a claim to fame, that's where I'd like to make my name: to start an organization or to spread education—*do something*. Use the power of one human being in a thousand to take the energy and money and time. It amazes me, the power of human beings, one in a thousand, to really do something, to be unselfish. And that's why we're going to be OK—probably.

Follow-Up

1. *Gretchen says "I love being protected, but I think there is a natural instinct to move on." She is expressing the tug and pull of the safety–growth conflict. Growth usually means that one must risk comfort and security to explore new ways of being. How has this safety–growth conflict emerged in your life and how have you reacted to it?*
2. *Select any two statements from this article and write or discuss your interpretations.*
3. *Gretchen states that she would eventually like a nice house, a lot of money, to travel, and to have children. But in reality she feels that she will probably never have all these. She perceives a large discrepancy between her dream life and her real one. How close is your dream life to your real one? What can you do to make it match more closely if there is a large gap?*
4. *Late adolescence and young adulthood is often a time for exploring alternative identities regarding career choices, relationship styles, appearance, and values. Describe your attempts in exploring identity choices.*

The Monster

Len Smith

It was a Saturday night and I had committed to going out with some friends to a new bar to shake some dust off of my social life. It had been several months since I had broken up with my girlfriend and my calendar was bare, with the exception of a national holiday or two. I was single so the possibility of finding the future "ex" was always looming on the horizon. I began the evening with the usual routine. I showered and then spent 20 minutes in front of a huge mirror in my bathroom using a hair dryer, a brush, three tons of hair gel, and every ounce of patience I could muster to get my hair to look "that certain way." The result probably would have looked the same if I had run a brush through it and called it a day. However, my skewed logic dictated that such attention to my hair builds confidence.

Next, I spent a half an hour trying to figure out what clothes I would wear. I started with a new shirt and jeans. Using a full-length mirror in my bedroom and a hand mirror, I began contorting myself and striking poses. Each move was an effort to determine whether the look I was going for was working. After five angles I determined the shirt wasn't right. I changed the shirt, then the jeans, then brought the shirt back, then the shirt with shorts and sandals, then a sweatshirt with sandals only including socks, then a button-down shirt, then every option only with boots, then a hat worn forward and backwards and after shedding more covering than a snake I found myself back in the original ensemble. The amount of consideration I had given this outfit proved to me that it was the right outfit. I had built more confidence. I doused myself in cologne, brushed my teeth, gargled with mouthwash, practiced my smile, and strutted out to my car.

When I arrived at my buddy's house, he was just getting out of the shower. He threw on a shirt, ran a brush through his hair and in under ten minutes he was ready to go. Ten minutes! I can't even change my mind in ten minutes! Obviously he wasn't as interested in meeting someone as I was. His lack of preparation would almost certainly leave him standing in a corner, one hand in his pocket—alone. Maybe the woman I would meet might have a friend. Finally after I took one last look in the bathroom mirror, we were in the car and heading downtown. Our destination was the Circle Center Mall's bar district, in particular a bar known as Flashbaxx.

When we arrived at the mall I reached up and contorted the rear view mirror so it was facing vertically towards the passenger seat. I had to primp one last time. A stray hair was neatly tucked back in place, the smile was practiced again, and my entire face was checked over to make sure there was nothing out of the ordinary that might cause a perspective date to point and yell, "Freak!" I thought to myself, "Maybe I should have worn a hat." I felt my confidence reaching peak levels. As we walked towards the mall, I brought my shoulders back, sucked in my stomach, swelled my neck muscles, put one hand in my pocket and began the stroll towards Flashbaxx. Mr. Cool.

We arrived at the Flashbaxx and to our delight ran into some friends we did not expect to meet. My little ship was sailing at full speed on a sea of confidence. We cut up a little, had a few beers and began sizing up the crowd. At about 10 o'clock the club was becoming very crowded. Flashbaxx was a thematic bar. Decked out with all the gaudiness and flores-cence of the 80s, walls adorned with memora-bilia from the 60s and 70s, I soon understood that the bar was named Flashbaxx because it played nothing but older tunes. It was when the D.J. fired up "Dancing Queen" by ABBA that I knew it could be a fun night. The bar was comprised of a wide variety of people—young and old, preppy and grunge, athletic and cos-mopolitan. The atmosphere was great. Three beers had relaxed me, my attention to my ap-pearance had built my confidence, and I was ready to meet someone.

Then it happened. Out of nowhere, fear came along and torpedoed my happy little boat; within seconds all hands were abandon-ing ship. I had thought of everything to pre-pare myself for the moment when I would be required to approach a total stranger and initiate a conversation. What I had not consid-ered, though, was how to actually go up and begin the conversation. Fresh out of a five-year relationship, my conversation skills with unknown women were as sharpened as a wooden spoon. There I stood in a crowded club with "Night Fever" by the Bee Gee's blar-ing while hundreds of closet disco kings and queens imitated John Travolta. I tried to re-hearse what I would say. Phrases like "Hey, isn't this music cool?" or "Great bar, eh!" or even "Do you come here often?" began to race around my head. I could not believe it. It was like my encyclopedia of clever conversation lines came from a *Brady Bunch* episode. After all my preparation, the fear of rejection had re-duced me to a piece of wet bread. I would have had a better chance of meeting someone if I had been wearing Speed-O's and a biking helmet. I tried to use the smile. I would catch a person's eye and I would think to myself, "I think she smiled back at me!" but the fear had risen so high that I just stood there. That is, until I had to move out of the way to make room for some guy that wasn't a mental

doughnut and didn't have a problem talking to strangers.

During my anxiety attack, my buddy had made his way up to the dance floor and was dancing with three women. I couldn't believe it. He had spent all of ten minutes getting ready. He had slept up until twenty minutes before we were supposed to leave! There he was six-foot-six, hair still a little wet from the shower, jumping up and down with three cute women to the tune of "My Sharona." On the other hand, I was frantically peeling the label off of my beer and striking a pose to look cool. If I had been watching myself from a distance I probably would have pointed and yelled "Freak!"

After a few hours of shifting my weight from one foot to the other, swelling my chest and acting cool I was sure I had made a com-plete fool out of myself. By about one o'clock we decided to leave. My buddy had a phone number, a good buzz, and an endless amount of stories about dancing for hours with three cute women. On the other hand, I could tell you every way to peel a beer label off and how to stand and look completely ridiculous while trying to meet someone without saying a word. What had I been afraid of? Did I think someone would actually yell "Leave me alone, idiot!" if I tried to make conversation? Or was it a fear that my attempts to make conversa-tion with a woman would cause all the music to stop, the lights to come on, and the entire bar to point and laugh while at the same time chanting, "Look at that guy's outfit, and that hair, and those teeth, and why isn't he wearing a hat?"

As we left Flashbaxx we ran into some friends from college. One of these friends was a young lady I had been attracted to but had not pursued because of my relationship with my ex-girlfriend. After some coy conversation and an exchange of phone numbers I realized that without knowing it I had flirted, had a po-lite conversation, and had not torn the label off of anything. All of this occurred without even a dry run to practice my smile. I'm not sure how it will go when I call this girl but one thing's for certain, the next time I hear "My Sharona" I'm going to be on a dance floor having fun—well, and maybe trying to look just a little cool.

Follow-Up

1. *The author faces a number of pressures and fears in an attempt to revitalize his romantic life. If you have had a similar circumstance, describe how you handled it. What seems to be the best way to lessen fears to a manageable level?*
2. *Write about or discuss any other aspect of this piece that relates to your life and how you face your fears.*

Ending the Battle between the Sexes

Aaron R. Kipnis
and Elizabeth Herron

Have you noticed that American men and women seem angrier at one another than ever? Belligerent superpowers have buried the hatchet, but the war between the sexes continues unabated. On every television talk show, women and men trade increasingly bitter accusations. We feel the tension in our homes, in our workplaces, and in our universities.

The Clarence Thomas–Anita Hill controversy and the incidents at the Navy's Tailhook convention brought the question of sexual harassment into the foreground of national awareness, but it now appears that these flaps have merely fueled male–female resentment instead of sparking a productive dialogue that might enhance understanding between the sexes.

Relations between women and men are rapidly changing. Often, however, these changes are seen to benefit one sex at the expense of the other, and the mistrust that results creates resentment. Most men and women seem unable to entertain the idea that the two sexes differing perspectives on many issues can be equally valid. So polarization grows instead of reconciliation, as many women and men fire ever bigger and better-aimed missiles across the gender gap. On both sides there's a dearth of compassion about the predicaments of the other sex.

For example:

- Women feel sexually harassed; men feel their courting behavior is often misunderstood.

- Women fear men's power to wound them physically; men fear women's power to wound them emotionally.
- Women say men aren't sensitive enough; men say women are too emotional.
- Women feel men don't do their fair share of housework and child care; men feel that women don't feel as much pressure to provide the family's income and do home maintenance.
- Many women feel morally superior to men; many men feel that they are more logical and just than women.
- Women say men have destroyed the environment; men say the women's movement has destroyed the traditional family.
- Men are often afraid to speak about the times that they feel victimized and powerless; women frequently deny their real power.
- Women feel that men don't listen; men feel that women talk too much.
- Women resent being paid less than men; men are concerned about the occupational hazards and stress that lead to their significantly shorter life spans.
- Men are concerned about unfairness in custody and visitation rights; women are concerned about fathers who shirk their child support payments.

It is very difficult to accept the idea that so many conflicting perspectives could all have intrinsic value. Many of us fear that listening to the story of another will somehow weaken our own voice, our own initiative, even our own identity. The fear keeps us locked in adversarial thinking and patterns of blame and alienation. In this frightened absence of empathy, devaluation of the other sex grows.

In an attempt to address some of the discord between the sexes, we have been conducting gender workshops around the country. We invite men and women to spend some time in all-male and all-female groups, talking about the opposite sex. Then we bring the two groups into an encounter with one another. In one of our mixed groups this spring, Susan, a 35-year-old advertising executive, told the men, "Most men these days are insensitive jerks. When are men going to get it that we are coming to work to make a living, not to get laid? Anita Hill was obviously telling the truth. Most of the women I work with have been harassed as well."

Michael, her co-worker, replied, "Then why didn't she tell him ten years ago that what he was doing was offensive? How are we supposed to know where your boundaries are if you laugh at our jokes, smile when you're angry, and never confront us in the direct way a man would? How am I supposed to learn what's not OK with you if the first time I hear about it is at a grievance hearing?"

We've heard many permutations of this same conversation:

Gina, a 32-year-old school teacher in Washington, D.C., asks, "Why don't men ever take no for an answer?"

Arthur, a 40-year-old construction foreman, replies that in his experience, "some women *do* in fact say no when they mean yes. Women seem to believe that men should do all the pursuing in the mating dance. But then if we don't read her silent signals right, we're the bad guys. If we get it right, though, then we're heroes."

Many men agree that they are in a double bind. They are labeled aggressive jerks if they come on strong, but are rejected as wimps if they don't. Women feel a similar double bind. They are accused of being teases if they make themselves attractive but reject the advances of men. Paradoxically, however, as Donna, a fortyish divorcée, reports, "When I am up front about my desires, men often head for the hills."

As Deborah Tannen, author of the bestseller about male-female language styles *You Just Don't Understand,* has observed, men and women often have entirely different styles of communication. How many of us have jokingly speculated that men and women actually come from different planets? But miscommunication alone is not the source of all our sorrow.

Men have an ancient history of enmity toward women. For centuries, many believed women to be the cause of our legendary fall from God's grace. "How can he be clean that is born of woman?" asks the Bible. Martin Luther wrote that "God created Adam Lord of all living things, but Eve spoiled it all." The "enlightened" '60s brought us Abbie Hoffman, who said: "The only alliance I would make with the women's liberation movement is in bed." And from the religious right, Jerry Falwell still characterizes feminism as a "satanic attack" on the American family.

In turn, many feel the women's movement devalues the role of men. Marilyn French, author of *The Women's Room,* said, "All men are rapists and that's all they are." In response to the emerging men's movement, Betty Friedan commented, "Oh God, sick . . . I'd hoped by now men were strong enough to accept their vulnerability and to be authentic without aping Neanderthal cavemen."

This hostility to the men's movement is somewhat paradoxical. Those who are intimately involved with the movement say that it is primarily dedicated to ending war and racism, increasing environmental awareness, healing men's lives and reducing violence, promoting responsible fatherhood, and creating equal partnerships with women—all things with which feminism is ideologically aligned. Yet leaders of the men's movement often evoke indignant responses from women. A prominent woman attorney tells us, "I've been waiting 20 years for men to hear our message. Now instead of joining us at last, they're starting their *own* movement. And now they want us to hear that they're wounded too. It makes me sick."

On the other hand, a leader of the men's movement says, "I was a feminist for 15 years. Recently, I realized that all the men I know are struggling just as much as women. Also, I'm tired of all the male-bashing. I just can't listen to women's issues anymore while passively watching so many men go down the tubes."

Some of our gender conflict is an inevitable by-product of the positive growth that has occurred in our society over the last generation. The traditional gender roles of previous generations imprisoned many women and men in soul-killing routines. Women felt dependent and disenfranchised; men felt distanced from feelings, family, and their capacity for self-care.

With almost 70 percent of women now in the work force, calls for women to return to the home full time seem ludicrous, not to mention financially impossible. In addition, these calls for the traditional nuclear family ignore the fact that increasing numbers of men now want to downshift from full-time work in order to spend more time at home. So if we can't go back to the old heroic model of masculinity and the old domestic ideal of femininity, how then do we weave a new social fabric out of the broken strands of worn-out sexual stereotypes?

Numerous participants in the well-established women's movement, as well as numbers of men in the smaller but growing men's movement, have been discovering the strength, healing, power, and sense of security that come from being involved with a same-sex group. Women and men have different social, psychological, and biological realities and receive different behavioral training from infancy through adulthood.

In most pre-technological societies, women and men both participate in same-sex social and ceremonial groups. The process of becoming a woman or a man usually begins with some form of ritual initiation. At the onset of puberty, young men and women are brought into the men's and women's lodges, where they gain a deep sense of gender identity.

Even in our own culture, women and men have traditionally had places to meet apart from members of the other sex. For generations, women have gathered over coffee or quilts; men have bonded at work and in taverns. But in our modern society, most heterosexuals believe that a member of the opposite sex is supposed to fulfill all their emotional and social needs. Most young people today are not taught to respect and honor the differences of the other gender, and they arrive at adulthood both mystified and distrustful, worried about the other sex's power to affect them. In fact, most cross-gender conflict is essentially *conflict between different cultures.* Looking at the gender war from this perspective may help us develop solutions to our dilemmas.

In recent decades, cultural anthropologists have come to believe that people are more productive members of society when they can retain their own cultural identity within the framework of the larger culture. As a consequence, the old American "melting pot" theory of cultural assimilation has evolved into a new theory of diversity, whose model might be the "tossed salad." In this ideal, each subculture retains its essential identity, while coexisting within the same social container.

Applying this idea to men and women, we can see the problems with the trend of the past several decades toward a sex-role melting pot. In our quest for gender equality through sameness, we are losing both the beauty of our diversity and our tolerance for differences. Just as a monoculture is not as environmentally stable or rich as a diverse natural ecosystem, androgyny denies the fact that sexual differences are healthy.

In the past, perceived differences between men and women have been used to promote discrimination, devaluation, and subjugation. As a result, many "we're all the same" proponents—New Agers and humanistic social theorists, for example—are justifiably suspicious of discussions that seek to restore awareness of our differences. But pretending that differences do not exist is not the way to end discrimination toward either sex.

Our present challenge is to acknowledge the value of our differing experiences as men and women, and to find ways to reap this harvest in the spirit of true equality. Carol Tavris, in her book *The Mismeasure of Women,* suggests that instead of "regarding cultural and reproductive differences as problems to be eliminated, we should aim to eliminate *the unequal consequences that follow from them.*"

Some habits are hard to change, even with an egalitarian awareness. Who can draw the line between what is socially conditioned and what is natural? It may not be possible, or even desirable, to do so. What seems more important is that women and men start understanding each other's different cultures and granting one another greater freedom to experiment with whatever roles or lifestyles attract them.

Lisa, a 29-year-old social worker from New York participating in one of our gender workshops, told us, "Both Joel [her husband] and I work full time. But it always seems to be me who ends up having to change my schedule when Gabe, our son, has a doctor's appointment or a teacher conference, is sick at home or has to be picked up after school. It's simply taken for granted that in most cases my time is less important than his. I know Joel tries really hard to be an engaged father. But

the truth is that I feel I'm always on the front line when it comes to the responsibilities of parenting and keeping the home together. It's just not fair."

Joel responds by acknowledging that Lisa's complaint is justified; but he says, "I handle all the home maintenance, fix the cars, do all the banking and bookkeeping and all the yard work as well. These things aren't hobbies. I also work more overtime than Lisa. Where am I supposed to find the time to equally co-parent too? Is Lisa going to start mowing the lawn or help me build the new bathroom? Not likely."

In many cases of male-female conflict, as with Lisa and Joel, there are two differing but *equally valid* points of view. Yet in books, the media, and in women's and men's groups, we only hear about most issues from a woman's point of view or from a man's. This is at the root of the escalating war between the sexes.

For us, the starting point in the quest for gender peace is for men and women to spend more time with members of the same sex. We have found that many men form intimate friendships in same-sex groups. In addition to supporting their well-being, these connections can take some of the pressure off their relationships with women. Men in close friendships no longer expect women to satisfy *all* their emotional needs. And when women meet in groups they support one another's need for connection and also for empowerment in the world. Women then no longer expect men to provide their sense of self-worth. So these same-sex groups can enhance not only the participants' individual lives, but their relationships with members of the other sex as well.

If men and women *remain* separated, however, we risk losing perspective and continuing the domination or scapegoating of the other sex. In women's groups, male-bashing has been running rampant for years. At a recent lecture we gave at a major university, a young male psychology student said, "This is the first time in three years on campus that I have heard anyone say a single positive thing about men or masculinity."

Many women voice the same complaint about their experiences in male-dominated workplaces. Gail, a middle management executive, says, "When I make proposals to the all-male board of directors, I catch the little condescending smirks and glances the men give one another. They don't pull that shit when my male colleagues speak. If they're that rude in front of me, I can only imagine how degrading their comments are when they meet in private."

There are few arenas today in which women and men can safely come together on common ground to frankly discuss our rapidly changing ideas about gender justice. Instead of more sniping from the sidelines, what is needed is for groups of women and men to communicate directly with one another. When we take this *next step* and make a commitment to spend time apart and then meet with each other, then we can begin to build a true social, political, and spiritual equality. This process also instills a greater appreciation for the unique gifts each sex has to contribute.

Husband-and-wife team James Sniechowski and Judith Sherven conduct gender reconciliation meetings—similar to the meetings we've been holding around the country—each month in Southern California. In a recent group of 25 people (11 women, 14 men), participants were invited to explore questions like: What did you learn about being a man/woman from your mother? From your father? Sniechowski reports that "even though, for the most part, the men and women revealed their confusions, mistrust, heartbreaks, and bewilderments, the room quickly filled with a poignant beauty." As one woman said of the meeting, "When I listen to the burdens we suffer, it helps me soften my heart toward them." On another occasion a man said, "My image of women shifts as I realize

they've been through some of the same stuff I have."

Discussions such as these give us an opportunity to really hear one another and, perhaps, discover that many of our disagreements come from equally valid, if different, points of view. What many women regard as intimacy feels suffocating and invasive to men. What many men regard as masculine strength feels isolating and distant to women. Through blame and condemnation, women and men shame one another. Through compassionate communication, however, we can help one another. This mutual empowerment is in the best interests of both sexes, because when one sex suffers, the other does too.

Toward the end of our meetings, men and women inevitably become more accountable for the ways in which they contribute to the problem. Gina said, "I've never really heard the men's point of view on all this before. I must admit that I rarely give men clear signals when they say or do something that offends me."

Arthur then said, "All my life I've been trained that my job as a man is to keep pursuing until 'no' is changed to 'yes, yes, yes.' But I hear it that when a woman says no, they want me to respect it. I get it now that what I thought was just a normal part of the dance is experienced as harassment by some women. But you know, it seems that if we're ever going to get together now, more women are going to have to start making the first moves."

After getting support from their same-sex groups and then listening to feedback from the whole group, Joel and Lisa realize that if they are both going to work full time they need to get outside help with family tasks, rather than continuing to blame and shame one another for not doing more.

Gender partnership based on strong, interactive, separate but equal gender identities can support the needs of both sexes. Becoming more affirming or supportive of our same sex doesn't have to lead to hostility toward the other sex. In fact, the acknowledgment that gender diversity is healthy may help all of us to become more tolerant toward other kinds of differences in our society.

Through gender reconciliation—both formal workshops and informal discussions—the sexes can support each other, instead of blaming one sex for not meeting the other's expectations. Men and women clearly have the capacity to move away from the sex-war rhetoric that is dividing us as well as the courage necessary to create forums for communication that can unite and heal us.

Boys and girls need regular opportunities in school to openly discuss their differing views on dating, sex, and gender roles. In universities, established women's studies courses could be complemented with men's studies, and classes in the two fields could be brought together from time to time to deepen students' understanding of both sexes. The informal discussion group is another useful format in which men and women everywhere can directly communicate with each other (see *Utne Reader* issue no. 44 [March/April 1991]). In the workplace the struggle for gender understanding needs to go beyond the simple setting up of guidelines about harassment; it is essential that women and men regularly discuss their differing views on gender issues. Outside help is often needed in structuring such discussions and getting them

under way. Our organization, the Gender Relations Institute, trains and provides "reconciliation facilitators" for that purpose.

These forums must be fair. Discussions of women's wage equity must also include men's job safety. Discussions about reproductive rights, custody rights, or parental leave must consider the rights of both mothers and fathers—and the needs of the children. Affirmative action to balance the male-dominated political and economic leadership must also bring balance to the female-dominated primary-education and social-welfare systems.

We call for both sexes to come to the negotiating table from a new position of increased strength and self-esteem. Men and women do not need to become more like one another, merely more deeply themselves. But gender understanding is only a step on the long road that must ultimately lead to fundamental institutional change. We would hope, for example, that in the near future men and women will stop arguing about whether women should go into combat and concentrate instead on how to end war. The skills and basic attitudes that will lead to gender peace are the very ones we need in order to meet the other needs of our time—social, political, and environmental—with committed action.

Follow-Up

1. *Explain why you agree or disagree with the authors' contention that in cases of male–female conflict there are two differing but equally valid points of view.*
2. *Discuss or write about your views on any two statements in this article.*
3. *What is one major issue or question you would like answered by the opposite gender? Consider asking a few members of the opposite gender and report the responses and your analysis.*
4. *To attempt the authors' strategy for attaining gender peace, see the end of this section and the Applied Activity entitled "Men and Women: A Dialogue."*

On Being a Man

Sam Keen

The year I was seventeen I received many messages from my classmates, my family, and my culture about what was required to be a *real man:*

> *Join the fraternity.*
> *Get a letter in football, baseball, or basketball.*
> *Screw a lot of girls.*
> *Be tough; fight if anybody insults you or your girl.*
> *Don't show your feelings.*
> *Drink lots of beer (predrug era).*
> *Be nice—don't fight or drink.*
> *Dress right—like everybody else: penny loafers, etc.*
> *Get a good job, work hard and make a lot of money.*
> *Get your own car.*
> *Be well liked, popular.*

* * *

Today I look at an old picture of that seventeen-year-old boy.... His clandestine life included many activities not on any list of requirements for being a *real man:* keeping a diary; exploring nearby woods and longing for the wilderness;...wondering about the limits of his mind; exploring his dark moods; writing poetry;...loving his parents;...wanting to do something to make the world better....

The popular cliché says that men think and do, women feel and emote. It's a half-truth worth playing with. Most of us learned that real men were supposed to control their feelings.... Little did we understand that by doing the manly thing, girding up our loins, pulling in our guts, pushing out our chests, tightening our jaws, and constricting our breathing, we forced most feelings into exile in our unconscious....

Perhaps the greatest price men have paid for their obsession with fearlessness is to have become tough on the outside but empty within. We are hollow men. The connection between fearlessness and feelinglessness should be obvious.... Men and women seem to have different styles of fearing. Men's fears focus around loss of what we experience as our independence, and women's around the loss of significant relationships....

...Men are more fearful of death than women.... Men make lousy patients. Ask any doctor. Disease and disability frighten us more than they do women.... Sickness raises the specter of all that men have been taught to fear: weakness, dependency, passivity....

Men usually do not talk much about their sexual fears and disappointments. Sex is a big thing for us. And we judge it in more absolute terms than women do. It is either/or. Up or down.

Follow-Up

1. *Either as a man, or in your experiences with men, how accurate are Keen's views about manhood today?*
2. *Select one of Keen's statements and discuss your reaction.*

From Both Sides

Lillian Rubin

Stop a woman in mid-sentence with the question, "What are you feeling right now?" and you might have to wait a bit while she reruns the mental tape to capture the moment just passed. But, more than likely, she'll be able to do it successfully. More than likely, she'll think for a while and come up with an answer.

The same is not true of a man. For him, a similar question usually will bring a sense of wonderment that one would even ask it, followed quickly by an uncomprehending and puzzled response. "What do you mean?" he'll ask. "I was just talking," he'll say.

To a woman, the world men live in seems a lonely one—a world in which their fears of exposing their sadness and pain, their anxiety about allowing their vulnerability to show, even to a woman they love, is so deeply rooted inside them that, most often, they can only allow it to happen "late at night in the dark."

Yet, if we listen to what men say, we will hear their insistence that they *do* speak of what's inside them, *do* share their thoughts and feelings with the women they love. "I tell her, but she's never satisfied," they complain. "No matter how much I say, it's never enough," they grumble.

From both sides, the complaints have merit. The problem lies not in what men don't say, however, but in what's not there—in what, quite simply, happens so far out of consciousness that it's not within their reach. For men have integrated all too well the lessons of their childhood—the experiences that taught them to repress and deny their inner thoughts, wishes, needs, and fears; indeed, not even to notice them. It's real, therefore, that the kind of inner thoughts and feelings that are readily accessible to a woman generally are unavailable to a man. When he says, "I don't know what I'm feeling," he isn't necessarily being intransigent and withholding. More than likely, he speaks the truth.

Boy in Blue Tutu

Lisen Stromberg

My son is a cross-dresser. Most mornings he gets up, puts on a hand-me-down dress, wraps an old pillowcase around his head with a ribbon (to create his "long blond hair"), and prances around singing "The hills are alive with the sound of music." My son is 3 years old.

At the toy store, he does not want a Batman doll. "I want Batgirl," he cries. When he begs to play with his friend Margo, it is because she has an extensive collection of Barbie dolls and outfits in which he can dress them.

He loves preschool for the teachers, but also for the wonderful selection of tutus, party shoes, and costume jewelry. His grandmother received the shock of her life when she went to pick him up at school one day and he was wearing a blue tutu with beaded gold slippers. His teacher tells us that he is "highly in touch with his feminine side."

Not everyone is so empathetic. "Boys should be playing baseball, not Barbie," my mother-in-law exclaims. "He keeps taking my daughter's Cinderella slippers!" my neighbor tells my other neighbor, who then tells me. Strangers ask, "So when do you think he will grow out of it?" and "How does your husband feel?"

I've tried to explain to these people that my son approaches life with a unique flair. He loves soccer, and he often plays in a silk cape that flutters in the wind when he runs. My husband can't wait for Little League to start because our son can already hit the ball out of the backyard. Our son can't wait for baseball, either, but for a different reason: He says the cleats are "just like tap shoes."

No one seems to be the least bit disturbed about my son's friend Gillian. At the age of 5, she refuses to wear dresses, plays T-ball and soccer, and is skilled at climbing trees and collecting bruises. Gillian is a tomboy. "Isn't she cute?" a friend exclaims to me. But my son, I remind myself, is not cute when he dresses up and re-enacts the glass slipper scene from *Cinderella*.

If Gillian is a tomboy because she likes to do boylike things, does that make my son a janegirl? As far as I can tell, there isn't an equivalent word in the English language. More importantly, while it's OK—even cute—for a girl to "behave like a boy," my son's "girlish" behavior is viewed as less than acceptable. Watching my son grow up, I have begun to ask myself: What is normal? My son also loves trucks, cars, and trains. Last fall, during his terrible twos, he was accused of being a bully because he bit a girl at the playground. How can a child go from bully to sissy in just 12 months?

While our sex-role stereotypes have expanded for girls, they have contracted for boys. We're doing research to help ensure that girls will excel in math, overcome the repression of adolescence, and get elected to corporate boards. I'm thrilled. Trust me: I have a 1-year-old daughter. But what about my son? It is not just in my house that the days of "boys will be boys" seem to be over. Prescriptions for Ritalin are at an all-time high, and, increasingly, boys are expected to be less rambunctious and more docile—that is, be more like girls. My mind reels: Is society saying that a 3-year-old boy should be more like a man, but a 12-year-old should be more like a girl?

Sometimes, I have to admit, even I am embarrassed by my son's behavior. His recent declaration to my father-in-law that he wants to be a ballet dancer when he grows up almost created a family feud. When the father of one of his preschool classmates unintentionally called him a girl—he was wearing that blue tutu—I cringed just a little. And I am often confused about the messages I'm sending him. I don't mind if he wants to wear pink lipstick to a birthday party—"Mom, you wear lipstick when you dress up!" he reminds me—but how do I protect him from the taunting that inevitably will occur as he ages?

I come back to my original question: What is normal? My husband and I are learning all too early in our son's life that the boundaries of normalcy are narrow. On the other hand, my son, who at the moment is pretending to be Belle from *Beauty and the Beast,* complete with pearl-drop earrings, doesn't know this yet. With luck and a little parental intervention, he won't for a long time. Until then, Beauty, at least in our household, will reign.

Follow-Up

1. *Select two statements from this article and offer your interpretations. Ask at least two others about their views on these same statements. Obtain at least two views that differ from your own. Describe your reaction and learnings.*
2. *The author says that it is more acceptable for a girl to act like a boy than vice-versa. Do you agree? Should there be more equity in this?*
3. *Stromberg claims that sex-role stereotypes have expanded for girls but have contracted for boys. Explain why you agree or disagree with this view.*
4. *See "X: A Fabulous Child's Story" by Lois Gould for issues that relate to this article.*

X: A Fabulous Child's Story

Lois Gould

Once upon a time, a baby named X was born. This baby was named X so that nobody could tell whether it was a boy or girl. Its parents could tell, of course, but they couldn't tell anybody else. They couldn't even tell Baby X, at first.

You see, it was all part of a very important Secret Scientific Xperiment, known officially as Project Baby X. The smartest scientists had set up this Xperiment at a cost of Xactly 23 billion dollars and 72 cents, which might seem like a lot for just one baby, even a very important Xperimental baby. But when you remember the prices of things like strained carrots and stuffed bunnies, and popcorn for the movies and booster shots for camp, let alone 28 shiny quarters from the tooth fairy, you begin to see how it adds up.

Also, long before Baby X was born, all those scientists had to be paid to work out the details of the Xperiment, and to write the *Official Instruction Manual* for Baby X's parents and, most important of all, to find the right set of parents to bring up Baby X. These parents had to be selected very carefully. Thousands of volunteers had to take thousands of tests and answer thousands of tricky questions. Almost everybody failed because, it turned out, almost everybody really wanted either a baby boy or a baby girl, and not Baby X at all. Also, almost everybody was afraid that Baby X would be a lot more trouble than a boy or a girl. (They were probably right, the scientists admitted, but Baby X needed parents who wouldn't *mind* the Xtra trouble.)

There were families with grandparents named Milton and Agatha, who didn't see why the baby couldn't be named Milton or Agatha instead of X, even if it *was* an X. There were families with aunts who insisted on sending tiny baseball mitts. Worst of all, these were families that already had other children who couldn't be trusted to keep the secret. Certainly not if they knew the secret was worth 23 billion dollars and 72 cents—and all you had to do was take one little peek at Baby X in the bathtub to know if it was a boy or a girl.

But, finally, the scientists found the Joneses, who really wanted to raise an X more than any other kind of baby—no matter how much trouble it would be. Ms. and Mr. Jones had to promise they would take equal turns caring for X, and feeding it, and singing lullabies. And they had to promise never to hire any baby-sitters. The government scientists knew perfectly well that the baby-sitter would probably peek at X in the bathtub, too.

The day the Joneses brought their baby home, lots of friends and relatives came over to see it. None of them knew about the secret Xperiment, though. So the first thing they asked was what kind of baby X was. When the Joneses smiled and said, "It's an X!" nobody knew what to say. They couldn't say, "Look at her cute little dimples!" And they couldn't say, "Look at his husky little biceps!" And they couldn't even say just plain "kitchy-coo." In fact, they all thought the Joneses were playing some kind of rude joke.

But, of course, the Joneses were not joking. "It's an X" was absolutely all they would say. And that made the friends and relatives very angry. The relatives felt embarrassed about having an X in the family. "People will think there's something wrong with it!" some of them whispered. "There is something wrong with it!" others whispered back.

"Nonsense!" the Joneses told them all cheerfully. "What could possibly be wrong with this perfectly adorable X?"

Nobody could answer that, except Baby X, who had just finished its bottle. Baby X's answer was a loud, satisfied burp.

Clearly, nothing at all was wrong. Nevertheless, none of the relatives felt comfortable about buying a present for a Baby X. The cousins who sent the baby a tiny football helmet would not come and visit any more. And the neighbors who sent a pink-flowered romper suit pulled their shades down when the Joneses passed their house. The *Official Instruction Manual* had warned the new parents that this would happen, so they didn't fret about it. Besides, they were too busy with Baby X and the hundreds of different Xercises for treating it properly.

Ms. and Mr. Jones had to be Xtra careful about how they played with little X. They knew that if they kept bouncing it up in the air and saying how *strong* and *active* it was, they'd be treating it more like a boy than an X. But if all they did was cuddle it and kiss it and tell it how *sweet* and *dainty* it was, they'd be treating it more like a girl than an X.

On page 1,654 of the *Official Instruction Manual*, the scientists prescribed: "plenty of bouncing and plenty of cuddling, *both*. X ought to be strong and sweet and active. Forget about *dainty* altogether."

Meanwhile, the Joneses were worrying about other problems. Toys, for instance. And clothes. On his first shopping trip, Mr. Jones told the store clerk, "I need some clothes and toys for my new baby." The clerk smiled and said, "Well, now, is it for a boy or a girl?" "It's an X," Mr. Jones said, smiling back. But the clerk got all red in the face and said huffily, "In *that* case, I'm afraid I can't help you, sir." So, Mr. Jones wandered helplessly up and down the aisles trying to find what X needed. But everything in the store was piled up in sections marked "Boys" or "Girls." There were "Boys' Pajamas" and "Girls' Underwear" and "Boys' Fire Engines" and "Girls' Housekeeping Sets." Mr. Jones went home without buying anything for X. That night he and Ms. Jones consulted page 2,326 of the *Official Instruction Manual*. "Buy plenty of everything!" it said firmly.

So they brought plenty of sturdy blue pajamas in the Boys' Department and cheerful flowered underwear in the Girls' Department. And they bought all kinds of toys. A boy doll that made pee-pee and cried, "Pa-pa." And a girl doll that talked in three languages and said, "I am the Pres-i-dent of Gen-er-al Mo-tors." They also bought a storybook about a brave princess who rescued a handsome prince from his ivory tower, and another one about a sister and brother who grew up to be a baseball and a ballet star, and you had to guess which was which.

The head scientist of Project Baby X checked all their purchases and told them to keep up the good work. They also reminded the Joneses to see page 4,629 of the *Manual*, where it said, "Never make Baby X feel *embarrassed* or *ashamed* about what it wants to play with. And if X gets dirty climbing rocks, never say 'Nice little Xes don't get dirty climbing rocks'."

Likewise, it said, "If X falls down and cries, never say 'Brave little Xes don't cry.' Because, of course, nice little Xes *do* get dirty, and brave little Xes *do* cry. No matter how dirty X gets, or how hard it cries, don't worry. It's all part of the Xperiment."

Whenever the Joneses pushed Baby X's stroller in the park, smiling strangers would come over and coo: "Is that a boy or girl?" The Joneses would smile back and say, "It's an X." The strangers would stop smiling then, and often snarl something nasty—as if the Joneses had snarled at *them*.

By the time X grew big enough to play with other children, the Joneses' troubles had grown bigger, too. Once a little girl grabbed X's shovel in the sandbox, and zonked X on the head with it. "Now, now, Tracy," the little girl's mother began to scold, "little girls mustn't hit little—" and she turned to ask X, "Are you a little boy or a little girl, dear?"

Mr. Jones, who was sitting near the sandbox, held his breath and crossed his fingers.

X smiled politely at the lady, even though X's head had never been zonked so hard in its life. "I'm a little X," X replied.

"You're a *what*?" the lady exclaimed angrily. "You're a little b-r-a-t, you mean!"

"But little girls mustn't hit little Xes, either!" said X, retrieving the shovel with another polite smile. "What good does hitting do, anyway?"

X's father, who was still holding his breath, finally let it out, uncrossed his fingers, and grinned back at X.

And at their next secret Project Baby X meeting, the scientists grinned, too. Baby X was doing fine.

But then it was time for X to start school. The Joneses were really worried about this, because school was even more full of rules for boys and girls, and there were no rules for Xes. The teacher would tell boys to form one line, and girls to form another line. There would be boys' games and girls' games, and boys' secrets and girls' secrets. The school library would have a list of recommended book for boys. There would even be a bathroom marked BOYS and another one marked GIRLS. Pretty soon boys and girls would hardly talk to each other. What would happen to poor little X?

The Joneses spent weeks consulting their *Instruction Manual* (there were 249½ pages of advice under "First Day of School"), and attending urgent special conferences with the smart scientists of Project Baby X.

The scientists had to make sure that X's mother had taught X how to throw and catch a ball properly, and that X's father had been sure to teach X what to serve at a doll's tea party. X had to know how to shoot marbles and how to jump rope and, most of all, what to say when the Other Children asked whether X was a Boy or a Girl.

Finally, X was ready. The Joneses helped X button on a nice new pair of red-and-white checked overalls, and sharpened six pencils for X's nice new pencilbox, and marked X's name clearly on all the books in the nice new bookbag. X brushed its teeth and combed its hair, which just about covered its ears, and remembered to put a napkin in its lunchbox.

The Joneses had asked X's teacher if the class could line up alphabetically, instead of forming separate lines for boys and girls. And they had asked if X could use the principal's bathroom, because it wasn't marked anything except BATHROOM. X's teacher promised to take care of all those problems. But nobody could help X with the biggest problem of all—Other Children.

Nobody in X's class had ever known an X before. What would they think? How would X make friends?

You couldn't tell what X was by studying its clothes—overalls don't even button right-to-left, like girls' clothes, or left-to-right, like boys' clothes. And you couldn't guess whether X had a girl's haircut or a boy's long haircut. And it was very hard to tell by the games X liked to play. Either X played ball very well for a girl, or else X played house very well for a boy.

Some of the children tried to find out by asking X tricky questions, like "Who's your favorite sports star?" That was easy. X had two favorite sports stars: a girl jockey named Robyn Smith and a boy archery champion named Robin Hood. Then they asked, "What's your favorite TV program?" And that was even easier. X's favorite TV program was "Lassie," which stars a girl dog played by a boy dog.

When X decided that its favorite toy was a doll, everyone decided that X must be a girl. But then X said that the doll was really a robot, and that X had computerized it, and that it was programmed to bake fudge brownies and then to clean up the kitchen. After X told them that, the other children gave up guessing what X was. All they knew was they'd sure like to see X's doll.

After school, X wanted to play with the other children. "How about shooting some baskets in the gym?" X asked the girls. But all they did was make faces and giggle behind X's back.

"How about weaving some baskets in the arts and crafts room?" X asked the boys. But they all made faces and giggled behind X's back, too.

That night, Ms. and Mr. Jones asked X how things had gone at school. X told them sadly that the lessons were okay, but otherwise school was a terrible place for an X. It seemed as if Other Children would never want an X for a friend.

Once more, the Joneses reached for their *Instruction Manual.* Under "Other Children," they found the following message: "What did you Xpect? *Other Children* have to obey all the silly boy-girl rules, because their parents taught them to. Lucky X—you don't have to stick to the rules at all! All you have to do is be yourself. P. S. We're not saying it'll be easy."

X liked being itself. But X cried a lot that night, partly because it felt afraid. So X's father held X tight, and cuddled it, and couldn't help crying a little, too. And X's mother cheered them both by reading an Xciting story about an enchanted prince called Sleeping Handsome, who woke up when Princess Charming kissed him.

The next morning, they all felt better, and little X went back to school with a brave smile and a clean pair of red-and-white checked overalls.

There was a seven-letter-word spelling bee in class that day. And a seven-lap boys' relay race in the gym. And a seven-layer-cake baking contest in the girls' kitchen corner. X won the spelling bee. X also won the relay race. And X almost won the baking contest, except it forgot to light the oven. Which only proves that nobody's perfect. Other Children noticed something else, too. He said "Winning or losing doesn't seem to count to X. X seems to have fun being good at boys' skills *and* girls' skills."

"Come to think of it," said another one of the Other Children, "maybe X is having twice as much fun as we are!"

So after school that day, the girl who beat X at the baking contest gave X a big slice of her prize winning cake. And the boy X beat in the relay race asked X to race him home.

From then on, some really funny things began to happen. Susie, who sat next to X in class, suddenly refused to wear pink dresses to school any more. She insisted on wearing red-and-white checked overalls—just like X's. Overalls, she told her parents, were much better for climbing monkey bars.

Then Jim, the class football nut, started wheeling his little sister's doll carriage around the football field. He'd put on his entire football uniform, except for the helmet. Then he'd put the helmet in the carriage, lovingly tucked under an old set of shoulder pads. Then he'd start jogging around the field, pushing the carriage and singing "Rockabye Baby" to his football helmet. He told his family that X did the same thing, so it must be okay. After all, X was now the team's star quarterback.

Susie's parents were horrified by her behavior, and Jim's parents were worried sick about his. But the worst came when the twins, Joe and Peggy, decided to share everything with each other. Peggy used Joe's hockey skates, and his microscope, and took half his newspaper route. Joe used Peggy's needlepoint kit, and her cookbooks, and took two of her three baby-sitting jobs. Peggy started running the lawn mower, and Joe started running the vacuum cleaner.

Their parents weren't one bit pleased with Peggy's wonderful biology experiments, or with Joe's terrific needlepoint pillows. They didn't care that Peggy mowed the lawn better, and that Joe vacuumed the carpet better. In fact, they were furious. It's all that little X's fault, they agreed. Just because X doesn't know what it is, or what it's supposed to be, it wants to get everybody *else* mixed up, too!

Peggy and Joe were forbidden to play with X any more. So was Susie, and then Jim, and then *all* the Other Children. But it was too late; the Other Children stayed mixed up and happy and free, and refused to go back to the way they'd been before X.

Finally, Joe and Peggy's parents decided to call an emergency meeting of the school's Parents' Association, to discuss "The X Problem." They sent a report to the principal stating that X was a "disruptive influence." They demanded immediate action. The Joneses, they said, should be *forced* to tell whether X was a boy or a girl. And then X should be *forced* to behave like whichever it *was*. If the Joneses refused to tell, the Parents' Association said, then X must take an Xamination. The school psychiatrist must Xamine it physically and mentally, and issue a full report. If X's test showed it was a boy, it would have to obey all the boys' rules. If it proved to be a girl, X would have to obey all the girls' rules.

And if X turned out to be some kind of mixed-up misfit, then X should be Xpelled from the school. Immediately.

The principal was very upset. Disruptive influence? Mixed-up misfit? But X was an Xcellent student. All the teachers said it was a delight to have X in their classes. X was president of the student council. X had won first prize in the talent show, and second prize in the art show, and honorable mention in the science fair, and six athletic events on field day, including the potato race.

Nevertheless, insisted the Parents' Association, X is a Problem Child. X is the Biggest Problem Child we have ever seen!

So the principal reluctantly notified X's parents that numerous complaints about X's behavior had come to the school's attention. And that after the psychiatrist's Xamination, the school would decide what to do about X.

The Joneses reported this at once to the scientists, who referred them to page 85,759 of the *Instruction Manual.* "Sooner or later," it said, "X will have to be Xamined by a psychiatrist. This may be the only way any of us will know for sure whether X is mixed up—or whether everyone else is."

The night before X was to be Xamined, the Joneses tried not to let X see how worried they were. "What if—?" Mr. Jones would say. And Ms. Jones would reply, "No use worrying." Then a few minutes later, Ms. Jones would say, "What if—?" and Mr. Jones would reply, "No use worrying."

X just smiled at them both, and hugged them hard and didn't say much of anything. X was thinking, What if—? And then X thought: No use worrying.

At Xactly 9 o'clock the next day, X reported to the school psychiatrist's office. The principal, along with a committee from the Parents' Association, X's teachers, X's classmates, and Ms. and Mr. Jones, waited in the hall outside. Nobody knew the details of the tests X was to be given, but everybody knew they'd be *very* hard, and they'd reveal Xactly what everyone wanted to know about X, but were afraid to ask.

It was terribly quiet in the hall. Almost spooky. Once in a while, they could hear a strange noise inside the room. There were buzzes. And a beep or two. And several bells. An occasional light would flash under the door. The Joneses thought it was a white light, but the principal thought it was blue. Two or three children swore it was either yellow or green. And the Parents' Association missed it completely.

Through it all, you could hear the psychiatrist's low voice, asking hundreds of questions, and X's higher voice, answering hundreds of answers.

The whole thing took so long that everyone knew it must be the most complete Xamination anyone had ever had to take. Poor X, the Joneses thought. Serves X right, the Parents' Committee thought. I wouldn't like to be in X's overalls right now, the children thought.

At last, the door opened. Everyone crowded around to hear the results. X didn't look any different; in fact, X was smiling. But the psychiatrist looked terrible. He looked as if he was crying! "What happened?" everyone was shouting. Had X done something disgraceful? "I wouldn't be a bit surprised!" muttered Peggy and Joe's parents. "Did X flunk the *whole* test?" cried Susie's parents. "Or just the most important part?" yelled Jim's parents.

"Oh, dear," sighed Mr. Jones.

"Oh, dear," sighed Ms. Jones.

"*Sssh,*" ssshed the principal. "The psychiatrist is trying to speak."

Wiping his eyes and clearing his throat, the psychiatrist began, in a hoarse whisper. "In my opinion," he whispered—you could tell he must be very upset—"in my opinion, young X here—"

"Yes? Yes?" shouted a parent impatiently.

"*Ssshh!*" ssshed the principal.

"Young *Sssh* here, I mean young X," said the doctor, frowning, "is just about—"

"Just about *what*? Let's have it!" shouted another parent.

" . . . just about the *least* mixed-up child I've ever Xamined!" said the psychiatrist.

"Yah for X!" yelled one of the children. And then the others began yelling, too. Clapping and cheering and jumping up and down.

"*SSSH!*" SSShed the principal, but nobody did.

The Parents' Committee was angry and bewildered. How *could* X have passed the whole Xamination? Didn't X have an *identity* problem? Wasn't X mixed up at *all*? Wasn't X *any* kind of a misfit? How could it *not* be, when it didn't even *know* what it was? And why was the psychiatrist crying?

Actually, he had stopped crying and was smiling politely through his tears. "Don't you see?" he said. "I'm crying because it's wonderful! X has absolutely no identity problem! X isn't one bit mixed up! As for being a misfit—ridiculous! X knows perfectly well what it is! Don't you, X?" The doctor winked. X winked back.

"But what *is* X?" shrieked Peggy and Joe's parents. "We still want to know what X is!"

"Ah, yes," said the doctor, winking again. "Well, don't worry. You'll all know one of these days. And you won't need me to tell you."

"What? What does he mean?" some of the parents grumbled suspiciously.

Susie and Peggy and Joe all answered at once. "He means that by the time X's sex matters, it won't be a secret any more!"

With that, the doctor began to push through the crowd toward X's parents. "How do you do," he said, somewhat stiffly. And then he reached out to hug them both. "If I ever have an X of my own," he whispered, "I sure hope you'll lend me your instruction manual."

Needless to say, the Joneses were very happy. The Project Baby X scientists were rather pleased, too. So were Susie, Tim, Peggy, Joe, and all the Other Children. The Parents' Association wasn't, but they promised to accept the psychiatrist's report, and not make any more trouble. They even invited Ms. and Mr. Jones to become honorary members, which they did.

Later that day, all X's friends put on their red-and-white checked overalls and went over to see X. They found X in the back yard, playing with a very tiny baby that none of them had ever seen before. The baby was wearing very tiny red-and-white checked overalls.

"How do you like our new baby?" X asked the Other Children proudly.

"It's got cute dimples," said Jim.

"It's got husky biceps, too," said Susie.

"What kind of baby is it?" asked Joe and Peggy.

X frowned at them. "Can't you tell?" Then X broke into a big, mischievous grin. *"It's a Y!"*

Follow-Up

1. *Explain why you agree or disagree with the author's idea of an X gender. Discuss whether this approach would be better or worse than the current gender identities.*
2. *Attempt to remember how you were taught, directly and indirectly, to act like a female or male. Discuss this process.*
3. *How does your gender identity enhance and/or hinder your development at this time?*
4. *If you have or are planning to have children, what are your beliefs regarding appropriate gender behavior? For example, in what ways, if any, should a son be treated differently than a daughter?*
5. *For additional reading see "Ending the Battle between the Sexes," "On Being a Man," and "Boy in Blue Tutu" (all in this section).*

Occupational Exploration

Christopher A. Schaefer

When I first entered college as an undergrad, I was a product of my parents' wishes—they wanted me to become a physician, so that's what I worked toward. But the courses were mind numbingly boring, and I realized that the course they had set for me was not what I wanted. The problem was, I didn't know what I wanted either.

After dropping out of school, finding a job and supporting myself for several years, I decided that being a blue collar worker (a shipping dock worker at a meat packing plant in Chicago) wasn't really me either. I enjoyed the money and the independence, but felt I was not fulfilling my potential, that I could do better and find a fulfilling career. So I decided to go back to school and get a very practical business degree (this after several other part-time "false starts"). While pursuing my business degree, I took a required computer course and decided—Ah, this is something I enjoy, that I want to do. This was a key turning point in my life—it was the first time I discovered something I really wanted to do and pursued it.

After graduation, I got a position in the computer field and enjoyed the challenge of my new responsibilities and the prestige of my own office. I now felt much closer to "Me," but there was still something missing, something within me still unfulfilled. I had always enjoyed helping others, and found the most enjoyable aspect of my new job was the time I spent training and teaching them. This was a life thread that felt like "Me." So in need of some extra money anyway, I decided to look for a part-time teaching job. To do this, I had to cope with a lifelong fear of public speaking. It wasn't easy, but the reward was worth the risk. I feel I have finally found a direction for myself that's "with the grain."

Follow-Up

1. *Sometimes it takes some actual experience to find out what you like and dislike in a job. This person kept trying jobs and taking courses until he found a position that matched his strengths and identity. What has been your job history and level of satisfaction? Do you think you will be in a continual search to find or create a job that matches your identity?*

Woodworker

Craig Mosher

As my hands press the plane forward, a smooth shaving curls up from the keen edge, filling the air with the tangy scent of freshcut pine. There is a soothing rhythm to the strokes of the plane and a delightful uniqueness in each spiraled shaving.

My chisel and mallet seek some more-organic form hidden within a block of Hawaiian koa wood. The power saw that cuts the block is no respecter of the flowing lines of light and dark that mark the pattern of growth. Sometimes, when my efforts at seeking the lifelines in the wood succeed, the form seems to take on a liveliness reminiscent of the forces that shaped the once tall and supple tree.

Now, as I seek to shape my life in more flexible, natural ways, the schools and offices that claimed so many of my years seem like a buzz saw that cut me into blocks irrespective of the life forms hidden within.

There are so many joys in my new vocation I wonder that I did not find it sooner. Perhaps, my life had to be cut into blocks in order for me to know that was not the form I sought. Yet, there are connections, too. The enjoyment I once got from organizing ideas and programs and peace marches I now find in planning the sequence of tasks and gathering materials to build a table. It is satisfying to see my hands transforming boards and glue into functional and even beautiful objects.

Working for myself I have a flexibility and a discipline that is rarely found in offices that structure work into eight-hour days and fifty-week years. I find freedom within my work, not just during my "time off." Even when I choose to discipline myself to eight-hour days, I feel more free knowing that I am choosing that schedule, either as self-discipline or so I can conveniently work with others. I struggle, when working for myself, to find a balance between demanding regular eight-hour days of myself in order to earn money, learn new skills, and do quality work, on the one hand, and taking time to play with my family, on the other.

I have time between jobs for other activities. I can take a day off each week to build projects for my own pleasure. In fact, the line between work and play blurs because I have such fun at my work. Tools become toys when I go to play in the shop.

As a free-lance woodworker I work for myself or for a client with whom I have some personal contact. The client knows that it is I and not some impersonal factory or machine creating the product. Both praise and criticism come directly to me. Expectations for the form and quality of the job are set by me, alone or in dialogue with the client. In either case I participate directly in setting expectations for my work, and thereby find myself committed to them. This brings pleasure when the product meets the standard and anguish when I sometimes fall short. As in any demanding personal endeavor, part of myself becomes invested in my work, so that I am happy when it is going well and sometimes depressed when I do poorly.

I am also learning more about my relationship to authority. I find it easier to use external authority—like a foreman's or client's expecting me on the job at 8 a.m. each morning—to motivate myself to work. Yet, I find greater satisfaction when I can internalize the authority and muster the self-discipline to go to work regularly in my own shop when only I know how many hours I work. I learned such self-discipline as a student, but then it was under the external threat of grades and disapproving teachers, which I came to internalize as guilt. The wide range of available jobs, from wood carving in my own shop to framing houses on a crew or even working in a factory, provides many levels of internal and external authority, so I have some flexibility to choose the level at which I feel comfortable at any given time.

There is clarity and concreteness in the woodworking craft. I work with materials rather than ideas or personalities. Most of my work is sequential, orderly, and structured. Work proceeds step by step. Foundations must be built before walls, wood cut before being finished. Progress is easily seen as walls are raised and rafters set. Sometimes work goes fast and sometimes slow, but at the end of every day I can see what I have done. I find this continually rewarding.

These rewards are immediate and "self-bestowed." I need not wait for a teacher or boss to tell me whether a cabinet is square or a floor level. Once I have learned the standards of high quality for a particular type of work, I decide for myself whether the job is properly done. I enjoy the freedom to judge my own work and also the challenge to my integrity that is implicit in every decision I make about quality.

I find satisfaction in discovering the direct link between the form and the function of the things I build. There is pleasure in erecting a house that will warmly shelter a family and provide spaces that facilitate their particular living patterns. The same is true of a child's pull toy, which both evokes laughter and withstands considerable knocking about. When I understand and observe the direct relation between the form and the function of a project, I get a sense of clarity that makes the work flow more smoothly.

Every job seems to pose new challenges to my growing skills. There is such variety in the types of work available that when I get bored I simply choose a different area of my work. When I tire of framing houses, I build furniture. When I get lonely in the shop, I seek bigger jobs with other workers. The range of skills that can be developed is so broad that I know I will spend many years as an active learner, enduring the frustrations and cherishing the joys of that process.

The many different woodworking skills can be generalized and transferred, so I rarely feel completely at a loss about how to solve a new problem. Relevant past experience is usually available to guide new learning. This range of transferable skills also gives me the secure feeling that I will likely be able to find work in almost any place at almost any time. The work is not always steady. There are seasonal fluctuations and changes dependent upon the state of the economy, but there are so many kinds of work that something is almost always available.

The key to finding plenty of work seems to be developing a reputation for quality and efficiency (that is, reasonable cost). I am encouraged by an increasing demand in the nation for quality hand craftsmanship. Perhaps it is a passing fashion, or perhaps it is a real trend away from the dreary uniformity of mass-produced goods, large factories, anonymous, alienated employees, and concentrations of power and wealth in the hands of a few capitalists.

A client once told me that he felt guilty asking me to remodel his garage for him while he sat in his office, since he was capable of doing the job himself. I realized that I was very happy it was he and not I going to his office every day in a suit and tie and that I was glad he had the money to pay me to do work I enjoy.

Most of the skills I have were learned on the job—what John Dewey and his followers called "learning by doing." Sometimes I learn slowly by my own trials and errors. I learn more quickly when I work with someone more skilled than I who can offer advice and answer questions. Apprenticeship is one of the oldest and most effective teaching-learning strategies. This teacher-apprentice relationship has, in my experience, also been an opportunity for forming friendships that make the work flow more smoothly. My woodworking teachers shared their skills and knowledge so that together we could do the work more quickly and accurately—quite unlike some authoritarian teaching styles I experienced in classrooms.

I am intrigued by the possibilities for cooperation inherent in the crafts and trades. Their variety, flexibility, and lack of officially determined credentials make for fewer barriers caused by specialization and less emphasis on hierarchical measures of status, all of which should make it easier for people to form cooperative work groups in which they can share their tools and skills, as well as themselves.

The friendships and group cohesion that can develop in such a cooperative endeavor make the work all that much more enjoyable.

I now find myself with a set of useful skills that contribute to a sense of identity based on concrete work and achievements. These skills and the work I can produce give meaning to my life, meaning that is tangible, self-renewing, and growing—and very personal. To the extent that my craft becomes art my individuality is expressed through work that others can use and enjoy.

It is, after all, more healthy, both personally and socially, for me to gain pleasure and self-esteem through the quality of my craftsmanship and the beauty and functionality of my work than through struggling for a position of wealth, authority, and power over other people. And it is certainly more fun.

Follow-Up

1. *Woodworker Mosher feels that being self-employed provides him with several intrinsic satisfactions: flexible scheduling, using his skills, designing products, creating quality work, discipline, pride in his work. What aspects of Mosher's career appeal to you and why? Which do not?*
2. *Bureaucratic organizations, according to Mosher, "cut me into blocks irrespective of the life forms hidden within." Explain how this statement does or does not apply to your life. If it does, what are some of your choices?*
3. *Select two statements from this article and offer your commentary.*

Don't Look Too Closely

Nels Goud

Almost everyone I know feels that a job is out there which is just right. It offers everything we desire—challenge, money, recognition, use of capacities, and the feeling of looking forward to going to work. We know these jobs exist because other people have them.

Since high school I've always dreamed of being a big band lead trumpeter. Now *there* is a perfect job. Playing gigs all around the country, screaming off high ones to the applause of an appreciative audience, and of course the inevitable groupies. I have talked to many professional trumpeters. When I was 17, I chatted with a trumpeter of the Jimmy Dorsey band. He didn't want to talk too much about trumpeting, except for telling me he did not like what he had to play. He was lonely for his children, about my age, he said. The traveling for ten months each year was now too much for him. "But what else can I do at my age?" Twenty years later I was talking with the lead trumpeter of the Buddy Rich band. This guy had been hitting notes a few minutes earlier that must now be soaring past Saturn. I asked him how he liked playing. "I'm getting tired of this lead trumpet stuff." He was all of 25 years old. As with the trumpeter I met two decades earlier, I figured he was having a bad night. He couldn't really mean that. I mean, he could hit double high C! What more could any human want?

Then at another time I met a famous psychologist who had left the university life and started a center for human growth. Having myself reached a point where classes were a bit repetitive, and feeling restricted by the publishing game, I felt this guy had it made. We spent a day talking about our lives and jobs. His main advice was "Stay with the uni-versity. I often wish I had. It is a real hassle to keep a center like this going. I'm more of an administrator than anything." Well, must have been one of those days.

One of my favorite places is a large nature preserve owned by the university. I was taking a leisurely stroll along a trail bounded by tall oaks and stopped at an outlook over a large lake. Every time I take this walk I envy the staff out here who get to run outdoor education programs in surroundings like these. The Associate Director happened by and we talked for a few minutes. I asked him what it was like working here. He looked up at the trees and said "You know this is the first chance I've had to notice the new leaves on the oaks this spring. It seems I'm always in the office answering the phone, writing memos, or trouble shooting a maintenance or personnel problem. I'd rather just be a student or visitor out here. Then maybe I would get to see the trees." Obviously I had caught him at a low moment.

I don't give up easily. While I was taking a break on a spring biking expedition in Florida, an old, dust-covered Buick pulled off the road and parked next to me. The driver, the only occupant, leaned over and rolled down the passenger window.

"Hey, I'm curious. What kind of biking group are you with? I've been seeing groups of bikers with orange flags like yours all day." I explained that we were just a bunch of Hoosiers who think that biking a couple hundred miles along the Florida Atlantic coast is the proper way to spend a relaxing spring vacation. Noticing his out-of-state license, I asked him what he was doing here. He handed me a business card that said Vern C—

Acrobat, Juggler, Unicyclist. This was not your usual Florida tourist.

"I go around to schools and do my act. Been doing it for 31 years now."

I looked a little closer. He had wavy hair, mainly gray with intermittent black strands. His face resembled what Errol Flynn would have looked like at 66. He was dressed in all black, slacks and a long sleeved turtleneck. Only a small paunch showed on an otherwise athletic frame. I was wondering how crowds of high school students reacted to a late middle-aged man juggling bowling pins while riding a unicycle. Then I realized ol' Vern had tapped another of my job fantasies. I had long considered putting together a dynamite program for public schools on human relations. Besides saving the youth of America, I would get the chance to travel and live the free life on the road. Shades of Kerouac. Here was a chance to get some ideas on how to do it.

"Vern, tell me a little bit what it's like going around to schools all year giving programs."

"Well, first of all, I'm going to quit next year. I'm tired. I'm tired of the motels. The one I'm staying in tonight doesn't even have a telephone or cable TV. The one in Daytona Beach cost five dollars less and had a TV and telephone."

"Uh, yeah, sounds like a bummer. But tell me more about your career, like how do you get these school assembly jobs?"

"First of all you have to get an agent. There's all sort of circuits in this business, you know. You need to get the publicity and a name for yourself. I come down here during the winter months. Do the midwest in the fall. I do about ten schools a week. Man, I'm tired. Gave three shows today and no time for lunch or anything. Just give the program, pack up, and rush over to the next school. Tonight all I'm going to do is watch some TV and drink beer. Then two more shows tomorrow. Do you know of any good motels in Titusville?"

"Not really, Vern. We throw down sleeping bags in school gyms or churches. No cable TV there either. How did you get started in this?"

"My old man was a circus acrobat. I learned the trade from him. He and Uncle Sam—I was in the Army once—have been my only bosses. I'm an independent contractor." He was proud of that.

"I have been married three times," he added without prompting. He needed to talk. But then again, so did I. We were barroom buddies on the berm of state road A1A. "My first wife ran off with my brother. Guess I wasn't around home enough. The second one got cancer and died. I got a regular job then for a few years. Got married again and the third wife got cancer too. She is still alive but, you know, didn't want to see anyone so I just went out on the circuit again. I call her every once in a while to see how she's doing." He paused for a minute and stared ahead. "I bought a home in Virginia last year. Planning to retire there. Just sit around and enjoy life and no more motels and three shows a day. But this has been my life. I don't know if I could just sit around. I am so tired, though."

We both had to go. I invited him to visit us where we were staying that night. Vern never showed up. Probably downed a few beers and went to sleep in that motel room without a cable TV. I had a lot of sympathy for Vern. But it would be different for me giving those school programs. I know it would.

Talking with people who have perfect jobs has taught me one thing—make sure I catch them on a good day next time.

Follow-Up

1. *For many, an occupation is a central component of their identity. They believe it is important to find just the right work to express themselves and find fulfillment. What are the characteristics of a "perfect job" for you? Is there such a thing?*

2. *The author, a persevering malcontent, kept encountering people who did not like their "perfect jobs." Interview people who have what you consider to be an ideal job. See if this ideal work is what you expected.*
3. *If you're interested in reading about ways to find a balance between personal and professional lives, you may want to check out* Down-Shifting: Reinventing Success on a Slower Track *by Amy Saltzman, 1991, HarperCollins.*

Thoreau on Work

Make getting a living not merely honest and honorable, but altogether inviting and glorious; for if getting a living is not so, then living is not.

* * *

It is not necessary that a man should earn his living by the sweat of his brow, unless he sweats easier than I do.

* * *

I say, beware of all enterprises that require new clothes, and not a new wearer of clothes.

* * *

[Take heed] of spending the best part of one's life earning money in order to enjoy a questionable liberty during the least valuable part of it.

* * *

Most of the luxuries, and many of the so-called comforts of life, are not only not indispensable, but positive hindrances to the elevation of mankind.

* * *

Men labor under a mistake.... [They] are so occupied with the factitious cares and superfluously coarse labors of life that its finer fruits cannot plucked by them.... [They have] no time to be anything but...machine[s].

* * *

The life which men praise and regard as successful is but one kind. Why should we exaggerate any one kind at the expense of the others?

* * *

Most men appear never to have considered what a house is, and are actually thought needlessly poor all their lives because they think that they must have such a one as their neighbors have.

* * *

It would be glorious to see mankind at leisure for once. It is nothing but work, work, work . . . I think that there is nothing, not even crime, more opposed to poetry, to philosophy, ay, to life itself, than this incessant business.

* * *

If a man walks in the woods for love of them half of each day, he is in danger of being regarded as a loafer. But if he spends his whole day as a speculator, shearing off those woods and making earth bald before her time, he is esteemed an industrious and enterprising citizen.

* * *

The aim of the laborer should be, not to get his living, to get "a good job," but to perform well a certain work.

* * *

If I should sell both my forenoons and afternoons to society, as most appear to do, I am sure that for me there would be nothing left worth living for.

* * *

The cost of a thing is the amount of what I call life which is required to be exchanged for it, immediately or in the long run.

Follow-Up

1. *Select one or more Thoreau quotes and discuss/write your reaction.*

If I Were a Car, I'd Be a Lemon

Denise Karuth

This morning the plumber for my building stopped by. I assured him that my barking Labrador retriever wouldn't bite by explaining that she was a seeing eye dog.

"You aren't blind are you?"

"Yes, but I used to be able to see better."

"But you're . . . you're in a wheelchair . . . You're not," he hesitated, "a cripple, too, are you?"

"I have multiple sclerosis," I answered. "Some of us just have all the luck."

"Holy Jesus! God bless you, ma'am. I'm really sorry. God bless you. If you ever have any trouble with your sink or electricity you just call this number." He placed his card on the arm of the couch. "Call any time, even at night. Just tell them you're a handicapped apartment and they'll come right out. God bless you. Jesus God!"

Sometimes the reactions are even stronger.

I would never willingly cause pain to anyone, so it makes me sad when perfect strangers walk up to me and burst into tears. My first reaction is to think that their tears are somehow my fault. As it happens, some of the people who cry have lost family members or friends to disabling illness, and in two instances, deaf senior citizens cried from a sense of empathy and community with me. In most cases, though, the tears are shed because of peoples' bleak notions of what life must be like for me, the "helpless blind cripple."

I'm not talking only about "the man in the street." The same misconceptions are held as well by students and professionals. Back when I was "just" blind, a middle-aged man passed me on campus and remarked to his companion, "Oh my God, Martha. Look at that. She's blind!"

"Yes," I replied, "but she isn't deaf!"

Then, of course, there are the rehabilitation counselors and the doctors, professionals who deal with disabled people *on a regular basis*. How much they, too, have yet to learn. For example, during my last eye exam at a leading teaching hospital in Boston, one of the top ophthalmologists said (in my presence) to three of his students: "When the retinal damage is not too severe, many of these patients can lead a normal life. But in a case like this, a normal life is impossible."

This pro may have known about my eyes. He knew very little about me.

Another doctor once told me, "You can't possibly have MS. Lightning just doesn't strike twice in the same place." Would that he had been right.

I would like to be able to sit people down and say, "Look, I appreciate your concern, but my life isn't that bad. Sure, it's not quite uninterrupted bliss, but whose life is? It's a good life. I work and play and have friends and make love and mistakes and get bored now and again just like you. So put your handkerchiefs away. First impressions aside, I'm a lot more like you than you probably imagine."

MORNING THOUGHTS

It's 6:30 a.m., and the solar alarm clock beckons through the patio doors; it refuses to be ignored. I savor a few last moments of rest and begin to plan the day ahead. It's Saturday. My weekend shower and hairwash are behind me, as are bladder irrigation and bowel care; with regard to personal care, this should be an easy day. I read over a long list of ongoing projects and responsibilities compiled over the last 2 days and select several items to work on. (With MS, memory can be affected, and mine needs all the help it can get; hence, the list.)

What's this? A Stravinsky attack! I am back at Symphony Hall where last night I heard the Dumbarton Oaks Concerto, a piece long familiar to me from my years as a music major and an orchestral musician. I must hear it again—now—and am compelled to roll over in bed to search for it in a small box of cassettes. I find it and slip it in the deck.

Having been an orchestral musician was one of the high points of my life. Orchestral playing has to be one of the most complex and beautiful group endeavors (a team sport, if you will) yet devised by humanity. Football pales to insignificance in comparison.

As a 17-year-old who had been ardently playing double bass for only 2 years, Chamber Orchestra helped me discover the exhilaration of overcoming overwhelming inexperience, the joy of sharing in the creation of something unsurpassingly wonderful, and of intimate involvement with a plane of music that I would have thought far beyond my understanding.

My intense involvement with music was like an express train to enlightenment: Regardless of what happens at the end of the line, one is always grateful for the ticket. People often wonder that I am not bitter about having to give up my orchestral playing. Sometimes I miss it so much that I cry. Mostly, though, I am grateful for having had the opportunity and for having learned, importantly, from it. So I cannot complain. My life now presents me with many of the same challenges and opportunities as did Stravinsky's music. The stakes, of course, are higher, but the price of defeat is more than I am willing to pay.

The joy of living with meaning and with purpose is worth considerable effort. In the long run, I do not have a great deal of control over what is happening to me physically. But if I let my physical disability paralyze my spirit, my life would become a well of self-pity, anger, and despair. I cannot allow that to happen.

THE NORMAL ASPECTS

What's my life been like? I was born 2 months prematurely in November 1954, the middle child of three. My family lived in the Adirondack Mountains and in Buffalo, New York. I attended public schools in Cheektowaga and Amherst, both neighbors to Buffalo. In 1972 I won a New York State Regents' Scholarship that paid my tuition to the State University of New York at Buffalo. In 1976 I graduated magna cum laude with a degree in music. That September, my brother Ed, our closest friend Fred, and I moved to Boston where I attended graduate school and received a master's degree in rehabilitation counseling.

My faith education stressed the importance of serving others and working for justice and peace. I am a member of the local chapters of the American Friends' Service Committee, Mobilization for Survival, Amnesty International, and IMPACT, a national ecumenical political action network. I have also lobbied at both state and national levels concerning U.S. involvement in Latin America, U.S. food policy, nuclear disarmament, civil rights for the disabled, and human services legislation and cutbacks. I have supported the Infant Formula Action Coalition, INFACT, which fights the unethical promotion of infant formula in Third World countries and helped organize a Legal Defense Fund for a friend who was unjustly arrested at the Seabrook nuclear power plant site in New Hampshire (all charges against him were later dropped). I have written a review of an accessible art exhibit for the Cambridge women's magazine *Sojourner,* and have had requests to do further writing. I also have been involved with two area food co-ops.

For fun, I run Irene, my black Labrador retriever, around Jamaica Pond every week in good weather. I entertain and visit friends, play some piano and recorder, and take walks in my motorized wheelchair either with friends or on my own.

So much for the many "normal" aspects of my life. As I focus on my experience as a disabled individual, I hope that you, the reader, will not lose sight of the similarity of the life we share.

COUSIN CAROL'S PREGNANT?

Being legally blind, with a small amount of residual vision, is like living in a bizarre fun house where what you see is not necessarily what you get. First off, I can see things up close far better than things any distance away. I can see my fingers, for example, if I hold them 2 inches from my face, but I cannot see my toes (although, when the lighting is right, I can see a blur where my foot is). If the contrast is right, I can make out Irene's dark shape; but, then, I have also mistaken a low stool or my black skirt or my black coat lying on the bed for Irene, even in the best light.

As my sight deteriorated, I found myself asking questions of store mannequins, I mistook full-length mirrors for doorways, and I tried to find the "Push for Walk" button on trees.

Many people think that either you can see or you can't. How difficult it is to write about vision, since no common vocabulary exists that adequately explains the variability of sight.

Being blind with residual vision means that you "see" your relatives and friends on the Boston trolleys and buses . . . even though those relatives never left Buffalo. It means looking both ways before crossing the street and then walking out into the side of a schoolbus. It means entering an unfamiliar room and being visually bombarded by confusing patterns of light and dark. It means getting so accustomed to familiar places that your friends accuse you of being able to see, or worse, they forget to warn you about newly placed obstacles.

Being blind means getting so thoroughly lost that sometimes you have no idea where you are, much less how to get where you're going. It means having people come up to you in the street, say "Hi!" and disappear, before you can figure out who they were. (*Always* identify yourself to your blind friends, especially if your meeting occurs in a place where they're not used to seeing you.)

Being blind means not knowing that Aunt Trudy has lost weight, or that cousin Carol is 8 months pregnant (until you embrace them). It means brushing up against wet paint, waltzing down the street with silver-streaked coat and hair, and wondering why people are taking notice of you. It means being the only person in the theater who does not dive under a chair when Audrey Hepburn's ankle is grabbed by her assailant in "Wait Until Dark." It means being utterly confused by cars making right and left turns on red. It means spending too much time looking for housekeys, dark glasses, the checkbook, or the vegetable steamer. And it means knowing how to take notes into exams by a method so wonderfully clever that I will not reveal it here.

In my case being blind is compounded by poor memory, difficulty with sense of touch, and the fact that I rely on others to do so much for me that things are often put away without my knowing where to find them again.

In short, being blind means having to become adept at assembling an image of reality from a jumble of jigsaw puzzle pieces—and doing so in the shortest possible time.

MS. It stands for multiple sclerosis, a chronic, disabling, neurologic disease. In my book it also stands for the Marquis de Sade, who, if given the chance to invent a disease, would have been hard pressed to come up with anything more diabolical.

No one knows what causes MS or how to cure it. There isn't even a fool-proof diagnostic test to see if you've got it. Many MS'ers are told that their symptoms are caused by depression, anxiety, hysteria, and even conversion reaction. It's not uncommon for as many as 8 years to elapse before the diagnosis is confirmed.

MS presents with dozens of different symptoms and affects each individual who has it quite differently. Textbook cases of MS are found only in textbooks.

One of the most disabling aspects of the disease is fatigue. There are 168 hours in a week. In a good week I can spend about 15 hours away from home in a wheelchair doing things like working, socializing, attending meetings and church, and the like. About 85% of my time is spent in bed in a mixture of work, resting up, and planning ahead. Being able to condense much of life into 15 hours a week and developing strategies for a constructive invalidism should earn me an honorary degree as a management consultant.

When I finally moved into an accessible apartment and acquired my two electric wheelchairs (the second because my first was unsuitable for outdoor use), the sense of freedom came rushing in like a wave. The second day I had my outdoor chair, I took it and Irene on an 8 mile walk, four times longer than any walk I'd been able to take in 5 years! The wheelchair had liberated me from the limits of my walking, and from a fair amount of the pain that walking and standing had intensified.

There are times now when I almost take for granted my ability to glide down streets for distances that were formerly unthinkable. I pass places where I spent hours waiting for buses to go distances I can now wheelchair in minutes. I remember how much it hurt to stand and wait for trains and buses, how I sat down on curbs and on floors of trolleys, banks, and supermarkets in an attempt to lessen the overwhelming pain and fatigue. I remember the times I cried walking down the street, doing dishes, or waiting for transit.

Whose turn is it to ask for a ride to church? (My dislike of asking people for rides to church is outmatched only by my love of choir, which rehearses earlier than the local wheelchair transit service can get me there.) Some would think that dependency and illness simplify life in that one is no longer faced with the burdens of work and self-reliance. On the contrary, a severely disabled person generally has more details to keep track of and a harder time doing it.

An able-bodied person does not have to:

- Know exactly where everything is in the house (from Elmer's Glue and electrical tape to hair barrettes and catheter clamps) because the able-bodied person can easily get up and search for things. A disabled person who spends a great deal of time in bed has to be able to tell others where things can be found.
- Set aside substantial amounts of time or plan in advance for things like bowel movements and catheter irrigation.
- Plan activities 5 business days in advance to meet the requirements of the wheelchair transit system.
- Make sure that a list of approximately 20 medical and surgical supplies are in stock and close at hand, along with whatever prescription drugs are required.
- Keep a particularly close watch on the budget so he or she can afford to pay attendants even when the reimbursement checks from Medicaid are 3 to 4 months behind.
- Budget time so that not more than 5 hours a day are spent out of bed.
- Hassle with things like wheelchair acquisition, maintenance, and repair or bills that providers did not submit to Medicaid.

In general, the less you are able to do for yourself, the more health problems you have that require specialized care. Also, as it gets harder to remember things, the more things there are to be remembered, planned, and kept track of.

The more disabled you are, the more of a magician you have to be simply to lead a normal life.

My best friend is most remarkable. She has congenital deformities of both hands, no intelligible speech, and she functions at a 3- to 4-year level. She is nearsighted, color blind, short statured, and dependent on others for assistance with personal care. She is also black, which many would agree is an additional handicap in today's society.

Yet, after a 3-month vocational training program, and with only a minimum of adaptive equipment, my best friend is now successfully employed in a skilled job that many able-bodied individuals would find daunting.

My best friend's name is Irene. Irene is my guide dog.

She has a black silky coat that looks like it's been polished, and a wonderfully expressive face with big brown eyes that could melt glaciers. Her favorite pastimes are eating, sleeping, playing, and being lovable. Her favorite food is virtually anything organic.

Irene, I am told, is a Greek word meaning peace. My best friend couldn't have a better name.

Irene is loyalty incarnate. She even goes with me into the too-little stalls in public bathrooms. As I write this, she is sleeping in a chair at the foot of my bed. The space is much too cramped for her, but she prefers to stay there, close to me, rather than stretching out comfortably on the double bed or the couch in the other room.

Irene and I have been together for the past 5½ years. Twenty-four hours a day. Seven days a week. We've enjoyed a truly symbiotic relationship.

How does Irene guide me? In the wheelchair I am so close to the ground that I can hold the leather leash very near to her collar. In this way, I'm able to follow her moves without having to hold the metal harness. She, of course, stops for curbs and steps, just as she did when I could walk. But now, in addition, she aims for curb-cuts and driveways.

Oh love of my life, dog of my dreams, hound of my heart. How can I possibly describe this relationship of ours? Should I write of our first week in training school when we were waiting to cross Massachusetts Avenue? You were eager and pulling my arm, but I told you that the light was against us. "Relax," I said. You looked up at me as if to say, "You mean that?" and promptly lay down (in complete disregard of standard guide dog behavior). Or should I tell about the time we went to see the Boston Ballet and you reacted to a bizarre, musically dissonant piece by climbing in terror upon my lap? Or should I write about the 160 or more days we've spent together in various hospitals? How you always knew when to put on the "Lassie act" to impress administrators and Nursing Supervisors.

Remember the time we walked on the subway platform and a disturbed lady greeted us with a cry of "Lord, strike down this demon dog led by a demon!"? Or when you had a gland infection and couldn't wag your tail? Or when you held your ground, even after I'd given the "Forward" command, and saved me from being hit by a car on Newbury Street?

Maybe I should write about how you joyously proceed with choir on Sunday mornings, snore during the sermon, and always know when the worship is over. Or about all the great romps we've had together. (How you love to play and make friends.) Or about how I'm convinced I can tell what you're thinking at any point in time.

I should write about your talent for being able to remember routes we've taken or people we've met only once before. Or about your adaptability in learning to locate curb-cuts, driveways, and elevators. Or your eagerness to shepherd others who travel with me. Maybe I should even mention that I've only run over your paws once in the 2 years I've been in a wheelchair.

I'm so proud of you that I don't care if people stare as we glide together down the street with your leash in my left hand and the wheelchair control in my right.

All in all, you are my pride, my love, and my joy. I can't conceive of life without you. If someone gave me a choice between losing my right arm or losing you permanently, I would part, reluctantly, with my right arm.

But then, what are best friends for?

MY BODY, MY WIMP

Right now it is 8:45 on a Sunday night, and I've been in bed for 5 hours. I want to continue to write, but my body wants to sleep. Can you remember being a little kid and wanting to stay up late, but your mother wouldn't let you? It's frustrating and aggravating to have a mother who never gives in, not even once. Sometimes I want to shout: "I'm 27 years old! Can't I even stay up until 10:00?" But I know from long experience that my protests are of no avail, that my only option is to give in. But not before I negotiate.

"Give me just 20 minutes," I say. "Maybe even 15." I find that I negotiate with my body a lot. "If we go to Jamaica Pond this afternoon and to choir this evening, I promise to stay in all day tomorrow." Or, "I know you're tired, but it's an important meeting, and I really should

be there." I even apologize to it: "Chastity (one of my nicknames for my genital area), I'm sorry. Being catheterized is a bitch. What can I say? Let's hope we don't have to do it again for awhile."

For years before it became irrefutably clear that my increasing weakness, fatigue, and pain were the result of illness, I was at war with my body, always pushing it beyond its limits. Now I realize that I treated it like a traitor instead of a besieged ally. I gave it years of grief that it did nothing to deserve,

Time's up. It's 9:00. I got my 15 minutes in. Now I'm negotiating with a body that is busy spacing out. "Let's put the writing board away, take our evening medications, pull up the covers, and go to sleep."

I'll have to leave the lights on since Fred is out. I used to feel badly that I had to trouble someone else to close doors and turn out lights that I couldn't get to. The paradox of their physical closeness and inaccessible distance hit home. Now I rarely think about it. I guess that's adjustment.

It's 9:05, and I'm reluctantly going to sleep. That's adjustment, too. "You know, body," I tease affectionately, "you're really a wimp."

Follow-Up

1. *If you do not have a physical disability: Think of instances in your life when you have seen or interacted with people who have physical disabilities. Describe your thoughts and feelings from these encounters. Are you confused about how to talk to a person who has a disability or to know what is "proper"?*

   If you do have a physical disability: What have been your experiences with people without disabilities? Were they similar to those described by Denise Karuth?

2. *Select one or more of these statements and offer your reactions:*
   - *I do not have a great deal of control over what is happening to me physically. But if I let my physical disability paralyze my spirit, my life would become a well of self-pity, anger, and despair.*
   - *As I focus on my experience as a disabled individual, I hope that you, the reader, will not lose sight of the similarity of the life we share.*

- *To her best friend Irene, Denise says "If someone gave me a choice between losing my right arm or losing you permanently, I would part, reluctantly, with my right arm."*
- *I was at war with my body, always pushing it beyond its limits. Now I realize that I treated it like a traitor instead of a besieged ally.*

3. *In another section of the article, Denise Karuth says that the biggest environmental barriers faced by individuals who use wheelchairs are, of course, architectural. She estimates that 60% of "accessible" architecture is flawed, with about 20% posing insurmountable difficulties. If you do not use a wheelchair, as you go through your day imagine doing your activities in a wheelchair. If you know someone who uses a wheelchair, ask about the challenges of getting around. If you do use a wheelchair, would you agree or disagree with Karuth?*

4. *Karuth could spend a maximum of 15 hours per week away from home in a wheelchair. Faced with similar constraints, what would your life be like?*

5. *Try one or more of the suggestions in the accompanying piece titled "Think 'People First'."*

6. *See the Applied Activity at the end of this section titled "A New Identity." Choose a disability for your identity transformation.*

Think "People First"

Language is a reflection of how people see each other. That's why the words we use can hurt. It's also why responsible communicators are now choosing language which reflects the dignity of people with disabilities—words that put the person first, rather than the disability. Read on for a short course on using language that empowers.

1. Think "people first." Say "a woman who has mental retardation," rather than "a mentally retarded woman."
2. Avoid words like "unfortunate," "afflicted," and "victim." Also, try to avoid casting a person with a disability as a superhuman model of courage. People with disabilities are just people, not tragic figures or demigods.
3. A developmental disability is not a disease. Do not mention "symptoms," "patients" or "treatment," unless the person you're writing about has an illness as well as a disability.
4. Use common sense. Avoid terms with obvious negative or judgmental connotations, such as "crippled," "deaf and dumb," "lame," and "defective." If you aren't sure how to refer to a person's condition, ask. And, if the disability is not relevant to your story or conversation, why mention it at all?
5. Never refer to a person as "confined to a wheelchair." Wheelchairs enable people to escape confinement. A person with a mobility impairment "uses" a wheelchair.
6. Try to describe people without disabilities as "typical" rather than "normal."

To a Body, with Love

Abe Arkoff

One rather fascinating and ingenious way of getting to know your body better involves opening a new channel of communication. Ira Progoff (1975) recommends that you have a dialogue with your body. (Benjamin Franklin's conversation with his gout is an example of this approach.) You can start by writing down all the salient memories you have of your body, such as the time you broke your leg, learned to swim, were first aware of your sexual feelings, and so on. Next, drawing upon these memories, write a brief summary of your relationship to your body. Then relax, sense the presence of your body as though it were a person, speak to it, allow it to speak to you, and write down your dialogue.

A similar but somewhat simpler method is one called "Body Letters." You simply sit down and without stopping to think, write a letter to your body, saying everything you wish to say to it. Then you become your body (you are anyway, of course) and without pausing, write a reply.

Here, as an example for those who don't mind reading the mail of others, is an exchange of letters:

Dear Body,

Well, I've resisted writing to you, just as I've sometimes resisted living in you these past many years. I haven't thought too much of you as a body (at least, what met the eye below the neck)—you were too short, too unmuscled, too nearsighted, too allergy-prone, too this, too that. I've put you down and largely abandoned you to take up residence in my (or is it "your" or "our") head. Now, I'm back in some surprise to say: I think I like you, and what was all the fuss about?

I stand in front of the mirror and look at you. There you are—a bit dilapidated after many years of wear, tear and deferred maintenance—but still all in one piece and functioning well enough for my purposes. You have passion. You almost never catch a cold or get the flu. You don't need much sleep. You only bulge a little despite our sweet tooth. You're content with long walks and hardly cast an envious glance at the joggers and runners zipping by.

Sometimes I wonder what I would have become had you developed in accordance with my boyhood dream. Instead, I spent my adolescence in the library and a lot of the rest of my life as well. My life has worked out well for me: I have a family that's dear, good friends, and enjoyable work in a beautiful place. We've been companions on an increasingly pleasant journey.

So this is an apology, thank-you, and let's-get-better-acquainted letter. I know I've made you promises, and I hereby promise to come down out of my head and start keeping them. Now that I think you're okay—well, even better than okay—I'm looking forward to a happier and happier association.

With love,
Abe

Dear Abe,

After all these years, it was good to get your letter showing (if you will permit a body metaphor) some change of heart. You know, having you for an inhabitant hasn't been the easiest thing in the world for me. There are moments and even days when you seem to care, but you are (oops, here comes another one) something of a backslider.

But give credit where it's due, I always say. You're a faithful walker. You watch your diet (except for, ah yes, that tooth and midnight raids on the refrigerator). You don't smoke, and there's only an occasional vodka martini (well, make that a double). The results of our last physical were okay, considering the mileage. It's only that we could be so much more to each other (notice how I'm trying to put this in a positive and cooperative way). Remember that series of massages so long ago—how good they felt? Why did we stop? Let's get some more. The "chi" class was nice, but you said it might be followed by some more. What happened? And, since we're walkers, how about some serious hiking and even backpacking (notice that no mention has been made of the north face of Mount Everest).

I think there is more in me than you suspect. You seem so concerned these days with your spiritual growth, and you proceed almost as if you want to rise above your body—me, that is. But don't forget that body, mind, and spirit proceed together, and body discipline can be an avenue to what's above.

Now that we have some communication started, let's try to (brace yourself) stay in touch. We've got some good years ahead, and I'll be with you every step of the way.

Faithfully,
Your Body

References
1. Franklin, B. (1945). *A Benjamin Franklin reader* (N. G. Goodman, Ed.). New York: Thomas Y. Crowell Company.
2. Progoff, I. (1975). *At a journal workshop: The basic text and guide for using the Intensive Journal*. New York: Dialogue House.

Follow-Up

1. *Do you own your body? To answer this question, discuss how responsible you have made yourself for what you and others do to your body.*
2. *Do you accept your body? What relationship do you see between your acceptance or rejection of your body and your overall self-esteem?*
3. *How much do you love your body? To answer this question, write a love letter to your body. Then, as your body, write a reply.*

Applied Activities for Section One

ARE YOU AN ADULT?

Most people offer psychological reasons rather than legal ones when describing how they knew they were an adult. Richard Cohen, for example, discovered he was an adult when he paid a restaurant tab. Here are some other events that trigger the adulthood realization (as obtained from interviews): the first day on a full-time job; buying a house; filling out income tax returns; attending the funeral of a friend or a parent; being referred to as *lady* by a patient; being asked to leave home by parents and pursuing a dream (such as playing rock music for a living) that others consider impractical. One 23-year-old, a married college grad and a health professional, still does *not* feel like an adult "because my husband now does everything for me that my father used to do." Try to complete one of the following items:

1. I became an adult when

   _____

   _____

   _____

   _____

   _____

2. I do *not* believe I am an adult yet because

   _____

   _____

   _____

Follow-Up
1. Ask others outside of class if they think they are adults.
2. Ask older family members when they considered themselves adults. Are you considered an adult by the people in your family?
3. Analyze the responses to the adulthood question for underlying themes (responsibility, independence, etc.).
4. Discuss (or write about) your findings.

ROLES AND AUTHENTICITY

Culturally defined roles constitute a major portion of one's identity. Some major roles include: male/female, acting your age, spouse or significant other, father/mother, son/daughter, employee or employer, student, member of a social or professional group, ethnic/racial identity, spiritual/religious orientation, volunteer. A role may use and draw out one's authentic needs, values, and aptitudes. Or a role may demand behaviors which contradict one's authentic needs, values, and aptitudes. The degree of fit between roles and authenticity is a primary determinant of well-being.

In this activity, examine how roles match your authentic needs, values, and aptitudes.

Directions:
1. Select a major role in your life and write it in the space provided (some examples of roles were listed previously or you can list another of your choosing).
2. Analyze your self-role behavior according to the four categories described below. Try to list actual examples for each of the four categories if possible.

ROLE _____

Self-role behavior categories	Examples from your life
A. True to self and true to role: When the role expectations fit your needs, values, aptitudes.	
B. True to self but may not be true to role: Individualistic and authentic behavior which falls outside the "regular way of doing things." Sometimes results in signs of disapproval or actual sanctions.	
C. Not true to self but true to role: When you act because "you have to" but it runs counter to your authentic needs, values, aptitudes.	
D. Not true to self and not true to role: When you act in ways contrary to both role expectations and your authentic self (e.g., self-destructive/illegal behaviors).	

Follow-Up

1. Which of the self-role categories ranks *first* in reference to the time and energy invested in it? Discuss or write what this means to you.
2. There are strategies for enhancing one's self-role functioning. Here are a few to consider:
    (a) Attempt to increase the A category behaviors, and/or decrease behaviors in the B, C, and D categories.
    (b) In extreme situations you might consider *eliminating* a role when this is a possible choice.
    (c) Sometimes *adding a new role* may draw out more of your authentic needs, values, and aptitudes.
    Attempt and experiment with one of these options to see if it enhances your well-being.
3. Repeat this activity with a different role or two.

A NEW IDENTITY

You had a good night's sleep, but as you start to wake up you sense something is different, even strange. Crawling out of bed you pass a mirror and stop and stare. Somehow overnight you've changed into a person of the opposite gender. Take a few moments to ponder this change and try to address the following items:

1. Describe some major ways in which your life would be different.
2. Name one positive aspect of this new identity. Name one negative aspect of this new identity.
3. If given the choice to stay with this new identity or to revert back to your former one, which one would you choose? Why?

Describe your learnings and interpret them.

Variations: Instead of gender change, consider changes of race, age, nationality, or historical period. Answer the above questions for any of these other identity changes.

GENDER ROLES: POSITIVE AND NEGATIVE

Directions: Complete steps 1 and 2 individually. Form groups (2–6 members of the *same* gender) and discuss your results. Attempt one or more of the Follow-Up activities.

1. List two advantages and two disadvantages of being a *male* today.

Advantages   _____

_____

Disadvantages   _____

_____

2. List two advantages and two disadvantages of being a *female* today.

Advantages   _____

_____

Disadvantages   _____

_____

Follow-Up

Compare and discuss* your results in one or more of the following ways:

1. In *mixed* gender groups (2–6 members).

2. Post all the lists on the wall. Have all participants read them. Conduct a whole class discussion on the perceptions and questions from these lists.

3. Discuss the following question in either mixed gender groups and/or with the whole class: What can be done to maximize the advantages and minimize the disadvantages for each gender?

4. Write about what you've learned after completing one or more of the above activities.

Note: Listening skills are essential with any of the above activities.

MEN AND WOMEN: A DIALOGUE

The intent of this activity is to perceive the different worlds of men and women.

1. Form all-men and all-women groups. If possible, each group should have 4–7 members.

2. The groups are to discuss a common topic concerning the *opposite* gender. Some sample topics are:
   • The advantages and disadvantages of being a man/woman.
   • Things I *don't* understand, like, or agree with about most men/women. (Why do they. . . ?)
   • Identity transformation. See the Applied Activity entitled "A New Identity" at the end of Section I.
   • A current national or local issue concerning gender rights.

3. Spend at least 20 minutes discussing the common topic. Have someone record the main points of the discussion and appoint a spokesperson who will present these points to the whole group.

4. Have each group spokesperson summarize the main points and questions raised by the group. Other groups listen and try to understand these points and do *not* offer their views. Once all groups have presented their findings, post the lists of each group's main points on a wall. Take a few minutes to let all participants look at these lists.

5. Depending on time constraints, try one or both of the following:
   - Form mixed gender groups of 4–8 members. Discuss one or more of the points mentioned in the earlier steps. The intent is to have each gender *understand* a point of view, not to persuade or to argue it.
   - Have the whole group meet. Address one of the points generated in the earlier steps—especially if a participant does not understand why someone feels a certain way. Again, the intent of the exercise is to understand, not to argue, lecture, or persuade. It may be helpful to appoint a facilitator to make sure this intent is followed (this person is usually the instructor).

6. Write about your reactions and what you learned from this experience.

SYMBOLIC IDENTITY

Emerson said that objects in nature have corresponding mental likenesses. Carl Jung believed that one's inner life can be represented by outward objects. This activity is a strategy for discovering facets of one's identity through seeking parallels in one's environment. It is crucial to conduct this activity in a relaxed, receptive manner. Let the symbolic discoveries come to you rather than striving for them.

Instructions: Go for a solitary stroll for at least 30 minutes. On this stroll you are to be receptive to something that reflects you as a person. You may see something, feel it, hear it, smell it, taste it, or even sense it intuitively. It is important to *not* force this parallel. Do not make it an intellectual task. Allow the surroundings to present you with the discovery. Just watch and observe with a free-floating attention. If this symbolic reflection appears, pause and enter it without analysis. Let it express itself to you. Once you feel that you have learned all you can, try to write it down. If nothing appears, then try again another time.

Here is one example of this technique: "On campus there is this pedestrian walkway over a busy street. It is tunnel shaped with a clear plastic enclosure. I was walking through this tunnel and gazing at the traffic passing below, couples walking hand-in-hand, and people hurrying to classes. It was then that I realized I was living my whole life in a tunnel. A big project had consumed so much of my life for over a year that I could only observe, but not participate in, a full life. To paraphrase a line in a Hemingway short story, I was there in real life but did not go to it anymore."

PERSONAL GOALS—IDENTITY

Within the next year I will more fully understand who I am by:

Goal 1:

Needed actions, support, and resources:

Timeline:

Progress notes (use extra pages if necessary):

Goal 2:

Needed actions, support, and resources:

Timeline:

Progress notes (use extra pages if necessary):

SECTION TWO

HUMAN COMMUNICATION

One of the things you can do that a squirrel cannot is talk. Another is to wonder why you are being compared to a squirrel. You can talk and wonder because of a part of the human brain called the cerebral cortex. Talking does not necessarily make us any wiser than the squirrel or other animals that do not have a cerebral cortex. We just do it a lot. We spend a good amount of our time hearing and watching others in person, in print, on TV, on the radio, and on all kinds of electronic technology. We tell about our experiences and listen to others' stories. We even talk to ourselves.

Humans seemingly have a need to put into words almost anything they experience. Communication research has shown that humans devote approximately 70 percent of their waking time in verbal communication. We communicate for instrumental reasons—our messages are a means to get information, objects, attention, affection, or influence, or to explain. We also communicate for expressive reasons. Our messages are valued for their own sake—we just enjoy the process of communicating. Being human means to communicate.

Underlying all the reasons to communicate is the need to make a connection with another person (or even with yourself). We all have a basic need to express what is going on in our life and have someone hear it in the way we intended. If this connection is appropriately made, we have genuine communication. If this connection is not consistently achieved, humans often become angry, lonely, alienated, or even sick. The articles in this section feature some of the more significant concepts and techniques for making communication connections.

- In "Interpersonal Communication" Warner Burke provides a basic model of communication. He explains effective and ineffective approaches for sending and receiving messages.
- Psychologist Carl Rogers offers a personalized account of his experiences as a listener in "To Hear and to Be Heard." Rogers says that true listening is a source of deep joy and satisfaction.
- A teacher describes several kinds of classroom listening in "A Teacher Hears."
- In "Self-Disclosure" Nelson Goud discusses the dynamics of how to make disclosures to others, examining under- and over-disclosure as well as appropriate disclosure. He offers guidelines for becoming an effective self-discloser. This article introduces the concept of fusion communication.
- The seemingly different wavelengths for men and women and their communication behavior are the theme of Deborah Tannen's "You Just Don't Understand." Six ways men and women differ are described in a highly practical fashion.
- Intuition, the mode of knowing without thinking, is explained by Frances Vaughan in "Awakening Intuition."
- Making sense of those strange dreams is the topic of Ernest Hartmann's "The Nature and Uses of Dreaming."
- Lou Beeker Schultz describes the rationale and practical suggestions for personal journal writing in "Personal Journaling as a Life Companion."
- Arthur J. Lange and Patricia Jakubowski distinguish three forms of expressing needs and rights in "Assertive, Nonassertive, and Aggressive Behavior." Applied suggestions for engaging in assertive communication are the focus of this article.
- In "King of the Purple Tree" author Nels Goud essentially tells a story of his failures in communication. Interactions with a club musician lead Goud and some of his students to new understandings.

Interpersonal Communication

Warner Burke

Communication, by definition, involves at least two individuals, the sender and the receiver. Consider yourself, first of all, as the sender of some message. There are certain filters or barriers (internal) which determine whether or not the message is actually transmitted. These barriers may be categorized as follows: (1) Assumptions about yourself—Do I really have something to offer? Am I safe to offer suggestions? Do I really want to share the information? Will others really understand? How will the communication affect my self-esteem? (2) Attitudes about the message itself—Is the information valuable? Do I see the information correctly, or understand it well enough to describe it to others? (3) Sensing the receiver's reaction—Do I become aware of whether or not the receiver is actually understanding? Or in other words, can I "sense" from certain cues or reactions by the receiver whether or not we are communicating?

Now consider yourself as the receiver. As a receiver you may filter or not hear certain aspects (or any aspect for that matter) of a message. Why? Because the message may seem unimportant or too difficult. Moreover, you may be selective in your attention. For example, you may feel that the sender is being redundant, so you quit listening after the first few words. You may be preoccupied with something else. Or your filtering or lack of attention may be due to your past experience with the sender. You may feel that "this guy has never made a point in his life and never will!"

Many times the receiver never makes use of his "third ear." That is, trying to be sensitive to nonverbal communication. The sender's eyes, gestures, and sometimes his overall posture communicate messages that the insensitive listener never receives.

There may be barriers that exist between the sender and the receiver, e.g., cultural differences. Environmental conditions may also cause barriers, e.g., poor acoustics. More common, however, are the differences in frames of reference. For example, there may not be a common understanding of purpose in a certain communication. You may ask me how I'm feeling today. To you the phrase, "How ya doing?" is nothing more than a greeting. However, I may think that you really want to know and I may tell you—possibly at length.

Now that some of the problems in interpersonal communication have been mentioned, let us delve somewhat deeper into this process of transferring a message from the brain and emotion of one person to the brain and emotion of another human being.

SENDING THE MESSAGE

In communicating a message effectively to another person, there are several obvious factors which are beneficial. Such things as correct pronunciation, lack of distracting brogue, dialect, or accent, or a pleasant resonance in one's voice usually facilitate the sending of a message.

Assuming the sender of a message really has a desire to be heard and understood and not just speak for the sake of speaking, he wants some assurance that he has communicated. The key to effective communication on the part of the speaker, then, is to obtain some feedback, of one form or another, from his listener(s). Some bright persons who really have something to say are ineffective speakers, be it lecturing or speaking to someone at a cocktail party, because they are unable to tell or care whether their listener(s) is understanding, or they do not make any effort to check on their effectiveness as a communicator. For example, many lecturers in a classroom situation are often unaware of when a listener is sound asleep. Unless there is interaction of some type between the speaker and his listener, the speaker is susceptible to "losing" his listener. Often the speaker must take the initiative in order to receive any feedback regarding the effectiveness of his communication. When speaking before a large group, I often resort to the simple act of requesting my audience to shake their head "yes" if they understand what I have just said, or "no" if they did not understand. Even though this technique is simple, I usually get considerable feedback quickly and I know immediately what I must do at that point to make my speech more effective or whether to continue on with my next point.

Even when talking to just one other person the speaker must often take the initiative, in an interactive sense, to determine whether his message is being understood. Even though I sometimes take the risk of "bugging" my listener, I often stop and ask him if he understands what I mean, or I occasionally ask him to tell me what he thinks I meant in my message.

There is a fairly small percentage of people who speak articulately and clearly enough to be understood most of the time. Most of us have to work at it, especially when we are attempting to communicate a message which is fairly abstract or when we want to tell something which is quite personal or highly emotional. In sending the message effectively, we must do two things simultaneously: (1) work at finding the appropriate words and emotion to express what we want to say, and (2) continually look for cues from the listener to get

some feedback even if we must ask our listener for some.

RECEIVING THE MESSAGE

In considering interpersonal communication, we might, at first thought, think that listening is the easier of the two functions in the process. If we assume, however, that the listener really wants to understand what the speaker is saying, then the process is not all that easy. The basic problem that the listener faces is that he is capable of thinking faster than the speaker can talk. In their *Harvard Business Review* article, Nichols and Stevens state that the average rate of speech for most Americans is about 125 words per minute. Most of our thinking processes involve words, and our brains can handle many more words per minute than 125. As Nichols and Stevens point out, what this means is that, when we listen, our brains receive words at a very slow rate compared with the brain's capabilities.

As you have experienced many times, you know that you can listen to what someone is saying and think about something else at the same time. As the "cocktail party" phenomenon illustrates, the human brain is truly remarkable in its ability to process a considerable amount of input simultaneously. Sometimes, at a cocktail party, I want to hear not only what the person in my small gathering is saying, but also what that lovely creature is talking about in the group about six feet away. If the overall noise level is not too loud, I can hear and understand both conversations.

The problem with listening, then, is that we have "spare" time in our thinking processes. How we use that spare time determines the extent of our listening effectiveness. It is easy for us to be distracted in listening, especially if the speaker talks slowly or haltingly or if he says something that stimulates another thought. For example, suppose you are listening to a friend who is telling you about a problem he is having in his department. In the process of describing the problem, he mentions a person whom you know, whereupon you start thinking about the person at length. Later, when your friend asks you what you would do about his problem, you're apt to respond, "what problem?"

Thus, a fundamental problem the listener must consider in the communicative process is the fact that his brain is capable of responding to a speaker at several different levels simultaneously. Naturally, this can be an asset to the listener rather than a problem. For example the listener can attend to nonverbal cues the speaker gives, e.g., facial expression, gesture, or tone of voice, as well as listen to the words themselves.

Besides a highly active brain, an effective listener has another factor to consider in the communicative process. This factor involves the process of trying to perceive what the speaker is saying from his point of view.

A BARRIER AND A GATEWAY

According to Carl Rogers, a leading psychotherapist and psychotherapy researcher, the major barrier to effective communication is the tendency to evaluate. That is, the barrier to mutual interpersonal communication is our very natural tendency to judge, to evaluate, to approve or disapprove the statement or opinion of the other person or group. Suppose someone says to you, "I didn't like what the lecturer had to say." Your typical response will be either agreement or disagreement. In other words, your primary reaction is to evaluate the statement from your point of view, from your own frame of reference.

Although the inclination to make evaluations is common, it is usually heightened in those situations where feelings and emotions are deeply involved. Thus, the stronger our feelings, the more likely it is that there will be no mutual element in the communication.

There will be only two ideas, two feelings, two judgments, missing each other in the heat of the psychological battle.

If having a tendency to evaluate is the major barrier to communication, then the logical gateway to communication is to become an active listener, to listen with understanding. Don't let this simple statement fool you. Listening with understanding means to see the expressed idea and attitude from the other person's point of view, to see how it feels to him, to achieve his frame of reference concerning his subject. One word that summarizes this process of listening with understanding is "empathy."

In psychotherapy, for example, Carl Rogers and his associates have found from research that empathetic understanding—understanding with a person not about him—is such an effective approach that it can bring about major changes in personality.

Suppose that in your next committee meeting you were to conduct an experiment which would test the quality of each committee member's understanding. Institute this rule: "Each person can speak up for himself only after he has first related the ideas and feelings of the previous speaker accurately and to that speaker's satisfaction." This would mean that before presenting your own point of view, it would be necessary for you to achieve the other speaker's frame of reference—to understand his thoughts and feelings so well that you could summarize them for him.

Can you imagine what this kind of approach might mean if it were projected into larger areas, such as congressional debates or labor-management disputes? What would happen if labor, without necessarily agreeing, could accurately state management's point of view in a way that management could accept; and management, without necessarily approving labor's stand, could state labor's case in a way that labor agreed was accurate? It would mean that real communication was established, and conditions would be more conducive for reaching a workable solution.

TOWARD MORE EFFECTIVE LISTENING

Some steps the listener can take to improve interpersonal communication have been stated. To summarize and be more explicit, let us consider these steps.

1. Effective listening must be an active process. To make certain that you are understanding what the speaker is saying, you, as the listener must interact with him. One way to do this is to paraphrase or summarize for the speaker what you think he has said.
2. Attending to nonverbal behavior that the speaker is communicating along with his verbal expression usually helps to understand the oral message more clearly. Often a facial expression or gesture will "tell" you that the speaker feels more strongly about his subject than his words would communicate.
3. The effective listener does not try to memorize every word or fact the speaker communicates, but, rather, he listens for the main thought or idea. Since your brain is such a highly effective processor of information, spending your listening time in more than just hearing the words of the speaker can lead to more effective listening. That is, while listening to the words, you can also be searching for the main idea of the message. Furthermore, you can attempt to find the frame of reference for the speaker's message as well as look at what he is saying from his perspective. This empathetic process also includes your attempting to experience the same feeling about the subject as the speaker.

These three steps toward more effective listening seem fairly simple and obvious. But the fact remains that we don't practice these steps very often. Why don't we?

According to Carl Rogers, it takes courage. If you really understand another person in this way, if you are willing to enter his private world and see the way life appears to him without any attempt to make evaluative judgments, you run the risk of being changed yourself. This risk of being changed is one of the most frightening prospects many of us face.

Moreover, when we need to utilize these steps the most, we are likely to use them the least, that is, when the situation involves a considerable amount of emotion. For example, when we listen to a message that contradicts our most deeply held prejudices, opinions, or convictions, our brain becomes stimulated by many factors other than what the speaker is telling us. When we are arguing with someone, especially about something that is "near and dear" to us, what are we typically doing when the other person is making his point? It's certainly not listening empathetically! We're probably planning a rebuttal to what he is saying, or we're formulating a question which will embarrass the speaker. We may, of course, simply be "tuning him out." How often have you been arguing with someone for 30 minutes or so, and you make what you consider to be a major point for your point of view, and your "opponent" responds by saying, "But that's what I said 30 minutes ago!"

When emotions are strongest, then, it is most difficult to achieve the frame of reference of the other person or group. Yet it is then that empathy is most needed if communication is to be established. A third party, for example, who is able to lay aside his own feelings and evaluation, can assist greatly by listening with understanding to each person or group and clarifying the views and attitudes each holds.

When the parties to a dispute realize that they are being understood, that someone sees how the situation seems to them, the statements grow less exaggerated and less defensive, and it is no longer necessary to maintain the attitude, "I am 100% right and you are 100% wrong."

SUMMARY

Effective communication, at least among human beings, is not a one-way street. It involves an interaction between the speaker and the listener. The responsibility for this interaction is assumed by both parties. You as the speaker can solicit feedback and adjust your message accordingly. As a listener, you can summarize for the speaker what you think he has said and continually practice the empathetic process.

One of the joys of life, at least for me, is to know that I have been heard and understood correctly and to know that someone cares enough to try to understand what I have said. I also get a great deal of satisfaction from seeing this same enjoyment on the face of a speaker when he knows I have understood him.

Follow-Up

1. *Choose one statement from this reading that describes one of your* strengths *as a communicator. Choose one statement that describes an area where you* need improvement *as a communicator.*
2. *Burke says that he sometimes initiates getting feedback from a listener to be sure he was understood. Consider trying this idea for times when you are not sure your message is understood.*
3. *Burke states that human thought is much faster than human speech. This fact often results in distracted thoughts and ineffective listening. Does this often happen to you? Try to focus on your listener more if it does.*
4. *Empathy is the ability to perceive another person's world as they do. Another option is to perceive a statement only from your own point of view. Try to understand what other people say from their point of view before you offer your viewpoint. What differences do you notice in the way you relate to one another? See the Applied Activity "Point of View" at the end of this section for a way to develop this skill.*
5. *Burke mentions that it takes courage to be an empathic listener because you run the risk of being changed yourself. You may hear something contrary to your existing beliefs that makes sense. Then you have to reexamine your beliefs and possibly make major changes, and this is threatening. Has this ever happened to you? Can you recognize when this is happening?*
6. *Burke states that when emotions are intense, true listening is especially important. But, of course, this is the time when listening is the most difficult. Experiment a few times with being a good listener during times when you can sense "hot" emotions. If this is done correctly, the defensiveness should decrease.*
7. *The Applied Activities at the end of this section allow you to apply most of the ideas mentioned in this article.*

To Hear and to Be Heard

Carl Rogers

The first simple feeling I want to share with you is my enjoyment when I can really *hear* someone. I think perhaps this has been a long standing characteristic of mine. I can remember this in my early grammar school days. A child would ask the teacher a question and the teacher would give a perfectly good answer to a completely different question. A feeling of pain and distress would always strike me. My reaction was, "But you didn't *hear* him!" I felt a sort of childish despair at the lack of communication which was (and is) so common.

I believe I know why it is satisfying to me to hear someone. When I can really hear someone it puts me in touch with him. It enriches my life. It is through hearing people that I have learned all that I know about individuals, about personality, about psychotherapy, and about interpersonal relationships. There is another peculiar satisfaction in it. When I really hear someone it is like listening to the music of the spheres, because beyond the immediate message of the person, no matter what that might be, there is the universal, the general. Hidden in all of the personal communications which I really hear there seem to be orderly psychological laws, aspects of the awesome order which we find in the universe as a whole. So there is both the satisfaction of hearing this particular person and also the satisfaction of feeling oneself in some sort of touch with what is universally true.

When I say that I enjoy hearing someone I mean, of course, hearing deeply. I mean that I hear the words, the thoughts, the feeling tones, the personal meaning, even the meaning that is below the conscious intent of the speaker. Sometimes, too, in a message which superficially is not very important, I hear a deep human cry, a "silent scream," that lies buried and unknown far below the surface of the person.

So I have learned to ask myself, can I hear the sounds and sense the shape of this other person's inner world? Can I resonate to what he is saying, can I let it echo back and forth in me, so deeply that I sense the meanings he is afraid of yet would like to communicate, as well as those meanings he knows?

I think, for example, of an interview I had with an adolescent boy, the recording of which I listened to only a short time ago. Like many an adolescent today he was saying at the outset of the interview that he had no goals. When I questioned him on this he made it even stronger that he had no goals whatsoever, not even one. I said, "There isn't anything you want to do?" "*Nothing* . . . Well, yeah, I want to keep on living." I remember very distinctly my feeling at that moment. I resonated very deeply to this phrase. He might simply be telling me that, like everyone else, he wanted to live. On the other hand he might be telling me, and this seemed to be a distinct possibility, that at some point the question of whether or not to live had been a real issue with him. So I tried to resonate to him at all levels. I didn't know for certain what the message was. I simply wanted to be open to any of the meanings that this statement might have, including the possible meaning that he might have at one time considered suicide. I didn't respond verbally at this level.

That would have frightened him. But I think that my being willing and able to listen to him at all levels is perhaps one of the things that made it possible for him to tell me, before the end of the interview, that not long before he had been on the point of blowing his brains out. This little episode constitutes an example of what I mean by wanting to really hear someone at all the levels at which he is endeavoring to communicate.

I find, in therapeutic interviews, and in the intensive group experiences which have come to mean a great deal to me in recent years, that hearing has consequences. When I do truly hear a person and the meanings that are important to him at that moment, hearing not simply his words, but *him,* and when I let him know that I have heard his own private personal meanings, many things happen. There is first of all a grateful look. He feels released. He wants to tell me more about his world. He surges forth in a new sense of freedom. I think he becomes more open to the process of change.

I have often noticed, both in therapy and in groups, that the more deeply I can hear the meanings of this person the more there is that happens. One thing I have come to look upon as almost universal is that when a person realizes he has been deeply heard, there is a moistness in his eyes. I think in some real sense he is weeping for joy. It is as though he were saying, "Thank God, *somebody* heard me. Someone knows what it's like to be me." In such moments I have had the fantasy of a prisoner in a dungeon, tapping out day after day a Morse code message, "Does anybody hear me? Is there anybody there? Can anyone hear me?" And finally one day he hears some faint tappings which spell out "Yes." By that one simple response he is released from his loneliness, he has become a human being again. There are many, many people living in private dungeons today, people who give no evidence of it whatever on the outside, where you have to listen very sharply to hear the faint messages from the dungeon.

I LIKE TO BE HEARD

Let me move on to a second learning, which I would like to share with you. I like to *be heard.* A number of times in my life I have felt myself bursting with insoluble problems, or going round and round in tormented circles or, during one period, overcome by feelings of worthlessness and despair, sure I was sinking into psychosis. I think I have been more lucky than most in finding at these times individuals who have been able to hear me and thus to rescue me from the chaos of my feelings. I have been fortunate in finding individuals who have been able to hear my meanings a little more deeply than I have known them. These individuals have heard me without judging me, diagnosing me, appraising me, evaluating me. They have just listened and clarified and responded to me at all the levels at which I was communicating. I can testify that when you are in psychological distress and someone really hears you without passing judgment on you, without trying to take responsibility for you, without trying to mold you, it feels *damn good.* At these times, it has relaxed the tension in me. It has permitted me to bring out the frightening feelings, the guilts, the despair, the confusions that have been a part of my experience. When I have been listened to and when I have been heard, I am able to reperceive my world in a new way and to go on. It is amazing that feelings which were completely awful, become bearable when someone listens. It is astonishing, how elements which seem insoluble become soluble when someone hears; how confusions which seem irremediable turn into relatively clear flowing streams when one is understood. I have deeply appreciated the times that I have experienced this sensitive, empathic, concentrated listening.

I have been very grateful that by the time I quite desperately needed this kind of help, I had trained and developed therapists, persons in their own right, independent and unafraid of me, who were able to go with me through a dark and troubled period in which I underwent a great deal of inner growth. It has also made me sharply aware that in developing my style of therapy for others, I was without doubt, at some unconscious level, developing the kind of help I wanted and could use myself.

WHEN I CANNOT HEAR

Let me turn to some of my dissatisfactions in this realm. I dislike it in myself when I can't hear another, when I do not understand him. If it is only a simple failure of comprehension or a failure to focus my attention on what he is saying, or a difficulty in understanding his words, then I feel only a very mild dissatisfaction with myself.

But what I really dislike in myself is when I cannot hear the other person because I am so sure in advance of what he is about to say that I don't listen. It is only afterward that I realize that I have only heard what I have already decided he is saying. I have failed really to listen. Or even worse are those times when I can't hear because what he is saying is too threatening, might even make me change my views or my behavior. Still worse are those times when I catch myself trying to twist his message to make it say what I want him to say, and then only hearing that. This can be a very subtle thing and it is surprising how skillful I can be in doing it. Just by twisting his words a small amount, by distorting his meaning just a little, I can make it appear that he is not only saying the thing I want to hear, but that he is the person I want him to be. It is only when I realize through his protest or through my own gradual recognition that I am subtly manipulating him that I become disgusted with myself. I

know too from being on the receiving end of this how frustrating it is to be received for what you are not, to be heard as saying something which you have not said and do not mean. This creates anger and bafflement and disillusion.

WHEN OTHERS DO NOT UNDERSTAND

The next learning I want to share with you is that I am terribly frustrated and shut into myself when I try to express something which is deeply me, which is a part of my own private, inner world, and the other person does not understand. When I take the gamble, the risk, of trying to share something that is very personal with another individual and it is not received and not understood, this is a very deflating and a very lonely experience. I have come to believe that it is that experience which makes some individuals psychotic. They have given up hoping that anyone can understand them and once they have lost that hope then their own inner world, which becomes more and more bizarre, is the only place where they can live. They can no longer live in any shared human experience. I can sympathize with them because I know that when I try to share some feeling aspect of myself which is private, precious, and tentative, and when this communication is met by evaluation, by reassurance, by denial, by distortion of my meaning I have very strongly the reaction, "Oh, what's the use!" At such a time one knows what it is to be *alone*.

So, as you can see, a creative, active, sensitive, accurate, empathic, non-judgmental listening, is for me terribly important in a relationship. It is important for me to provide it. It has been extremely important especially at certain times in my life to receive it. I feel that I have grown within myself when I have provided it. I am very sure that I have grown and been released and enhanced when I have received this kind of listening.

1. *Try to think of a time when you, like Carl Rogers, felt a sense of enjoyment and satisfaction from really hearing someone.*
2. *Rogers claims that when you are really heard there is an inner release, a feeling of freedom, and a desire to share more of yourself. Has this been true for you? Has there been, in your life, a listener who hears you deeply?*
3. *Rogers is a highly influential therapist and theorist. However, even he dislikes himself "when I cannot hear the other person because I am so sure in advance of what he is about to say that I don't listen." And "still worse are those times when I catch myself trying to twist his message to make it say what I want him to say, and then only hearing that." Most of us engage in one or both of these non-listening behaviors. Monitor your listening behavior; attempt to catch yourself listening poorly. See if you can change your approach and just listen without imposing your thoughts.*
4. *Select any other point that Rogers makes in this article and offer your view on its validity.*
5. *Develop your listening skills by attempting one or more of the Applied Activities at the end of this section.*

John Steinbeck on Listening

We had had many discussions at the galley table and there had been many honest attempts to understand each other's thinking. There are several kinds of reception possible. There is the mind which lies in wait with traps for flaws, so set that it may miss, through not grasping it, a soundness. There is a second which is not reception at all, but blind flight because of laziness, or because some pattern is disturbed by the processes of the discussion. The best reception of all is that, which is easy and relaxed, which says in effect, "Let me absorb this thing. Let me try to understand it without private barriers. When I have understood what you are saying, only then will I subject it to my own scrutiny and my own criticism." This is the finest of all critical approaches and the rarest.

The smallest and meanest of all is that which, being frightened or outraged by thinking outside or beyond its pattern, revenges itself senselessly; leaps on a misspelled word or a mispronunciation, drags tricky definition in by the scruff of the neck, and, raging like a small unpleasant dog, rags and tears the structure to shreds. We have known a critic to base a vicious criticism on a misplaced letter in a word, when actually he was venting rage on an idea he hated. These are the suspicious ones, the self-protective ones, living lives of difficult defense, insuring themselves against folly with folly—stubbornly self-protective at too high a cost.

A Teacher Hears

Listening, and hearing deeply, I feel, are the most important skills I must constantly strive to improve. Listening to my students tells me what they understand as opposed to what they can regurgitate. It tells me how they feel about the subject, about me, and about themselves.

Sometimes what I hear is silence. My classes are very active. No one goes quietly through the period. In the beginning of the year this surprises some students and even makes some uncomfortable. But soon they become accustomed to it. William was one of my new seventh-grade students this year. Early in the year I called on him. "So what law allows us to say that 3 + 7 is the same as 7 + 3? William? William? . . ." Nothing. No sound. No eye contact. Nothing. I approached him. My normal reaction was to tease. "Is there anybody in there?" Something in me said "not this time." I had never seen a reaction like this. I was to find out later that William was a victim of abuse. He was terrified of being hurt—of being wrong. Gradually as the year has progressed, William has learned to trust me. Although it has not been easy for either of us, I now can call on him, and he will look at me and softly, very softly, tell me what he knows.

Sometimes what I hear is non-verbal. Meghan is a bubbly, bright, tiny little girl in the same class as William. Meghan works very hard on a consistent basis to keep herself at the top of this class. In early June she took her final and completely fell apart. I recognized a full-blown case of test anxiety. The following day, the last day the class would meet, there was time left at the end of the period and the class visited among themselves. I approached Meghan's desk. As I began to ask her about how she felt taking the final, I saw eyes filling with tears, and a strong little girl trying very hard not to cry. We talked about what had happened, about her competitive drive, about how important her math *grade* had become in her mind, and about how we could attempt to conquer the problem next year. The entire time she sank lower in her chair, trying to answer my questions, but without much success. What a painful chord we had struck. As I left school later that day, I noticed a note attached to my windshield wipers. "Mrs. R., This year has been really great. I can't wait till next year. Meghan." It seems both of us had listened.

Sometimes I hear boredom. One day last year I looked up at my seventh-grade class and not one single student was "in attendance." Furthermore they weren't even being disruptive. It was like they had run into a really bad TV program! They were slouching and looking down or out the window. Total boredom had invaded that room. I was still in shock as I headed home that day. What I had heard in that room that period could not have been more clear if they, as a class, had gotten up and left!

Sometimes I hear confusion, frustration. Dara is an outstanding math student. She learns easily and well. Very often, however, when I am teaching a new concept, I often hear Dara say that "This is stupid" or "I don't like this." It was after a number of times of hearing this from her that I realized what I was really hearing was "I don't quite understand" or "I haven't completely processed what you are saying." In fact, she doesn't think it is stupid at all but rather is openly expressing a moment of confusion that she is experiencing.

And sometimes I fail to hear at all. Josh had done a beautiful job in math for three quarters. I'd had his older brother in past years, so he came to me already motivated. Suddenly in the fourth quarter he quit—missing or lost or half-done assignments, inattention in class. My response was annoyance, almost anger. After about three weeks of this, his mother called. Josh, it seemed, had had some bouts with depression and self-doubt in the past. Again it had flared up. He felt he had disappointed me and that I didn't "like" him. How could I have interpreted his behavior so wrongly? How could I have failed to hear what he was saying to me?

There are all kinds of hearing skills to be cultivated in teaching. It is the main link to the student-teacher chain, and perhaps is the most underrated of all the communication skills.

—A middle school teacher

Self-Disclosure

Nelson Goud

*No man can come to know himself except as
an outcome of disclosing himself to another
person. . . . if we want to be loved, we must
disclose ourselves.*

—Sidney Jourard

*I am afraid to tell you who I am, because, if I
tell you who I am, you may not like who I am,
and it's all that I have.*

—John Powell

Self-disclosure is what we reveal about ourselves to others. As the above quotes illustrate,
self-disclosure has the potential for great gains
but also contains significant risks. We are continually faced with the choice of revealing or
concealing ourselves from others.

Growth psychologists contend that the
quality of authenticity is one of the marks of a
mature, healthy person. In contrast is the
person who primarily acts in the form of false
fronts or facades. With an authentic person we
do not have to always wonder "What is she or
he *really* like?" Authenticity contains a good
dose of naturalness and reality. The ability to
self-disclose is one component of authenticity.
Rogers (1994, 1961) believes that a movement
away from facades to genuineness is a key
sign of personal growth. Pearson (1985) sum-
marized several studies that demonstrated a
close relationship between self-disclosure
and a person's level of self-esteem and self-
actualization.

Learning to appropriately self-disclose is
essential for establishing intimate relationships, avoiding social alienation, and knowing
oneself. Some of the major dimensions of effective self-disclosure will be examined in the
following discussion.

DISCLOSURE BREADTH AND DEPTH

Self-disclosure can be classified according to
both breadth and depth. Breadth refers to the
range of topics disclosed. Depth refers to the
degree of intimacy and completeness (feelings and ideas) of a disclosure. In general, the
more the depth, the more the risk and vulnerability. For example, casual relationships usually have breadth but little depth. Or, it is
possible to have a relationship characterized
by intense depth in one domain but little
depth or breadth in other domains (a brief love
affair would be an example).

What is considered low, moderate, and
high disclosure varies greatly among individuals. You may feel very comfortable discussing your feelings about your age, but
another may find this deeply personal and of
a high disclosure nature. A person must be
aware of these individual disclosure preferences if effective communication is to occur.
Additionally, there are wide cultural differences in the appropriateness of disclosure
levels (this article will emphasize general
American norms). You may even experience
variations in your willingness to disclose on
the same topic to different people, or under
different circumstances. Even with these individual variations, there are some common
findings which relate to most people.

Several studies of self-disclosure have
found that positive mental health is characterized by high disclosure to a few significant
others; poorly adjusted persons tend to over-
disclose or under-disclose to almost everyone
(Cozby, 1973; Derlega & Chaikin, 1975; Johnson, 1993). Optimum disclosure depends on

many factors: the purpose of disclosing, the nature of the relationship, the context of the disclosure, and the possible consequences. Most negative consequences result from either under- or over-disclosing.

UNDER-DISCLOSURE

There are many reasons why people may not reveal themselves. Derlega and Chaikin (1975) state that low revealers may not trust in the good will of others and may be "afraid of ridicule, rejection, or the possibility that the listener will reveal the information to others" (p. 14). Sometimes the low revealer is perceived to be a person of little emotion and having few major problems. That person's uniqueness also is masked. If concealment becomes the predominant way of relating to others, there may be a number of detrimental consequences: loneliness, mistrust from others because they do not know how this person thinks or feels, little shared intimacy, loss of a major source of self-knowledge, and a higher-than-normal amount of psychological energy expended to maintain a persona.

Sidney Jourard (1971) contends that how people choose to fulfill their life roles can influence disclosure levels. Life roles refer to the expected behaviors based on gender, occupation, and age. A healthy person can perform these roles and also express other dimensions of personhood. However, some people define themselves entirely by the roles they perform and are unaware of their interior life. Self-disclosure depends on an awareness of this interior life. Role conformity can lead to a "normal existence" but, as Jourard says, "it is possible to be a normal personality and be absolutely miserable" (p. 28).

Low self-revelation may be purposeful for some but not for others. Verbal self-disclosure depends on the ability to first recognize what you are feeling and thinking, and second, to place these interior states into words. Some people have deficiencies in one or both of these capabilities. In many ways, self-disclosure is a learned skill. Without experience in recognizing emotions and how to verbalize them, it is not possible to disclose them. Ask a young child to express emotions and the majority fall into the "sad, bad, glad" categories. Many persons do not develop beyond this level because they are not taught or encouraged to do so. Even today, conventional socialization still tends to favor females over males in these abilities. Pearson (1985) cites many studies that demonstrate the greater facility of females in verbal and non-verbal emotional expression (and recognizing the same).

OVER-DISCLOSURE

> There's this girl on my floor in the dormitory who's really weird. She tells people she's just met about really personal things, like all these guys she's sleeping with. Everyone tries to avoid her. I think she really needs help (A college coed, as quoted in Derlega & Chaikin, p. 10).

In one of my first graduate counseling courses we formed a group and the instructor told us to share how we felt about ourselves. A man on my right was the first to volunteer. He said, "My name is John and for the past year I have been in a psychiatric hospital. For quite awhile I had been hallucinating about cadavers and talking with them. I decided to get help. It worked. I do not have my hallucinations very much anymore." No one knew how to react to John's revelation. His openness was respected, but we felt uneasy. His disclosure was introduced before most of us were really capable of hearing him. We did not know enough about each other to place his deeply revealing comment in context. Instead of creating a closeness, I felt more distanced from John—Was he really okay now? If he reveals at this level so readily, will he be able to keep our in-class disclosures confidential?

These instances are examples of what most would consider over-disclosing. Over-disclosing is characterized by immediate revelations of high intimacy without considering the context or others' readiness to hear. Instead of encouraging closeness, over-disclosing tends to produce avoidance behaviors. Many over-disclosers are perceived as strange or deviant. Being so open about their own private lives, over-disclosers may not be trusted with reciprocal disclosures from others. Over-disclosers may initially solicit some sympathy, but if they continue, others will begin to ignore them or become annoyed.

To engage in effective disclosure, a person must observe many cues. A good deal of sensitivity is required to accurately judge the changing conditions of trust, vulnerability, and context. Some guidelines to consider on the topic of self-disclosure are offered next.

GUIDELINES FOR EFFECTIVE SELF-DISCLOSURE

Interpersonal Relationships

The degree of intimacy in a relationship closely parallels the level of mutual self-disclosure. The more that you know of another, the deeper the foundation for trust (or in some cases, mistrust, as with some over-disclosers). Self-disclosure is a primary path to discovering shared interests, values, and life perceptions—all major components of intimacy (both romantic and non-romantic). Some basic findings are listed next.

1. For early stages of a relationship, the preferred pattern is to initially share a lot of information at low disclosure levels. Higher degrees of disclosure follow at a gradual rate. Each disclosure level change is generally reciprocated by each partner if the relationship is to deepen. Changing levels of disclosure requires one of the parties to take a risk. If the other party is willing to strengthen the relationship at that moment, a reciprocating disclosure will usually occur. The reciprocity of disclosure may not be as significant in advanced, established stages of intimacy. Here trust has already been developed and attention can be focused on the topic being divulged by one of the parties (Jourard, 1971; Pearson, 1985; Johnson, 1993).

2. Should I conceal or reveal? Some disclosures are so powerful that they can cause major shifts, positive or negative, in a relationship. You love her but you do not know if she "likes or loves" you. One night she says "I love you." This propels the relationship to a new dimension. A few months later you want to share your whole life because of this deep intimacy but it includes (choose at least one): sexual fantasies with others, shameful past experiences, a disliked aspect of your partner. Will it be dishonest if you do not share yourself completely, or are some things best left unsaid?

Even the experts vary in their guidance on these issues. Harry Browne in Arkoff (1993) says that if you strive to be an honest person then "the only way to demonstrate your honesty is by simply responding honestly to everything (and to everyone)." Morton Hunt in Arkoff (1993) believes that people should be selective in what they reveal to intimates because often they release their own pain only to transfer it unnecessarily to the partner. "There are limits to intimacy," says Hunt, "not only for our own good, but for the good of those we love."

Carl Rogers, one of the most influential psychologists of this century, offers this example and guideline. He described a wife who was becoming increasingly sullen, angry, guilty and expressing these feelings in ways that were damaging her marriage. She realized that some unresolved issues from affairs with married men prior to her marriage were part of the problem, but felt that she could not express these to her husband. He might change his mind about what kind of person she was to him (which was as a loving, "nice girl"). Deciding that concealing was doing as much or more harm, she revealed her feelings. She did not go into details, but focused on the effects of those affairs. In her case it was heard and understood, and cleared the way for a deeper relationship with her husband. She believed that her desire for a good marriage was worth the risk of disclosure.

Rogers offers a helpful guideline on whether to disclose or not in an intimate relationship: ". . . in any continuing relationship any persistent feeling had better be expressed. Suppressing it can only damage the relationship. The first sentence is not stated casually. Only if it is a significant continuing relationship, and only if it is a recurring or persistent feeling, is it necessary to bring the feeling into the open in the relationship. If this is not done, what is unexpressed gradually poisons the relationship" (Rogers, 1972, pp. 20–21).

Jennifer and Scott have gradually developed a close, intimate relationship. They find it exhilarating to be able to trust each other with deep disclosures. They both believe that they want a relationship based on total honesty. However, Jennifer still finds herself attracted to other men, though she does not act on these feelings. She wonders if she should share this with Scott (in order to be totally honest). She also knows that Scott is somewhat insecure about losing her. In this instance it would probably be premature for Jennifer to disclose her feelings of attraction to other men. The relationship would be unnecessarily threatened by feelings that are quite common and not strong enough to warrant a major negative shift in their developing relationship. If these feelings persist and influence her relationship with Scott, then disclosure should be considered.

There are many other instances where nondisclosure is the appropriate choice given the multiple circumstances surrounding a relationship. What good does it do to mention a flaw of a friend, lover, or parent when it is not significant to a continuing relationship? There are many times when a leader, parent, or others in an authority position must *not* disclose their fears in order to keep a problem situation manageable for others. I remember how my own parents were somehow strong and lively during the whole period that I had a mild case of polio. If they had shared their fears with me as a ten year old, I would have been frightened for the duration of the illness. Through their actions I remained relatively confident and positive during my hospitalization and recovery.

Purposes of Self-Disclosure

As a sender and receiver it is important to realize the intent of a self-revelation. Knowing another's motive helps to determine the kind of response to offer. Here are selected motives of self-disclosure, both negative and positive:

1. A genuine desire to establish more closeness or intimacy.
2. A catharsis or release of burdensome emotions. It is crucial here to consider the effects of this release on the receiver. Imagine that Carol has been suffering intense shame and hurt from abusive childhood experiences. She needs to express this to someone. Carol should consider talking to someone who can offer sound guidance, such as a counselor, spiritual advisor, or family doctor. In general, for disclosures that are primarily cathartic and confessional in nature, it is usually wise to share them initially with non-involved third parties.
3. Sometimes a person self-discloses to avoid responsibility. Instead of taking responsibility to right a wrong or to solve a problem, a person may intentionally tell

someone, hoping that person will shoulder the load.

4. Knowing that self-disclosure often creates affection and closeness, some persons take advantage of this knowledge in a self-serving manner, in what might be called manipulative intimacy. People may reveal just the right amount of information to be trusted, but the trust is used for their gain only (sexual, financial, or status). They have no intent of establishing a genuine relationship through this kind of self-disclosure.

Multiple Receivers

It is helpful to have several persons to whom you can disclose on different topics and intimacy levels. It is almost impossible for one person, even a spouse or close friend, to be an appropriate receiver for all your feelings and experiences. For example, you may need to talk *about* your spouse/friend, and this requires someone else you can trust. Most often a single receiver does not have all the needed background to understand everything you want to share. Think of a time when you tried to share an intense experience from your job, hobby, or school major but your receiver had no relevant experience. You undoubtedly found yourself explaining background information rather than the experience you wanted to share. I find there are some aspects of university life that are inaccessible to those outside of the university. Here I seek a university friend if I have a need to communicate. The same holds true for my trumpet-playing.

Context

For effective self-disclosure to occur, the circumstances must be considered. Some of the major circumstances include the following.

Emotional and Physical Readiness. It is difficult to send or receive high levels of disclosure when you are tired, rushed, anxious, in the midst of problem solving, and so on. While a person does not always have to be in a perfect mental or physical condition, make sure that at least minimal readiness levels are met.

Time Framework. Is there sufficient time to comprehend and discuss the disclosure (especially high level ones)? Try to avoid the last minute disclosure. In this approach a person delays a disclosure until the last possible moment to avoid possible further discussion or consequences. For example, counselors often hear the most important revelations in the last five minutes of a counseling session. Or imagine an ongoing couple at the end of a regular date. While about to leave, Rodolfo turns and says, "Oh, by the way, I think it might be good if we spent a little time apart—G'night."

Physical Setting. Attempt to be aware of the effects of the physical environment, such as temperature, noise level, and the presence of other people. Susie may be very comfortable disclosing in a crowded restaurant but Jake is not. Sometimes movement is a factor. I know of many people, including myself, who prefer to self-disclose while going on a walk, during breaks on a long bike ride, or driving in a car. My son and I have our best disclosure times during these kinds of activities. My daughter and I have our mutual disclosures while sitting out on the patio.

Dyad Effect. A two-person group (dyad) has been found to be the preferred number for self-disclosure (Pearson, 1985). Trust and confidentiality seem to occur more readily in dyads. Effective disclosure is possible in larger groups but there is more initial resistance.

Some Exceptions. There are two contextual circumstances where high disclosure occurs faster than normal. One is during crisis situations such as disasters, accidents, serious illness or death of a loved one, or being trapped in an enclosed space. In these situations, participants share a common and intense bond of danger or loss. The normal rules of disclosure are often shelved in order to restore a sense of safety and support.

The second instance is the stranger phenomenon first mentioned by the German sociologist Georg Simmel in the late 1800s. Here a person discusses intimate topics to a complete stranger at a bar, on a plane, in a hotel restaurant, on a park bench, and so on. Another and more recent version is to reveal oneself to strangers in cyberspace on the Internet. There are several reasons why a stranger may be the recipient of high self-disclosures. A stranger has little likelihood of using the information against the sender—in short, there is little threat. An Internet user does not have to worry about following up a disclosure or getting further involved. Sometimes a stranger may offer an outsider's point of view of your situation. Disclosures to strangers may be helpful, but only if not used as regular substitutes for genuine and consistent intimate relationships.

Fusion Communication

Usually the sender and receiver of a message are different people. It is possible for a person to be both the sender and receiver. I call this fusion communication. There are times when there are no appropriate receivers available to hear your disclosure. Or you cannot adequately verbalize certain feelings or experiences to others in a way they could understand, but you must express yourself. In this instance you may appoint yourself as the receiver. Some forms of fusion communication are discussed below.

Internal Dialogues. Internal dialogues include talking to yourself (silently or out loud); writing interpretive diaries or journals; or expressing your inner world through art forms —poetry, song, or dance. Anne Frank used

fusion communication during her confinement by keeping a diary "in order to bring out all kinds of things that lie buried deep in my heart. . . . The reason for my starting a diary . . . is that I have no . . . real friend."

Boomerang Dialogues. In boomerang dialogues, individuals seem to be disclosing to something else, but they are really communicating to themselves. You may, for example, speak to a pet about a current life dilemma or problem. Your message is bounced off the pet to you. Almost any external object can be a target of boomerang dialogue—plants, trees, a car, walls, the sky, or the ocean. Young children often disclose to real or stuffed animals or to invisible friends. Some forms of prayer function as fusion communication.

Deceased loved ones can also be recipients of self-disclosures. In *The Winter of Our Discontent,* John Steinbeck explains the essence of this form of fusion communication: "Much of my talk is addressed to people who are dead . . . Nothing mysterious or mystic about that. It's asking for advice or an excuse from the inner part of you that is formed and certain" (p. 57).

Kempler (1987) discusses how some inner experiences have stages of maturity. To disclose them prematurely may damage their full expression. This is particularly true for new inspirations, emotional self-insights, and intuitive illuminations. Forms of fusion communication should be considered in these instances.

Fusion communication is one valuable self-disclosure strategy under the conditions described above. If it is the only form of self-disclosure, that indicates something is amiss. Interpersonal and fusion communication are both essential for a balanced life.

Self-Disclosure and Self-Knowledge

We gain knowledge of ourselves through several means. Two major sources are feedback from others and knowledge gained from our experiences. Talking about our inner reactions to experiences is also a primary path to self-awareness. Johnson (1993) says, "When you explain your feelings, perceptions, reactions, and experiences in words, they become clearer, better organized, and take on new meanings" (p. 35).

While disclosing some confused feelings or intuitions with someone you trust, you may suddenly stumble over an insight, or discover "I didn't know I felt this way." Jourard (1971) contends that without sufficient self-disclosure individuals may learn to conceal their own identities from themselves. One path to deep inner knowledge, he continues, is this: "When a person has been able to disclose himself utterly to another person, he learns how to increase his contact with his real self, and he may then be better able to direct his destiny on the basis of this knowledge" (p. 6).

Gender and Self-Disclosure

There are some gender differences on self-disclosure behavior. Below are selected findings as reported by Pearson (1985). These are group tendencies and do not automatically apply for every male or female:

- Women self-disclose more easily and more often than men.
- Women self-disclose more negative information.
- Women self-disclose more on intimate topics; both men and women self-disclose at similar levels on non-intimate topics.
- Increased eye contact and a closer personal space encourage self-disclosure for women, but decrease it for men.
- Positively interpreted touch increases self-disclosure for both men and women.
- Both men and women tend to disclose more as they get older; females disclose at higher levels at all age stages.

"Dumping Station"

A sign points to the spot where campers can cast their rubbish. Campers leave the dumping station with lighter backs and more room in their tents.

Our minds could use a dumping station. A mind, too, functions better if it is lighter and has more room. It means that one must try to jettison unnecessary guilt, prolonged worry, immobilizing fear, or chronic mourning. It may mean talking it out with someone, doing more or doing less, or getting help. But cleaning out emotional debris is essential if life is to be lived as intended. Cleaning the mind starts with first knowing what to throw away. What would make your mind lighter?

CONCLUSION

One requirement of an individual identity is boundaries. Without boundaries it is difficult to perceive where one person begins and another ends. Sometime it feels nice to merge identities for awhile (such as the infant-mother bond or the initial stages of intense intimacy). Continuing these merged identities for too long, however, will eventually stunt full development. Our growth depends on realizing unique and individual potentialities.

Self-disclosure is closely tied to identity boundaries. Becoming close to another can be described as allowing another to enter—to pass through a boundary gate and see what is there. The further along another is allowed to pass boundary gates, the deeper the intimacy. In the most intimate of relationships there still may be some boundary gates that remain closed. We may have parts of ourselves that we wish not to reveal, or it may be that we just cannot explain some knowings of our interior life. Some of our unconscious stirrings are unknown to anyone, including us. Finally, we may purposely choose to have a hideaway that gives privacy in order to produce a sense of uniqueness, mystery, and constructive surprise.

The choice is ours. We can let everyone pass through our boundary gates at the costs of indistinct identities and interpersonal sameness. We can let no one in at the expense of loneliness, mistrust, and the loss of a major source of understanding oneself. Keeping our gates locked also means we cannot venture out; we, too, are locked out of others' lives. Or we can learn selectivity. We experiment and observe and even "goof." Eventually we will create and discover the art of knowing when to open and when to close our boundary gates, when to embrace the world and when to seek some privacy.

References

Arkoff, A. (1993). *Psychology and personal growth* (4th ed.). Boston: Allyn & Bacon.

Cozby, P. C. (1973). Self-disclosure: A literature review. *Psychological Bulletin, 79,* 73–91.

Derlega, V., & Chaikin, A. (1975). *Sharing intimacy.* Englewood Cliffs, NJ: Prentice-Hall.

Johnson, D. (1993). *Reaching out.* Boston: Allyn & Bacon.

Jourard, S. (1971). *The transparent self.* New York: Van Nostrand Reinhold Co.

Kempler, B. (1987). The shadow side of self-disclosure. *Journal of Humanistic Psychology, 27,* 109–117.

Pearson, J. (1985). *Gender and communication.* Dubuque, IA: Wm. C. Brown.

Rogers, C. (1961). *On becoming a person.* Boston: Houghton Mifflin.

Rogers, C. (1972). *Becoming partners: Marriage and its alternatives.* New York: Delacorte Press.

Rogers, C., & Freiberg, H. (1994). *Freedom to learn* (3rd ed.). New York: Merrill/Macmillan.

Follow-Up

1. *Select two statements from the article that have relevance for your life.*
2. *Describe a time when you self-disclosed but wish you had not. What happened to make you feel this way? What did you learn about disclosure from*

this experience? (You do not have to reveal private details here, just general situations.)

3. *Try to remember a time when you took a risk and self-disclosed and it turned out well. What did you learn about disclosure from this experience?*
4. *Overall, are you an under-discloser, an over-discloser, or an appropriate discloser? Explain why you see yourself this way.*
5. *Try to describe any experience or preference in fusion communication strategies. Under what conditions, if any, do you find them helpful?*
6. *Select one or more Guidelines for Effective Self-Disclosure and apply them in your current situation.*

You Just Don't Understand

Deborah Tannen

A married couple was in a car when the wife turned to her husband and asked, "Would you like to stop for a drink?"

"No, thanks," he answered truthfully. So they didn't stop.

The result? The wife—who had indeed wanted to stop—became annoyed because she felt her preference had not been considered. The husband, seeing his wife was angry, became frustrated. *Why didn't she just say what she wanted?*

Unfortunately, he failed to see that his wife was asking the question not to get an instant decision, but to begin a negotiation. And the woman didn't realize that when her husband said no, he was just expressing his preference, not making a ruling. When a man and woman interpret the same interchange in such conflicting ways, it's no wonder they can find themselves leveling angry charges of selfishness and obstinacy at each other.

As a specialist in linguistics, I have studied how the conversational styles of men and women differ. We cannot, of course, lump "all men" or "all women" into fixed categories—individuals vary greatly. But research shows that the seemingly senseless misunderstandings that haunt our relationships can at least in part be explained by the different conversational rules by which men and women often play.

Whenever I write or speak about this subject, people tell me how relieved they are to learn that what they had previously ascribed to personal failings is, in fact, very common. Learning about the different (though equally valid) conversational frequencies men and women are tuned to can help banish blame and help us truly talk to one another. Here are some of the most common areas of conflict.

STATUS VS. SUPPORT

Men grow up in a world in which a conversation is often a contest—either to achieve the upper hand or to prevent other people from pushing them around. For many women, however, talking is typically a way to exchange confirmation and support. I saw this firsthand when my husband and I had jobs in different cities. When people made comments like "That must be rough" and "How do you stand it?" I accepted their sympathy.

But my husband would react with irritation. Our situation had advantages, he would explain. As academics, we had long weekends and vacations together.

Everything he said was true, but I didn't understand why he chose to say it. He told me that he felt some of the comments implied: "Yours is not a real marriage. I am superior to you because my wife and I have avoided your misfortune." It had not occurred to me there might be an element of one-upmanship, though I recognized it when it was pointed out.

I now see that my husband was simply approaching the world as many men do: as a place where people try to achieve and maintain status. I, on the other hand, was approaching the world as many women do: as a network of connections, in which people seek consensus.

INDEPENDENCE VS. INTIMACY

Since women often think in terms of closeness and support, they struggle to preserve intimacy. Men, concerned with status, tend to focus on establishing independence. These traits can lead women and men to starkly different views of the same situation.

When Josh's old high-school friend called him at work to say he'd be in town, Josh invited him to stay for the weekend. That evening he told Linda.

Linda was upset. How could Josh make these plans without discussing them with her beforehand? She would never do that to him. "Why don't you tell your friend you have to check with your wife?" she asked.

Josh replied, "I can't say I have to ask my wife for permission!"

To Josh, checking with his wife would mean he was not free to act on his own. It would make him feel like a child or an underling. But Linda actually enjoys telling people, "I have to check with Josh." It makes her feel good to show her life is entwined with her husband's.

ADVICE VS. UNDERSTANDING

Eve had a benign lump removed from her breast. When she confided to her husband, Mark, that she was distressed because the stitches changed the contour of her breast, he answered, "You can always have plastic surgery."

This comment bothered her. "I'm sorry you don't like the way it looks," she protested, "but I am not having any more surgery!"

Mark was hurt and puzzled. "I don't care about a scar," he replied. "It doesn't bother me at all."

"Then why are you telling me to have plastic surgery?" she asked.

"Because *you* were upset about the way it looks."

Eve felt like a heel. Mark had been wonderfully supportive throughout her surgery. How could she snap at him now?

The problem stemmed from a difference in approach. To many men, a complaint is a challenge to come up with a solution. Mark thought he was reassuring Eve by telling her there was something she could *do* about her scar. But often women are looking for emotional support, not solutions.

INFORMATION VS. FEELINGS

A cartoon I once saw shows a husband opening a newspaper and asking his wife, "Is there anything you'd like to say before I start reading?" We know there isn't—but that as soon as the man begins reading, his wife will think of something.

The cartoon is funny because people recognize their own experience in it. What's not funny is that many women are hurt when men don't talk to them at home, and many men are frustrated when they disappoint their partners without knowing why.

Rebecca, who is happily married, told me this is a source of dissatisfaction with her husband, Stuart. When she tells him what she is thinking, he listens silently. When she asks him what is on his mind, he says, "Nothing."

All Rebecca's life she has had practice verbalizing her feelings with friends and relatives. To her, this shows involvement and caring. But to Stuart, like most men, talk is for information. All his life he has had practice in keeping his innermost thoughts to himself.

Yet many such men hold center stage in a social setting, telling jokes and stories. They use conversation to claim attention and to entertain. Women can wind up hurt that their husbands tell relative strangers things they have not told them.

To avoid this kind of misunderstanding, both men and women can make adjustments.

A woman may observe a man's desire to read the paper, for example, without seeing it as rejection. And a man can understand a woman's desire to talk without feeling it an intrusion.

ORDERS VS. PROPOSALS

Diana often begins statements with "Let's." She might say, "Let's park over there" or "Let's clean up before lunch." This makes Nathan angry. He has deciphered Diana's "Let's" as a command. Like most men, he resists being told what to do. But to Diana, she is making suggestions, not demands. Like most women, she wants to avoid confrontation and formulates requests as proposals rather than orders. Her style of talking *is* a way of getting others to do what she wants—but by winning agreement first.

With certain men, like Nathan, this tactic backfires. If they perceive someone is trying to get them to do something indirectly, they feel manipulated and respond more resentfully than they would to a straightforward request.

CONFLICT VS. COMPROMISE

In trying to prevent fights, some women refuse to openly oppose the will of others. But at times it's far more effective for a woman to assert herself, even at the risk of conflict.

Dora was frustrated by a series of used automobiles she drove. It was she who commuted to work, but her husband, Hank, who chose the cars. Hank always went for automobiles that were "interesting," but in continual need of repair. After Dora was nearly killed when her brakes failed, they were in the market for yet another car.

Dora wanted to buy a late-model sedan from a friend. Hank fixed his sights on a 15-year-old sports car. Previously, she would have acceded to his wishes. But this time Dora bought the boring but dependable car and steeled herself for Hank's anger. To her amazement, he spoke not a word of remonstrance. When she later told him what she had expected, he scoffed at her fears and said she should have done what she wanted from the start if she felt that strongly about it.

As Dora discovered, a little conflict won't kill you. At the same time, men who habitually oppose others can adjust their style to opt for less confrontation.

When we don't see style differences for what they are, we sometimes draw unfair conclusions ("You're illogical," "You're self-centered," "You don't care about me"). But once we grasp the two characteristic approaches, we stand a better chance of preventing disagreements from spiraling out of control. Learning the other's ways of talking is a leap across the communication gap between men and women, and a giant step toward genuine understanding.

Follow-Up

1. *Describe an instance when you and someone of the opposite gender seemed to communicate on different wavelengths (or from distinctly separate frames of reference). Can you understand the other's framework?*
2. *Tannen shows how different gender mindsets result in different interpretations of the same situation. She gives examples from six conflicting patterns.*

Do you act in accordance with your gender in each of these six patterns? Explain why or why not.

3. *Which of the six gender communication patterns were practiced by your parents or guardians in the way Tannen describes? How has this influenced your communication preferences?*

4. *Observe men–women conversations to see if Tannen's ideas hold true.*

5. *Attempt the He Said, She Said Applied Activity at the end of this section.*

Awakening Intuition

Frances Vaughan

Carl Jung has defined intuition as one of four basic psychological functions, the other three being thinking, feeling, and sensation. He characterizes intuition as the function that explores the unknown, and senses possibilities and implications which may not be readily apparent. Intuition perceives what is hidden, and thus enables one to perceive obscure meanings in symbolic imagery, or subconscious motives in oneself and in others. It is also associated with insight, or the ability to understand the dynamics of a personality or situation. Jung distinguished between the introverted intuitive person, whose intuition focuses primarily on the inner world of the psyche, and the extroverted intuitive, whose perceptions of the external world consistently lead to frontiers of exploration. Many successful entrepreneurs who have an uncanny ability to know what will happen next in their businesses are of the latter type.

Intuition is also the psychological function operative in scientific inventions or discoveries. Mathematicians, for instance, readily acknowledge the value of intuition in formulating new hypotheses, and exercise proof and verification as secondary processes. Likewise in physics and other sciences, it is intuition which provides researchers with new possibilities to pursue with the instruments of science. The history of science shows clearly that great breakthroughs in human understanding have been the result of intuitive perceptions that are only later tested and verified.

> This term [intuition] does not denote something contrary to reason, but something outside the province of reason.
>
> C. G. Jung: *Psychological Types*

Having defined intuition as a mode of knowing and a psychological function which is potentially available to everyone, let us turn our attention to examining the variety of human experiences which are commonly called intuitive. Intuitive experiences include, but are by no means limited to, mystical insights into the nature of reality. Experiences which are commonly called intuitive also include discovery and invention in science, inspiration in art, creative problem solving, perception of patterns and possibilities, extrasensory perception, clairvoyance, telepathy, precognition, retrocognition, feelings of attraction and aversion, picking up "vibes," knowing or perceiving through the body rather than the rational mind, hunches, and premonitions.

Intuition is often associated with having a hunch or a strong feeling of knowing what is going to happen. Often these hunches are vague, and since they are rarely recorded they are seldom verifiable.

At times hunches may seem negative, such as the hunch that you will forget something when you go on a trip. At other times they may be positive, such as the hunch that you will get a job you applied for even though the competition is stiff, or the hunch that you will do well in an exam despite inadequate preparation. What is necessary in the beginning, regardless of whether the hunch is positive, negative, or neutral, is to learn to distinguish genuinely intuitive hunches from those which are simply a product of anxiety or wishful thinking.

The best way to do this is to keep a record of your hunches in a journal or a diary. In this way you can check up on yourself, to see how often your hunches turn out to be accurate.

Subjectively you may begin to notice that intuitive hunches feel different from those which turn out to be purely imaginary. The only way you can learn to make the distinction for yourself is to learn by trial and error. At first, when you begin to keep a record of your hunches, you may find a high percentage of errors. As your sensitivity to nonverbal cues, both internal and external, is refined, your record may improve. Don't be discouraged by errors. Every time you make an error you have the opportunity to learn something about yourself. If you are willing to acknowledge yourself as the source of your error—that is, to take responsibility for it rather than blaming it on outside circumstances—you may quickly learn to see how your personal interests distort your perceptions and get in the way of clear intuition.

The conscious mind, or ego, frequently interferes with intuitive perception. The more you want something to happen, the less you are able to sense whether it will happen or not. For example, if you want someone you love to call you, you may think it is him or her every time the phone rings, only to be disappointed each time. On the other hand, someone you hardly know, or whom you have not thought about in weeks, may come into your mind inexplicably, and then, a few minutes later, that person may call. Fear and desire both interfere with intuitive perception. If you are anxious, angry, or emotionally upset, you are not likely to be receptive to the subtle messages which can come into consciousness via intuition.

Lack of acceptance of intuition in the culture at large certainly contributes to its suppression in individuals who do not want to be "different." Many adults in my groups have said that they felt they were more intuitive as children, and that they learned to keep their intuitive perceptions to themselves after encountering skepticism or ridicule from adults. One woman who attended an intuition workshop recalled an incident in her life when she was about five years old. On a Friday she announced to her mother that Grandmother would not be coming to dinner on Sunday because she had hurt her foot. Her mother did not pay much attention to her remark, as she assumed she was making it up. To her amazement, the following day Grandmother called and said she would not come to dinner the next day because she had sprained her ankle the previous afternoon.

Such incidents may be frightening to adults who do not understand them or consider them paranormal. Parents who are afraid of what seems incomprehensible often respond angrily to intuitive observations by their children. They may attempt to explain them away, or to deny the child's experience, saying something like, "You couldn't possibly know that. Don't lie to me." At best, the child's remarks may be ignored.

Young children learn very quickly that there are some things they are not supposed to talk about. For many this reticence persists into adulthood. Participants in intuition workshops often express appreciation for having the opportunity to talk about experiences which they would ordinarily not discuss for fear of being considered "weird" or "crazy." Children seldom share their inner world of fantasy and perception with adults, because sympathetic, understanding adults are rare.

In general, intuition flourishes only when it is valued, and clearly certain lifestyles and experiences facilitate or nourish it. Inspiration needs space and attention if it is to take shape in a creative endeavor. Attention acts as psychic energy and enhances the process it values. The artist who is highly intuitive in his or her perceptions of reality knows that inspiration always seems to come of its own accord. Effort is invariably involved in the creative process, but flashes of inspiration tend to occur spontaneously. Seeking inspiration requires a receptive mode of consciousness and is comparable to trying to remember something you know but have forgotten. Tarthang Tulku, a Tibetan Lama, writes: "If we wish to regain some memory or insight that is 'there,' but is temporarily elusive, it is often most effective to put aside any grasping or tight achievement-orientation and become passively receptive. By quietly opening the mind, the hidden element is allowed to present itself on its own. In a similar manner, artists seeking inspiration used to go to sleep, hoping for a visit from a muse, who would speak to them—and then through them—in their art. People courting divine intercession have long understood that they must *open* themselves to divine messages and purposes, as in the cases of prayer and oracles. According to all these various orientations, the importance of surrendering the self has been emphasized."

In a sense, everyone is an artist in charge of designing his or her life. If the unexamined life is not worth living, what about the uninspired life? Certainly many, if not most, people in our society would not consider their lives to be particularly inspired. Yet the possibility is there for *everyone* to tap the creative source of inspiration which comes from well-developed intuition.

Perhaps you have had the experience of struggling with a problem or a decision until you were sick of it, and then deciding to forget it for a while. Very often the solution pops into your head when you least expect it. The expression "sleep on it" refers to allowing this intuitive process to be completed during sleep. Many people report finding solutions to apparently insoluble dilemmas through their dreams and daydreams. When you stop trying to make something happen, intuition is allowed to operate.

If you are serious about wanting to fully experience the potential of both the right and left hemispheres of the brain and find a lifestyle that is truly satisfying to you, then you must give yourself the time and space necessary for allowing your intuition to come into conscious awareness. Remember, there is

nothing you can do to make intuition happen, but there is much that you can do to allow it to happen. Be gentle. There is no need to force anything.

The regular practice of meditation is the single most powerful means of increasing intuition. Taking time to do the exercises in this book is a good first step, but once you have decided that clear intuition is a valuable asset in your life, you will want to continue to sharpen and expand your awareness of it. The silent mind, cultivated in many different forms of meditation, is the matrix of intuition. When you are in touch with the stillpoint at the center of your being, there is no need to use imagery or verbal exercises to activate intuition. It flows by itself, unimpeded by fears and preoccupations.

The wisdom of intuition does not follow the rules of logic. It will never make rational, discriminating choices for you. It is no substitute for careful research or data gathering. It is a purveyor of possibilities, not an evaluating faculty. Critical judgment may inhibit intuition, yet intuition never becomes a substitute for discrimination. Discriminating judgments are essential to making choices in the world, but let the mind be guided by reason, not bound by it. Your intuition can show you alternatives; it can give you a sense of what is possible for you. It does not tell you what is right or wrong, but it is a reliable indicator of what you need at a particular time. How you feel about trusting your intuition inevitably affects its functioning. If you value it and affirm it, it will flourish. How you think about intuition will determine how you use it, whether you bend it to egotistical purposes, or follow where it leads you. Pure intuition remains unaffected by thoughts and feelings, and will always take you beyond the boundaries of present conscious knowledge.

References

Tulku, T. (1977). *Time, space, and knowledge.* Emeryville, CA: Dharma Publishing.

Von Franz, M. L., & Hillman, J. (1971). *Jung's typology.* New York: Spring Publications.

Weil, A. (1972). *The natural mind.* Boston: Houghton Mifflin.

Follow-Up

1. *Select two statements from Vaughan's article and offer your interpretations.*
2. *Do you value and encourage intuition in your life? Explain your answer.*
3. *Vaughan says that fear and desire interfere with intuitive perception. Have you found this to be true? Why? Explain how you can detect when emotional needs are blocking intuitive reception.*
4. *Vaughan recommends keeping a record of your "hunches" in order to distinguish true intuition from wishful or anxious thinking. Try this and report the results.*

The Nature and Uses of Dreaming

Ernest Hartmann, M.D.

A 20-year-old college student barely escaped with his life from a fire that killed several members of his family. A few nights later, he had a vivid dream: "I was on a beach when a huge tidal wave came along and engulfed me. I was flipped over and over; there was nothing I could do. I was just about to drown when I woke up." On another night, he also dreamt: "I was swept away in a whirlwind. I was helpless, just blown away." These dreams clearly do not picture the details of what happened to him—the fire. Rather, they picture his emotional state—his feeling of fear, terror, and helplessness.

I have collected and studied many series of dreams after major trauma and repeatedly have come across such dreams as tidal waves, whirlwinds, or being chased by gangs of thugs. I am convinced that these dreams are a sort of paradigm, a place where we can see most clearly what is happening in all dreams. Such dreams are by no means nonsense. They picture the emotional state of our minds.

My collaborators and I have been developing a view of dreams which differs considerably from accepted wisdom on the subject. Nevertheless, it turns out to be very compatible with the commonsense experience of those who remember their dreams and have developed an interest in them.

Over all, dreams have not gotten much respect in the past few decades. There have been two dominant schools of thought. One view championed by some biologists is that dreams basically are random nonsense, the products of a poorly functioning brain during sleep. If there is any meaning to dreams, it is "added on later" as our brains try to "make the best of a bad job." A related view proposed by other biologists is that dreaming may function as an "unlearning" procedure: a dream is garbage being thrown out by a computer to keep itself from being clogged up. In this view, we dream specifically about what we do *not* need to remember.

The other view of drums, more common among psychoanalysts and therapists, derives broadly from the work of pioneering psychoanalyst Sigmund Freud. He did take dreams seriously in one sense, calling them the "royal road" to the workings of the unconscious. However, Freud felt that his main contribution—his discovery of the secret of dreams—was his finding that, when properly analyzed, every dream turns out to be a fulfillment of a wish. Further, although Freud appears to take dreams much more seriously than the biologists do, he does not place much value on the dream itself, which he calls the "manifest dream." He repeatedly refers to the dream as an irrational mental product, whose value emerges only when one subjects it to a process of free association leading eventually to an underlying "latent dream" containing the underlying wish.

After having spent many years conducting research on the biology of dreaming, I disagree with both these broad views. Indeed, there now is available a tremendous amount of information about the biology of sleep and specifically the biology of REM (rapid eye movement) sleep, the part of sleep in which most of our memorable dreams occur. However, this knowledge of the underlying biology of dreaming does not tell us the true nature or functions of dreaming, and it certainly is not a reason for dismissing the psychological meaning of dreams. Why should the developing understanding of the biology underlying it make dreaming meaningless, any more than the developing understanding of the biology underlying thought makes thought meaningless?

I have spent many years analyzing my own and my patients' dreams in my clinical work. Establishing the necessary climate of safety comes from a sense of alliance between patient and therapist. The patient is allowed to tell his or her story about the trauma or new event over and over again, making connections to other material, gradually seeing it in a new light. I believe this happens in dreaming as well. The safe place is provided by a bed and the muscular inhibition of REM sleep, which assures that the sleeper will lie quietly in bed, rather than running around acting out the dream. Once safety is established, the broad connections gradually are made.

Finally, in addition to the basic function of dreaming, which I believe probably helps us even when we do not remember dreams, there are many ways in which dreams can be useful to us when we do remember them. For example, the women who dreamt some version of "Jim turned into my father" generally found this a useful insight, a new way of looking at things that helped in their relationship. Sometimes, the new and broader connections made by dreaming can be helpful in our work and in artistic and scientific discovery.

A number of creative people have made use of dreams in their discoveries. Some of the best known examples are the French chemist Auguste Kekulé, who saw snakes biting their tails in a dream, which led him to the correct ring structure for the benzene molecule. Inventor Elias Howe attributed the discovery of the sewing machine to a dream in which he was captured by cannibals. He noticed as they danced around him that there were holes at the tips of spears, and he realized this was the design feature he needed to solve his problem. Vladimir Horowitz and several other well-known pianists have described playing piano pieces in their dreams and discovering a new fingering they had not tried previously and

which turned out to work perfectly. Robert Louis Stevenson said that his book, *The Strange Case of Dr. Jekyll and Mr. Hyde*, came to him in a dream.

In these cases, I am not saying that all the hard work of discovery happened in the dream. Generally, the artist or scientist made one new connection in a dream and then developed the work in the waking state. Stevenson probably saw a respectable doctor turning into a monster—this is, in fact, quite a typical nightmare image—and then his waking writing skills took over from there. In each case, the dreamers were well-versed in their fields and were worrying hard about a particular problem, which thus had become an emotional concern and was pictured in a dream.

I believe that, by its broader connective features, dreaming has obvious uses of this kind and we probably can make a good deal more of our dreams than we do. For instance, many Native American and South American cultures have adopted a methodology for career choice. In puberty, a young man—or, in some cases, young woman—is sent out into the desert to have a dream or a vision. Often, the young person will return with a powerful dream which, with or without help from the elders, leads to a decision about a future life course.

We might tend to dismiss this as superstition having no relevance to our lives. However, I suggest that we can benefit from the techniques of these cultures. I believe they are making good use of the broader connective powers of dreaming. The young person, who clearly has his future role or "career" in mind as an emotional concern, goes out and has a dream that makes connections more broadly than he does in waking life, which pictures something for him based on his concerns, wishes, or fears, and this often turns out to be very useful to him.

I have known a few people who informally have made use of such a technique. In our culture, we generally ask a young person to consider carefully his or her possible choices for a career, make a list of pros and cons, and so on. There is nothing wrong with this, but I have known several cases in which the decision truly came together or felt right only after a dream.

Sometimes, dreams can be extremely useful in our personal lives, scientific or artistic work, or even something as basic as career choice. I certainly am not suggesting substitut-ing the dream for waking thought, but why leave it out entirely? Dreaming is one end of the continuum, a way of making connections more broadly than our focused waking thought, but guided by what is important to us. Why should we not use everything we have and allow ourselves to notice and employ this additional connecting power?

Follow-Up

1. *Hartmann claims that dreams provide a context for emotional concerns, make new connections among our experiences, and can be helpful in making choices. Explain why you agree or disagree with his ideas.*
2. *How have dreams played a role in your life?*
3. *Select two ideas from this article and offer your interpretations.*
4. *For a related reading, see "Awakening Intuition" by Frances Vaughan in this section.*

Personal Journaling as a Life Companion

Lou Beeker Schultz

"Question—I'm not presently keeping a diary, but sometimes I do feel the need to sit down and write down my feelings. So I decide I will write a diary; I get everything ready, open the book, and then comes the question: where do I start?

Anais Nin—Put yourself right in the present. This was my principle when I wrote the diary—to write the thing I felt most strongly about that day. Start there and that starts the whole unravelling, because that has roots in the past and it has branches into the future. The main thing is that what you feel strongly about today is where you're at today, and that is what the purpose of the diary is....I chose the event of the day that I felt most strongly about, the most vivid one, the warmest one, the nearest one, the strongest one."

Anais Nin, *A Woman Speaks*, p. 163

The people's faces change from journal class to journal class, but the beginning questions are the same, "How do I begin to keep a journal?" and "What is the purpose and benefit of keeping one?"

This one life activity can be a catalyst to increased productivity, deepening life's meanings, enriching one's creativity, and connecting into the inner wisdom we have.

Many famous people have experienced the benefits from keeping a journal. A few are: George Washington, Leonardo da Vinci, Georgia O'Keeffe, May Sarton, Henry David Thoreau, Thomas Edison, Walt Whitman, Charles Lindbergh, Elizabeth Cady Stanton, Susan B. Anthony, and Ralph Waldo Emerson.

You are about to begin a significant journey with paper and pen friends that can always be with you through the ebbs and flows of your life. A constant companion—*Your Personal Journal.*

WHAT IS JOURNALING?

As we travel through life, we are always with ourselves. The journal can be a steadfast companion through life's journey. It will always be there, receptive of our deepest internal thoughts, feelings, and truths—a written documentation of what is happening in the individual moments of life and how we interpret the experiences.

It is essential to remember that journal writing is not a panacea. It is not a record of our daily activities. However, it is an effective tool to record our honest feelings, thoughts, and beliefs at a specific moment in time. We are photographing, in words, a slice of time. We can release on paper what we believe is within our hearts, even buried within our inner-being. Then later, as we reread our journals, we can let our entries feedback to us of where we have been, what has been accomplished, and let the experience weave into our life.

Journaling provides a place to chart life's progress, record treasured memories, and accept, know, and value oneself. It becomes an oasis to contemplate memorable times, value ordinary moments, and listen to inner hunches.

By developing the regular habit of recording thoughts in a journal, many people have come to see and feel greater ease in effective communication with both oneself and others. Insoluble problems at the time of a writing seem resolved later when reading back through the entries. Over time this notebook can be valued as an abiding and trusting friend.

SPECIALIZED JOURNALS

Blank journals can be customized and tailored to fit individual needs. Workshop participants have claimed the following notebooks earmarked for their special interest have served them well:

Life Goals	Health
Career	Family
Spirituality	Ideas
Counseling	Travel
Gratitude	Diet
Gardening	Exercise
Financial	A Child
Dreams	Transitions
Illness	Simplify Life
Family Entries	Nature
Meditation	Life's Milestones
Feng Shui	Synchronicity

Explore the activities in your life and contemplate the kind of journal most beneficial for you during this season of your life. Some readers may prefer utilizing one notebook with jottings from the above topics. This is appropriate, too.

JOURNALING MUSTS

The mechanics of journal writing are easy. There are two primary guidelines. One, date every journal entry. If there is any cardinal rule, this would be the one. Second, write in the honesty of the moment. Because of these few basic guidelines, the journal provides us with a significant component—its non-judgmental quality.

WRITING TOOLS

Materials for this endeavor are minimal. Peruse through your local bookshop and office supply store and select either a spiral notebook, bound blank book, a three-ring binder with loose leaf paper, artist sketch book, lined or un-lined paper. With over 5,000,000 blank books sold annually, you will find the best one for you.

Experiment with a pen or pencil that fits with ease into your hand. Explore the use of fountain pens, roller balls, ball points, gel-inks, colored pencils, and various point styles of colored markers. Remember to use the style of journal and writing implement appropriate and comfortable for you.

Some journalers prefer using a computer. If this is your preferred method, keep a few things in mind. Utilize your own personal computer and not one that is connected to the work of your professional organization, even if it is password protected. With privacy issues today within a corporate structure, one does not know who may have access to reading what you enter online. Ultimately, a journal is personal and for your eyes only. Sometimes participants will print out a copy of their entry to keep in a notebook, and store the daily entry in their own personal computer disk file. In essence, use what works for your lifestyle.

PRIVACY

Journal privacy is a universal theme. When you are not writing in your journal, keep it in a safe place. Be careful where you leave your journal. This is not the type of leisure reading you want to lie around on the coffee table for family and friends, tempting them to read its pages while visiting. Some journal writers place their notebooks in closets, metal boxes, shoe boxes, suitcases, safes, briefcases, large handbags, trunks or glove compartments, or drawers. There are as many various places to store your writings as there are people. Explore the nooks and crannies in your home and find the best place for your journal.

For some journalers for whom privacy is of extreme importance, consider writing names, phrases, events, and so on in a code.

Remember to translate your code and store it somewhere different from your journal. Over time, as you see the benefits of jounaling your life, you may discover this is not as big of an issue as initially perceived.

If you plan to carry your journal with you, place your name, address, telephone number, and e-mail address on the initial inside page. Consider adding a privacy statement such as "Please respect my privacy and refrain from reading this notebook." Some journal writers will add a subsequent addendum stating, "Financial reward given upon its return."

JOURNAL WRITING GUIDELINES AND EXERCISES

1. At the beginning of each journal I leave a few blank pages. These can be used for volume number, titling, key topics/issues, beginning and ending dates, and disclaimers. In addition, I write on only one side of each page. This provides space on the reverse side for additional notes during the reading back process. At the end, I leave several pages for the writing of the feedback process. This may include additional writings, questions, thoughts, follow-up activities, and informal indexing.

2. Some people prefer writing at the same time each day, either early morning or late evening, in the same location. Set the timer for ten to fifteen minutes. Others may prefer keeping their journals portable, transporting them and writing as the time and urges unfold naturally throughout the day. Still others enjoy a combination of both.

Remember that "waiting times" are an excellent gift of time to write an entry. A few minutes in the post office line, grocery store line, airports, dentist's and doctor's offices can add up to hours of journal writing time.

3. As you transition into this solitude time of writing, be observant of yourself: What am I thinking? What am I feeling? Think of using descriptive words in the journal entry. What are the actions planned or already taken? Include sensory details—the sounds, the tastes, the touches, the sights. If possible, consider the sense of smell; it can be the most powerful. Add adjectives that are descriptive, providing distinctive and clear information. Are there humorous situations? What are the metaphors and similes conveying deeper meanings of an experience?

4. What follows is an exercise applying Carl Jung's concept, "stream of consciousness." It is an intuitive process, encouraging our conscious and subconscious minds to empty out whatever is inside us. As you sit comfortably with your open journal and pen, take three or four deep breaths from the lower part of your abdomen. Relax. Give yourself permission to write whatever comes to you. Place the current date in your notebook then proceed to write quickly for five to ten minutes, continuously. Keep your hand moving. Write your initial thoughts. Write what is coming into your mind, from the depths of your being. The thoughts may appear logical, or they may not. They could be pictures, images, ideas, snippets of songs, movie clips, hunches, and/or insights. There may be negative thoughts; there may be positive thoughts. In the journal there is no wrong. There only *is*. All are welcomed in this open moment. There is no one to be judgmental here of you or your writing. Let yourself be "free in the moment." Write the truth of how you believe, see, feel, think, and/or value today. Surrender to the moment's flow. Write naturally. Be not concerned with misspellings, correct grammar, cross-outs, capital letters, dotting every *i*, and crossing every *t*. The personal journal is not the resident for English Format 101. A free-writing exercise of this type consistently practiced over time can provide us with a myriad of insights, creative ideas, and depth into the truth of our higher self and bring forth our best gifts we have to claim for ourselves, provide to others, and develop for our life's purpose. In essence, be willing to risk on the writing page.

5. A spin-off of this exercise can be "Journaling in the Round." As you read over a stream of consciousness entry, notice the sentence, phrase, or paragraph resonating within you. What is whispering for additional attention? Take this sentence, write it at the top of the next page in your journal and continue writing whatever comes to you. From this second exercise, transfer another line to the next page, continuing with a third entry, then a fourth. Repeat this as often as you desire. This exercise will take you in unexpected and unexplored directions.

The journal can be a source of decision making for multiple opportunities coming simultaneously. Explore the decisions you make daily in your life. At the top of the blank page write the current date. Title the page, "Conscious Choices I Made Today." Underneath, list the deliberate decisions you selected. Expand it to include the various options you had presented before you. At the day's end reflect back over your list and appreciate the conscious choices you made to live your life truest to your authentic internal values and goals.

6. Your notebook can be a place of acceptance and space to vent your feelings and emotions through catharsis writing. A place to write until you are empty. It is a safe and secure haven to release temporary intense feelings of loss and helplessness due to death, job loss, divorce, trauma, or severe illness.

7. Sometimes images are able to deeply express what words cannot. The journal can be a place to doodle, draw, and sketch images you feel within. One does not have to have artistic talent to express the symbols and forms that are within. After a written entry, some journalers on the receptive page will briefly outline or sketch an image symbolizing what is felt inside.

Include photographs in the journal if you desire. With the picture, consider adding a reflective and meaningful commentary to it.

Sometimes the combination of using both written words and visual images, engaging both hemispheres of the brain, can ultimately be a sense of feeling freedom and lightness within.

8. When there are multiple people, ideas, and things competing for attention simultaneously, one tool for realignment and regaining centeredness is to propose two basic questions in the journal:

1. What do I *have* to do today?
2. What do I *want* to do today?

Ensure a combination of both are achieved to foster greater sense of balance and wholeness within.

9. When reading newspapers, magazines, and books, there may be quotes that capture your attention and stay in your thoughts. Seize this writing opportunity. Cut out and insert or tape the clipping in your notebook. Ponder your thoughts and ideas on the journaling page. Write the maxim down, then write what comes to you next. What does this mean to you? Is it motivating you? Is it something you want to live your life by? Write the adage several times. Follow where your consciousness leads you.

10. Sometimes you may sit down at the blank page and wonder what to write or think "I have nothing to write." Following are a few of my favorite prompts to help with this temporary state. Almost immediately upon writing the beginning sentence I am transformed. I begin thinking a plethora of information, details, insights, connections that I had no dream I could have thought of in just the previous moments:

Today I accomplished . . .
Today I had a meaningful conversation with _____. I learned from this encounter . . .
Last night I dreamed . . .
I remember the time . . .
Deep inside my being I hear . . .

JOURNAL FEEDBACK

Over the weeks, months, and years of keeping a journal, perhaps you begin thinking, "What can I do with all these accumulated writings?" This is part of the feedback process. This can be a significant, productive time of solitude. Begin with an open frame of reference. Anticipate receiving beautiful and meaningful gifts. The book, *Harvesting Your Journals* (Deer/Strickland, 1999), provides numerous ideas. The authors highly recommend using the following stem statements after reading a journal notebook:

"I learned . . .
I relearned . . .
I discovered . . .
I regret . . .
I appreciate . . .
Right now, I feel . . .
I will . . . "

Another exercise while reading the journal is to highlight action words, or *verbs,* used in the journal. Focus on the movement of your life. Recognize, value, and appreciate your accomplishments, growth, and development. If necessary, note the areas where taking action is avoided.

A favorite feedback approach I use is to read a journal entry. Pause. Reflect on the time period I was in and where I am now, gaining a new perspective. On the opposite or reverse page of the initial writing, place the present date of this feedback entry and begin writing in a stream-of-consciousness flow. If applicable, I will write about recognizing specific small action steps taken in moving toward a desired goal, or recall and appreciate a meaningful moment invested with family and friends. As additional observations and insights appear, they are captured in the notebook.

As this article comes to a close, it is your turn to decide what you will do with this information. Will it be just an interesting article and then you move on to the next one? Or will you find a pen and a piece of paper and experiment with one of the various exercises provided?

With the birth of this upcoming hour, may you embark on your own discovery into the creativity awaiting you with your own indispensable journal companion.

References

Adams, K. (1990) *Journal to the Self: Twenty-Two Paths to Personal Growth*, NY: Warner Books.

Baldwin, C. (1991) *Life's Companion: Journal Writing as a Spiritual Quest*, NY: Bantam.

Heart, R. D., & Strickland, S. (1999) *Harvesting Your Journals: Writing Tools to Enhance Your Growth and Creativity*, NM: Heart Link Publications.

Progoff, I. (1975) *At a Journal Workshop*, NY: Dialogue House Library.

Rainer, T. (1978) *The New Diary: How to Use a Journal for Self Guidance and Expanded Creativity*, CA: Tracer, Inc.

Schwa, M. (1996). *A Voice of Her Own: Women and the Journal Writing Journey*, New York: Fireside Book/Simon & Schuster.

Follow-Up:

1. *Experiment with keeping a personal journal. Write three to five entries weekly for four weeks. After this experience:*
   - *What are the pluses and/or minuses of this activity for you?*

- Is this a worthwhile investment of your time and energy? Explain.
- Is this journal writing experience an activity you will further explore? Why or why not?

2. The author recommends several journal writing exercises. Select one and explore it. On a separate sheet of paper write your response to this activity.

3. Beeker Schultz implies keeping a journal can be the closest companion one has in life. Write your response to this implication based on your life experiences.

4. Select one of the quotes and explore how this maxim translates meaningfully for you. If it does not, write about these thoughts, also.

Assertive, Nonassertive, and Aggressive Behavior

Arthur J. Lange and
Patricia Jakubowski

Assertion involves standing up for personal rights and expressing thoughts, feelings, and beliefs in *direct, honest,* and *appropriate* ways which do not violate another person's rights.[1] The basic message in assertion is: This is what I think. This is what I feel. This is how I see the situation. This message expresses "who the person is" and is said without dominating, humiliating, or degrading the other person.

Assertion involves respect—not deference. Deference is acting in a subservient manner as though the other person is right, or better, simply because the other person is older, more powerful, experienced, or knowledgeable, or is of a different sex or race. Deference is present when people express themselves in ways that are self-effacing, appeasing, or overly apologetic.

Two types of respect are involved in assertion: respect for oneself, that is, expressing one's needs and defending one's rights, as well as respect for the other person's needs and rights. An example will help clarify the kind of respect involved in assertive behavior.

A woman was desperately trying to get a flight to Kansas City to see her mother who was sick in the hospital. Weather conditions were bad and the lines were long. Having been rejected from three standby flights, she again found herself in the middle of a long line for the fourth and last flight to Kansas City. This time she approached a man who was standing near the beginning of the line and said, pointing to her place, "Would you mind exchanging places with me? I ordinarily wouldn't ask, but
it's extremely important that I get to Kansas City tonight." The man nodded yes, and as it turned out, both of them were able to get on the flight.

When asked what her reaction would have been if the man had refused, she replied, "It would have been OK. I hoped he would say yes, but after all he was there first."[1]

In this example the woman showed self-respect for her own needs by asking whether the man would be willing to help her. Also, she respected the man's right to refuse her request and not fulfill her need.

How is respect shown when refusing another's request? It depends on how that request is refused. A request may be refused aggressively: "What do you mean you want to borrow my car! I don't know where you get your nerve!" Such aggressive refusals involve only one-way respect; that is, respect for one's right to refuse but not for the other person's right to ask. A request may also be refused nonassertively: "What can I say . . . I feel just awful saying this, really bad . . . I can't loan you my car. Oh gee, what a terrible thing to say!" Here the person refused the request, but did it in a way that showed lack of self-respect: It suggested that the refuser was a bad person who should not have denied the request. In addition, the nonassertive refusal did not respect the other person's right to be treated as a capable person who can handle a disappointment. In contrast, an assertive refusal would be: "I'd like to help you out, but I feel uncomfortable loaning my car." The assertive refusal shows the two-fold respect: self-respect in the self-confident way the request is refused and respect for the other person's right to ask.

In our view, the goal of assertion is communication and "mutuality"; that is, to get and give respect, to ask for fair play, and to leave room for compromise when the needs and rights of two people conflict. In such compromises neither person sacrifices basic integrity and both get some of their needs satisfied. The compromise may be one in which one person gets her needs taken care of immediately while the other party gets taken care of a little later. For example, one weekend the friends see a movie and the next weekend they bowl. Or the compromise may involve both parties giving up a little. They attend *part* of an outdoor concert and then take a short walk and talk. When personal integrity is at stake, a compromise is inappropriate and nonassertive.

We are opposed to viewing assertion as simply a way "to get what one wants" for three reasons. First, this view emphasizes success in attaining goals. Thus it can cause people to become passive when they believe that acting assertively will not get them what they want. Second, this view concentrates only on the asserter's right and not on the personal rights of both parties. Such an attitude increases the chances of people using aggressive or manipulative methods to get what they want. Third, it may lead to irresponsible behavior in which assertion is used to take advantage of other people. We have frequently heard people say that they can assertively ask for favors and it's just too bad that the other person is not strong enough to refuse their requests. In contrast, we advocate *responsible* asserting which involves mutuality, asking for fair play, and using one's greater assertive power to help others become more able to stand up for themselves. Interestingly, a byproduct of responsible assertion is that people often do get what they want. Why? Because most people become cooperative when they are approached in a way which is both respectful of self and respectful of others.

Nonassertion involves violating one's own rights by failing to express honest feelings, thoughts, and beliefs and consequently permitting others to violate oneself, or expressing one's thoughts and feelings in such an apologetic, diffident, self-effacing manner that others can easily disregard them.[1] In the latter type of nonassertion, the total message which is communicated is: I don't count—you can take advantage of me. My feelings don't matter—only yours do. My thoughts aren't important—yours are the only ones worth listening to. I'm nothing—you are superior.

Nonassertion shows a lack of respect for one's own needs. It also sometimes shows a subtle lack of respect for the other person's ability to take disappointments, to shoulder some responsibility, to handle his own problems, etc. The goal of nonassertion is to appease others and to avoid conflict at any cost.

Aggression involves directly standing up for personal rights and expressing thoughts, feelings, and beliefs in a way which is often dishonest, usually inappropriate, and always violates the rights of the other person. An example of "emotionally dishonest" aggression is a situation where individuals who feel saddened by another person's mourning for the death of a loved one sarcastically degrade the mourner ("That's just what I like to see—a grown person sniveling like a two-year-old brat"), instead of revealing their own sad and helpless feelings.

The usual goal of aggression is domination and winning, forcing the other person to lose. Winning is insured by humiliating, degrading, belittling, or overpowering other people so that they become weaker and less able to express and defend their needs and rights. The basic message is: That is what I think—you're stupid for believing differently. This is what I want—what you want isn't important. This is what I feel—your feelings don't count.

NONVERBAL COMPONENTS OF ASSERTIVE, NONASSERTIVE, AND AGGRESSIVE BEHAVIOR

So far we've discussed the verbal components of assertive, nonassertive, and aggressive behavior. The nonverbal components of these behaviors are equally important, if not more so. Research has shown that the vast majority of our communication is carried out nonverbally.[2] Take a moment to consider how the statement "I like you" can be said as a sincere statement, a question, or a sarcastic remark, by simply changing voice inflection, facial expression, and hand gestures. Likewise, an otherwise verbal assertive statement can become nonassertive or aggressive depending on the nonverbal behaviors which accompany the verbal statement.

Eisler, Miller, and Hersen[3] have pinpointed some of the nonverbal behaviors which may be important in assertion: duration of looking at the other person, duration of speech, loudness of speech, and affect in speech. Research has generally supported the importance of these nonverbal behaviors[3] with the exception of the length of time it takes the person to respond to the other individual.[4] Other nonverbal behaviors which may be important in assertion, nonassertion, and aggression are described below.

In assertive behavior, the nonverbals are congruent with the verbal messages and add support, strength, and emphasis to what is being said verbally. The voice is appropriately loud to the situation; eye contact is firm but not a staredown; body gestures which denote strength are used; and the speech pattern is fluent—without awkward hesitancies—expressive, clear, and emphasizes key words.

In nonassertive behavior, the nonverbal behaviors include evasive eye contact, body gestures such as hand wringing, clutching the other person, stepping back from the other person as the assertive remark is made, hunching the shoulders, covering the mouth with the hand, nervous gestures which distract the listener from what the speaker is saying, and wooden body posture. The voice tone may be singsong or overly soft. The speech pattern is hesitant and filled with pauses and the throat may be cleared frequently. Facial gestures may include raising the eyebrows, laughs, and winks when expressing anger.

In general, the nonassertive gestures are ones which convey weakness, anxiety, pleading, or self-effacement. They reduce the impact of what is being said verbally, which is precisely why people who are scared of acting assertively use them. Their goal is to "soften" what they're saying so that the other person will not be offended.

In aggressive behavior, the nonverbal behaviors are ones which dominate or demean the other person. These include eye contact that tries to stare down and dominate the other person, a strident voice that does not fit the situation, sarcastic or condescending tone of voice, and parental body gestures such as excessive finger pointing.

EXAMPLES OF ASSERTIVE, NONASSERTIVE, AND AGGRESSIVE BEHAVIOR

In each example, the first response is aggressive, the second, nonassertive, and the third is assertive.

Confronting a Professor Who Gives Inappropriate and Excessive Amounts of Work—

1. Dr. Jones, you have some nerve giving me this kind of work. I know you have control over me, but I don't have to take this stuff. You professors think you can use grad students for anything you please—Well not this time!
2. OK, Dr. Jones, I'll do it. I guess you must have a reason for asking me to do this stuff . . . even if it isn't related to my assistantship. I don't suppose you'd consider letting me off the hook this time? Huh?

3. Dr. Jones, when you give me work that's not related to your class, I'd have to put in extra hours beyond what's appropriate for my assistantship. For those reasons I need to say no on this extra work.

Talking with Someone Who Has Just Made a Sexist Remark—

1. Who the hell do you think you are? God's gift to women?
2. Oh come on (ha ha). You know how much that irritates me when you say things like that (ha ha).
3. Frankly, I think that remark demeans both of us.

Refusing an Extra Helping of Food at a Dinner Party—

1. You'd just love me to put on a few pounds of fat!
2. Gee . . . ah . . . Well, since you insist . . . I'll change my mind. Yeah, give me another piece.
3. That food does look good but I don't want any more.

Trying to Get a Group on the Subject After They've Wandered into Tangential Areas—

1. Can't you people get back to work and stop this goofing off?
2. I guess it's just my hang-up. Do you think it'd be OK if we got back to the original subject? I've forgotten it myself (ha ha).
3. What we're talking about is interesting; however, I'm feeling the need to get back to the original subject.

TYPES OF ASSERTION

Basic Assertion

Basic assertion refers to a simple expression of standing up for personal rights, beliefs, feelings, or opinions. It does not involve other social skills, such as empathy, confrontation, persuasion, etc. Examples of basic assertions are:

When being interrupted—
Excuse me, I'd like to finish what I'm saying.

When being asked an important question for which you are unprepared—
I'd like to have a few minutes to think that over.

When returning an item to a store—
I'd like my money back on this saw.

When refusing a request—
No, this afternoon is not a good time for me to visit with you.

When telling a parent you don't want advice—
I don't want any more advice.

Basic assertion also involves expressing affection and appreciation toward other people:

I like you.
I care for you a lot.
Having a friend like you makes me feel happy.
You're someone special to me.

The following is a particularly touching example of assertively expressing affection:

A father overheard his five-year-old child saying to a playmate: "Are you having a good time?" When the playmate replied "Yes," the child continued, "I am too. I'm so glad that I invited you to come over and play!"

Empathic Assertion

Often people want to do more than simply express their feelings or needs. They may also want to convey some sensitivity to the other person. When this is the goal, the empathic assertion can be used. This type of assertion involves making a statement that conveys recognition of the other person's situation or feelings and is followed by another statement which stands up for the speaker's rights.[1] Examples of empathic assertions are:

When two people are chatting loudly while a meeting is going on—

You may not realize it, but your talking is starting to make it hard for me to hear what's going on in the meeting. Would you keep it down?

When having some furniture delivered—

I know it's hard to say exactly when the truck will come, but I'd like a ball park estimate of the arrival time.

When telling a parent that you don't want advice—

I know that you give me advice because you don't want me to get hurt by mistakes I might make. At this point in my life, I need to learn how to make my own decisions and rely on myself, even if I do make some mistakes. I appreciate the help you've given me in the past and you can help me now by not giving me advice.[1]

There is considerable personal power in the empathic assertion because other people more easily respond to assertion when they have been recognized first. This power, however, should not be used as a manipulation to merely gain one's own ends, without genuine respect for the other person. Repeatedly saying, "I understand how you feel but . . . " can be just "mouthing" understanding and conning other people into believing that their feelings are being taken into account when in fact their feelings are really being discounted. Such behavior does not involve empathic assertion.

Another important benefit of the empathic assertion is that it causes the speaker to take a moment to try to understand the other person's feelings before the speaker reacts. This can help the speaker keep perspective on the situation and thus reduces the likelihood of the speaker's aggressively overreacting when irritated.

Escalating Assertion

According to Rimm and Masters,[5] escalating assertion involves starting with a "minimal" assertive response that can usually accomplish the speaker's goal with a minimum of effort and negative emotion and a small possibility of negative consequences. When the other person fails to respond to the minimal assertion and continues to violate one's rights, the speaker gradually escalates the assertion and becomes increasingly firm. We have observed that often it is not necessary to go beyond the initial minimal assertion; but if it is necessary, the person can become increasingly firm without becoming aggressive. The escalating assertion can occur from a request to a demand, from a preference to an outright refusal, or, as the following example illustrates, from an empathic assertion to a firm basic assertion.

> *The speaker is in a bar with a woman friend, and a man repeatedly offers to buy them drinks—*
>
> That's very nice of you to offer, but we came here to catch up on some news. Thanks, anyway!
>
> No, thank you. We really would rather talk just to each other.
>
> This is the third and last time I am going to tell you that we don't want your company. Please leave![6]

In this example, the final blunt refusal was appropriate because the earlier escalating assertions were ignored. If the woman had started with the highly escalated assertion the first time the man had approached, her response would have been inappropriate. Since assertion involves direct, honest, and *appropriate* expressions of thoughts and feelings, her reaction would be aggressive, rather than assertive. Likewise when a person has not objected to taking the minutes of a meeting, but one day suddenly says, "I'm getting sick and tired of being the secretary just because I'm the only woman in the group," her response would be aggressive, rather than assertive. Only if her comment had been preceded by successively escalated assertions which had been ignored would her comment be appropriate and assertive.

A final point about the escalating assertion is that just before making the final escalated assertion, we suggest that one consider offering a "contract option," in which the other person is informed what the final assertion will be and is given a chance to change behavior before it occurs. For example, when a repair shop repeatedly refuses to settle an unreasonable bill, one may say, "I'm being left with no other alternative than to complain to the Better Business Bureau and your distributor. I'd prefer not to do that but I will if this is the only alternative I'm left with." Often people only recognize that one means business at the contract option point.

Whether the contract option is simply a threat depends on how it is said. If it is said in a menacing tone of voice which relies on emotionality to carry the argument, it is a threat. When the contract option is carried out assertively, it is said in a matter-of-fact tone of voice which simply gives information about the consequences which will occur if the situation is not equitably resolved.

Confrontive Assertion

Confrontive assertion is used when the other person's words contradict his deeds. This type of assertion involves objectively describing what the other person said would be done and what the other actually did do, after which the speaker expresses what he wants.[1] The entire assertion is said in a matter-of-fact, nonevaluative way, as the examples below show:

I was supposed to be consulted before the final proposal was typed. But I see the secretary is typing it right now. Before he finishes it, I want to review the proposal and make whatever corrections I think are needed. In the future, I want to get a chance to review any proposals before they're sent to the secretary.

I thought we'd agreed that you were going to be more considerate toward students. Yet I noticed today that when two students asked for some information you said that you had better things to do than babysit for kids. As we discussed earlier, I see

showing more consideration as an important part of your job. I'd like to figure out what seems to be the problem.

I said it was OK to borrow my records as long as you checked with me first. Now you're playing my classical records without asking. I'd like to know why you did that.

The above are examples of initial confrontive assertive statements. In most cases the ensuing conversation would be an extended interaction between the two people. This is particularly true in the last two examples in which the speaker wanted additional information and the resulting discussions would be problem-solving ones.

In contrast to assertive confrontation, aggressive confrontation involves judging other people—rather than describing their behavior—and trying to make others feel guilty. For example:

Hey, those are my records! Evidently your word means absolutely nothing to you! Just for that I want my records right now and in the future you're going to find them locked up. Then you'll have to ask me first.

SUMMARY

Assertion involves standing up for personal rights and expressing thoughts, feelings, and beliefs in direct, honest, and appropriate ways which respect the rights of other people. In contrast, aggression involves self-expression, which is characterized by violating others' rights and demeaning others in an attempt to achieve one's own objectives. Nonassertion involves behavior which violates one's own self by failing to express honest feelings or thoughts. It may also involve diffident, overly apologetic, or effacing expression of personal rights and preferences.

It is important that assertive skills be used responsibly, that is, used in ways which treat others fairly and help facilitate others becoming more assertive.

Losing others' approval is a major fear which prompts many individuals to act nonassertively. For those who are frequently aggressive, a typical fear concerns their losing control and power over other people. A major reason for acting assertively rather than unassertively is that assertion increases one's own sense of self-respect and personal control.

References

1. Jakubowski, P. (1977). Assertive behavior and clinical problems of women. In E. Rawlings & D. Carter (Eds.), *Psychotherapy for women: Treatment towards equality.* Springfield, IL: Charles C. Thomas.
2. Mehrabian, A. (1972). *Nonverbal communication.* Chicago: Aldine/Atherton.
3. Eisler, R. M., Miller, P. M., & Hersen, M. (1973). Components of assertive behavior. *Journal of Clinical Psychology, 29,* 295–299.
4. Galassi, J. P., Galassi, M. D., & Litz, M. C. (1974). Assertive training in groups using video feedback. *Journal of Counseling Psychology, 21,* 390–394.
5. Rimm, D. C., & Masters, J. C. (1974). *Behavior therapy: Techniques and empirical findings.* New York: Academic Press.
6. Jakubowski, P. (1977). Self-assertion training procedures for women. In E. Rawlings & D. Carter (Eds.), *Psychotherapy for women: Treatment towards equality.* Springfield, IL: Charles C. Thomas.

Follow-Up

1. *Give examples of instances when you acted in these ways: nonassertively, assertively, aggressively (as explained in the article). What is your predominant style in expressing your rights and beliefs? Give a brief explanation supporting your answer.*
2. *While there is a difference between assertive and aggressive behavior, some see both as pushy. Is this true for you? Explain your response.*
3. *If you have been aggressive in expressing your rights and beliefs, what have been the consequences?*
4. *Choose one or more of the following types of assertion and attempt to be more skillful expressing them: basic assertion, empathic assertion, escalating assertion, confrontive assertion.*
5. *Assertive behavior is closely related to self-esteem. One approach to enhancing your own esteem level is to become more appropriately assertive. Try some gradual and appropriate risks in assertiveness to see if this is true for you.*
6. *For further reading on this topic go to almost any major bookstore and browse the self-help or psychology sections. One highly recommended practical book on assertiveness is the most recent edition of* Your Perfect Right *by Alberti and Emmons.*

King of the Purple Tree

Nels Goud

"Why don't we go out and get something to eat and talk about it more there?"

The others liked the idea and grabbed their notebooks and started to leave the classroom. One turned to me and asked "How about joining us? Maybe we'll see what you are really like outside of the prof role," she smiled.

Well, that would be true, but then they weren't around to see everything that happened later. I don't know if a prof should have acted as I did, but it was what I was "really like."

We went to a lounge called The Purple Tree. It was a large room with tables arranged in lop-sided circles around a huge purple tree like the kind you see in Japanese paintings. Most of the tables were filled. Some people were singing under the direction of the performer of the month, Rey Morada. *Rey* means king in Spanish, a student told me. The King sat on a stool in a far corner and was surrounded by speakers, consoles, microphones, guitar amplifier, synthesizer, and lines of cords. The King could also hook up an amplified harmonica around his neck if he wanted. The King had built an electronic castle.

The King was a performer who tried to excite his audience and get them to participate. If a tune triggered a few shouts or singing, he would turn up the volume and urge the patrons to sing louder. If a few more tables joined in, then the speakers would be turned up even higher. Four tables crowded with conventioneers were right in front of the King, and they sang almost every song. There is a strange kind of loneliness at conventions.

You run out of things to talk about. The loneliness starts coming, and singing chases it away for awhile. The conventioneers were singing loudly.

We wanted to talk and found a table in the opposite corner from the King. The waitress brought a couple of pitchers of beer and took the food orders. We listened to the King for a few minutes. The King stopped to adjust his electronic empire. A student leaned over and continued the class discussion: "How can you really be honest most of the time without hurting another's feelings?" She was serious and wanted some guidance.

"But if you aren't honest then you are a phony and that is worse," said another student. "I'm tired of just trying to please everybody," he added.

"Are these the only choices?" I asked.

"What did you say?" asked another. The King had found a crowd pleaser. "Cuando? Cuando? Cuando?" shouted the conventioneers. The King paused a moment to turn several knobs on his console.

"What are other choices besides being honest or a phony?" continued the student.

"You could choose to be true to another value besides honesty," I said.

"I don't get it," said one of the students.

"Suppose a friend starts dating a new guy but does not tell her current boyfriend this. The boyfriend asks you if your friend is dating anyone else. Will you be true to loyalty, or honesty?"

"Are you saying then you have to choose what truth to be honest to?"

"Yes."

"Yeah, but . . ." a student started to add. He could not be heard because the King had turned up the speakers and all you could hear was the amplified clangor of "Cuando? Cuando? Cuando?"

A student shouted across the table "I wish he would turn it down!" Everybody nodded. It was a common reaction in the other tables too. A few people were gesturing to the King to tone it down. The King smiled and pulled the mike closer to him and in grand fortissimo sang "Cuando? Cuando? Cuando?" The conventioneers responded in kind. The King called the tune at The Purple Tree.

"Why don't you ask him to quiet it some, Nels?" Mary asked. I was still the authority and could change things.

"Mary, what is your class project?"

"Assertiveness," she said.

"Well," I said, "Here's a chance to try it. What would an assertive person say?"

"Okay, Okay, I get your point. But what if he doesn't turn it down?"

"Hey," said another student, "All you can do is try and be honest."

"I guess you're right." Mary got up and walked over to the King. We could see her talk and smile and the King smiled and strummed his guitar. Mary returned, all excited, and said, "I did it! I was assertive!" We applauded her and the King shouted "Cuando? Cuando? Cuando?" and the whole song was repeated. The Purple Tree shivered from the tweeters and woofers of the large speakers.

"It's all right, Mary. You gave it a try," said someone. We tried to continue our conversation by shouting. You could not hear anyone more than two seats away. Except for the conventioneers in front of the King, all the other patrons were leaning forward and shouting their conversations, and all this did was increase the sound level. I became irritated and got up.

"Guess I'll give it a try," I said.

"Let's see how a pro does it," shouted a student.

"Say, Rey," I said as the King was adjusting his console, "How about playing those nice tunes a bit softer so we can talk. It is really hard to hear." The King sat up and stared at me. I continued, "You have some fine equipment, but it's overwhelming even back there." I pointed to our table.

"I'm paid to provide entertainment," the King said.

"You *are* entertaining, but we would like to talk, too."

"Too bad," the King said. He was smirking now.

"A real musician could entertain without blasting, Rey," I said and walked back to the table. Well, that was a notch beyond assertiveness, I thought. It was an honest statement, though. Honest to my anger.

"Cuando? Cuando? Cuando?" rang out as I sat down. I was beginning to dislike this song that I had liked before coming to The Purple Tree. I gestured to our group that it was hopeless. "Assertiveness and honesty aren't in tonight, gang. At least for us."

The King finally took a break and we could talk for a few minutes on being honest and authentic. The King was returning for another set and someone said, "I'm going home. It's going to get noisy again." The whole group agreed. We left our tip and walked by the purple tree on our way out. Someone called out, "Hey Nels, come on over." A couple of former students were at a table with a large group. They had just arrived.

"Hi, Steve. What's the occasion?"

"We just finished our crisis hotline training and are celebrating a bit. Come join us."

"Okay."

The crisis people were in the second layer of tables from the King's electronic empire. It was going to be very loud sitting there, but they didn't know this yet. I sat at the end of the table with the King at my back. We talked for a minute or so about their training sessions and when they would be starting on the phone lines.

"Nels," Steve said with a worried, puzzled look, "The musician guy behind you is talking about you."

I turned around and the King was perched on his stool with his guitar, glaring at me. I looked at him, then turned back to Steve and asked, "What did he say, Steve?"

"He told everyone he won't play with you here."

I turned around again and the King was still staring. He bent over to his mike and said, "I will not play if this guy stays here." He pointed at me.

The lounge was as quiet as it was going to get. Several tables of patrons were looking at the King and me and asking each other what was going on. I turned back. The crisis people sat looking at me, not knowing what to do, either. Hey, crisis counselors, I thought, here's a chance to use your training. Well, they aren't on duty yet.

The King repeated his command and I turned and said, "I'm not leaving, Rey. What is your problem?" The King looked out to the crowd and said "He has got to go." He was angry now and pointing with a clenched fist.

"I am not leaving, Rey." Something was going to happen soon. The King was pushing the point. I could feel my heart slamming my chest and adrenaline had kicked in. Why stay? To not stay would be wrong and cowardly. I had done nothing but ask him to quiet down, as many had that evening. He responded smartly and so did I, so we were even. Until now. I sat still and sipped my drink and waited. It was his move.

The King glowered and the lounge crowd was getting uneasy, not knowing what was going on or what to do. The crisis people were silent and wide eyed. I was alone and knew I had to stay. It was the right thing to do. Too bad my students had left. We could have had a good discussion on being honest and true after this thing was over. I was hoping for it to be over soon, but this would have to wait, too.

The King was hoping I would pack and leave and I could not show any sign that I was.

Someone in the back shouted, "Rey, sing something."

"Not with this guy here," said the King.

"Aw come on, Rey, how about 'Cuando? Cuando? Cuando?' "

The King shuffled on the stool and said "All right. I'll do it for you but not for him." I sat still. You will not make me leave acting like that, Rey. I sat through three more songs. The crowd was singing along and it was back to the normal din. I explained to Steve what had happened earlier and got up to leave. It was all right to leave now. It was my choice and not the King's.

I walked slowly past the table and the large purple tree. Now that the fear and the confrontation were settled a strong sense of indignation surfaced. The King had insulted a customer. If I were true and honest, the management should hear about this. Truth and honesty were taking a beating so far, but that would change now. I was right. So right that I was feeling righteous. If you feel right you may or may not act. If you feel righteous, then you act—and this is not always the right thing to do.

"Where's the manager?" I asked of a waitress behind the bar.

"He's not here. What do you need?" she asked.

"I want to talk about the way your musician treats customers."

The waitress motioned to the bartender and said, "He's the guy who caused all the trouble."

"What are you saying?" I asked.

"You are the one who caused the commotion," she repeated in a righteous and loud voice.

"Yeah, sure." I walked out.

In the parking lot it was turning cool and dark enough to see the moon and a few stars. I could hear "Cuando? Cuando? Cuando?" through the walls of the Purple Tree.

Follow-Up

1. *Offer your views on the author's thoughts and actions after being challenged by the singer to leave.*
2. *Much to the author's surprise, he was told by the staff that he, not the singer, was the problem. Describe an instance and how you reacted when you thought you were obviously "in the right" but found out that others' opinions differed.*
3. *Offer your views and give examples for one or more of the following statements:*
   - *If you feel right you may or may not act. If you feel righteous, then you act—and this is not always the right thing to do.*
   - *If you aren't honest then you are a phony.*
   - *Sometimes you have to choose between competing truths (e.g., loyalty versus honesty).*
4. *Choose any other statement or idea in the article and provide your reaction.*

Applied Activities for Section Two

SENDER–RECEIVER EXCHANGE

This activity combines self-disclosure, listening, and self-knowledge. It has the most value when participants have some beginning acquaintance and are willing to disclose new dimensions of themselves. The procedure is as follows:

1. Read the articles on self-disclosure and listening in this book or other resources.
2. Choose a partner (there might be one three-member group).
3. Find a location with a minimum of distractions. It is recommended that 60 minutes be given to this activity (with a minimum of 30 minutes).
4. The basic task is for each participant to finish the sentences below. Each person is to complete an item before going on to the next. If you are in the sender role, complete the sentence in the most genuine manner possible (which can be the choice of *not* talking). If you are in the receiver role, your mission is to understand but not to offer reactions or interpretations.
5. It is more important to take quality time per item than to race through the list. If you cannot think of an adequate response to an item, skip it and go on to the next (you can always return to the skipped item if you choose).

Sender–Receiver Items

1. The name I'm to be called is _____ .

2. One of the best experiences I had during the past year was _____
   _____ .

3. Two traits or qualities others say I have are _____ and
   _____ .

4. One of my favorite free-time activities or hobbies is _____ .

5. One impression I seem to give to others that isn't totally true is _____
   _____ .

6. If, for some reason, I could only keep three possessions (excluding houses, vehicles, properties), they would be _____ , _____ ,
   and _____ .

7. If given *one* of the following at this time in my life, it would be _____
   _____ because _____ .

(a) a week alone in a favorite spot
(b) an activity with excitement, adventure
(c) a new friend to share experiences with
(d) an answer to what I should be in life
(e) an intimate, loving relationship
(f) accepting myself as I am
(g) a chance to help make a positive change in another's life
(h) to be recognized as being an expert in some field
(i) a deep spiritual/religious experience
(j) learn a new skill or special knowledge

8. Given some time with any person of my choice (current or historical), it would be _____ because _____ .

9. One thing I would like to change about myself is _____ .

10. My age is _____ and how I feel about it is _____ .

11. (a) I *like* being a male/female because _____ .

    (b) I *dislike* being a male/female because _____ .

    (c) One way I interact differently with the opposite sex is _____

    _____ .

12. The degree of satisfaction and fulfillment with my occupation or major is

    _____ .

13. I am fully accepted for who I am (no conditions) by _____ .

14. Compared to age 15, how are you different? _____

    _____ .

    The same? _____ .

15. A way I am the *same* as one or both of my parents (guardians) is _____

    _____ .

16. For at least two of the following emotional states, explain what normally causes them and how you react:

Worried-anxious-nervous	Wonder-awe-amazement
Lonely-not belonging-alienated	Joy-ecstasy
Angry-frustrated	Loved-intimate-belonging
Inadequate-inferior-failure	Confident-self respect
Confused-uncertain-lost	Sense of purpose and direction

17. My spiritual beliefs emphasize _____ .

18. A potential or ability that I have not fully developed, and want to, is _____

_____ .

19. Describe two activities that tend to produce for you a sense of well-being, centeredness, or harmony with life. How often do you experience these activities?

20. Within the next year it will be very important for me to _____

_____ .

Follow-Up

1. Discuss in small groups and/or with the whole class the following: What ideas in the article on self-disclosure applied to this experience (for example, trust, over-/under-discloser, appropriate discloser)?
2. Write a brief reaction paper on what you learned from this activity.
3. Try this activity with someone outside class (if they agree to the conditions).
4. Estimate how one of your significant others would respond to some or all of these items (check it out with their permission).
5. Select one item from the Sender-Receiver list to explore in more depth (either through writing, talking, or reflection).
6. Complete this activity one year from now.

POINT OF VIEW

1. Choose a topic about which you have strong beliefs and feelings; for example, the death penalty, prayer in schools, Republicans, Democrats, assisted suicide, a current crime trial, a current world/national/local issue, or a controversial person, movie, or book.
2. Interview others on this topic until you find two persons who essentially have the same views as yours and two persons who have opposing views. Your interview should last at least 4–5 minutes to gather sufficient information.
3. During each interview you are to remain as nonjudgmental as possible. The other person should not know your stance on the topic as you converse. Your sole mission is to find out the other person's thoughts and feelings on the topic. You may ask questions, but only those that are necessary to clarify the other person's views. You could consider yourself a news reporter who is interviewing people for their views on a story. You may have to explain your role to others prior to the interview.

Complete the above actions before continuing to the next steps.

4. Describe your thoughts and feelings while interviewing those who disagreed with you. Do the same for those who agreed.

- Did you have any interfering listening reactions during the interviews (e.g., strong urges to present your ideas, thinking of other arguments while listening, impatience, and so on)? If yes, how did this influence your understanding of the other person?
- How did the others respond when you showed that you understood their positions without a challenge?
- What have you learned, if anything, from this experience that can be used elsewhere?

(If this activity was difficult to accomplish, consider trying it several times until you have mastered this skill.)

THE WORLD OF _____

One of the most basic skills in relating and communicating is empathy—the ability to sense how another perceives the world. The World Of _____ activity is a direct attempt to experience empathy. Here are the directions.

1. Describe in writing how someone or something other than yourself might perceive the world. You may choose a living or non-living subject.
2. You may have to observe your subject for a period of time in order to get a feel for its world. Place yourself in the position of your subject and attempt to describe how it feels and responds. The time perspective can range from a few minutes to years.
3. Complete your description on one side of a sheet of paper. Place the name of your subject on the back (do not name the subject in your description).
4. When all descriptions are completed, form groups of 3–5 members. Members read their descriptions. The others try to guess the correct answer.
5. Discuss or write about what you learned from this experience.
6. Discuss or write about one or two situations where it would be beneficial to practice more empathy.

Examples of The World Of _____ Descriptions Are Seen Below

(a) My mate and I have been here about two years. It is incredible the things we hear and encounter. Most people take us for granted. They use us for their own convenience with little or no regard for us. Sometimes the rough treatment, the wrath, the scorn, and the abusive language are unbearable. We have also heard the sorrow, suffering, and anguish of many. It's enough to break one's heart. But then, there are the loving caresses, sweet words, and kisses that make it all bearable and worthwhile. In spite of everything we are content to be what we are. We are here to serve humanity.

(b) My day often starts very early in the morning and sometimes I don't get to sleep until way past midnight. I see people when they awake and at bedtime. Usually my location is stationary, but things around me are always moving. I guess I feel important because almost always when someone passes by they give me a look. Their look is longer than a mere glance, but they really aren't looking at *me*! Some people make funny faces at me. I see people as they are, but they see only what they want to see. My life is sad because I never can see myself. But I often bring superficial pleasure to each individual who passes by. Some of my relatives are usually in motion but they are handicapped because they can only view what has already passed by—never able to see ahead. Most of us can see only one side of any circumstance. Although I am very fragile, people can never fake their true emotions with me.

Answers:
(a) pair of pay telephones
(b) mirror

EFFECTIVE COMMUNICATOR CHECKLIST

Sending and listening skills are listed below. Rate your skill at each one, using the code provided. (If you prefer, ask someone else to rate you.)

1 = Very Poor   2 = Poor   3 = Adequate
4 = Good   5 = Excellent

Sending Skills

___ Have something useful to say

___ Have necessary knowledge of the topic

___ Attempt to detect how the message is understood by the receiver(s)

___ If possible, use multiple methods (such as writing, talking, nonverbal expressions)

___ Be aware of the *context* (the time factor, noise level, distractions, and emotional state) of the situation

___ Make your verbal and non-verbal messages match (for example, do not smile when angry, look concerned if you say you are)

Listening Skills

___ Can understand (or attempt to understand) the speaker from his or her point of view

___ Can focus on the speaker without getting caught up in distracting thoughts or your own ideas

_____ Can understand another even when emotions or beliefs are at a high intensity level (especially if you differ)

_____ Give verbal and nonverbal feedback to the speaker on how they are being received

_____ Can pick out the main idea or feeling without getting distracted by secondary points

Consider choosing at least one sending and one listening skill to further develop. Discuss your learnings.

HE SAID, SHE SAID

Observe several men and women as they communicate. Observe in a variety of formal and informal situations and try to sample from different age categories. Consider pairing with a partner of the opposite gender for an observation session or two. Your own interactions can count. Circle the choice which *most frequently* communicates in the manner indicated.

1. Conversation topics are about events, issues, things.	Men	Women	Both	Neither
2. Conversation topics are about people and/or themselves.	Men	Women	Both	Neither
3. Touch the other person while talking.	Men	Women	Both	Neither
4. Establish frequent eye contact, often engage in "facial mirroring."	Men	Women	Both	Neither
5. Smile while talking.	Men	Women	Both	Neither
6. Tend to use sweeping gestures versus smaller, controlled ones.	Men	Women	Both	Neither
7. Prefer to interact face to face.	Men	Women	Both	Neither
8. Prefer to interact side to side.	Men	Women	Both	Neither
9. Tend to lean back when interacting.	Men	Women	Both	Neither
10. Most at ease with self-disclosures.	Men	Women	Both	Neither
11. Often engage in several topics during one interaction.	Men	Women	Both	Neither
12. More often interrupt when interacting with opposite gender.	Men	Women	Both	Neither
13. Use hostile words, profanity.	Men	Women	Both	Neither
14. Use qualifying language (i.e., "If it is okay..."; "What do you think?"; "Maybe..."; end sentences with a questioning tone).	Men	Women	Both	Neither

Follow-Up

- Discuss your findings with classmates and compare your observations.
- Discuss or write how these gender communication differences reflect cultural norms for men and women.
- Rate yourself on the above items and provide a brief interpretation.
- Consider adding more items from your observations of men and women as they communicate.

A COMMUNICATION MEDLEY

Try one or more of these communication experiences to enhance your sending or listening skills:

1. Watch a few TV talk shows with the intent of observing communication skills, particularly listening. Observe the effects of good and poor sending and listening behaviors (the Effective Communicator Checklist located in this section may be of help here).
2. Watch a TV drama or rented video *without* sound. Attempt to understand what is happening by observing only nonverbal actions (gestures, facial expressions, movements). If the show is recorded, rerun the tape with audio to check your accuracy.
3. Some hints that indicate you need work on sending skills: others often ask you to clarify something you said; you notice others get that glazed look after several minutes of listening to you; others nod politely but find an excuse to leave before you have finished.
4. Approximately two-thirds of our emotions are sent and received through nonverbal channels. If you are experiencing difficulty in having others understand your emotions, try experimenting with nonverbal behaviors. For example, warmth and caring is expressed with a genuine smile, consistent but nonpiercing eye contact, and closer proximity. Enthusiasm is generally expressed with active gestures, vocal variety, and facial vitality. It is also helpful to observe others who are good at showing the particular emotion you want to convey and watch their nonverbal communication.

INTUITION HISTORY

While the intuitive mode prefers nonverbal forms, there are some "verbal bridges" that get at its meaning and intent. Here are a few phrases often heard when one is describing the intuitive state:

"My instinct tells me . . . "
"I have this gut feeling . . . "
"The idea just came out of the blue (or nowhere)."
"I had this strong hunch . . . "

"I followed my heart."
"I can't explain it, I just have this strong attraction to . . . "
"I had these powerful stirrings, inner rumblings urging me to . . . "
"I don't think about it, I just act."
"There was this instant and uncanny connection."
"Don't ask me how, I just *know*."

List two instances in your life in which your actions were (are) strongly influenced (at least 50%) by intuition. Here are some categories to consider: school/college experiences, relationships (entering or leaving), geographical move, career decisions/choices, non-career interests (hobbies, pursuits), taking a trip/vacation, making a major purchase, changing an aspect of your lifestyle or personality.

1.

2.

Name an instance when you *did not* follow your intuitive urgings and things did not turn out right.

Name an instance when you acted *mainly* on intuition and things did not turn out right.

Follow-Up

1. Describe your learnings and views about the role of intuition in your life.

PROBLEM SOLVING: RATIONAL AND INTUITIVE STRATEGIES

1. Briefly describe a current decision, choice, or problem you are facing.
2. What is your *rational* side expressing about this issue? (Your logical, cognitive, and analytical processes).
3. What does your *intuitive* side seem to be saying about this issue? (Your inner sensings, feeling tones, gut reaction.) Can you separate the latter from momentary impulses and/or feelings of getting approval?
4. If the rational and intuitive expressions conflict, what has been your experience with a similar decision in your past? If there has been a relevant experience, what has it taught you that you can use now?
5. If little resolution has occurred, try to let the problem incubate for awhile (i.e., do not actively pursue it, let the subconscious work on it).
6. Consider writing a dialogue between you and the decision/problem.

Follow-Up

1. Describe your learnings from this activity.

INTUITIVE PROBLEM-SOLVING THROUGH GUIDED IMAGERY

Take some time now to think about a problem that you are currently facing. It can be any situation, any unresolved question concerning relationships, work, growth, or anything else that is important to you.

The first step in this exercise is to formulate a question. Ask any question. In formulating the question, make it as clear as possible. What is the question you want to resolve? When you have a question clearly in your mind, write it down, or make a note of it so that it is clearly stated in your mind. The next step in this exercise is to begin your relaxation practice. Focus your awareness on your body. Take your awareness up to the top of your head and move it slowly down over your whole body, penetrating deeply inside your body, as well as moving it over the surface of your skin. Take as long as you want. When you have focused your awareness, and your mind is quiet, remember the question that you posed earlier. There is nothing you have to do about the question; just hold it in your awareness.

> Imagine now that you are at the shore of a large body of water. You get into a small boat and settle comfortably down with a blanket. The boat begins to drift away from shore and is carried gently by the current in the water further and further from the shore. Listen to the sound of the water lapping against the sides of the boat and imagine the rocking motion of the gentle current as you drift slowly further and further away. There is no cause for worry or anxiety because the current will carry you where you need to go. After a time you notice that the light is fading and you see that you have drifted into an underground passage. It gets darker and darker but the movement of the water continues and you drift along feeling quiet and peaceful. After some time you see a light in the distance and you realize that your boat is being carried toward the light. The light becomes brighter and brighter as you get closer to it. The intensity is almost unbearable. Finally your boat emerges into brilliant sunshine and you find yourself on a gently moving stream in a beautiful quiet meadow. The boat comes to a stop and you get out on the bank of the stream. In this place someone or something will bring you a message. The message may not seem to answer the question you asked, but don't worry about that. Trust that it will tell you something you need to know for the solution to your problem. Allow yourself to be quiet and still and wait for whatever image or message comes to you. When you have heard or seen whatever it is that is there for you, get back in the boat and turn on the motor. Very quickly you will find yourself back at the shore where you started. You can leave the boat now and bring your awareness

back to the present time and place, to your physical body, feeling comfortable and relaxed. Take a few minutes now to write down what happened in the meadow. If there was anything you heard, anything you saw, write it down. It may not make sense at the moment, but something of value to you can emerge from it.

JOURNAL BEGINNINGS

Following are additional prompts to support your journaling goals. Set the timer for 5 minutes. Read the prompts and select one that stands out to you. Write continuously until the timer rings.

- Three things I plan to accomplish this week are . . .

- The thought that keeps coming to my mind is . . .

- Today's newspaper headlines read . . . my reaction to this is . . .

- A risk I plan to take is . . . The benefits are . . . Why this risk is important to me is . . . I will do this by _____ [date].

- This moment, I am thinking/feeling . . .

- Today, for fun I did . . .

- One thing I would genuinely like to change about myself is . . .

- My biggest fear is . . .

- What did I accomplish today?

- Look out your window. Write what you see.

- One thing in my life time I want to achieve is _____ because . . .

LIFESTORIES

This is an open-ended activity best experienced in a relaxed, informal atmosphere with people you already know and trust. Not only will you learn a little more about yourself, but a bit more about the others in your life. Some general guidelines:

- Two to five members.
- One person chooses and discusses an item from the list below. The other group members just listen and/or offer comments after the speaker is finished.
- Everyone should get a turn. There is also the option to pass.
- Discuss as many items as you wish (and in any order).

1. Your earliest memory
2. Your first good friend
3. A favorite place in your childhood home
4. A special moment with a parent (guardian)
5. What you did in summers before high school
6. How you are like and unlike one of your parents (guardians)
7. Favorite subjects in school
8. Least favorite subjects in school
9. A favorite teacher
10. A childhood vacation that stands out
11. A major hero as a child or adolescent
12. One of your current favorite sounds or tastes
13. Describe one major success in your life
14. A failure or dead end
15. Two little joys (small pleasures)
16. One of your current favorite places to be
17. One major experience or accomplishment yet to occur which you desire
18. A treasured possession
19. A person (excluding a significant other or family member) you would like to spend time with (can be a historical figure if you choose)
20. Something that inspires you
21. A fear
22. When do you feel lonely?
23. How are you different now compared to age 16? How are you the same?
24. Something you'd like to do for another person
25. Something you want and need further growth in

Editor's note: An excellent reference for further pursuing this activity is *The Common Ground Book: A Circle of Friends* by Remar Sutton and Mary Abbott Waite. British American Publishing, 1992.

PERSONAL GOALS—HUMAN COMMUNICATION

Within the next year I will improve my communication skills by:

Goal 1:

Needed actions, support, and resources:

Timeline:

Progress notes (use extra page if necessary):

Goal 2:

Needed actions, support, and resources:

Timeline:

Progress notes (use extra page if necessary):

GROWTH DYNAMICS

Change is inherent in growth. In the accompanying magnolia photo we see this change in the stages of bloom—full, partial, and buds representing potential flowering. Similarly, human potentialities exist in various stages of maturity. Growth psychologists contend that there is a basic underlying force directing growth.

> Whether one calls it a growth tendency, a drive toward self-actualization, or a forward-moving directional tendency, it is the mainspring of life. . . . It is the urge which is evident in all organic and human life—to expand, extend, become autonomous, develop, mature—the tendency to express and activate all the capacities of the organism. The actualizing tendency can be thwarted or warped, but it cannot be destroyed without destroying the organism. (Rogers, 1980, p. 118; 1961, p. 35).

> We have, each one of us, an essential inner nature which is instinctoid, intrinsic, given, "natural". . . and which tends strongly to persist. . . . Each person's inner nature has some characteristics which all other selves have (species-wide) and some which are unique to the person (idiosyncratic). . . . This inner core or self grows into adulthood only partly by (objective or subjective) discovery. . . . Partly it is also a creation of the person himself. . . . If this essential core is frustrated, denied or suppressed, sickness results (or one becomes) a "diminished or stunted person" (Maslow, 1968, pp. 190–93).

137

"Magnolia"

Barry Stevens (Rogers & Stevens, 1971) refers to this growth tendency as her "built-in pathfinder" which, if listened to, helps a person to see clearly even in times of turmoil. This growth tendency can be inhibited or enhanced by interactions with the outside world (especially other people), and by individual decisions. A person's growth status is the outcome of the continual interaction of this actualizing tendency and demands from the outside world.

Carl Rogers (Rogers, 1961; Rogers & Stevens, 1971; Rogers & Freiberg, 1994) describes some valued directions of persons moving toward greater growth and maturity.

- A movement away from facades, pretense, defensiveness, and putting up a front.
- A movement away from pleasing others as a goal in itself.
- Being real and genuine is positively valued. A person tends to move toward his or her real self and real feelings.
- Self-direction is positively valued. A person discovers an increasing pride and confidence in making choices and guiding his or her life.
- A person becomes more open to experience, becomes increasingly able to sense inner experience and external reality *as it is,* rather than distorting it to fit a preconceived pattern.

The person can react more readily to new people and situations and tolerate more ambiguity with this kind of perception.

- Being a process is positively valued. A person accepts himself or herself as a stream of becoming, not a finished product. A person prefers the process, both fascinating and uncertain, of being in the midst of constantly developing potentialities.
- Others are increasingly appreciated for what they are, just as the person has come to appreciate his or her being. The person seeks to achieve close and real relationships, including the deeply intimate.

Abraham Maslow (1970, 1968) also found the qualities listed above in his studies of self-actualizing persons. He added the following items to the list of self-actualizing characteristics.

- A problem-centered versus an ego-centered orientation. A person devotes much energy to a life mission, a cause, or a task beyond his or her own existence.
- An ability to appreciate, again and again, basic life experiences with awe, pleasure, and wonder.
- A special kind of creativity evident in a person's attitude and unique ways of doing even everyday things.
- There is a framework of values, a philosophy to live by.

References

Maslow, A. H. (1970). *Motivation and personality.* New York: Harper & Row.

Maslow, A. H. (1968). *Toward a psychology of being.* New York: Van Nostrand Reinhold.

Rogers, C. R. (1980). *A way of being.* Boston: Houghton Mifflin.

Rogers, C. R. (1961). *On becoming a person.* Boston: Houghton Mifflin.

Rogers, C. R., & Freiberg, H. J. (1994). *Freedom to learn,* 3rd ed. New York: Merrill.

Rogers, C. R., & Stevens, B. (1971). *Person to person: The problem.* New York: Pocket Books.

READINGS OVERVIEW

Factors that impede or promote growth are the central topics of the readings in this section.

- In "The Meaning of Personal Growth," Abe Arkoff discusses the multiple dimensions of growth. The propensity to grow, as well as the burdens of growth, are highlighted.
- Nels Goud engages in a one-person dialogue on the question of "Uniqueness." He offers arguments both pro and con on whether an individual human is truly unique.

- What does it mean to realize one's potentialities? Humanistic psychologist Abraham Maslow discusses nine aspects of self-actualization in "Self-Actualizing and Beyond."
- Tom Keating introduces a common man, "Herbie." We are asked at the end of the article whether Herbie fulfills the criteria of healthy growth.
- Harold Bloomfield and Robert Kory present many practical ideas for overcoming feelings of stagnation and powerlessness in "Getting Unstuck: Joyfully Recreating Your Life."
- Ending one's life on purpose, the extreme growth inhibitor, is explored in Poe Ballantine's "Advice to William Somebody," and in "Left Behind" by Jenny Montgomery.
- "Vital Moments" by Nelson Goud examines how brief life-validating moments influence human growth. Included are peak experiences, wonder, psychological epiphanies, and flow.
- The place of courage in making growth decisions is the theme of Rollo May's "Courage."
- In "The Lesson of the Cliff," Morton Hunt provides a guide for facing fears that can block our growth. He discusses how this idea enabled him to face his growth fears in a variety of circumstances.
- Amy Gross demonstrates how daily encounters can have the same qualities as heroic adventures. She explains how common challenges produce "Small Terrors, Secret Heroics."
- Three short pieces introduce the issue of pace in healthy development: "Just a Regular Kid" by a fifth grade teacher, and "The Pace of Growth" by novelist John Knowles, an undergraduate student, and Nikos Kazantzakis.
- Daphne Haygood-Benyard ends the section with her poem "No One's Perfect."

You are invited to attempt one or more of the Applied Activities at the end of this section. These exercises are designed to apply the concepts of this section to your life. The questions posed at the end of each article also aim at personalizing the selections.

The Meaning of Personal Growth

Abe Arkoff

Personal growth, as it is defined here, is simply change in a desired or valued direction. Values, of course, vary from person to person. I may feel I have grown when I have freed myself from dependence on my parents. You may experience personal growth when you change your conception of yourself and begin to respond to the world in a new and freer way. My parents, however, may not agree that my new-found autonomy is growth, and your spouse may be threatened by your new self-definition and put pressure on you to revert to the person you were.

Potentiality refers to inherent capacity for growth. What's possible for us? What can we become? What can keep us from becoming all we wish to become? How can we find a path of growth that's right for us? These are some of the questions we will consider in the material that follows.

THE POTENTIAL FOR GROWTH

A Russian scientist has estimated that with our brain working at only half capacity, we could learn 40 languages with no difficulty (Otto, 1972). Many of us, however, find it something of a struggle to learn more than one. From this perspective, we certainly seem to be less than we could be.

What has come to be called the "human potential movement" began during the 1960s and was dedicated to helping people make the most of their capacities. An underlying assumption—sometimes called "the human potential hypothesis"—was that most people function at only a small fraction of their po-

tential. A further assumption was that by proceeding in certain ways much more of this potential could be realized.

Nearly a century ago William James, one of the earliest American psychologists, estimated that humans, on the average, functioned at about 10% of their capacity. Later, anthropologist Margaret Mead put this figure at 6%. Human potentialist Herbert Otto's original estimate of average fulfillment was a modest 5%, which he later reduced to 4%. He writes that the estimated percentage has been decreasing because "we are discovering that every human being has more powers, resources, and abilities than we suspected ten years ago, five years ago" (1972, p. 14).

A trio of psychologists—Arthur Combs, Donald Avila, and William Purkey (1978)—maintain that human beings are "overbuilt." They write, "One of the most exciting discoveries of this generation is the idea that human capacity is far greater than anything ever thought possible. The fascinating thing about human beings is not their limitations, but their immense capabilities. . . . From everything we can observe, it seems clear that few of us ever remotely approach the potentialities for effective behavior that lie within us. Most of us use but a small fraction of our capabilities" (pp. 69–70, 71).

Obstacles to Growth

Why don't we make more of ourselves and our lives? Why don't we realize more of our potential? These are important questions—and ones many philosophers and psychologists and stuck, bewildered souls have pondered.

A Diminished Conception of Ourselves. One reason we don't make more of ourselves is that we may have a diminished view of who we are and what we can become. To some extent, we are who we *think* we are, and some of us may not think we're much. Although research suggests we are more likely to overestimate than underestimate ourselves, two psychologists, Ellen Langer and Carol Dweck (1973) write, "We maintain that there are few, if any, of us who have a truly satisfying self-concept. People occasionally put on a good show and seem to others to be on top of it all, but these very same people often think: 'if they only knew the real me'" (p. 29).

The basic goal of many personal growth programs and psychotherapies is to get the individuals concerned to enhance their self-concept and to accept, love, and prize themselves more. A basic goal of some transpersonal approaches is to inspire persons with awe or reverence for themselves and their place in the universe. As such individuals come to see more in themselves, they attempt and accomplish more, and accomplishing more they further enhance their conception of themselves.

The following true story (recalled by a woman psychologist from her prepsychology days) indicates how important an obstacle a negative self-concept can be, and how a positive self-concept can both instigate and stem from growth:

> I was living out in San Francisco at the time. While coming home from work one day I got involved in an accident and required the attention of a doctor. A friend of mine mentioned the accident to his friend, an eager, but not yet established, young lawyer. The lawyer contacted me, and then proceeded to persuade me that I had a case and that he was the one to handle it.
>
> That was the way I met Hank. The impression I got of him after talking over the phone for the next week or so was that he was enthusiastic, good humored, and sort of charming. When he came over to my house to discuss the case further, I had to add unattractive to the list of adjectives.

> After we concluded our discussion of business matters, we got involved in a friendly and rather personal conversation. Hank had recently come to San Francisco from New York. He was divorced and was eager to tell me about the marvelous changes in his life. It seemed that his ex-wife had constantly told him how ugly he was. I thought that that was both cruel and accurate—but kept the latter thought to myself. Hank explained how inhibited this made him with other people. "I had little confidence in myself and was enormously shy." I said I couldn't believe that he was very shy. He recounted some experiences he had had at parties and with clients to convince me. He was successful in gaining my sympathy.
>
> Then he told me how different he was now. He had traveled across the country with the thought that he just might not be as homely looking as she said—so he took some risks. He gradually improved his opinion of himself. He put this a little differently though: "I slowly started to recognize how wrong she was. Now I know I'm good looking. When I walk into a room people take notice of me and believe it or not (I didn't) the girls are all over me at parties." We talked some more, and then a horn started honking outside. He said it was his new girlfriend picking him up. We went over to the terrace to see if it were she—it was, and she was simply beautiful. For a moment I couldn't believe the whole episode. What was even more bewildering was that I started finding him attractive.
>
> Although Hank's somewhat dramatic tale is not unique, most people with negative self-concepts never bother to test out other hypotheses about themselves, as he did. While at first he accepted his wife's opinion as indisputable truth, he later formulated an alternative positive view, "I am *not* ugly," and set out to confirm it. Now Hank tells people how to respond to him. His new manner has an air of confidence, and the subtle and not so subtle cues are effective. It is not surprising that most people listen. (Langer and Dweck, 1973, pp. 40–42)

A Fixed Conception of Ourselves. A second reason we don't grow as much as we might is that we fix our conception of ourself. We begin to think, "Well, I've always been this way." We each begin to think of ourself as a person who can do this but can't do that. In this situation, growth concedes to "destiny."

To find out where our "I've always been this way" originated, Bloomfield and Kory (1980) recommend that we quiz the significant others of our childhood days. How did they see us? What labels did they apply to us? We may hear from their lips the same labels we have come to apply to ourselves. If we announce we're going to change, how do they respond? Does their response seem to say: "Lots of luck and you'll need it because 'you've always been this way.'" For illustration, here is a case presented by Bloomfield and Kory:

> John, a college student, complains, "I can count the number of dates I've had on one hand and not run out of fingers." He's obviously got a sense of humor, but he is afraid to be himself around women. "I'm shy," he says. "That's my nature." John recalls his mother telling people that he was "the shy one." He never realized that his mother had an emotional investment in keeping him tied to her apron strings. John spent his childhood and adolescence living up to the family label of "the shy one." No doubt he had a tendency to be shy as a little boy, but with their labeling, his parents helped him develop that tendency into a full-blown personality characteristic. The question is whether John is going to continue justifying his fears of women with the rationale: "Shyness is my nature." (p. 167)

A fixed notion of who we are can easily result when we continue to move around in the same old sub-environments that call forth the same old response. We can develop a kind of comfort in leading our familiar life and in being our familiar self. To change and grow might bring welcome hope and pleasurable excitement, but it might also bring unwelcome anxiety. More about this in the material that follows.

The Need for Safety. A third obstacle to growth concerns an unwillingness to leave safe places. Maslow (1968) hypothesized that in addition to growth forces, each person also has safety forces and these two sets work in opposition to each other. Maslow noted that the conflict between these forces could block the individual. He diagrammed this process as follows:

$$\text{Safety} \leftarrow \text{PERSON} \rightarrow \text{Growth}$$

Elaborating on these opposing forces, Maslow wrote,

> Every human being has *both* sets of forces within him. One set clings to safety and defensiveness out of fear, tending to regress backward, hanging on to the past, *afraid* to grow away from the primitive communication with the mother's uterus and breast, *afraid* to take chances, *afraid* to jeopardize what he already has, *afraid* of independence, freedom and separateness. The other set of forces impels him forward toward wholeness of Self and uniqueness of Self, toward full functioning of all his capacities, toward confidence in the face of the external world at the same time that he can accept his deepest, real, unconscious Self. (p. 46)

Maslow noted that both safety and growth have drawbacks and attractions for the individual. The person grows when the drawbacks of safety and the attractions of growth are greater than the attractions of safety and the drawbacks of growth. Parents, teachers, and therapists sometimes are able to step in to change the weight of safety and growth vectors. As our conception of ourselves is enhanced, safety becomes less attractive and necessary and growth becomes more attractive and even irresistible.

When I consider the lives of my mother and father, it is easier for me to think of my mother's life as a success. Both my parents were immigrants, my mother from Latvia, my father from Russia. Both were looking for better lives in a new land, and both made their way to a small Midwestern city where they found each other, married, and raised five children.

Success in life, according to Freud's bare-bones set of criteria, requires success in loving and working but I never felt my father found his true work or calling. He was a brilliant and spiritual man who would have been fulfilled as a rabbi or teacher. Instead, for almost all of his adult life, he spent six-and-one-half long days a week in a little store, an occupation for which he exhibited little zest or talent. In his late-middle years, he became for awhile quite depressed—his response, I believe, to his inability to move his life along.

Some years ago, I went back to my hometown just to wander again around old boyhood places. My parents were long since dead, and no relatives or close friends remained, but I found a man who had known my father quite well. We had coffee together and talked about the old days. He remembered how my father had been a force in the usually rabbi-less Jewish community and one who took it upon himself to round up 10 mostly reluctant men so that a Friday night sabbath prayer meeting could be held. "But," he added, "one thing about your father, he wasn't willing to take a chance."

I wondered about that: my father, a man who went AWOL from the Czar's army and came to a far-away land whose language and culture was completely strange to him, who fell in love, married, started a business, had five children, became a pillar of his religious community. He had taken chances, made commitments, achieved. What had happened to him along the way? How had he gotten so mired, so stuck?

In her book *Pathfinders*, Gail Sheehy describes a group of "people of high well being"—those who successfully negotiate the crises of life. She concludes that the "master quality" possessed by pathfinders is their willingness to take risks. In her study of lives she found that a continuing sense of well-being generally required a continual willingness to risk change. Similar findings came out of a longitudinal study of men and women by social scientists at the University of California at San Francisco (Lowenthal, 1980). Although the researcher expected those adults who showed a strong sense of continuity in values and goals would show the greatest sense of well-being instead it was those who demonstrated change.

The Fear of Growth. A fourth obstacle to growth concerns fear of what growth may bring. A number of students of human nature have noted an absolute fear of growth in some individuals. Why should some of us fear to grow? One reason may be that we fear the unknown. Even if we do not like or are not comfortable with who we are, at least we are accustomed to ourselves. We hesitate to risk what we have (even though it's not all we want) to get something that may be less or worse.

A second reason we fear growth is that we may see growth as bringing responsibilities we doubt we will be able to meet. If we succeed, more will be expected of us and we may doubt our ability to continually meet these expectations. "The higher you climb, the harder you fall," we tell ourselves, "so maybe it's better not to reach too high."

There is a third fear of growth that Maslow (1971) called "the Jonah Complex." This complex (named after Jonah who wound up in the whale when he ran from a mission he had been given from on high) refers to our fear of our own greatness. Maslow hypothesized that in the presence of very special individuals (saintly persons, geniuses, beauties, etc.) we may tend to feel uneasy, envious, or inferior and therefore countervalue (or depreciate) them or their qualities. Maslow suggests that if we could bring ourselves "to love more purely the highest values in others," we would become better able to discover and love and make the most of these qualities in ourselves.

PATHWAYS TO GROWTH

All of life is concerned with growth, as is all of this book. It would be impossible and unnecessary here to review every pathway to growth that has been proposed or pursued. But it may be helpful to distinguish between two main paths that have aroused some controversy.

One path to growth is an individual way. Its emphasis is on oneself and involves developing one's own potentiality and making the most of one's life and spirit. It is an essentially inner path, although it may move out like a widening spiral to encompass more than oneself.

A second path is an outer and collective path—one of social activism and change. It involves finding ways to change the institutions of society—for example, the home and school and marriage—to enhance the lives of all people. It involves taking responsibility for the betterment of everyone everywhere and especially those less fortunate than oneself.

Some advocates of the second path have called the first a "narcissistic" one because they view it as a selfish pursuit. To them, it is a kind of self-absorption when the times call for social change and the reconstruction of social agencies. They fear that in frustration, people are "searching within" when they should be "reaching out."

Proponents of the first path vigorously disagree. They feel that personal growth or enhancement is a necessary first step—that one cannot reach out if one's center is hollow. If one wants a better world, the way to begin is to make oneself a better or fuller person. They ask how those who do not and cannot respect and love and help themselves hope to relate to and help others.

Roberts Samples (1977) calls the first path "selfness." This is "the state in which self is celebrated in a nonexploitative mode." It is distinct from selfish, the exploitation of others for the benefit of oneself and also distinct from selfless, the exploitation of oneself for the benefit of others.

There is, it seems, nothing essentially incompatible in the two paths. Service to others is a time-honored avenue to transcendence and so is the deep inner pursuit of oneself. One can grow from the inside out or from the outside in or both ways at once. There are many kinds of growth and many routes—each of us can find our own way.

References

Astin, A. W. (1977). *Four critical years.* San Francisco: Jossey-Bass.

Bloomfield, H. H., & Kory, R. B. (1980). *Inner joy.* New York: Wyden.

Combs, A. W., Avila, D. L., & Purkey, W. W. (1978). *Helping relationships: Basic concepts for the helping professions* (2nd ed.). Boston: Allyn & Bacon.

Davis, K. (1947). Final note on a case of extreme isolation. *American Journal of Sociology, 52,* 432–437.

Langer, E. J., & Dweck, C. S. (1973). *Personal politics: The psychology of making it.* Englewood Cliffs, NJ: Prentice-Hall.

Lowenthal, M. F. (1980). *Changing hierarchies of commitment in adulthood.* In N. J. Smesler & E. H. Erikson (Eds.), *Themes of work and love in adulthood* (pp. 238–264). Cambridge, MA: Harvard University Press.

Maslow, A. H. (1968). *Toward a psychology of being* (2nd ed.). New York: Van Nostrand Reinhold.

Maslow, A. H. (1972). *The farther reaches of human nature.* New York: Viking.

Otto, H. A. (1971). New light on human potential. In College of Home Economics, Iowa State University (Ed.), *Families of the future* (pp. 14–25). Ames: Iowa State University Press.

Samples, B. (1977, May). Selfness: Seeds of a transformation. *AHP Newsletter*, pp. 1–2.

Szent-Gyoergyi, A. (1974). Drive in living matter to perfect itself. *Synthesis, 1,* 14–26.

Wallechinsky, D. (1986). *Midterm report: The class of '65—Chronicles of an American generation.* New York: Viking.

Follow-Up

1. *Do you have any sense of a drive within yourself toward growth, enhancement, or perfection? Discuss this aspect of yourself.*
2. *Have you felt any guilt because of your failure to make more of yourself? Do you have a nostalgia for the person you might have become? Discuss these aspects of yourself.*
3. *Are you a risk-taker or a security-seeker? What are the relative strengths of safety and growth forces in your life? Discuss this aspect of yourself.*
4. *Apply two statements in this article to your life.*

Uniqueness

Nelson Goud

As a kid I spent many hours daydreaming what I would be when I grew up. I had this intuition that I had some kind of specialness. The intuition was a faint but persistent voice, somewhat like sensing the dim signals sent by a distant star.

I grew up. I look about me for evidence of what I was destined to uniquely accomplish. Maybe I need help—please let me know if you have spotted it. I am even finding out that my special destiny fantasy is quite common, perhaps you have experienced it also. Even my daydreams aren't original.

Sometimes this special destiny illusion persists and lingers until just the right circumstances arise to release it. Then "if only's" get in the way: "I could be great if only I had more time; if only I had the resources and opportunity; if only others didn't make so many demands; if only the sun wasn't in my eyes; if only the world would adjust itself solely to me." Most of us, though, gradually learn that only a rare few invent a cure for a major disease, create pieces of art and music that express the human soul for millions, or develop a theory that completely changes how people view the world and themselves. How humbling to know whatever your accomplishments, only a few will have intimate knowledge of them. Most of what we do in life has either been done before or is, at best, a new variation of themes others have created. Surprisingly I remain unconvinced by my own arguments. The faint inner voice still says, "You are a unique person." So the dialogue must continue.

One comment that makes us feel unique is "You're one in a million." Then we read that the current U.S. population is around 275 million. This means that there are 275 Americans just like you. If extended to the world population, there are 6,000 people just like you. You could form a small town made up of persons exactly like you. You would never need a mirror or snivel that "no one understands me." If we buy the estimate that there are 100 billion planets in our galaxy alone that are capable of supporting life forms, then what are our chances of being special or significant?

I still feel unique. Okay, let's try another angle. We can examine our significance and specialness over time. In *The Dragons of Eden,* Carl Sagan condensed the 15 billion year lifetime of the universe into a single calendar year. Here are a few events in the history of the universe, including your life, if they had occurred in twelve months.

- Big Bang—
  January 1
- Origin of the Milky Way Galaxy—
  May 1
- Our solar system—
  September 9
- Earth appears—
  September 14
- First life on Earth—
  September 25
- Invention of sex (by microorganisms)—
  November 1
- Oldest photosynthetic plants—
  November 12
- First humans—
  December 31 (10:30 p.m.)
- Invention of agriculture—
  December 31 (11:59:20 p.m.)
- European Renaissance—
  December 31 (11:59:59 p.m.)

What we studied in history took place in less than a second. Our current lives would not even merit a rapid eye-blink. We are not even cosmic trifles. We make no difference at all. In a way, after some initial chin dragging, this could be welcome news. No longer do we have to despair at a low grade, or get upset by an unfair supervisor, or losing a lover—what difference do they make anyway?

It seems, you may say, that the arguments here are one-sided. You would be correct. There are some unresolved questions concerning human uniqueness. Why is it, for example, that one of life's most fundamental impulses is to produce such astounding variety? Why are there over 1,000,000 species of bugs? At least 175,000 species of trees? Even the green stuff we see on ponds and the seas, algae, has 25,000 forms. Experts won't even venture a guess at how many species of fish there are. There are so many kinds of living organisms that some scientists devote whole careers trying to classify them. My personal favorite, the one-celled Euglena, is so unique that experts cannot determine whether it is a plant or animal—now that's originality!

We are part of a universal life force that presses toward variation and individuality. It is our first affirmation that we have the potential for uniqueness.

Our bodies show uniqueness. With some exceptions for identical twins, each of us has distinctive cell protein makeup; scents; blood antigen combinations; teeth surface patterns; and, naturally, fingerprints. Differences become even more pronounced between individual humans when we examine the psychological, social, and various mental behaviors. Even identical twins can show wide variations in the latter areas.

Each minute of existence is a changing combination of sensory inputs, other people, and your inner world of thoughts and feelings. How you make sense of these demands minute-by-minute is a distinctive act. No one experiences the world exactly like you, nor can your experience be duplicated. "Every new mind is a new classification . . . and is new in nature," exclaims Emerson (Edman, ed., 1926). This continuing process of unique experiencing is a fundamental source of original ideas and behavior, and of being in the world.

Pulitzer Prize–winning author Annie Dillard claims that our creative uniqueness helps keep the universe together. According to the law of entropy, things eventually disintegrate. Citing Buckminster Fuller, she says that "by creating things, by thinking up new combinations, we counteract this flow of entropy. We make new structures, new wholenesses, so the universe comes out even. A shepherd on a hilltop who looks at a mess of stars and thinks, 'There's a hunter, a plow, a fish,' is making mental connections that have as much real force in the universe as the very fires in those stars themselves."

This whole discussion is starting to get a bit confusing and contradictory. First we see that attaining cosmic uniqueness and significance is futile. We are told that anything we do is not truly original, but a variation on existing themes. Our "special destiny" is but an illusion. Then we are presented with the view that a basic life force compels variety and individuality in all living organisms, even in a one-celled Euglena. In humans this variation is demonstrated in both bodily and psycho-social traits. How we experience life in each moment is offered as a kind of uniqueness.

There is more. . . . The least discussed kind of uniqueness is our *way of being*. The distinctive manner in which we carry out life's activities, the way we do things—this can be a source of true uniqueness. It is not unique to be a teacher, secretary, executive, friend, lover, or parent. But we have a choice on how to perform these and other major life roles. We can perform them in a standard, conventional manner, or we can choose to have them be mediums of our own individual personality.

Sometimes style is substance. Imagine two of your favorite singers singing the same song. It is the style of each performer which makes the performances unique. John Steinbeck describes a woman who was valued for her unique style of human interaction. "She had a way of laughing appreciatively at everything anyone said, and, to merit this applause, people tried to say funny things when she was about. . . . She made people feel good. No one could ever remember that she said anything, but months after hearing it, they could recall the exact tones of her laughter." We know a person has developed an individuality of style when it is said, "I don't know quite how to explain it, but he has a way about him."

Role models can help us develop a way of being. There comes a point, though, when we have to say that we have learned all we could from them and then venture out to find our own voice. Miles Davis, the pioneering jazz trumpeter, is known for his special tone and phrasing. When asked how he learned this style, Davis said that he did not play in this manner at first. Instead, he started by playing like other jazz trumpeters. Eventually he decided to blend techniques from them with his own "feel" of the music. He concluded that "it takes a long time to play like yourself." Thanks, Miles, for taking that time. It will take some time, some experimenting, but we too can learn to "play like ourselves."

Earlier it was contended that only the "greats" create the ideas and products of the first magnitude, the grand themes. This does not mean that there is no room left for originality in our creations—they are just of another magnitude. As the naturalist John Audubon pointed out, "The fields would be

"Unique"

very silent if no birds sang there except those who sang best." What a loss if only the best chirpers sang and they were all in a distant village. What a loss if only the greatest could perform life's tasks—could we exist for long this way? All our voices, especially those which show our special way of being, are needed if life is to function as it is intended.

I've always been a bit puzzled by the philosopher Martin Buber's idea that if there were other persons just like us, then there would be no need for us to be in the world. It is now starting to make sense. Life is *asking us* to share our specialness. This is not a selfish or oddball act. Choosing to share our uniqueness is a profound way to follow a primary life directive and to form a connection with the world. We can contribute a dimension of required newness. It is our choice though.

So, how are you expressing your specialness?

Follow-Up

1. *Did you, like the author, have a "special destiny intuition" as a child? What has happened to it? If it still persists, what direction is it pointing toward?*

2. It is stated that "Most of what we do in life has either been done before or is, at best, a new variation of themes others have created." Do you agree with this? Explain your answer.

3. Relate one or more of the following statements to your life:
   - The distinctive manner in which we carry out life's activities, the way we do things—this can be a source of true uniqueness.
   - "It takes a long time to play like yourself." (Miles Davis)
   - Choose any other statement which evoked a reaction in you.

4. In what ways are you unique without doing anything but just existing? In what ways do you have to make a conscious choice and effort to develop your uniqueness?

Self-Actualizing and Beyond

Abraham Maslow

What does one do when he self-actualizes? Does he grit his teeth and squeeze? What does self-actualization mean in terms of actual behavior, actual procedure? I shall describe [nine] ways in which one self-actualizes.

First, self-actualization means experiencing fully, vividly, selflessly, with full concentration and total absorption. It means experiencing without the self-consciousness of the adolescent. At this moment of experiencing, the person is wholly and fully human. This is a self-actualizing moment. This is a moment when the self is actualizing itself. As individuals, we all experience such moments occasionally. As counselors, we can help clients to experience them more often. We can encourage them to become totally absorbed in something and to forget their poses and their defenses and their shyness—to go at it "whole-hog." From the outside, we can see that this can be a very sweet moment. In those youngsters who are trying to be very tough and cynical and sophisticated, we can see the recovery of some of the guilelessness of childhood; some of the innocence and sweetness of the face can come back as they devote themselves fully to a moment and throw themselves fully into the experiencing of it. The key word for this is "selflessly," and our youngsters suffer from too little selflessness and too much self-consciousness, self-awareness.

Second, let us think of life as a process of choices, one after another. At each point there is a progression choice and a regression choice. There may be a movement toward defense, toward safety, toward being afraid; but over on the other side, there is the growth choice. To make the growth choice instead of the fear choice a dozen times a day is to move a dozen times a day toward self-actualization. *Self-actualization is an ongoing process;* it means making each of the many single choices about whether to lie or be honest, whether to steal or not to steal at a particular point, and it means to make each of these choices as a growth choice. This is movement toward self-actualization.

Third, to talk of self-actualization implies that there is a self to be actualized. A human being is not a *tabula rasa*, not a lump of clay or Plasticine. He is something which is already there, at least a "cartilaginous" structure of some kind. A human being is, at minimum, his temperament, his biochemical balances, and so on. There is a self, and what I have sometimes referred to as "listening to the impulse voices" means letting the self emerge. Most of us, most of the time (and especially does this apply to children, young people), listen not to ourselves but to Mommy's introjected voice or Daddy's voice or to the voice of the Establishment, of the Elders, of authority, or of tradition.

As a simple first step toward self-actualization, I sometimes suggest to my students that when they are given a glass of wine and asked how they like it, they try a different way of responding. First, I suggest that they *not* look at the label on the bottle. Thus they will not use it to get any cue about whether or not they *should* like it. Next, I recommend that they close their eyes if possible and that they "make a hush." Now they are ready to look within themselves and try to shut out the noise of the world so that they may savor the wine on their tongues and look to the "Supreme Court" inside themselves. Then, and only then, they may come out and say, "I like it" or "I don't like it." A statement so arrived at is different from the usual kind of phoniness that we all indulge in.

At a party recently, I caught myself looking at the label on a bottle and assuring my hostess that she had indeed selected a very good Scotch. But then I stopped myself: What was I saying? I know little about Scotches. All I knew was what the advertisements said. I had no idea whether this one was good or not; yet this is the kind of thing we all do. Refusing to do it is part of the ongoing process of actualizing oneself. Does *your* belly hurt? Or does it feel good? Does this taste good on *your* tongue? Do *you* like lettuce?

Fourth, when in doubt, be honest rather than not. I am covered by that phrase "when in doubt," so that we need not argue too much about diplomacy. Frequently, when we are in doubt we are not honest. Clients are not honest much of the time. They are playing games and posing. They do not take easily to the suggestion to be honest. Looking within oneself for many of the answers implies taking responsibility. That is in itself a great step toward actualization. This matter of responsibility has been little studied. It doesn't turn up in our textbooks, for who can investigate responsibility in white rats? Yet it is an almost tangible part of psychotherapy. In psychotherapy, one can see it, can feel it, can know the moment of responsibility. Then there is a clear knowing of what it feels like. This is one of the great steps. Each time one takes responsibility, this is an actualizing of the self.

Fifth, we have talked so far of experiencing without self-awareness, of making the growth choice rather than the fear choice, of listening to the impulse voices, and of being honest and taking responsibility. All these are steps toward self-actualization, and all of them guarantee better life choices. A person who does each of these little things each time the choice point comes will find that they add up to better choices about what is constitutionally right for him. He comes to know what his destiny is, who his wife or husband will be, what his mission in life will be. One cannot choose wisely for a life unless he dares to listen to himself, *his own self*, at each moment in life, and to say calmly, "No, I don't like such and such."

The art world, in my opinion, has been captured by a small group of opinion- and taste-makers about whom I feel suspicious. That is an *ad hominem* judgment, but it seems fair enough for people who set themselves up as able to say, "You like what I like or else you are a fool." We must teach people to listen to their own tastes. Most people don't do it. When standing in a gallery before a puzzling painting, one rarely hears, "That is a puzzling painting." We had a dance program at Brandeis University not too long ago—a weird thing altogether, with electronic music, tapes, and people doing surrealistic and Dada things. When the lights went up everybody looked stunned, and nobody knew what to say. In that kind of situation most people will make some smart chatter instead of saying, "I would like to think about this." Making an honest statement involves daring to be different, unpopular, nonconformist. If clients, young or old, cannot be taught about being prepared to be unpopular, counselors might just as well give up right now. To be courageous rather than afraid is another version of the same thing.

Sixth, self-actualization is not only an end state but also the process of actualizing one's potentialities at any time, in any amount. It is, for example, a matter of becoming smarter by studying if one is an intelligent person. Self-actualization means using one's intelligence. It does not mean doing some far-out thing necessarily, but it may mean going through an arduous and demanding period of preparation in order to realize one's possibilities. Self-actualization can consist of finger exercises at a piano keyboard. Self-actualization means working to do well the thing that one wants to do. To become a second-rate physician is not a good path to self-actualization. One wants to be first-rate or as good as he can be.

Seventh, peak experiences (85, 89) are transient moments of self-actualization. They are moments of ecstasy which cannot be bought, cannot be guaranteed, cannot even be sought. One must be, as C. S. Lewis wrote, "surprised by joy." But one can set up the conditions so that peak experiences are more likely, or one can perversely set up the conditions so that they are less likely. Breaking up an illusion, getting rid of a false notion, learning what one is not good at, learning what one's potentialities are *not*—these are also part of discovering what one is in fact.

Practically everyone does have peak experiences, but not everyone knows it. Some people wave these small mystical experiences aside. Helping people to recognize these little moments of ecstasy (124) when they happen is one of the jobs of the counselor or metacounselor. Yet, how does one's psyche, with nothing external in the world to point at—there is no blackboard there—look into another person's secret psyche and then try to communicate? We have to work out a new way of communication. I have tried one. It is described in another appendix in that same book, *Religions, Values, and Peak-Experiences,* under the title "Rhapsodic Communications." I think that kind of communication may be more of a model for teaching, and counseling, for helping adults to become as fully developed as they can be, than the kind we are used to when we see teachers writing on the board. If I love Beethoven and I hear something in a quartet that you don't, how do I teach you to hear? The noises are there, obviously. But I hear something very, very beautiful, and you look blank. You hear the sounds. How do I get you to hear the beauty? That is more our problem in teaching than making you learn the ABC's or demonstrating arithmetic on the board or pointing to a dissection of a frog. These latter things are external to both people; one has a pointer, and both can look at the same time. This kind of teaching is easy; the other kind is much harder, but it is part of the counselor's job. It is metacounseling.

Eighth, finding out who one is, what he is, what he likes, what he doesn't like, what is good for him and what bad, where he is going and what his mission is—opening oneself up to himself—means the exposure of psychopathology. It means identifying defenses, and after defenses have been identified, it means finding the courage to give them up. This is painful because defenses are erected against something which is unpleasant. But giving up the defenses is worthwhile. If the psychoanalytic literature has taught us nothing else, it has taught us that repression is not a good way of solving problems.

Ninth,* in examining self-actualizing people directly, I find that in all cases, at least in our culture, they are dedicated people, devoted to some task "outside themselves," some vocation, or duty, or beloved job. Generally the devotion and dedication is so marked that one can fairly use the old words vocation, calling, or mission to describe their passionate, selfless, and profound feeling for their "work."

Put all these points together, and we see that self-actualization is not a matter of one great moment. It is not true that on Thursday at four o'clock the trumpet blows and one steps into the pantheon forever and altogether. Self-actualization is a matter of degree, or little accessions accumulated one by one. Too often our clients are inclined to wait for some kind of inspiration to strike so that they can say, "At 3:23 on this Thursday I became self-actualized!" People selected as self-actualizing subjects, people who fit the criteria, go about it in these little ways: They listen to their own voices; they take responsibility; they are honest; and they work hard. They find out who they are and what they are, not only in terms of their mission in life, but also in terms of the way their feet hurt when they wear such and such a pair of shoes and whether they do or do not like eggplant or stay up all night if they drink too much beer. All this is what the real self means. They find their own biological natures, their congenital natures, which are irreversible or difficult to change.

*Editor's Note: This last dimension appeared in a later work of Maslow's. It is included because Maslow emphasized this quality as an attribute of self-actualization.

Follow-Up

1. *Maslow poses nine dimensions of self-actualization. Describe how your life fulfills (or does not fulfill) four of these dimensions.*
2. *Which self-actualization dimension needs the most development in your life? Discuss how you could act on this improvement at this time.*
3. *Maslow states that self-actualizing persons are devoted to a call or work "larger than themselves." How does this statement apply to your life?*
4. *Select two statements from this article and offer your interpretations.*
5. *For further reading, see Maslow's* The Farther Reaches of Human Nature, *Esalen Books, 1971.*

Herbie

Tom Keating

If you have lived between 16th Street and Broad Ripple in the last 25 years you probably have seen him a dozen times and likely bought his goods.

He is a little old fellow, slightly stooped. He walks with a shuffle and always carries two shopping bags. And he always smiles.

His name is Herbert Wirth. Most people call him Herbie. He is 72 and has made his living since 1944 selling dishrags and wash cloths door to door.

He has never owned a car. He calculates he has walked more than 50,000 miles since he began his selling career at the age of 57 after losing his job at a dry goods company.

He works 9 a.m. to 6 p.m. six days a week and doesn't stop for lunch.

But, he doesn't just pick a street at random and start selling.

"Everything I do has been worked out systematically over the years through trial and error," he explained.

"I start at 46th Street and Winthrop Avenue and in one day will work up the east side of Winthrop to the canal in Broad Ripple. Then the next day I'll work the west side of Winthrop all the way to the canal again. After that I just keep moving over a street every day working from 46th to the canal until I reach Boulevard Place.

"After that I start again at 46th and Winthrop and this time work down to Fall Creek. Again I work one street at a time until I get to Pennsylvania Street. Every day I cover at least one whole side of a street, catching the side streets as I go along.

"It takes me about four months to complete the whole circuit. Then I start all over again. This way I get around to my customers three times a year.

"The reason I don't bother with lunch is because I found out that it takes me almost exactly nine hours to cover one street, and if I stop to eat it throws my schedule off. I do stop for a glass of water several times during the day. People are real nice about that."

Wirth starts each day with two large shopping bags filled to the brim with the six items he sells—dishrags, wash cloths, pot scrapers, large red handkerchiefs, two sizes of ladies hankies and black, brown and white shoelaces.

"I sometimes think the weight of the bags (25 pounds each at the start) acts as an incentive for me to sell.

"My feet never bother me. I guess once you get used to walking a lot, your feet get tough. It varies how much I sell each day. I usually average around 40 dishrags, 35 wash cloths and 25 pot scrapers. They all sell for a quarter."

"I use psychology in my work. There is a great art to selling. I try not to make a pest of myself. If people want my products, fine. If not, I thank them and be on my way. I don't try to play on people's sympathy. I don't want them to buy anything they can't use just because they feel sorry for me.

"I know many housewives are afraid of door-to-door salesmen, but by now most everyone knows me so I have somewhat of an advantage in this respect. I even have people who call me at home now to order articles.

"The Northside has changed a lot in the last 25 years, but the people have stayed about the same. Most are basically good. I get a door slammed in my face once in a while, but only once or twice a year.

"And regardless of what a lot of people say about youngsters, they are every bit as nice today as they were in the 1940s and 1950s.

"I get along with kids and dogs real well. I've always heard that postmen have trouble with dogs. I've never been able to figure that out. I guess some people just don't understand dogs."

Born in Lake Forest, Ill., Wirth moved here at the age of 13. He lives in a small house almost in the middle of his territory.

"When you get to be 72 you find yourself looking back and wondering what would have happened to your life if you had done this or that at a certain time. But, it's too late at my age to do anything but wonder. I guess that is the worst thing about growing old.

"I don't see any reason I can't keep working for many years. I feel great and I think I'd go out of my mind if I had to sit around and loaf every day.

"I've always taken life very seriously—probably too seriously. I've never had the time for many hobbies. In my free time about all I do is watch TV and read. I made the mistake of never getting married when I was young and now I don't have any close family. I live by myself and it's not too much fun.

"I know that selling dishrags is not the most important job in the world. I sometimes have envied men who are doing exciting and glamorous things.

"There won't be much of a dent in the world when I die, but at least I can say I made an honest to God try to do what I did as a nice man."

[One year later.] Despite the fact he was well known, he had no relatives so he lived alone for the last 20 years or so and worked at his job with few complaints and few fears.

But, he was afraid of one thing—that he wouldn't have anyone at his funeral.

He explained two years ago that he didn't mind living alone, except maybe at Christmas, but he didn't like the idea of dying without someone taking the time to say a few prayers

for him and remember that he had "tried to be a good man."

Saturday, Herbert Wirth died of a heart attack in a Northside supermarket. There was some concern for a while because no relatives could be found to handle the funeral arrangements.

But Herbie had known that this would be the case and on March 5, 1968, he had paid cash to the Flanner and Buchanan Mortuaries for a complete funeral and burial.

He requested that there be no service in the funeral home nor in a church. All he wanted was a graveside service.

And that some people be there.

Something kind of strange and warm and you might even say wonderful happened in Indianapolis yesterday.

More than 1,000 persons showed up for the funeral of a 73-year-old man who sold dishrags door to door.

Not a tycoon nor a big politician nor a sports idol—just a little old fellow who lived alone and peddled odds and ends on the Northside for 25 years and never did anything special except be himself.

His name was Herbie Wirth and he said a couple of years ago that he didn't want to be buried without someone there to say a prayer or two for him.

A newspaper story Tuesday mentioned this wish and everyone thought maybe 10 or 20 or even 30 people might show up for the graveside services at Crown Hill Cemetery.

But shortly before 10 a.m. a huge bell in the cemetery gate tower began ringing for the first time in more than 40 years and when the services started there were more people present than have attended a graveside funeral in this city in possibly 20 years, according to cemetery officials.

The people who were there were white and black, old and young, rich and poor.

They were soldiers in uniform, flower children with long flowing hair, businessmen in suits and overcoats, women carrying babies, truck drivers, elderly people who had to be helped up the icy hill to the grave, and teenagers cutting school.

Wives and husbands who hadn't told each other of their plans, met unexpectedly at the grave.

Many of these people said they didn't even know Herbie. Many others did. For whatever reason they came, not one stood to gain a thing, not even gratitude.

Coming to this funeral was not a casual stop. Many had to park their cars at least a mile from the grave and walk over hills in a snowstorm in 20-degree weather.

Why did so many come?

Well, you think it might have something to do with the almost universal fear of being alone, of having no one. You think it might also be because Herbie was well-liked and the simplicity of his life was what was being honored.

But when a thousand people stand in freezing weather to pay homage to a little man who was neither rich nor famous, you have to think above all that it is simply because a lot of people do care about others.

Someone brought a large guest book to the grave and most of the people present signed it before leaving.

Because Herbie had no relatives, the book was placed in the casket with him.

It was a very full book.

Follow-Up

1. *What are your feelings and thoughts about Herbie's story?*
2. *Tom Keating gave his conclusions on why so many people attended Herbie's funeral at the end of the article. Comment on his interpretations and possibly add your own if different from Keating's.*
3. *Did Herbie live a life in a healthy, responsible manner according to the concepts mentioned in the earlier articles by Goud, Arkoff, Peck, and the psychologists cited in the introduction?*

Getting Unstuck:
Joyfully Recreating Your Life

*Harold H. Bloomfield
and Robert B. Kory*

I feel trapped. I spend my days wiping runny noses, preparing meals that get cold before they get eaten, doing dishes, clipping supermarket coupons, cleaning house. No matter how hard Jim works, we always seem to be scrimping to get by. This isn't what I had in mind when I said "to have and to hold till death do us part." Some days I get the urge to pack up and leave. Other days I feel depressed, sort of sorry for myself. Most of the time I'm just bored.

These are the words of a young mother, married to a young aerospace engineer. They live in a quiet residential area, have a small house, two cars, and a future that promises them all the comforts of the suburban American lifestyle.

Jim and Barbara love each other, and their marriage has been stable. Neither raves about their sex life, but neither has sought extramarital sexual contact. Casually appraised, they are beneficiaries of the American dream, both college-educated, both products of middle-class families. Nevertheless, Barbara feels she is suffocating; Jim feels too pressured by his work to be of help. Both feel stuck . . . good and stuck.

The "I'm stuck" syndrome, an anhedonic* emotional trap if ever there was one, is reaching epidemic proportions. It's wide-

*Editor's Note: Anhedonic is a word derived from the Greek an- (not) and hedone (pleasure) and refers to the inability to experience pleasure. Anhedonic means inhibiting pleasure or interfering with pleasure. For more about anhedonia and anhedonic things, see their book Inner Joy *from which this reading was condensed.*

spread among young marrieds, but the same feelings of depression and resignation are showing up among adults at every stage of life. Perhaps you're feeling stuck in your job. If you're older, you may feel cornered by inflation or illness. Many a mother going back to work soon feels stifled by the limited opportunities. Having played out the singles scene, you may be pessimistic about your chances of finding a lasting relationship that will work. Or you may be twenty years into a bad marriage and unable to get out. The common denominator is the feeling of being caught by a situation beyond your control, it leaves you depressed about the present and resigned to the future.

If you've been bitten hard by the "I'm stuck" bug, you can marshal any number of reasons to justify your frustrations. You may get angry at the company that doesn't recognize your ability and give you the promotion you feel you deserve. You may complain about the government, which mishandles the economy and allows inflation and taxes to keep rising through the roof. If you're a woman, a black, a Chicano, or a member of any other group that has suffered discrimination, you can blame the system that denied you your opportunities. Spouses make excellent targets to blame for your distress.

The frustrations of the "I'm stuck" syndrome may be more or less legitimate: you are facing a very difficult and perhaps oppressive situation. But that insight doesn't accomplish very much other than to justify indulging in self-pity. The important questions are: Why do you let difficult situations make you feel powerless? What can you do to start molding your life to suit your desires?

PUTTING IT OFF

Some people get themselves stuck with what may seem to be the best of intentions. They don't want to make trouble for others, or don't want to risk losing what they have in order to create something better. Rather than take control of their lives and accept the risks of growth, they choose to put up with stifling jobs, lingering health problems, collapsing marriages, or destructive habits. It's an anhedonic trap. The longer they procrastinate, the more difficult change becomes, and the more desperate they are likely to feel.

John, a college student, complains, "I can count the number of dates I've had on one hand and not run out of fingers." He's obviously got a sense of humor, but he is afraid to be himself around women. "I'm shy," he says. "That's my nature." John recalls his mother telling people that he was "the shy one." He never realized that his mother had an emotional investment in keeping him tied to her apron strings. John spent his childhood and adolescence living up to the family label of "the shy one." No doubt he had a tendency to be shy as a little boy, but with their labeling, his parents helped him develop that tendency into a full-blown personality characteristic. The question is whether John is going to continue justifying his fears of women with the rationale: "Shyness is my nature." Whenever you resort to a label to explain a negative personality characteristic, you're only making excuses for avoiding the challenge of growth.

Gloria is twenty-six and overweight. She has tried every imaginable diet, managed on several occasions to lose over thirty pounds, but always put the weight back on. She says she wants to shed her excess poundage forever, but in the same breath she reveals why she has always been unsuccessful in

her attempts up to now. "I've always had a weight problem, ever since I was a little girl. I must have too many fat cells or a low metabolism or something." Gloria keeps herself stuck with the classic recall to her physiology. What she doesn't see is the hidden payoff. As long as she is fat she has a built-in excuse for feeling lonely and unattractive. Terrified by the prospect of rejection, she avoids it by rejecting herself, then hiding her self-rejection ("I've always been that way"). You may be tall, short, fat, thin, big-bosomed or small-breasted, bushy-headed or bald as a snowball. None of these physiological characteristics is justification for keeping yourself stuck and unhappy. They just aren't that important. Far more significant is your vitality, your friendliness, your self-confidence, your inner joy. These are the qualities you can choose to make outstanding in your life.

Vanessa at twenty-eight has been offered a major promotion at work. A vice-president has asked her to become his administrative assistant. The new job requires that Vanessa polish up on her basic math. Vanessa wants the job, but she is afraid to take it because she has always had difficulty with math. "I barely passed math in high school," she says. "Numbers make me nervous. I can't even balance my checkbook." For sixteen years Vanessa used this "I've always been" to avoid the extra effort required for her to become proficient in basic math. Now she has a choice. She can continue to use her "I've always been that way" as an excuse, or she can decide to focus whatever energy it takes for her to develop her math skills. The first choice is guaranteed to keep her stuck; the second opens broad new possibilities for success. Who knows why she has had difficulty with math in the past? It really doesn't matter, because she has the intelligence to acquire the skills the new job demands. All she needs now is the courage to challenge her "I've always been."

Tim is known for a short temper and frequent angry outbursts. His boss has told him that if he wants to make any kind of progress with the company he will have to learn to control his temper and develop his interpersonal skills. Tim's response has been consistent, "Sure, I have a short temper! I'm Irish." Ever since Tim got into fights on the school playground, his parents indulged his temper with this excuse. Now Tim sits at his desk in a sullen rage; his boss has told him that due to economic pressures on the company, Tim will be out of a job. His boss did not hide the fact that Tim, of all the junior executives, was dismissed because senior management found him hard to work with. This blow was finally enough for Tim to realize he had to make some changes. The alternative was to get stuck not only emotionally, but also economically. Having put all his excuses aside, Tim is now working on developing the emotional skills he needs to be a better manager.

SOME STEPS TOWARD SELF-DIRECTION

Once you have decided to take control, you *have* the power to create your own life according to your personal vision. You *can* establish your own values based on your own experience. To get unstuck, you need to seize this power to break free from your past and transform your intuitions into realities. The decision to take control of your life is a first step. Transforming that decision into action is the real test. Here are some suggestions that you may find useful:

Stop thinking of yourself as fragile.

Behind every anhedonic choice that keeps you stuck is the belief that you (or your life) will fall apart if you challenge the rules. This is a powerful myth! It can keep you absolutely paralyzed! The only way to rid yourself of it is to put your psychological strengths to the test. Few people realize how strong they really are until they stop putting up with the problems in their lives and take some steps toward change. It won't be easy. You may get knocked down a few times, but you won't fall apart. On the contrary, the more you assert your ability to take control over your life, the stronger you'll become. Developing psychological strengths is just like developing physical abilities. The more you exercise, the stronger you become.

Once and for all, you must eliminate the words wish, hope, and maybe from your vocabulary.

These are sedatives you administer to yourself to numb your sensitivity to your emotional realities. Like any narcotic, wishing and hoping weaken your power to take control of your life. In place of wishing and hoping, you have to substitute a new confidence in your willpower.

Substitute *"I will make it happen"* for "I hope things get better."

Substitute *"I am going to do x, y, z, so I'll feel better"* for "I wish things were better."

Substitute *"I will make my marriage work"* for "Maybe my marriage will still work out."

Start considering yourself too important to put up with anxiety about the obstacles in you life.

The best antidote for anxiety is action. Instead of bemoaning your problems or worrying about the long way to a major goal, take the first step. If your job is suffocating you, stop complaining and put together your résumé. Get any assistance you need to make certain it's the best résumé you can possibly write. If you're in a relationship that is faltering, gather up the courage to have a long talk about your future with your lover. Don't put it off until tomorrow. Do it today! Action, even one small step, breaks the illusion that makes personal problems seem insurmountable. You can only solve your problems one step at a time. Taking the first step has the amazing effect of reducing any problem to life size.

Choose one of your bigger dreams and start making it a reality.

One of my clients had always dreamed of exploring the Inca ruins in Peru. She had never been out of the United States and, as a secretary, didn't earn a large income. Nevertheless, this was the dream she chose. I suggested she contact travel agencies, museums, and local universities to explore all possibilities for her trip. The cost of a commercial tour was out of her reach, but she did discover that she could for a modest cost join an archaeological expedition from a local museum. She paid for some of her expenses and joined in the work as a volunteer. The result was the most rewarding vacation of her life. More: by actualizing just one of her dreams, she broke the cycle of defeatism that was keeping her stuck. Now at twenty-seven she is back at school to study archaeology. Fulfilling a dream is an exercise in discovering personal power. It can turn your life around.

Stop feeling you always have to have a plan.

Plans have their place, but planning involves only half of your brain, the verbal, analytic hemisphere. There is a huge silent dimension of your personality, the intuitive dimension, and you're probably not using it. Scientific research on creativity shows indisputably that the creative process depends just as much on the right brain functions (intuition) as on the left brain operations (analysis and language). If you insist on always having a plan, you cut yourself off from your intuitive self and the inner joy it provides. To break planning addiction, indulge in one freedom. Decide to spend a day exploring a park or a neighborhood with curiosity as your sole guide. Enroll in a local university and take a course that strikes your interest. You never know, it may lead you into a new occupation. The next time you feel attracted to someone you don't know, and want to introduce yourself, go ahead. You're likely to make a new friend. By giving yourself freedom to follow your hunches, even in small ways, you develop your sensitivity to your inner voice. You learn to hear the quiet messages that can make your life an adventure.

CREATE AN INTEGRATED SUCCESS PROFILE

Here are some techniques to help you reshape your success profile.

Begin by giving yourself full permission to succeed.

Most people are held back by the fear that they don't have what it takes. While they may pay lip service to believing in themselves, they turn right around and complain about all the obstacles that stand in the way: the boss, the company, too much work, too little work, too many "bad breaks." The fact is that many successful people do not have exceptional ability and many have limited education. They didn't score at the top in IQ tests, nor did they go to the best schools or get the best grades. Many come from humble backgrounds and have had bad breaks. The common denominator among all successful and happy people is desire, determination, and confidence. Your chance of success and fulfillment is just as good as anyone else's, and probably much better than you think. Only when you understand this key fact can you plunge ahead with enthusiasm and start functioning at your full potential.

Think of success as a process, not a final destination.

Highly successful people don't set out to achieve one grand goal and, on achieving it, pronounce themselves successful. They view their lives as an adventure and themselves as the heroic players. Perhaps this seems a little grandiose to you, but it's far better to think of yourself as a hero and play life to the fullest than to minimize your abilities and never give yourself a chance to exercise all your talents. You are the creator of your life; why not create it heroically? It doesn't matter how old you are or where you may be on the success ladder. You have the power to create a life that will exceed your highest expectations. All you have to do is learn how to use it.

Beware of any lingering fears of success.

It may surprise you to hear that many people block their success by fear, but the facts are there to be examined. Success implies change— in responsibility, life-style, relationships, and many other aspects of life—and for most people change is frightening. They're reluctant to surrender the safety of the routine and the familiar. Except in rare individuals, the instinct to resist change, do nothing, and accept the mediocre is measurably stronger than the desire to succeed.

People undermine their success in subtle ways. They choose wrong jobs, submit to employers who use them, behave in ways that undermine their chances of promotion, rely on weakness out of habit, and ignore strengths out of ignorance. To create a success profile of maximum opportunity you have to put an end to any lingering fears of success. You must be determined to discover your strengths and cultivate your talents; you must learn to relish your own growth.

Set attainable goals and learn to enjoy each small step of progress.

One of the most common ways people sabotage themselves is by trying to achieve too much too fast. There is a Wall Street saying that warns against this folly: "Bulls make money, bears make money, hogs never make money." While learning to take risks is important, foolish risks are nothing other than foolish.

Don't overschedule.

Most people have a tendency to assume they can accomplish more in a given period than they actually can. The problem arises from planning a project without allowing enough extra time for things to go wrong (as they always do). Deadlines are valuable, because most people are more efficient and creative when they accomplish a task within a given period. However, you would be wise in setting your deadlines to allow an extra 20 percent for things to go wrong. When deadlines are so short that they cause anxiety and a last-minute rush, you and your work suffer unnecessarily.

Insulate yourself as much as possible from interruption.

Nothing is more jarring to the nervous system than repeated interruptions when you're in the midst of concentrating on an important problem. One of the worst mistakes is to get into the habit of taking every phone call no matter what you're doing. A good way to handle the telephone is to concentrate your calls in one time segment, say between nine and ten in the morning or four and five in the afternoon. During that time you take all calls, and call people back who called you. You aren't being rude to refuse a call because you are busy. You are being wise. If you are a victim of the telephone, telephone screening can change your work life.

Consciously project ease and enjoyment.

For example, when you're at a meeting, sit back and relax. This is far more effective for listening than sitting on the edge of your chair. When you wish to speak, your movement forward will draw attention and quiet the group. Above all, don't hurry your speech. When you have something important to contribute, there is no rush! Your *words* are going to have an impact on your listeners. Take your time, be brief, and speak clearly. Intersperse pauses after key points. The value of silence is too often ignored. Be sure to enjoy yourself. That way you project maximum power and make others feel most comfortable. It's always a pleasure to listen to someone who is calm, speaks clearly, and projects a natural enthusiasm.

Become aware of your natural optimum work/play cycles.

Just as you have a unique personality, you have an optimum work cycle that is likely to be different than anyone else's. Some people do their best work in the morning, others have an intense burst of concentration toward the end of the day. There are also people who have concentration bursts for brief intervals throughout the day. We call these periods of maximum alertness "prime time." Once you understand your prime time, you can schedule your activities so that you'll tackle the important and challenging ones at your peak creative periods and relegate mundane activities to your low points. Substantial evidence indicates that your prime time and optimum work cycle are biologically or even genetically determined. Trying to force yourself into in unnatural pattern (such as doing your most difficult work in the morning when you concentrate best in the afternoon) is a big mistake. You will cause needless tension, your work will suffer, and you will cheat yourself out of the most important thing of all—enjoying what you're doing.

Identify the conditions that help you get into a "state of flow."

Almost everyone has had the experience of starting work on a project and getting so immersed that they completely forget time, fatigue, even where they are. Many hours later, when the task is complete, they become aware that they've been functioning at a unique, high level where creative energies pour out effortlessly. Psychologists call this a state of flow. This wonderful and productive state is not arbitrary. You can learn how to create it and then use it at will to accomplish a great deal of work in the shortest time. The key is learning what conditions trigger the inner shift from ordinary functioning to flow. For some people, quiet is necessary. Most people must be well rested. Time of day is almost always a key factor. Flow is much more likely during your prime time than during a low period. Perhaps you need to be working at a particular desk or computer for flow to happen. There could be any number of critical conditions. Once you have learned what they are, you have made a major discovery. Flow is one of the basic means of "doing less and accomplishing more." It is also a natural state of inner joy, even ecstasy.

Follow-Up

1. *Describe a "stuck" time in your life, indicating how you got stuck and how you got yourself unstuck (or are trying).*
2. *Review "Some Steps Toward Self-Direction." Choose one or more to apply to your life if you are stuck in your growth.*
3. *Select and apply one or more of the ideas mentioned in the section "Create An Integrated Success Profile."*

Advice to William Somebody

Poe Ballantine for Donna Brown

I can't count the number of times I have officially assembled the equipment to take my life: a knife, a handgun, a plastic bag, a bottle of codeine and a fifth of vodka. My motivations are never quite clear: perception of failure, futility, a sense of irremediable isolation, MTV—nothing everyone else hasn't suffered through. Yet I tend to magnify my gloomy outlook into a drive-in picture of the end of the world. I can't seem to remember that despair is a temporary state, a dark storm along the highway; that if I can just stick it out, keep the wipers going and my foot on the gas, I will make it through to the other side.

Once, while driving across the country writing suicide notes in my head for no good reason at all, I pulled off for gas in Las Vegas, New Mexico. I remember it exactly: a Phillips 66, pump number seven, $1.09 a gallon. When I went inside to pay, everyone in the store was speaking Spanish. I paid and asked the skinny Mexican kid behind the register where the coffee was. He pointed to the back. I used the restroom, then went over and got the coffee. I had decided to drive on through to Phoenix, approximately one million miles.

The store was big and new and sterile and hopeless, like the blossoming commercialism of everything. I set the large cup of coffee on the counter.

"Anything else?" asked the kid.

"Pack of Newport 100s."

He slid the cigarettes across, looking at me.

"How much?" I said.

"Two-fourteen," he said.

The price seemed too low. "For both?" I asked.

"Coffee's on me," he said.

I didn't ask him why. Maybe he was quitting after this shift. Maybe it was store policy: free coffee with every fill-up. Maybe he recognized my turmoil and understood the power of kindness from a stranger. Or maybe he represented the invisible divinity that runs through all humanity like an old FDR radio speech and appears only when you need it the most. Whatever the case, I drove on through to Phoenix without another thought of my demise.

Another time, in the other Las Vegas, where I couldn't get a job and was already five hundred in the hole and the air stank with shallow unfriendliness and mistrust, I was riding my bicycle down to the union office to see if they had found me a job. I had paid them two hundred dollars a month ago, and they still hadn't gotten me any work. (The union never did find me a job. I finally broke one of their picket lines—you know, I'm sorry, but I was five hundred in the hole and my rent was coming up.) That day, I was riding along in the hot June sun, secretly thinking about throwing myself in front of a truck, when I coasted by a garage across from Bob Stupak's Vegas World (a now defunct hotel and casino), and a black mechanic sitting on a tire in the dark, cool interior smiled at me and put up his thumb. I don't think he understood how important that single gesture was, what it meant to me.

I am ashamed to admit that I think so much about taking my life. I have no right. I am fit. I am independent. I am a member of a privileged society. A billion Third World people would give their left lung to be in my position. They would probably work hard and shut up for a minute and appreciate their lives. But I, like so many members of my generation, am overwhelmed by a certain modern black plague—call it depression, if you like.

I have known a dozen people who have taken their lives, all of them young, none of them, in my opinion, justified. I remember the girl in Number 1, who killed herself the day after I moved into a dilapidated, nearly empty apartment complex in Niagara Falls, New York. Though I'd spoken to her only once, I was horrified, struck hollow by the act. I met her father and brother that day on the stairs. They'd come to retrieve her belongings. They were haggard and gray with grief and reached out to me for some explanation, as if I could offer one. I grew angry with the girl and her thoughtless infliction of pain on the people who loved her. She had quit the game in the middle; like a spoiled child, she had thrown all her unopened Christmas packages out into the snow.

Or I'll be leafing through a newspaper in a laundromat and see that William Somebody has died of a self-inflicted gunshot wound at the age of thirty-eight, and I'll wonder, with a little rip in my stomach: Why couldn't he make it? Why couldn't he see the absolute permanence of his mistake? Why didn't he talk to someone? Why didn't he talk to *me*? I could've told him: Life is sacred. Suicide is wrong. You're going to die someday anyway; why speed the inevitable?

But when *my* unendurable dread descends, I don't remember my indignation at the selfishness of the girl in Number 1 or my cleareyed missionary advice to William Somebody. All I want is out.

The fact that I am still alive amazes me every morning. I wish I had a psychological formula, a rescue kit to hand out to my fellow melancholics. I wish I could say, *This is what saved me.* But each time it's something different: Kindness from a stranger. Lack of courage. Obligation to parents. Inability to write a good note. The possibility that I will have to start over again as a one-legged beggar in Tijuana or a housefly hatching out of a Dairy Queen swirl of yellow poodle droppings. Or I'll imag-

ine the appearance of my corpse, its state of decomposition by the time I am found, which always makes me think of the Jonestown mass suicides and how silly those people looked, all swollen in polyester heaps and black at the fingertips—the ultimate in bad fashion.

Recently, I took the worst trip of my life. It started out fairly well on a sunny, early-spring day in El Paso. I got on a Greyhound bus headed north. By the time I'd reached Colorado, I was consumed in the flames of a strep infection, my back was out, and snow was falling by the foot. I got stuck in South Dakota for three days. I began to miss all the appointments I had made with friends along the way. I ended up in New York City, not once, but twice in a period of twenty-four hours, both times against my will, the second time hobbling in a pointless, amoral fever around the labyrinth of the Port Authority Bus Terminal, talking to myself and smashing my fist into my face as hard as I could. I was trying to break teeth, draw blood, damage brains and vertebrae. People were staring at me, even the New Yorkers, who are accustomed to the insane. All the destinations looked the same to me. All the buses were the same. I stopped a woman with a clipboard whose job it was to rescue idiot travelers lost in the Port Authority.

"Can you tell me when the next bus leaves?" I said.

"Which bus?" she said.

"It doesn't matter," I said.

She seemed shocked, this woman who worked in the bowels of New York City, insane asylum of the world.

"How about LA?" I said.

She looked at her sheet. "Four o'clock," she said. "Three hours."

"What about Washington, D.C.?"

"Half an hour," she said, squinting at me, then glancing at her clipboard. "Gate 82. That's the Richmond bus."

I got on the Richmond bus, and all the way down to D.C., I plotted my demise as the snow flowed starlike across the glass. I wondered

CARRYING TO MANY BURDENS

what everyone would think when they heard the news. I wondered how my meager possessions would be distributed. I wondered who would care, who would laugh, who would secretly rejoice. I wondered if anyone would feel sorry for me, if anyone would miss me.

We were soon approaching D.C., and I had done nothing but daydream about my end. My neck was sore, my tooth was chipped, and my cheek was swollen to the eye.

God, please, just let me die.

Then three kids boarded the bus, ball caps on sideways. They swaggered down the aisle. Each wore a new snow white down jacket. I caught the dull nickel gleam of a gun handle in a waistband. Two of the kids dropped into

the seats directly behind me. They spoke loudly for everyone's benefit.

"What'chu lookin' at?"

"Lemme see that *gun*."

"You ain't afraid to *show* it.' "

"Lookit. I got a straight bead on the driver."

The woman next to me blanched and flattened against her seat. I felt my bladder float up into my chest cavity. Time stopped and draped itself like a braided pearl net across the aisle. One of the kids stood up. I saw the driver's eyes freeze in the mirror. I pictured the massacre photos in the next day's paper, my name misspelled, page four. Life was suddenly sweet. I prayed with a coward's softness. The snow flew past the windows.

Follow-Up

1. *Select two statements by Ballantine and offer your interpretations.*
2. *How do you respond when in a state of despair and gloom? What seems to (a) prolong and (b) get you out of this state? What have you found to be helpful for another person in a state of despair?*
3. *Ballantine writes about the power of kindness from a stranger. Describe a time when you were the recipient of such a kindness. A giver? How can you enhance this quality in your life?*
4. *For a related reading see "Left Behind" and the Applied Activity entitled "Depression Checklist" (in this section).*

Left Behind

Jenny Montgomery

On Sept. 13, more than 100 people gathered to pay respect to a man who had ended his own life just five days earlier. Warm embraces and comforting words were exchanged throughout the evening as people struggled to understand why Merle, 27, could not express his pain. His diminutive father sat solemnly in the same seat for hours, staring at the table as if he were looking for some meaning. No one knows exactly what he was feeling.

A good friend, during the informal memorial service, read Merle's explanatory note with great fortitude. Some were touched to hear that Merle looked forward to meeting his long-deceased mother in the afterlife, and that he had wanted to "go out on my own terms." But the most shocking news was that he had been considering suicide for awhile, yet he never asked for help.

He asked that his friends feel no responsibility for his decision, but, nevertheless, inner voices prompted many to ask themselves why they weren't more perceptive. Unfortunately, the only person who could have changed his ultimate decision was Merle.

Those who commit suicide never see the hollow eyes of the people they leave behind. They never hear the soft cries, humorous stories and cherished memories swirling like smoke through a room as loved ones huddle together for support.

They never see how people who shared only moments of their lives come to say goodbye, anyway.

These are the repercussions of suicide. And while it was obvious that each person was coping with the loss in a different way, those who knew Merle had lost a little part of themselves when he pulled the trigger. We wondered if he realized just how much he meant to so many people—maybe he just could not care.

As the evening grew long, old grudges were laid to rest, and estranged friends vowed to rekindle what they had lost. Many of us vowed to be better listeners and more supportive in our friendships. Most importantly, we swore that we would never cause anyone to feel what we were feeling then.

One of Merle's closest friends constructed a website, dedicated to his memory, complete with a guest book. One woman wrote, "Merle was truly a kind, funny man, and I can't stop thinking about how his life ended. Please, if anyone gets to this point, talk to your friends and find another way out."

Follow-Up

1. *What are your thoughts and feelings concerning this article?*

Vital Moments

Nelson Goud

Humans have the capacity to experience intense and vitalizing moments of joy, wonder, illumination, serenity, mastery, and ecstasy. These experiences can be collectively characterized as *vital moments*. Vital moments are instances of pure being when one feels completely and fully alive. In these moments a person becomes totally absorbed in the present and often feels connected to fundamental life sources and energies. Emerson (in Whelan, 1991) said that "there is a depth in those brief moments which constrain us to ascribe more reality to them than to all other experiences" (p. 64).

Vital moments serve many functions which include making life choices and decisions, providing therapeutic effects such as symptom removal, creativity, tolerance and acceptance, and philosophical shifts. Among their most basic value is to affirm the value of life. Maslow (1970), in his studies of peak experiences, stated that "they give meaning to life itself.... it proves to the experiencer that there are things or objects or experiences to yearn for which are worthwhile in themselves" (pp. 62–63). For more extensive reading in this area see Goud (1995).

Vital moments appear under several guises. Some of the most commonly experienced are described next.

PEAK EXPERIENCES

Here one may experience an immense infusion of joy and happiness or an immersion in great serenity. Often one believes that life can be viewed as it is, and has a sense that everything is connected. Some examples:

• "I always wondered how you know when you are truly in love. And then I found out it is something that can hardly be described with words. We had shared a wonderful weekend trip and I just wanted to hug the world on the drive home. I felt like I would explode with happiness and delight. I knew I loved him within weeks after meeting him but this was new. I wanted to share my life with him and the parts of me that I don't share with anyone. I wanted to run and laugh and yell and tell him I knew for sure that I was truly, madly and deeply in love with him. I wanted to tell everyone and I wanted to tell no one. I wanted to share this incredible feeling of completeness but I didn't want to share something so incredibly personal and real. I felt like I was in a whirlwind and I felt all of this while sitting quietly next to him during the car ride home. I still have fleeting moments of those feelings, although not as intensely as that particular day. I feel much more content and whole having experienced such joy and utter ecstasy from simply knowing another human being." (M. Laski)

• It was happening again. My mind was being invaded by a rushing torrent of insights, a volcanic explosion of truths. I had no choice but to just let it happen. I was caught in another "idea storm." Images, answers, questions, and insights were bombarding me with unusual ferocity and clarity. Puzzles that months of serious thinking couldn't unravel were solved for me. New associations were exploding all around. Glimpses of exciting new paths to explore were unveiled right before my eyes. It was like being in the midst of a forest where the trees had just shed rainbows of newly fallen leaves. Then suddenly a strong gust of wind would swoop in, encircling me with thousands of swirling leaves. To my wonderment each leaf had an idea on it. All I had to do was pluck one from mid-air and record its message. In a frenzy, I started to scribble a word or two from each leaf I grabbed. Each leaf lost in the wind was possibly an idea I wouldn't see again. I was missing as many as I caught. Ecstasy and frustration somehow coexisted in the same moment but there was no time to fully experience either one. Even though I only captured a small portion of this amazing shower of ideas, I have plenty to savor for months to come. I'm left with a nice blend of peaceful exhaustion, awe, and wonder. (N. Goud)

• "One day when I was four, I found myself standing at the beach, alone. The sea touched the sky. Breathing with the waves, I entered their rhythm. Suddenly there was a channeling of energy: the sun, the wind, the sea were going right through me. A door opened, and I became the sun, the wind, and the sea. There was no 'I' anymore. I had merged with everything else. . . . Sound, smell, taste, touch, shape—all melted into a brilliant light. The pulsating energy went right through me, and I was part of this energy." (E. Hoffman)

• "When I am at my best, as a group facilitator or as a therapist . . . when I am closest to my inner, intuitive, self . . . then whatever I do seems to be full of healing. Then, simply my presence is releasing and helpful. . . . It seems that my inner spirit has reached out and touched the inner spirit of the other. Our relationship transcends itself and becomes a part of something larger. Profound growth and healing and energy are present." (C. Rogers)

WONDER

Here one experiences complete awe and astonishment in the presence of some form of newness and mystery. Some examples:

• "Once it chanced that I stood in the abutment of a rainbow's arch, which filled the lower stratum of the atmosphere, tingeing the grass and leaves around, and dazzling me as I looked

through colored crystal. It was a lake of rainbow light, in which, for a short while, I lived like a dolphin." (H. Thoreau)

• When I was a second-grader, the teacher gave a homework assignment introducing the concept of zero. . . . Most of my classmates regarded this as simply another of the innumerable rules to be memorized. . . . But I sat alone in my room that night and stared with tears at the seemingly senseless problems. I wondered, 'How could I add something to a number and yet the number remain unchanged?' Suddenly, I understood— the immensity of the concept of nothingness overwhelmed me. I was awed that mathematicians were brilliant enough to capture this immensity in a little symbol . . . and decided to become a mathematician." (E. Hoffman)

• I first saw you in the newborn nursery. There was this large window and a couple rows of babies behind it—just like the movies. I was determined not to look like a goony father and to maintain my cool. A nurse came in and bent over this crib and picked up this tiny human organism and walked over the window and held you up to my face. You were a bit tired. Then you opened your eyes and we made a connection. There is nothing like it. An unseen current locked us in and I was so damn happy and proud that I pointed you out to everyone exclaiming all your virtues and potential greatness. Since the nurse was the only one there, I lost my cool status. But I was too absorbed and overwhelmed with your existence to even notice anything but you and me. (N. Goud)

PSYCHOLOGICAL EPIPHANY

This is a sudden revelation about one's identity or view of life. Some examples:

• "With dinner concluded, the waiter set the check down in the middle of the table. That's when it happened. My father did not reach for the check . . . my father did nothing. Finally, it dawned on me. Me! I was supposed to pick up the check. I whipped out my American Express Card. My view of myself was suddenly altered. With a stroke of a pen, I was suddenly an adult." (R. Cohen)

• "I was a workaholic, a crazy, crazy woman. I was on a plane four times a week. I just wanted to get to the top. One morning at home I opened the bathroom cabinet and counted 150 shampoo bottles brought back from these trips. All of a sudden, I realized that I was reaching that goal but wasn't happy. A year would go by and I wouldn't know what had happened. I left that work and eventually bought a small, neighborhood grocery store and am liking life again." (J. Castro)

FLOW

This is an extended state of pleasure gained through mastery. It is a time when one is fully functioning in an activity (for further reading see Csikszentmihalyi, 1990, 1997). Some examples:

• "You get it rolling, and all of a sudden, you just start clicking, and the basket seems to be as big as the ocean. It seems like the whole game, everything, is in slow motion, but you're going regular speed. . . . You can't force it. You have to let it flow, let it ride." (Bill Walton, after making 21 of 22 shots in a UCLA game.)

• "I used to fight and argue about practicing the piano. Then one day I was by myself and it came out just right, more than perfect. It was as though I hadn't played it but something in the world had played that piano just right . . . it was a mystery. After that, I played the piano my same old way, but I didn't argue about it anymore. I just wondered if it would ever happen again." (I. Progoff)

• "The only way I can describe what happens is that when I have a clear and powerful insight, and I am writing with attention to I, the words fairly dance on the page before me. I say things I am not conscious of ever having thought before, in ways that surprise me." (A. Greeley)

APPLICATIONS

There are ways to arrange a life to invite or inhibit vital moments from occurring. Contacting triggers is the main path for experiencing vital moments. *Triggers* are the stimuli which produce moments (e.g., nature, the arts, love, sex, mastery, contemplation, beauty, special places). Triggers alone are not sufficient, though. *How* one experiences a trigger is just as significant. Encountering loud and distracting behaviors while walking through a forest grove would be an example of an anti-trigger. Other anti-triggers include: treating everything as a means and not as an end in itself; an overscheduled and excessively busy life; anything that inhibits full absorption and being-in-the-moment.

Many find it difficult to express the feelings and meaning of vital moments. Unless you have the skill and a willing receiver, it may be best *not* to communicate a vital moment. An inadequate expression tends to diminish or lessen the experience. For some, journaling or other creative modes may be helpful. We may find, like Thoreau, that "the facts most astounding and most real are never communicated."

Vital moments are times when we experience life's ultimates—what we live for. They can also show us our true paths, paths which have the most likelihood of meaning and even bliss. One way to test this conclusion is to construct your own history of vital moments. What is it that has and still provides wonder, flow, or peak experiences? What have been your life-changing epiphanies? Constructing such a history is therapeutic in itself—you may even re-experience parts of these moments while recalling them.

• "Outside he stood for a while on the sidewalk, just breathing deeply and feeling the pleasure of being alive. . . . A sharp breeze tingled his flesh and made his eyes get a little watery, and when he blinked and opened them, it seemed for a moment as if everything was bathed in a soft gold light. . . . It was just for a moment but it gave Sonny a sudden sense of joy that seemed to spread through his whole being. He had known these moments before, in different times and places, and they had seemed so intense and so real that everything else was like sleep. Such moments made you feel completely alive, reminded you of being alive, and Sonny wondered if perhaps that's what 'real life' was after all—those moments." (D. Wakefield)

References

Castro, J. (1993). The Simple Life. In A. Arkoff (Ed.), *Psychology and personal growth* (4th ed.). Boston: Allyn & Bacon.

Cohen, R. (1998). Suddenly I'm the Adult? In *Psychology and personal growth* (5th ed.). Boston: Allyn & Bacon.

Csikszentmihalyi, M. (1990). *The psychology of optimal experience.* New York: Harper & Row.

Csikszentmihalyi, M. (1997). *Finding flow.* New York: Basic Books.

Goud, N. (1995). Vital moments. *J. of Humanistic Education and Development, 34,* 25–33.

Greeley, A. (1974). *Ecstasy: A way of knowing.* Englewood Cliffs, NJ: Prentice-Hall.

Hoffman, E. (1992). *Visions of innocence: Spiritual and inspirations experiences of childhood.* Boston: Shambhala.

Laski, M. (1961). *Ecstasy in secular and religious experiences.* Los Angeles: Jeremy P. Tarcher.

Maslow, A. (1970). *Religions, values, and peak-experiences.* New York: Viking Compass.

Progoff, I. (1992). *At a journal workshop.* New York: Jeremy P. Tarcher/Perigee Books.

Rogers, C. (1980). *A way of being.* Boston: Houghton Mifflin.

Thoreau, H. (1854/1962). In *Thoreau: Walden and other writings.* J. Krutch (Ed.), New York: Bantam Books.

Wakefield, D. (1970). *Going all the way.* Bloomington, IN: Indiana University Press.

Whelan, R. (1991). *Self-reliance: The wisdom of Ralph Waldo Emerson.* New York: Bell Tower.

Follow-Up

1. *Describe two "vital moments" from your life and their effects.*
2. *Attempt a Vital Moment History as described at the end of the article. Discuss your learnings.*
3. *Goud says that contacting a **trigger** is the main path for experiencing vital moments. What are some of your triggers which often lead to vital moments? Are you experiencing these triggers on a consistent basis? Discuss your answers.*
4. *Provide and discuss examples of anti-triggers as described in the article.*
5. *For a related reading see "Little Joys" by Abe Arkoff in the Emotions and Feelings Section.*

Courage

Rollo May

[*Editor's Note:* In his book *The Courage To Create,* Rollo May expresses his belief that we are between eras and that this involves radical changes in how we choose to live. We can respond with apathy, paralysis, or as May hopes, with courage. May discusses four kinds of courage.]

1. *Physical courage.* This is different from the kind of physical courage which stresses power over people. May proposes a new form which develops the "capacity to listen with the body . . . a learning to think with the body. It will be a valuing of the body as the means of empathy with others, as expression of the self as a thing of beauty and as a rich source of pleasure. . . . I propose the use of the body not for the development of musclemen, but for the development of sensitivity" (p. 6).

[*Editor's note*—Physical courage also refers to times when one purposely, but not foolishly, places oneself in situations where the body is potentially at risk.]

2. *Moral courage.* "Moral courage has its source in identification through one's own sensitivity with the suffering of one's fellow human beings . . . it depends on one's capacity to *perceive,* to let one's self see the suffering of other people. If we let ourselves experience the evil, we will be forced to do something about it. . . . The most prevalent form of cowardice in our day hides behind the statement 'I did not want to become involved'" (pp. 8–9).

[*Editor's note*—Although not explicitly stated by May, moral courage may also include acting on principle, or taking a stand on what you believe is right in the face of opposition.]

3. *Social courage.* "The courage to relate to other human beings, the capacity to risk one's self in the hope of achieving meaningful intimacy . . . to invest one's self over a period of time in a relationship that will demand an increasing openness. . . . Intimacy requires courage because risk is inescapable" (p. 9).

    The primary risks in entering or not enterimg an intimate relationship, according to May, are (a) we will change in some way, (b) facing the fear that one may lose a sense of individuality, and (c) facing the fear of being abandoned.

4. *Creative courage.* This is the courage to introduce new forms, symbols, or patterns within a society. Among these are original ideas which

emanate from your deepest centers. Not having creative courage, May contends, results in a betrayal of yourself and your community. In addition, "By the creative act, we are able to reach beyond our own death. . . . Creativity is a yearning for immortality . . . " (pp. 19, 27).

May discusses the paradox of courage: "We must be fully committed, but we must also be aware at the same time that we might possibly be wrong" (pp. 12–13). He contends that those who are convinced that their way is the only right way leads to dogmatism and fanaticism. Doubt is required to be open to new truths. "Commitment is healthiest," says May, "when it is not without doubt, but in spite of doubt" (p. 14).

May concludes that "in human beings courage is necessary to make being and becoming possible. An assertion of the self, a commitment, is essential if the self is to have any reality . . . a man or woman becomes fully human only by his or her choices and his or her commitment to them. People attain worth and dignity by the multitude of decisions they make from day to day. These decisions require courage" (pp. 4–5).

Follow-Up

1. *Describe an instance in your life when you demonstrated one or more kinds of courage as stated by Rollo May.*
2. *Describe a current situation in your life which is demanding one or more kinds of courage. Explain how you are behaving in this situation.*
3. *Describe at least one person who has consistently demonstrated one of the kinds of courage May outlines. How has this person influenced you?*
4. *Discuss or write a reaction to one or more statements from this article.*

The Lesson of the Cliff

Morton Hunt

It was a sweltering July day in Philadelphia—I can feel it still, 56 years later. The five boys I was with had grown tired of playing marbles and burning holes in dry leaves with a lens and were casting about for something else.

"Hey!" said freckle-faced little Ned. "I got an idea. We haven't climbed the cliff for a long while."

"Let's go!" said someone else. And off they went, trotting and panting like a pack of stray dogs.

I hesitated. I longed to be brave and active, like them, but I'd been a sickly child most of my eight years and had taken to heart my mother's admonitions to remember that I wasn't as strong as other boys and not to take chances.

"Come on!" called Jerry, my best friend. "Just because you've been sick is no reason to be a sissy." "I'm *coming!*" I yelled, and ran along after them.

Through the park and into the woods we went, finally emerging in a clearing. At the far side, 40 to 50 feet away, loomed the cliff, a bristling, near-vertical wall of jutting rocks, earth slides, scraggly bushes and ailanthus saplings. From the tumbled rocks at its base to the fringe of sod at its top, it was only about 60 feet high, but to me it looked like the very embodiment of the Forbidden and Impossible.

One by one, the other boys scrabbled upward, finding handholds and toeholds on rocky outcrops and earthen ledges. I hung back until the others were partway up; then, trembling and sweating, I began to climb. A hand here, a foot there, my heart thumping in my skinny chest, I made my way up and up.

At some point, I looked back—and was horrified. The ground at the base of the cliff seemed very far below; one slip and I would fall, bouncing off the cliff face and ending on the rocks. There, shattered and strangling on my own blood, I would gurgle, twitch a few times, and then expire, like the cat I had seen run over a few days earlier.

But the boys were chattering above me on an earthen ledge two-thirds of the way to the top. It was 5 to 6 feet deep and some 15 feet long. I clawed my way up to them; then I crawled as far back on the ledge as I could, huddling against the rock face. The other boys stood close to the edge and boldly urinated into space; the sight made me so queasy that I surreptitiously clutched at the rocks behind me.

In a few minutes, they started up to the top.

"Hey, wait," I croaked.

"So long! See you in the funny papers," one of them said, and the others laughed.

"But I can't . . . I . . . " That spurred them on: jeering and catcalling back to me, they wriggled their way to the top, from where they would walk home by a roundabout route. Before they left, they peered down at me.

"You can stay if you want to," mocked Ned. "It's all yours." Jerry looked concerned, but he went with the others.

I looked down and was overcome by dizziness; a nameless force seemed to be impelling me to fall off. I lay clinging to a rock as the world spun around. I could never climb back down. It was much too far to go, too hazardous; partway, I would grow feeble or faint, lose my grip, fall and die. But the way up to the top was even worse—higher, steeper, more treacherous; I would never make it. I heard someone sobbing and moaning; I wondered who it was and realized that it was I.

Time passed. The shadows gradually lengthened, the sun disappeared from the treetops beyond the clearing below, dusk began to gather. Silent now, I lay on my stomach as if in a trance, stupefied by fear and fatigue, unable to move or even to think of how to get back down to safety and home.

January 1945, Watton Air Base, East Anglia. This morning I found my name posted on the blackboard: Tomorrow I fly another weather reconnaissance mission over enemy territory. All day my mind was whirling; at dinner I felt as if I might throw up at any moment.

I knew that I needed a good night's sleep, so I took a pill and went to bed early, but I could not make myself stop imagining the endless flight in which I, as pilot, and my navigator would venture in our unarmed twin-engine Mosquito far into German-held territory.

Hour after hour I thrashed around in bed; from time to time I would drift off, only to wake with a dreadful start, gasping for breath, my heart flopping like a beached fish as I imagined the shellburst in the cockpit, the blood and the sickening white-hot pain, the fire, smoke and spurting oil, the Mozzie winging over into a spin while I, shattered and half-conscious, am too weak either to fight the controls or pull myself up and out the escape hatch as the plane screams down and down.

Next morning, in the locker room, as I get into my flight outfit, it is clear to me that I simply can't do it. The mission is a 1000-mile trip, three hours of it over German-held territory and Germany itself—too deep in to go unnoticed. I can't possibly strap myself into that defenseless little plane and, with my own hands and feet, make it climb 5 miles high,

guide it out over the winter sea and into a Europe bristling with Nazi anti-aircraft batteries, radar stations and fighter planes, and finally make it back to safety.

Even as I zip up my boots and pull on my helmet, I know I can't. I will get in the plane, warm up and check out the engines, but at the runway my hands will freeze on the controls, and I will be unable to make the plane move.

January 1957, New York. I'm delirious with joy.

I've always felt that if I didn't write a book by the time I was 40, I'd never do so. With only three years to go, I've been offered a book contract—by the most distinguished of American publishers. Alfred Knopf himself, after reading an article of mine, had written to invite me to submit a proposal. After months of hard work, I had turned in an outline and sample chapter. Now Knopf and his editors have said yes.

But, later in the day, I begin to fear that I have made a terrible mistake. I've suggested a history of love, tracing its evolution from the time of the early Greeks to the present—a vast project, but fun to think about and to sketch in outline form. Yet now that the moment of truth has come, I see how rash I've been. Having spent months researching and writing the sample chapter, I can look ahead—and what I see is frightening.

How could I have imagined I'd ever be able to learn what love meant to the ancient Greeks, to the imperial Romans, to the ascetic early Christians, to the knights and ladies of the Middle Ages, to—? Enough! It's hopeless, impossible, more than any one person can do.

Or, at least, more than I can do. Even if I found everything I needed in the library and took reams of notes, how could I ever make sense of it all? Or organize it? Or write about it entertainingly, sentence after sentence, page after page, chapter after chapter? Only now,

"Coming to a Roadblock" by tom mcCain. Copyright © 1996.

when a contract is being offered me, can I see clearly what I will have to do—and realize that I cannot.

June 1963, New York. I am lying in bed, sleepless, although it is 2 a.m.; I suspect that she, quiet in the dark next to me, is awake too. Tonight we agreed that it was useless to go on and that I should move out as soon as I can.

But I feel as if the ground is giving way beneath me, as if I am falling through space. How can we ever decide how to divide our possessions and our savings? How will we work out my rights as an absentee father? Will I

be able to find a place for myself and, without help, make it homelike? I have never lived alone, how will I feel when I close the door at night and am imprisoned in my solitude?

What will I tell my family, and how will they take it? Will my married friends shun me? What can I say to my 8-year-old son, and what will happen to his feelings about me? Where will I meet single friends? Whom will I talk to, eat with, share my life with? I haven't the least idea how to start; I haven't been single since my 20s.

Yet what if, somehow, after a while, I were to meet the right woman and feel desire stirring in me? But here my mind goes blank. I haven't been to bed with another woman in over 17 years; how should I behave, what should I do? What if my hesitant actions are scorned? What if I seem clumsy, gross, nervous, foolish?

And even if all goes well, how will I know whether what I feel is love or only lust? Can I trust myself to love again—or trust anyone else to love me? Will anyone, could anyone, ever do so? Will I ever want to marry again? There is so much to be said, learned, worked out first; so many hints, allusions, promises, bargains, plans; so many beliefs and tastes to be exchanged and harmonized—no, it is too hard a road to travel, too remote a goal. I can't do it.

Twilight, a first star in the sky, the ground below the cliff growing dim. But now in the woods the beam of a flashlight dances about and I hear the voices of Jerry and my father. My father! But what can he do? Middle-aged and portly, he cannot climb up here. Even if he could, what good would that do?

Staying well back from the foot of the cliff so that he can see me, he points the beam up and calls to me. "Come on down, now," he says in a perfectly normal, comforting tone. "Dinner's ready."

"I can't!" I wail. "I'll fall, I'll die!"

"You got up," he says. "You can get down the same way. I'll light the way."

"No, I can't!" I howl. "It's too far, it's too hard, I can't do it."

"Listen to me," my father says. "Don't think about how far it is, how hard it is. All you have to think about is taking one little step. You can do that. Look where I'm shining the light. Do you see that rock?" The beam bounces around on a jutting outcrop just below the ledge. "See it?" he calls up.

I inch over. "Yes," I say.

"Good," he says. "Now just turn around so you can put your left foot on that rock. That's all you have to do. It's just a little way below you. You can do that. Don't worry about what comes next, and don't look down any farther than that first step. Trust me."

It seems possible. I inch backward, gingerly feel for the rock with my left foot and find it. "That's good," my father calls. "Now, a little bit to the right and a few inches lower, there's another foothold. Move your right foot down there very slowly—that's all you have to do. Just think about that next step, nothing else." I do so. "Good," he says. "Now let go of whatever you're holding onto with your left hand and reach back and grab that skinny tree just at the edge, where my light is. That's all you have to do." Again, I do so.

That's how it goes. One step at a time, one handhold at a time, he talks me down the cliff, stressing that I have only to make one simple move each time, never letting me stop to think of the long way down, always telling me that the next thing I have to do is something I *can* do.

Suddenly I take the last step down onto the tumbled rocks at the bottom and into my father's strong arms, sobbing a little, and then, surprisingly, feeling a sense of immense accomplishment and something like pride.

January 1945. I taxi out onto the runway and firmly shove the throttles forward. I remember at last that I *know* how to do what I must. All I have to do is take off and climb to 25,000 feet, heading eastward over East Anglia; that's all I need think about right now. I can do that.

Later: The North Sea is just ahead. All I have to do, I tell myself, is stay on this heading for about 20 minutes, until we have crossed over Schouwen Island in the Netherlands. That's all; I can do it.

Over Schouwen Island, my navigator tells me to turn to a heading of 125 degrees and hold it for 10 minutes, until we reach our next checkpoint. Good; that's not so hard; I can do that.

That's how it goes. I drive the roaring little plane across Holland and Germany, high over fields and woods, cities, rivers and mountain ranges, never envisioning the whole trip but only the leg we are flying, never thinking of the hours ahead but concentrating on getting through each brief segment of time, each measured span of miles, until at last sunlight dazzles off the wrinkled sea ahead of us and in a few minutes we are out of enemy territory, safe and still alive.

January 1957. After tossing about much of the night, thinking about the impossibly ambitious book I had said I could write, I remember the old lesson once again: Though I know what the goal is, I can avoid panic and vertigo if I look only at the next step.

I'll keep my gaze on the first chapter. All I have to do is read whatever I can find in the library about love among the Greeks; that isn't impossibly hard. Then I'll tell myself that all I have to do is sort out my notes, dividing the chapter into a number of sections; I can do that. Then I'll make myself look no further ahead than writing the first section. And with that thought, I heave a great sigh and fall asleep.

And that's the way I spend more than two and a half years. Then, one exhilarating afternoon, the last of 653 pages emerges from my typewriter and, like a boy, I turn somersaults on the living room floor in sheer joy. Some months later, I hold in my hands the first copy of my book, *The Natural History of Love*—already chosen by the Book of the Month Club—and a few weeks after that I read my first major review, praising the book, in the *New York Times Book Review*. For a while, I occasionally leaf through the book, marveling that I could ever have done all this—and knowing that I learned how, long ago, in the dusk on the face of a small cliff.

September 1963. I unlock the door of my tiny apartment, carry my bags in and close the door behind me. I have taken one step; it wasn't so hard. I had remembered the lesson that I have applied again and again throughout my life; one step at a time, one step that I can manage.

The first was to find an apartment; I looked no further into the future until I had done that. Then I went about furnishing my two rooms, I looked no further ahead until that was done. Today, I am moving in; I have made my own little nest, and it looks pleasant. I unpack, make a few phone calls, fix lunch, feel at home. Good; I've taken that step.

By the next year, I have constructed a new life, gotten my final divorce decree, acquired the social and emotional skills that I need as a middle-aged single man (I would remain one for five years), and even have become a passable bachelor cook. And discovered once more, to my surprise, that I do know how to make my way toward a distant, difficult goal.

I have realized with the same surprise, time and again throughout my life, that, having looked at a far and frightening prospect and been dismayed, I can cope with it after all by remembering the simple lesson I learned so long ago. I remind myself to look not at the rocks far below but at the first small and relatively easy step and, having taken it, to take the next one, feeling a sense of accomplishment with each move, until I have done what I wanted to do, gotten where I wanted to be, and can look back, amazed and proud of the distance I have come.

Follow-Up

1. *Describe a problem that overwhelmed you, but which you might have dealt with successfully by working on it one step at a time.*
2. *Describe a problem that you dealt with successfully by working on it one step at a time.*
3. *Describe a formidable problem or task that you now face in your life. What is the first step that you might take toward its mastery?*

Small Terrors, Secret Heroics

Amy Gross

People think adventure is to be found outside the usual course of life. They set aside vacations for the pursuit of danger, they travel to it, buy equipment for it, and after their wrestle with the elements, or the rapids, or the mountain side, they return to hohum life. And they regard as heroes those who have made danger their way of life. It's not hard to understand the call of that sort of heroism, the seduction of the big dare. Entering that space between life and death, you taste perfect freedom.

People theorize that modern life is so tame, the opportunities for raw bravery and aggression so rare, that only through vigorous sports and dangerous play can we detonate our pent-up energies and remember our animalhood. That physical putting-to-the-test is the great escape from the predominantly mental lives we live. For many, work is an abstraction and its reward, money, is another abstraction, an essentially arbitrary gauge of achievement except for a gambler whose work is collecting money. The bodily tests of one's powers—win or lose, survive or not—is nothing if not concrete.

But it seems to me that these sports, these physical challenges are really only exercises. When you think of the adventures, the terrors, the possible leaps, the opportunities in everyday life to choose between heroism and cowardice, you know that you don't have to travel to danger. In fact, the stakes are higher at home. It is easier to risk death scaling a mountain than to risk being old and alone, or unloved and unneeded, or being thought stupid or insane. It is easier to die than to live as a failure. And so, every day, there are risks we refuse, possible terrors we avoid. We do what

other people expect from us, so they'll love and want us; we perform according to the rules of success and sanity; we remain silent when we should speak up and speak though we have nothing to say; and our lives stay small. We don't recognize as adventures the challenges that come to us, and we shrink from designing our own. Only in a somewhat extraneous experiment like riding the rapids or skydiving do we dash out of the tameness enforced on us by our own fears. I'm not saying that someone who lives courageously every day wouldn't want or need to spend a week in the wilderness; only that attention should be paid to the opportunities for wildness at home.

These more subtle heroics are seemingly small acts. The fact that they require enormous courage is usually known only to the protagonist. For one man, speaking in public is so terrifying he gratefully allows others in his work-group to talk for him. It would be a very small act if he were once to present his own work, a very private victory. For him, afraid of appearing afraid, certain he was about to make a fool of himself, the experience would be a free-fall. He would be risking everything. In anyone else's eyes, he would only have stopped being silly. These small acts have to do, often, with overcoming the terrors other people tell you are silly. The reason to overcome is not to please these other people. The reason is the one offered by the man who climbs the mountain—because it's there. The at-home fears block one's way more resolutely than any mountain.

For many people, silly as it sounds, going to a party is a small act of courage. Initiating a conversation with that stranger across the room, for some people, can be an act no less noble than facing a bull in a ring. I'm not being facetious here. I've stood at a party a step away from an author whose work awes me, mentally testing and rejecting opening lines, choking when one or another began to rise out of my throat. Getting back on a horse after you've been thrown is simple (and practical—how else are you going to get back to the stables?). To venture a conversation with a superior stranger is to risk everything—being seen as an ant. Your specialness is at stake. Will the superior being recognize your own superiority? Will you come off as just another face? Are you just another face? Dragons test only your strength. Strangers test your wit, or your face, or whatever it is you rely on to barter your way through the open market. If I ever approach that author and survive, I'll feel as though I'd vanquished dragons.

Daring to make a soufflé, to argue a grade, to tell the truth, to say yes or to say no, to admit "I want," or "I deserve," these can all be moments of heroism, invisible leaps that free you, if only from the fear of accepting the dare. I read that someone is going to motorcycle-jump a string of 17 trucks, a large and remarkably useless act. A woman who has been painting for years, who one day picks herself up and brings her work to a gallery, is leaping further than that. Risking being told she's no good, risking her hope that she is saying something unique with her paints, that *she* is unique—that's a very great risk. If she avoids the gallery judge's criticism, she can continue to cherish what are possibly fantasies of talent and success. To bring in her work is to subject her fantasies to the test of reality. There are all kinds of ways to deal with the rejection that might be her reward. Would she have the wisdom to apply those ways? Should she protect herself from such a challenge to her wisdom? Sure. Why not? It's not noticeable cowardice to play life safe, it's the way we all play it, one way or another. But to risk, to leap,

to throw one's fantasies into the ring is to pursue danger. Mighty exciting. The truth, we've been told, will set us free, one way or another.

There's a woman I know, a social worker who has to commute an hour and a half every day to the hospital where she's on staff. She hears about a job opening at a better hospital, only ten minutes from home; the job is bigger than hers and so is the salary. This is terribly upsetting news. She asks everyone what she should do, apply or not. Of course, everyone tells her to apply. But, she argues, what if she got the job and then couldn't do the work? A challenge like hers, when unmet, is obsessing. She talks and talks about applying. Finally, the decision is made for her—she hears the job is taken.

When people asked her, "What do you have to lose?" she thought they didn't understand what was at stake. Her definition of herself, her "ego" as she put it. She has a bank of negative judgments and if she were to apply and not get the job, or get the job and then be fired, all those judgments would be confirmed. Once and for all she would know herself—and the world would know her—to be a failure. The underlying premise is that her success to date is due to luck and the gullibility of her supervisors. By not applying for the bigger job, she protects herself from the confirmation of that premise, and retains the right to think she might have been able to do the job. It's a common bargain, but a bad one. Not risking defeat is always defeat. The fact is, she did have nothing to lose—by not applying she's already lost. Once a dare, the opportunity to leap presents itself, you can't escape a sense of failure until or unless you abandon yourself to the leap. And the defeat following a risk taken must be, at the least, a peaceful one. The defeat of not even trying is acidified by the anger of impotence.

Another woman has been living with a man for several months. The basis of her attachment is in its alternative—being alone, having to look for a new man. Now, nothing is ever so clear-cut that rationalization is impossible. She argues that she has some feeling for the man, she has not met anyone better, the man is easy, undemanding. In her mind, leaving him would be like cutting herself off from an anchor. She would be adrift. She doesn't see how she could take care of herself, what would happen to her . . . she might be alone forever. Her fear is the expectation of total catastrophe. Ignoring all the laws of probability, she is positing only one alternative and that one is unacceptable.

For her to break out would be a feat more astonishing, if less flamboyant, than any escape performed by a Houdini. She would be setting off on an adventure comparable to Robinson Crusoe's, as true a test of individual resources as his. No ferreting for berries, but could she nourish herself?

Her refusal to try—to leap into the fear—is not blatant cowardice. Her dread of aloneness is ubiquitous and natural. How many of us ever leave a bad setup without the towrope of The Other Man or The Other Woman? I never have. If she were to let go of her man—cleanly and crisply—it would be an ostensibly small act. In my eyes, at least, it would be heroic.

I remember a friend of mine telling a man who had just swallowed his first tab of LSD (remember LSD?), "If you see anything frightening, walk towards it." Afterwards, the man described what happened when he hallucinated grotesque faces. At first, he had shuddered and pulled back, and the faces continued to menace. Then he tried staring them down, moving towards them. The faces turned into fantastic Thai dancers, costumed in spangles, and apparently arranged just for his delight. It meant something to the man that he could defend himself against his own monsters. You could shrug off his adventure by saying that his fears were only hallucinations, but so are most fears hallucinations.

Staring down monsters is the essence of adventure, and the monster is never the mountain or the bull or the string of 17 trucks or the stranger. The monster is always your own self-doubts. And whether you're daring to explore a dark cave or daring to dial a certain telephone number, the aftereffects are the same. You've called on your own power and it's been there for you; you've learned, once again, that you have nothing to fear from yourself and so it seems there's really nothing at all to fear, and, for a while, anyway, you know you are larger than your fears. And when you feel the snap of that fear-band breaking—when you submit the piece of work, or close the oven door on the soufflé, that moment of letting go, falling free, taking your chances—what a rush that is. I don't know what residue is left by adrenaline after its surge has powered you through a crisis. But whatever the residue is, someone ought to bottle it. The high doesn't last long, but it's what makes the pursuit of danger so addictive.

I got hooked on fear four years ago. I was spending a week at Big Sur, taking a seminar at Esalen, a so-called "growth center," famous primarily for its hot-springs baths where men and women bathed in the nude. The place was on a cliff above the Pacific and the bathhouse was pronged into the side of the cliff, cantilevered out over the ocean. Idyllic setting. Tainted only by the fact that I was there with a man and between us, something had gone very wrong. Some poisonous combination of fear and rage had made us each other's enemies. So there we were, in this paradise, on teeth-edge with each other, and the second day, he said he was going to the baths and was I coming? I was not, in no way. He was impatient—no, disgusted is more accurate—with my uprightness. Okay, he said, and slapped a towel over his shoulder and walked away, down the thin rocky path to the bathhouse.

The grounds were deserted. I figured everyone was at the baths, or resting between seminars, and I started towards our room. And then I thought about never having been in a hot-springs bath, and from what I'd read, it must be luxurious, and my friend's sneer kept stabbing at me, and I knew that the only reason I wasn't going to the baths, and was instead going to spend a gorgeous afternoon hiding away in a dark room, was that I was afraid to take off my clothes in front of strangers. All the rage I'd been secretly storing suddenly turned itself on me. Coward. Idiot.

I remember clearly what it felt like to turn my body back towards the baths. Like an un-oiled robot, commanded by a distant brain. It is not an exaggeration to say I was trembling. My throat felt strangled, my stomach was clamped in a spasm, and various loud throbbings in my body distracted me from seeing or hearing as I went down that path. At the bath-house, there were a few stone steps and two signs, "Men" and "Women." I turned left towards "Women" and immediately knew the signs were vestigial. Half the bodies were male. There were four square cement tubs—shallow, about three feet deep—and one was empty of people. That's all I was looking for and all I saw. Mechanically, I ripped off my clothes and aimed the body towards my tub. I sank into a corner, immobile, and stared and saw nothing.

When I came to, sometime later, I noted that the bathhouse was three-sided, and I was facing the fourth side, open onto the sky and the ocean. Between the railing and the tubs were massage tables. On one was a naked young woman sitting in lotus position and playing a recorder. On the next, was a young man in an inverted lotus—head and shoulders on the mat, legs folded in air, also very naked. They were beautiful, those two, with their background of sky, and the music was perfect, and I decided I would come to Esalen and live, I would be a waitress.

Later I found my friend sitting on the steps of the lodge with his towel. Where were you? he asked.

I was at the baths.

He looked surprised, pleased. Oh, you must have been on the other side. I thought you weren't going.

I started to explain and then I started to cry, and then I noticed that my eyes were focusing peculiarly. Objects—trees, rocks, a porch railing—were startlingly three dimensional. I was seeing their spaces and the depth of space between them, and there seemed to be a fresh space in my own head. And looking at him, I saw just my old friend. Not the monster I'd been living with. I could see his kindness

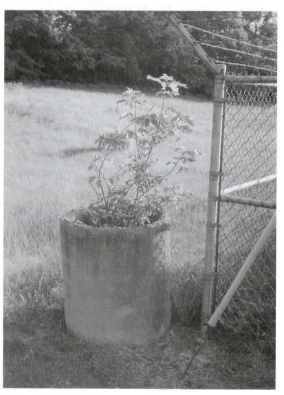

"One for the Tree"

A seed drops to the earth. Slowly the seed emerges, only to find itself surrounded by a hard, round wall. It grows the only way it can. Each year its spindly branches broaden and stretch a few more inches to the sky. This year it is showing off its first leaves of spring. It is becoming a tree. A tree that will one day outgrow its wall.

Some people are like this tree. A few, through no design of their own, have hard walls placed around them. Others seem to build hard walls around them, knowingly or not. But it takes only a few spurts of life to show that it is possible. That it is possible a life can still happen.

and his concern. He was just my friend. My usual eyes had slipped an evil mask over his face.

We had a good time together for the next few days. We had fun, I was light and playful. No self-consciousness, no need for it. Who was watching me? Whose judgment could I fear? What did a judgment have to do with me? I, anyone, was as impossible to judge as a stone. One can, of course, judge a stone, but does that judgment worry the stone?

In those few days, I was fearless. Fearless, as I remember it, feels like innocence. As though I didn't know what it was to be hurt, or to inflict hurt. No second thoughts. That automatic and unconscious rating of myself against other people was unnecessary—every person was my peer. Laughter was different too, sweeter.

The fog came down again, but those few days of superclarity were a taste of a possible state, a place I want to return to. The price of passage there was self-defiance, overruling powerful habits of defense. And the only route there was through the fear. There's always the chance now that another fear walked into might take me back.

It's pretty funny to talk about stripping as the way to Nirvana, but silly as it sounds, taking off my clothes was as much a plunge into terror, and the unknown, and freedom, as skydiving would be for me. My point is not to denigrate skydiving. It is, rather, to say that you don't have to rent a plane to fall free. Life is so playfully arranged, we can trust it to supply us with endless opportunities to turn our bodies around, and walk into terror. Why we are, most of us anyway, so afraid, I don't know. Maybe we're trained in fear, by people who are fortunate enough to have a lot to lose. But hoarding security, like hoarding money, leaves us nothing to show. A miser lives in destitution. Risking it all, pursuing danger, whether in the air or in the living room, seems to be the better way to play this game. The alternative is flight, constant flight.

Follow-Up

1. *Amy Gross writes, "When you think of the adventures, the terrors, the possible leaps, the opportunities in everyday life to choose between heroism and cowardice, you know that you don't have to travel to danger." Discuss and/or write a brief paper describing the challenges you find in your own everyday life, along with your heroic or cowardly responses.*
2. *Discuss and/or write a brief paper about the "secret heroics" you have shown in the face of one of your "small terrors."*
3. *Discuss and/or write a brief paper about the "blatant cowardice" you have shown in the face of one of your "small terrors."*
4. *Discuss and/or write a brief paper about some current "small terror" or fear in your life, indicating what it is, how it affects you, and how you deal with it.*

Just a Regular Kid

I teach fifth grade. The children are 10 years old. I would venture to say 99% of them think, learn and act like they are 10. It doesn't seem to be enough. Administrators, teachers, parents and members of the community seem to always want a 10 year old (or whatever age) *to be better than 10.*

Don't misunderstand, I am in favor of excellence or striving for it. I am for the gifted child. I am for intellectual and physical achievement. What I am against is the thought that there must be something wrong if a child thinks, acts, or feels his age.

Adults become ecstatic if at grade level 5.0 a child tests 8.2. If at 10, a child pitches a ball like a 12 year old, adults are impressed. How many accomplish these feats? I would venture to say one out of 100. What happens to the other 99? They have their moments, I'm sure, but seldom are parents or teachers satisfied. The world today is agog with achievements. I grant it would be a thrill to parent or teach a president, a Nobel Prize winner, an Olympic champion. Yet, why is it not enough to have been influential in the life of an intelligent, moral, healthy, productive human being?

Immaturity is often used as an excuse for the errors of the young. I don't think so. I think most youngsters are maturing through their successes *and* errors. Adults expect so much so soon. Yet, how many adults are error-free?

I should like a little more calm in the business of helping children grow. I should like a little less push. I should like us to all be more content with each individual child. When 10 year olds act or learn like they're 10, let's say hurrah! What a blessing! They'll only be 10 once. How great to flub and win, to fail and pass, to laugh and be hurt on a 10-year-old level when you're 10. Why must we expect children "to take it like a man" or "act like a lady"?

As a parent and teacher I have been caught up in this push for the young to "grow up." As my own children grow and leave childhood behind I realize perhaps we pushed too soon. We took their young lives and expected adult behavior and thinking from children. I see other parents do the same. Parents and teachers seem to forget a child's best has to be good enough. They want their child to be the best.

Children are children. Thank goodness! If I do nothing else as a teacher I hope I remember this fact. They will falter. They will be mischievous. They may even be bad. They will achieve. They will laugh.

And they will learn. I'm hopeful I can help the children, their parents, and myself to understand that it is quite acceptable to do all these things in a childlike way.

—A fifth grade teacher and graduate student

Follow-Up

1. *Do you agree with the main idea expressed in this essay?*
2. *Were you expected to be more than a child when you were young?*

The Pace of Growth

Below are excerpts from two novelists and an undergraduate student.

INDIAN SUMMER

"His goal was simply to be a full human man, making the best of himself. He was disgusted and fearful of what failure to do that had done to many people, to most people he knew. He did not want to be . . . twisted by subservience . . . ground down by poverty . . . slowly poisoned by contempt for (him)self. . . . Most of all, he did not want to be defeated as most people in the world were, that is, simply by not really living, eaten by the termites of a half life semilived.

All the same there was one wonderfully encouraging fact, which he kept the firmest possible grip on at all times. He actually knew one or two people who had broken past all these blocks and became real, true, full human beings.

Very soon now he was going to have to put a stop to this downward path he had let himself be persuaded to set out upon; he was going to have to halt this descent very soon or else, he sensed, it would be too late because he would have lost the power to escape. . . . If he took one gram too much of humiliation here, then the fuel of self-liking necessary to carry him away might be gone, and like so many . . . he would turn from a venturer into a clinger, caution would move one degree higher on the scale than ambition and so dominate it and finally crush it, doubt would inch ahead of certainty, fear would crowd out confidence, and his life would in all essentials be finished and its great issue lost.

We're out of phase with life; we live our lives out of season . . . [we] begin to fall behind too, like everybody else, into an Indian summer of brief, too late, doomed flowering."

—John Knowles

LEARNING THE WRONG THINGS

"I'm confused and frustrated. Humans are very adaptable to situations. We do learn from everything we do. What happens when you learn what you don't want to learn, but as a result of that exposure it becomes a part of you anyway? You should be very aware of the learning environments you find yourself in. If you're not, then in subtle ways you are going to become what you do. If you're in an environment you disagree with, you'd better do something before it changes you."

—An undergraduate student

THE BUTTERFLY

"I remembered one morning when I discovered a cocoon in the bark of a tree, just as the butterfly was making a hole in its case and preparing to come out. I waited a while, but it was too long appearing and I was impatient. I bent over it and breathed on it to warm it. I warmed it as quickly as I could and the miracle began to happen before my eyes, faster than life. The case opened, the butterfly started slowly crawling out and I shall never forget my horror when I saw how its wings were folded back and crumpled; the wretched butterfly tried with its whole trembling body to unfold them. Bending over it, I tried to help it with my breath. In vain. It needed to be hatched out patiently and the unfolding of the wings should be a gradual process in the sun. Now it was too late. My breath had forced the butterfly to appear, all crumpled, before its time. It struggled desperately and, a few seconds later, died in the palm of my hand.

That little body is, I do believe, the greatest weight I have on my conscience. For I realize today that it is a mortal sin to violate the great laws of nature. We should not hurry, we should not be impatient, but we should confidently obey the eternal rhythm. . . . Ah, if only that little butterfly could always flutter before me to show me the way."

—Nikos Kazantzakis

Follow-Up

1. *The first two authors warn against staying too long in an environment that stunts their growth. Can you think of an example where this happened to you or someone you know? Is it happening to you now?*
2. *Kazantzakis's excerpt provides a warning for pushing growth too quickly— forcing something before its time. Has this ever happened to you in some aspect of your life? How about now?*
3. *Do you tend to err in lingering too long or pushing too hard in your own personal growth? What are some specific steps you could take to create the best pace or tempo for your growth?*
4. *John Knowles's character mentions that he knew one or two people who were "real, true, full human beings." How many do you know (if any)? If you do, what makes them this way?*
5. *Discuss and/or write a reaction paper to one or more of these questions.*

No One's Perfect

Daphne Haygood-Benyard

No one's perfect . . . they say
Well I disagree!
I happen to be a perfect example of a perfect person
I'm perfectly good in my goodness
Perfect at being angry when I'm mad
I'm perfectly disagreeable when I argue
And make perfect mistakes in my errors
I develop a perfectly negative attitude when moody
I'm perfectly happy in my happiness
And will cry perfectly when sad
I'm perfectly calm in my coolness
Fall perfectly short in my shortcomings
And when I make a mess . . . it's a perfect wreck
I pout . . . shout . . . and strike out perfectly
In the insanity of living in this perfectly imperfect world.
So no one's perfect?
WELL!! PERFECTLY, I DISAGREE!

Applied Activities for Section Three

EVOLUTION OF A PERSON #1

1. **Lifeline.** List the major events and people that have significantly influenced your life development. These are the events and people that have made a difference in determining your self-image, interests, and skills; how you relate to other people; career and school choices; and values. As you examine your life, past and present, what have been some turning points? Perhaps a path you did not take but wonder about now? Or a decision which turned out right? What are some untried dreams or goals? Place these persons and events along a line starting with your birth and ending with the current date.

2. **Symbolic drawing.** On a single piece of paper draw a shape that symbolically represents your life from birth to the present. This drawing does not have to look artistic. Use shapes, lines, or even shadings and colors. Sometimes you have to think about your whole life in a gentle, reflective manner for a few minutes and wait for an image to appear. If an image does not immediately appear, do not force it. Wait a few hours or a day or two and probably one will emerge. A single drawing will be easier to remember and will tend to capture the emotional tones better than words.

3. In your lifeline and symbolic drawing, make sure to include all major influences, whether positive or negative. If you do not want anyone to see your work, disguise an event by using your own symbols (for example, you could use a number to represent a particular traumatic event).

4. Discuss what you have learned with classmates or write a reaction paper. Remember that you need only share what you are comfortable in disclosing.

5. An extension of this activity will be explored later in an Applied Activity appropriately called Evolution of A Person #2. (See the last section, A Quality Life.)

STRETCHING LIMITS

Knowing personal limits is necessary for making wise life choices. Often, however, a person constructs internal boundaries that are too constricting. Certain qualities are not expressed because opportunities to draw them out are not taken. Fears, a few failures, or plain inexperience restrain what we think we can do. Only when individuals do something they "are not capable of" are the internal boundaries challenged and usually expanded. When boundaries are extended, life is experienced more fully.

There are two ways to check whether your inner limits are too restrictive: (1) attempt to take a current strength to a higher or deeper level, (2) attempt a task which taps an undeveloped capacity, one you believe you have but have given little chance to develop.

The key is to design activities that challenge you to think and act at higher levels. In short, you are to set up realistic, but challenging, goals. For example, let's say that you have always wanted to try a few original ideas in your work but have not done so. You would then select the "best chance" new idea and design an action plan to try it out. You might consider telling a trusted other of your plan in order to develop a support person. Report what you learned about stretching your limits.

TRAIT EXAGGERATION

If you desire to strengthen a quality in your natural repertoire, you may have to overpractice it for awhile (like learning an athletic or musical technique). For example, let's say you want to become a better listener. For two weeks saturate yourself in learning and practicing listening—watch good listeners, read about listening, purposely emphasize listening in your normal interactions. This same approach can be used for almost any interpersonal or emotional quality. Describe your activities, results, and what you learned.

STRENGTHS RECOGNITION

A healthy self-perception depends in part on an awareness of personal strengths. In general, the more genuine strengths a person recognizes and values, the higher the level of self-esteem. It is not a common experience, though, to talk about your strengths without it being classified as bragging. However, it is socially acceptable to have someone else recognize and mention your strengths. It is important to talk about strengths, because this is a major way to maintain strength awareness. The following activities are two methods for recognizing strengths in others. You may be surprised how others react to these acknowledgments.

1. A strength is excellence in any skill, knowledge, or personal quality. In a proper time and context, directly tell three or more people what you believe to be one of their strengths. It is also helpful to provide an example of this strength. Note the immediate verbal and nonverbal reactions of those being acknowledged. Did they accept the recognition, or tend to sidestep or downplay it? Did they feel compelled to say something complimentary back to you?
2. If you have been part of an ongoing small group, in or outside of class, consider this activity. Tape a blank sheet of paper on the back of each group member. Distribute packets of Post-it notes. Then each person thinks of two strengths of every other group member. These are written on separate Post-it notes. After everyone has had time to finish writing, meander around and place your strengths notes on the back of the appropriate person. You may want to share your impressions and thoughts with the group after viewing your strengths notes.
3. Discuss or write about what you learned from one or both of these strengths recognition activities.

FIRST TIMES

One way to chart your life journey is to remember "first times." Each first time becomes a small or even a major threshold of your personal development. Try to list as many first times as you can. Here are some examples taken from several adults.

I'll never forget the first time I . . .

Rode a bike on my own
Drew an original picture
Went to school
Could read something
Flunked a test
Saw my baby sister
Bought a new baseball glove
Played a song on my trumpet
Kissed a boy
Played in a recital
Had a child

Had a period
Flew on an airplane
Went to a prom
Got my driver's license
Voted
Got drunk
Made a stand
Was totally out of line
Went to a funeral
Visited a foreign country

Now it's your turn. Write as many as you can on a separate piece of paper.

I'll never forget the first time I . . .

Follow-Up

1. Discuss one or more first times with someone.
2. Write a reaction paper on what these first times meant to you.
3. For further reading on this topic, see Robert Fulghum's *From Beginning To End: The Rituals of Our Lives,* 1995.

DEPRESSION CHECKLIST

Depression is linked with suicide, substance abuse, and several mental disorders. Clinical depression is a major health problem. It is an illness, not a character flaw or personality weakness. It is not the same as having a short-term case of the blues or the blahs. Below is a checklist of commonly noted signs of depression. It can be used for examining yourself or for someone you know. A key point in marking any item is to determine whether it has persisted for at least two weeks.

Body signs

_____ Major change in sleep patterns (less or more)

_____ Major change in appetite/weight

_____ Pronounced loss of energy

_____ Drug/chemical abuse

Emotional signs

_____ Deep sadness

_____ Intense feelings of hopelessness, worthlessness

_____ Pervasive loss of interest in everything (even former favorite activities)

_____ Irritable and angry

_____ Continual thoughts/statements of death and/or suicide

_____ Frequent crying spells

Cognitive signs

_____ Inability to concentrate

_____ Unable to make decisions

_____ Constant confusion

Interpersonal signs

_____ Social withdrawal ("I want to be alone.")

_____ No one cares or needs me

If you or someone you know has consistently shown one or more of these indicators for over a two week period, then professional help may be needed. Keep in mind that a depressed person often has little energy or desire to seek help; someone else may have to initiate this step. Professional help is necessary for successful treatment. Below are some resources to consider for depression information treatment interventions:

Local medical doctors and counseling services (in emergencies call 911 or your local suicide/crisis hotline number)

SOS: Signs of Suicide (1-800-973-2211) A phone site designed to teach people how to recognize someone who may be at risk for taking his/her life. This information is also available on the Web at www.mentalhealthscreening.org/parade.

National Depressive and Manic-Depressive Association (1-800-826-3632) Besides current screening information, this organization can also provide contacts for support groups. This information is available on the Web at www.ndmda.org.

Depression Awareness, Recognition, and Treatment (D/ART)
National Institute of Mental Health
Room 10-85
5600 Fishers Lane
Rockville, MD 20857
(Call 1-800-421-4211 for a free brochure.)

PERSONAL GOALS—GROWTH DYNAMICS

Within the next year I will move in the direction of actualizing my potentialities by:

Goal 1:

Needed actions, support, and resources:

Timeline:

Progress notes (use extra pages if necessary):

Goal 2:

Needed actions, support, and resources:

Timeline:

Progress notes (use extra page if necessary):

SECTION

FOUR

HUMAN RELATIONSHIPS

O ne of the best ways to learn the function of anything is to do without it. An injury to any part of your body readily shows its taken-for-granted purpose. A power outage highlights our pervasive dependence on electricity. Imagine a life without other people. Sometimes we may want such a thing, but only when we choose it. What we consider to be typical human behavior would not be possible without constant interaction with many persons in our lives. Observations of persons raised in isolation from an early age show great deficits in language, emotional expression, and a marked incapacity for a mature, sustained human interaction.

Most of us cannot escape the influence of our fellow humans even when we are alone—we think of them, we wonder what they are doing, we wonder if they miss us, we may even get mad at them, we might feel lonely. We are so enmeshed in our significant relationships that their influence permeates our existence even after their deaths.

Our human interactions differ according to their type, intensity, frequency, and duration. You can visually capture these dimensions by making a human web. Place a dot in the middle of a blank piece of paper—this dot represents you. Draw concentric circles around the dot. Place each of the following in an appropriate circle: relatives, friends, colleagues, teachers, professional relationships, authority figures, social groups, neighbors, acquaintances, heroes, mentors, role models, romantic encounters, disliked persons, and you can add any other relationship categories. When you place names by each of these circles, you begin to see how much of your life is spent in human interactions. You, too, are a member of many other webs.

Embedded deep within the human is the need to love and belong, in the dual sense of giving and receiving. Much of our lives is spent in attempting to fulfill these two needs. Abraham Maslow (1968) said that "no psychological health is possible unless the person is fundamentally accepted, loved and respected by others" (p. 196).

The reading selections in this section represent some of our most significant human relationships:

- In "Shoulders" Nels Goud argues that we have relied on others to become the person we are today.
- "Human Relationship Statistics" provides a snapshot of U.S. citizens according to recent statistics.
- Models of pairing (or non-pairing) are outlined in "Intimate Relationship Choices" by Abe Arkoff.
- The dynamics of effective and ineffective marriages are the topics of "Making Marriage Work" by John Gottman and Nan Silver.
- A day of joining and parting is described by Thomas R. Keating in "Sometimes It Rains."
- Handling money conflicts in intimate relationships is the theme of Dianne Hales's "Are Money Fights Ruining Your Marriage?"
- The excitements and difficulties of e-mail relationships are the topic of "Internet Romance" by Meghan Daum.
- Judith Viorst posits that we have six "Kinds of Friends."
- Mark Murrmann talks about past friends in "Lamenting the Fading of Friendships."
- A Little League player becomes a mirror of fundamental values and lessons in human relations in Nels Goud's true story of "The Human Potential of Whip Gimby."
- The struggle to become independent from parents and to accept them as distinct persons is the thesis of "Parents" by Martin Shepard. Exercises for parent dialogues are included.
- Parental sacrifice is the theme of "Eye for Sale" by Bob Greene.
- A teacher who cared is featured in "The Missing Halloween" by Nels Goud.
- Stephen Regan shares how a neighbor became a role model in "Think Nanny."

The Applied Activities and the Follow-Up study questions aid in expanding the ideas in the readings and how to apply them to your own life.

Reference
Maslow, A. (1968). *Toward a psychology of being.* New York: Van Nostrand Reinhold Co.

Shoulders

Nels Goud

I was about six years old when my parents took me to a parade. Standing there in a crowd of giants all I could see were knees and belt buckles. The bands, floats, and zany clowns passed by unseen. "I can't see! I want to see!" I yelled. Within a couple seconds two strong arms lifted me up high above the crowd. I had the best seat in the house up there on my father's shoulders. He didn't seem to mind at all that he was half strangled each time I got excited.

Two weeks ago I took some college students through a modified Outward Bound initiatives course. One task was to figure out how to get over a sheer 13-foot wall using only their minds and bodies. Gradually they decided to place a couple of people at the base of the wall. Sandy was elected to climb up on their shoulders. Sandy stretched and still was six inches from reaching the upper ledge. The two classmates she was standing on then pushed her up until she caught hold of the ledge and scrambled over. The rest of the class cheered Sandy. No one gave a hand to the two below with dirty shirts and sore shoulders.

It took actual shoulders to see the parade and climb the wall. Shoulders come in many other forms—teachings, models and mentors, others' past efforts. Our most accomplished persons readily acknowledged shoulders. "Many times a day I realize how much my life is built upon the labors of my fellow men, both living and dead," said Einstein. Eddie Robinson, immediately before the game which made him college football's winningest coach, said to his players "It's a record made up of men like you for the last 40 years."

Why is it, then, that most of us, most of the time, forget that we stand on shoulders? It appears that once our foundations are established, they are dropped from waking consciousness. Our attention becomes fully focused on current struggles, unattained goals, and ungratified needs. Successes are seen as the result of personal resourcefulness, perseverance, and possibly a few breaks. Occasionally we might throw in a plaudit for those we stand on, but it generally rings of the obligatory. I was reminded of this when someone asked me how I achieved a certain style of trumpet playing. My response centered on individual effort and practice. Later reflection revealed gaping holes in this answer. I forgot my shoulders. Any current trumpeting skill would have to be traced to my mom's encouragement while hearing me butcher pieces like 'The Carnival of Venice' in the back room; and to Hendrik Buytendorp, the music teacher who made it clear that trumpet scales were just as important as Little League baseball practice; and to Ferguson, Severinsen, Hirt, Mangione. An honest and true answer would have to acknowledge all these influences. Try it yourself—just attempt to fully explain how you are able to do something well. The answer will unveil a vast network of shoulders.

Forgetting shoulders may be linked to distorted notions of self-sufficiency. We value and reward self-direction, individual initiative, and taking responsibility. A healthy person possesses these qualities. It is when these traits are exaggerated out of proportion that problems begin. Healthy autonomy turns into neurotic self-reliance. A person gradually begins to believe he/she can master life's challenges by relying solely on personal resources, and that to even acknowledge the help of others is a 'weakness'. It may even work for awhile. Then prices must be paid. Some develop illusions of omnipotence or step into the trap Karen Horney called the pseudosolution of mastery. This "I don't need anybody, never had, never will" orientation propels one to the outpost of alienation.

One does not lose uniqueness by tracing an accomplishment or ability to the influence of others. The actual idea and action is an individual one; it has your stamp. That is what shoulders are for, they permit a stretching of the limits of what has gone on before. By remembering shoulders while perched up there, you get the bonus of a profound sense of belonging. One may even realize Thoreau's advice: "If I devote myself to pursuits and contemplations, I must first see, at least, that I do not pursue them sitting upon another man's shoulders. I must get off him first, that he may pursue his contemplations too."

Sometimes I realize my part in this shoulders network in simple ways. I am watching the Indianapolis 500 parade with 250,000 other giants. The bands, floats, and clowns pass by and I hear my four year old son hollering, "I can't see! I want to see!" I hoist him up on my shoulders and he half strangles me.

Follow-Up

1. *Goud maintains that we often forget the contributions of others toward our accomplishments. Discuss whether this is true in your life and in the lives of others.*
2. *Some people feel that acknowledging help from others is a form of weakness. Offer your thoughts on this idea.*
3. *Thoreau was quoted on the observation that at times a person must "get off another's shoulders" so that the latter can also freely pursue a life. Discuss your views on this idea.*
4. *The author suggested that you think of one of your skills or accomplishments and then trace it back to its origins. Try this and report on the role of others in this history.*

Human Relationship Statistics

- According to the 2000 Census Bureau, there are about 281 million U.S. citizens. In 1990 there were about 249 million; in 1930, 123 million; in 1879, 39 million; and in the first census in 1790, there were 4 million U.S. citizens.
- The median age of the U.S. population is 35.3 years. The median age of females is 37, and the median age of males is 34.6.
- In 1998, 56% of the adult U.S. population were married and living with their spouse.
- In 1998, approximately 10% of adult U.S. citizens were divorced.
- Approximately 50% of marriages end in divorce.
- 90% of all U.S. citizens marry at some time.
- About 75% of divorced U.S. citizens remarry. About 60% of remarriages fail.
- Studies indicate that those who co-habit prior to marriage are more likely to divorce than those who do not co-habit.
- In 1998, the median age at first marriage was 26.7 for men and 25 for women. In 1988 it was 25.9 for men and 23.6 for women; in 1978, 24.2 for men and 21.8 for women; in 1968, 23.1 for men and 20.8 for women, and in 1900 it was 25.9 for men and 21.9 for women.
- In 1999, there were approximately 70.2 million children (under age 18) in the United States—about 26% of the population. Since the mid-1960s, children have been decreasing as a proportion of the total U.S. population.
- In 1999, 65% of U.S. children were white, non-Hispanic; 15% were black, non-Hispanic; 16% were Hispanic; 4% were Asian/Pacific Islander, and 1% were American Indian/Alaska native.
- In 1999, 68% of U.S. children lived with two parents. This was down from 77% in 1980.
- In 1999, about 23% of children lived with only their mothers, 4% with only their fathers, and 4% lived with neither parent.
- In 1997, about 5.5% of U.S. children were living in homes maintained by their grandparents (with or without parental presence).
- In 1998, 33% of all births were to unmarried women. Approximately 40% of first births were to unmarried women.
- In 1999, 54% of children from birth through third grade received some form of child care on a regular basis from persons other than their parents.
- Approximately 23% of married couples identified the woman as the head of the household in 1998. In 1990 it was 7.4%.
- During the 1990s there was an average of 120,000 adoptions each year. About 42% were placed with relatives or stepparents.

- There are approximately 35 million people in the United States age 65 or older (about 13% of the population). This percent is expected to double by 2030.
- Life expectancy for U.S. citizens who were 65 in the year 2000 is 18 more years, on average.
- Of those 65 or older in 2000, about 84% were non-Hispanic whites. By 2050, this percent is estimated to be 64%.
- Approximately 11% of U.S. citizens 65 and over live in poverty (a decrease from 35% in 1959).
- About 4% of those 65 and older were in nursing homes in 1997.

Follow-Up

1. *Choose one or more of these statistical findings and discuss your interpretations. Try to get others' views on the same findings (especially ones which may differ from yours).*

Intimate Relationship Choices

Abe Arkoff

Below are brief descriptions of five models of pairing or, in one case, nonpairing. Read each description, and complete the incomplete statements following it by giving as many reasons as you can. If a model is generally unattractive to you, try to find something about it that you like. If a model is generally attractive to you, try to find something about it that you *don't* like.

1. The traditional model: The male is primarily the breadwinner while the female is primarily the homemaker.

   This model is attractive to me because

   This model is unattractive to me because

2. The shared-roles model: The parties share equally in the breadwinning and homemaking activities.

   This model is attractive to me because

   This model is unattractive to me because

3. The reversed-roles model: The female is primarily the breadwinner while the male is primarily the homemaker.

   This model is attractive to me because

   This model is unattractive to me because

4. The living-together model: The parties live together without being formally married and possibly with no intention to have children or permanency.

   This model is attractive to me because

   This model is unattractive to me because

5. The singlehood model: The person lives alone.

   This model is attractive to me because

   This model is unattractive to me because

Identify the pairing model that you prefer for yourself and explain in detail why it is your preference.

Making Marriage Work

John Gottman and Nan Silver

The chance of a first marriage ending in divorce over a forty-year period is 67 percent. Half of all divorces will occur in the first seven years. Some studies find the divorce rate for second marriages is as much as 10 percent higher than for first-timers. The chance of getting divorced remains so high that it makes sense for all married couples—including those who are currently satisfied with their relationship—to put extra effort into their marriages to keep them strong.

One of the saddest reasons a marriage dies is that neither spouse recognizes its value until it is too late. Only after the papers have been signed, the furniture divided, and separate apartments rented do the exes realize how much they really gave up when they gave up on each other. Too often a good marriage is taken for granted rather than given the nurturing and respect it deserves and desperately needs.

FRIENDSHIP VERSUS FIGHTING

At the heart of my program is the simple truth that happy marriages are based on a deep friendship. By this I mean a mutual respect for and enjoyment of each other's company. These couples tend to know each other intimately—they are well versed in each other's likes, dislikes, personality quirks, hopes, and dreams. They have an abiding regard for each other and express this fondness not just in the big ways but in little ways day in and out.

Take the case of hardworking Nathaniel, who runs his own import business and works very long hours. In another marriage, his schedule might be a major liability. But he and his wife Olivia have found ways to stay connected. They talk frequently on the phone during the day. When she has a doctor's appointment, he remembers to call to see how it went. When he has a meeting with an important client, she'll check in to see how it fared. When they have chicken for dinner, she gives him both drumsticks because she knows he likes them best. When he makes blueberry pancakes for the kids Saturday morning, he'll leave the blueberries out of hers because he knows she doesn't like them. Although he's not religious, he accompanies her to church each Sunday because it's important to her. And although she's not crazy about spending a lot of time with their relatives, she has pursued a friendship with Nathaniel's mother and sisters because family matters so much to him.

If all of this sounds humdrum and unromantic, it's anything but. Through small but important ways Olivia and Nathaniel are maintaining the friendship that is the foundation of their love. As a result they have a marriage that is far more passionate than do couples who punctuate their lives together with romantic vacations and lavish anniversary gifts but have fallen out of touch in their daily lives.

Friendship fuels the flames of romance because it offers the best protection against feeling adversarial toward your spouse. Because Nathaniel and Olivia have kept their friendship strong despite the inevitable disagreements and irritations of married life, they are experiencing what is known technically as "positive sentiment override." This means that their positive thoughts about each other and their marriage are so pervasive that they tend to supersede their negative feelings. It takes a much more significant conflict for them to lose their equilibrium as a couple than it would otherwise. Their positivity causes them to feel optimistic about each other and their marriage, to assume positive things about their lives together, and to give each other the benefit of the doubt.

Rediscovering or reinvigorating friendship doesn't prevent couples from arguing. Instead, it gives them a secret weapon that prevents quarrels from getting out of hand. For example, here's what happens when Olivia and Nathaniel argue. As they plan to move from the city to the suburbs, tensions between them are high. Although they see eye to eye on which house to buy and how to decorate it, they are locking horns over buying a new car. Olivia thinks they should join the suburban masses and get a minivan. To Nathaniel nothing could be drearier—he wants a Jeep. The more they talk about it, the higher the decibel level gets. If you were a fly on the wall of their bedroom, you would have serious doubts about their future together. Then all of a sudden, Olivia puts her hands on her hips and, in perfect imitation of their four-year-old son, sticks out her tongue. Since Nathaniel knows that she's about to do this, he sticks out his tongue first. Then they both start laughing. As always, this silly contest defuses the tension between them.

In our research we actually have a technical name for what Olivia and Nathaniel did. Probably unwittingly, they used a *repair attempt*. This name refers to any statement or action—silly or otherwise—that prevents negativity from escalating out of control. Repair attempts are the secret weapon of emotionally intelligent couples—even though many of these couples aren't aware that they are doing something so powerful. When a couple have a strong friendship, they naturally become experts at sending each other repair attempts and at correctly reading those sent their way. But when couples are in negative override, even a repair statement as blunt as "Hey, I'm sorry" will have a low success rate.

The success or failure of a couple's repair attempts is one of the primary factors in whether their marriage flourishes or flounders. And again, what determines the success of their repair attempts is the strength of their marital friendship. If this sounds simplistic or obvious, you'll find in the pages ahead that it is not. Strengthening your marital friendship isn't as basic as just being "nice." Even if you feel that your friendship is already quite solid, you may be surprised to find there is room to strengthen it all the more. Most of the couples who take our workshop are relieved to hear that almost everybody messes up during marital conflict. What matters is whether the repairs are successful.

In the strongest marriages, husband and wife share a deep sense of meaning. They don't just "get along"—they also support each other's hopes and aspirations and build a sense of purpose into their lives together. That is really what I mean when I talk about honoring and respecting each other.

Very often a marriage's failure to do this is what causes husband and wife to find themselves in endless, useless rounds of argument or to feel isolated and lonely in their marriage. After watching countless videotapes of couples fighting, I can guarantee you that most quarrels are really not about whether the toilet lid is up or down or whose turn it is to take out the trash. There are deeper, hidden issues that fuel these superficial conflicts and make them far more intense and hurtful than they would otherwise be.

Once you understand this, you will be ready to accept one of the most surprising truths about marriage: *Most marital arguments cannot be resolved.* Couples spend year after year trying to change each other's mind—but it can't be done. This is because most of their disagreements are rooted in fundamental differences of lifestyle, personality, or values. By fighting over these differences, all they succeed in doing is wasting their time and harming their marriage.

This doesn't mean there's nothing you can do if your relationship has been overrun by conflict. But it does mean that the typical conflict-resolution advice won't help. Instead, you need to understand the bottom-line difference that is causing the conflict between you—and to learn how to live with it by honoring and respecting each other. Only then will you be able to build shared meaning and a sense of purpose into your marriage.

HARSH STARTUP

When a discussion leads off this way—with criticism and/or sarcasm, a form of contempt—it has begun with a "harsh startup." Although Dara talks to Oliver in a very soft, quiet voice, there's a load of negative power in her words. After hearing the first minute or so of their conversation, it's no surprise to me that by the end Dara and Oliver haven't resolved their differences at all. The research shows that if your discussion begins with a harsh startup, it will inevitably end on a negative note, even if there are a lot of attempts to "make nice" in between. Statistics tell the story: 96 percent of the time you can predict the outcome of a conversation based on the *first three minutes* of the fifteen-minute interaction! A harsh startup simply dooms you to failure. So if you begin a discussion that way, you might as well pull the plug, take a breather, and start over.

THE FOUR HORSEMEN

Certain kinds of negativity, if allowed to run rampant, are so lethal to a relationship that I call them the Four Horsemen of the Apocalypse. Usually these four horsemen clip-clop into the heart of a marriage in the following order: criticism, contempt, defensiveness, and stonewalling.

Horseman 1: Criticism

You will always have some complaints about the person you live with. But there's a world of difference between a complaint and a criticism. A complaint only addresses the specific action at which your spouse failed. A criticism is more global—it adds on some negative words about your mate's character or personality. "I'm really angry that you didn't sweep the kitchen floor last night. We agreed that we'd take turns doing it" is a complaint. "Why are you so forgetful? I hate having to always sweep the kitchen floor when it's your turn. You just don't care" is a criticism. A complaint focuses on a specific behavior, but a criticism ups the ante by throwing in blame and general character assassination. Here's a recipe: To turn any complaint into a criticism, just add my favorite line: "What is wrong with you?"

Horseman 2: Contempt

Dara doesn't stop at criticizing Oliver. Soon she's literally sneering. When he suggests that they keep a list of his chores on the refrigerator to help him remember, she says, "Do you think you work really well with lists?" Next, Oliver tells her that he needs fifteen minutes to relax when he gets home before starting to do chores. "So if I leave you alone for fifteen minutes, then you think you'll be motivated to jump up and do something?" she asks him.

"Maybe. We haven't tried it, have we?" Oliver asks.

Dara has an opportunity here to soften up, but instead she comes back with sarcasm. "I think you do a pretty good job of coming home and lying around or disappearing into the bathroom," she says. And then she adds challengingly, "So you think that's the cure-all, to give you fifteen minutes?"

This sarcasm and cynicism are types of contempt. So are name-calling, eye-rolling, sneering, mockery, and hostile humor. In whatever form, contempt—the worst of the four horsemen—is poisonous to a relationship because it conveys disgust. It's virtually impossible to resolve a problem when your partner is getting the message you're disgusted with him or her. Inevitably, contempt leads to more conflict rather than to reconciliation.

Contempt is fueled by long-simmering negative thoughts about the partner. You're more likely to have such thoughts if your differences are not resolved. No doubt, the first time Peter and Cynthia argued about money, he wasn't so disrespectful. He probably offered a simple complaint like "I think you should wash your own car. It costs too much to always have someone else wash it." But as they kept disagreeing about this, his complaints turned to global criticisms, such as: "You always spend too much money." And when the conflict continued, he felt more and more disgusted and fed up with Cynthia, a change that affected what he said when they argued.

Belligerence, a close cousin to contempt, is just as deadly to a relationship. It is a form of aggressive anger because it contains a threat or provocation. When a wife complains that her husband doesn't come home from work in time for dinner, a belligerent response would be "Well, what are you going to do about it?" When Peter says to Cynthia, "What are you going to do, sue me?" he thinks he's making a joke, but he's really being belligerent.

Horseman 3: Defensiveness

It's no surprise, considering how nasty her husband is being, that Cynthia defends herself. She points out that she doesn't get her car washed as often as he thinks. She explains that it's more difficult physically for her to wash her car herself than it is for him to wash his truck.

Although it's understandable that Cynthia would defend herself, research shows that this approach rarely has the desired effect. The attacking spouse does not back down or apologize. This is because defensiveness is really a way of blaming your partner. You're saying, in effect, "The problem isn't *me*, it's *you*." Defensiveness just escalates the conflict, which is why it's so deadly. When Cynthia tells Peter how hard it is for her to wash her car, he doesn't say, "Oh, now I understand." He ignores her excuse—he doesn't even acknowledge what she's said. He climbs farther up his high moral ground, telling her how well he takes care of his vehicle and implying that she's

spoiled for not doing the same. Cynthia can't win—and neither can their marriage.

Criticism, Contempt, and Defensiveness don't always gallop into a home in strict order. They function more like a relay match—handing the baton off to each other over and over again, if the couple can't put a stop to it. You can see this happening as Oliver and Dara continue their discussion about cleaning their house. Although they seem to be seeking a solution, Dara becomes increasingly contemptuous—mocking Oliver in the guise of questioning him and tearing down every plan he devises. The more defensive he becomes, the more she attacks him. Her body language signals condescension. She speaks softly, her elbows resting on the table, her intertwined fingers cradling her chin. Like a law professor or a judge, she peppers him with questions just to see him squirm.

Horseman 4: Stonewalling

In marriages like Dara and Oliver's, where discussions begin with a harsh startup, where criticism and contempt lead to defensiveness, which leads to more contempt and more defensiveness, eventually one partner tunes out. This heralds the arrival of the fourth horseman.

Think of the husband who comes home from work, gets met with a barrage of criticism from his wife, and hides behind the newspaper. The less responsive he is, the more she yells. Eventually he gets up and leaves the room. Rather than confronting his wife, he disengages. By turning away from her, he is avoiding a fight, but he is also avoiding his marriage. He has become a stonewaller. Although both husbands and wives can be stonewallers, this behavior is far more common among men, for reasons we'll see later.

During a typical conversation between two people, the listener gives all kinds of cues to the speaker that he's paying attention. He may use eye contact, nod his head, say something like "Yeah" or "Uh-huh." But a stonewaller doesn't give you this sort of casual feedback. He tends to look away or down without uttering a sound. He sits like an impassive stone wall. The stonewaller acts as though he couldn't care less about what you're saying, if he even hears it.

Stonewalling usually arrives later in the course of a marriage than the other three horsemen. That's why it's less common among newlywed husbands such as Oliver than among couples who have been in a negative spiral for a while. It takes time for the negativity created by the first three horsemen to become overwhelming enough that stonewalling becomes an understandable "out." That's the stance that Mack takes when he and his wife Rita argue about each other's behavior at parties. She says the problem is that he drinks too much. He thinks the bigger problem is her reaction: She embarrasses him by yelling at him in front of his friends. Here they are, already in the middle of an argument:

RITA: Now I've become the problem, again. I started off with the complaint, but now I am the problem. That always seems to happen.

MACK: Yeah, I do that, I know. (Pause.) But your tantrums and childishness are an embarrassment to me and my friends.

RITA: If you would control your drinking at parties, puleese . . .

MACK: (Looks down, avoids eye contact, says nothing—he's stonewalling.)

RITA: Because I think (laughs) for the most part, we get along pretty well, really (laughs).

MACK: (Continues to stonewall. Remains silent, makes no eye contact, head nods, facial movements, or vocalizations.)

RITA: Don't you think?

MACK: (No response.)

RITA: Mack? Hello?

It may seem to Rita that her complaints have no effect on Mack. But nothing could be further from the truth. Usually people stonewall as a protection against feeling *flooded*. Flooding means that your spouse's negativity—whether in the guise of criticism or contempt or even defensiveness—is so overwhelming,

and so sudden, that it leaves you shell-shocked. You feel so defenseless against this sniper attack that you learn to do anything to avoid a replay. The more often you feel flooded by your spouse's criticism or contempt, the more hypervigilant you are for cues that your spouse is about to "blow" again. All you can think about is protecting yourself from the turbulence your spouse's onslaught causes. And the way to do that is to disengage emotionally from the relationship. No wonder Mack and Rita are now divorced.

Another husband, Paul, was quite up front about why he stonewalls when his wife, Amy, gets negative. In the following discussion he articulates what all stonewallers are feeling.

AMY: When I get mad, that's when you should step in and try to make it better. But when you just stop talking, it means, 'I no longer care about how you feel.' That just makes me feel one inch tall. Like my opinion or feelings have absolutely no bearing on you. And that's not the way a marriage should be.

PAUL: What I'm saying is, if you wanna have a serious conversation, you're gonna do it without yelling and screaming all the time. You start saying things that are hurtful.

AMY: Well, when I'm hurt, mad, and I wanna hurt you, I start saying things. And that's when we should both stop. I should say, "I'm sorry." And you should say, "I know that you wanna talk about this. And I really should make an effort to talk instead of just ignoring you."

PAUL: I'll talk when—

AMY: It fits your purpose.

PAUL: No, when you're not yelling and screaming and jumping up and down stomping.

Amy kept telling Paul how it made her feel when he shut down. But she did not seem to hear him tell her *why* he shuts down: He can't handle her hostility. This couple later divorced.

A marriage's meltdown can be predicted, then, by habitual harsh startup and frequent flooding brought on by the relentless presence of the four horsemen during disagreements. Although each of these factors alone can predict a divorce, they usually coexist in an unhappy marriage.

Just because your marriage follows this pattern, it's not a given that a divorce is in the offing. In fact, you'll find examples of all four horsemen and even occasional flooding in stable marriages. But when the four horsemen take up *permanent* residence, when either partner begins to feel flooded routinely, the relationship is in serious trouble. Frequently feeling flooded leads almost inevitably to distancing yourself from your spouse. That in turn leads you to feel lonely. Without help, the couple will end up divorced or living in a dead marriage, in which they maintain separate, parallel lives in the same home. They may go through the motions of togetherness—attending their children's plays, hosting dinner parties, taking family vacations. But emotionally they no longer feel connected to each other. They have given up.

REPAIR ATTEMPTS

It takes time for the four horsemen and the flooding that comes in their wake to overrun a marriage. And yet divorce can so often be predicted by listening to a single conversation between newlyweds. How can this be? The answer is that by analyzing any disagreement a couple has, you get a good sense of the pattern they tend to follow. A crucial part of that pattern is whether their repair attempts succeed or fail. Repair attempts . . . are efforts the couple makes ("Let's take a break," "Wait, I need to calm down") to deescalate the tension during a touchy discussion—to put on the brakes so flooding is prevented.

Repair attempts save marriages not just because they decrease emotional tension between spouses, but because by lowering the stress level they also prevent your heart from racing and making you feel flooded. When the four horsemen rule a couple's communication, repair attempts often don't even get noticed. Especially when you're feeling flooded, you're not able to hear a verbal white flag.

In unhappy marriages a feedback loop develops between the four horsemen and the failure of repair attempts. The more contemptuous and defensive the couple is with each other, the more flooding occurs, and the harder it is to hear and respond to a repair. And since the repair is not heard, the contempt and defensiveness just get heightened, making flooding more pronounced, which makes it more difficult to hear the next repair attempt, until finally one partner withdraws.

In emotionally intelligent marriages I hear a wide range of successful repair attempts. Each person has his or her own approach. Olivia and Nathaniel stick out their tongues; other couples laugh or smile or say they're sorry. Even an irritated "Hey, stop yelling at me," or "You're getting off the topic" can defuse a tense situation. All such repair attempts keep a marriage stable because they prevent the four horsemen from moving in for good.

SHARED MEANINGS

But it is also true that a rewarding marriage is about more than sidestepping conflict. The more you can agree about the fundamentals in life, the richer, more meaningful, and in a sense easier your marriage is likely to be. You certainly can't force yourselves to have the same deeply held views. But some coming together on these issues is likely to occur naturally if you are open to each other's perspectives. *A crucial goal of any marriage, therefore, is to create an atmosphere that encourages each person to talk honestly about his or her convictions.* The more you speak candidly and respectfully with each other, the more likely there is to be a blending of your sense of meaning.

Follow-Up

1. *Select two ideas from this article and comment on their meaning and application.*
2. *Choose one of the negative relationship factors and attempt to decrease it in an ongoing relationship.*
3. *Try to apply the concept of "repair attempts" in an ongoing relationship and report the results.*
4. *Complete the "Love Maps" Applied Activity at the end of this section and comment on your learnings.*
5. *For more detail on the ideas in this article, see* The Seven Principles for Making Marriage Work *by John Gottman and Nan Silver. Three Rivers Press, 1999.*

Sometimes It Rains

Thomas R. Keating

The rain was coming down in solid sheets, but the young man and woman holding hands as they ducked into the revolving door at the Delaware Street entrance to the City-County Building didn't notice at all.

Storms, even tornadoes, are relative on your wedding day.

Shaking the rain out of their hair and laughing, they bounced along the main floor of the building and grinned at each other steadily as they stepped onto the escalator to the basement.

The young man was 20. The girl was 18.

They looked very much like any other young couple except that they were dressed in their best clothes and looked like they had just discovered one of the world's top secrets.

In the basement they met another young man and woman who were even more exuberant. The men shook hands while the girls exchanged hugs and brief kisses on the cheek.

After a minute of excited talk, they all gathered in the chambers of the Center Township justice of the peace for the ceremony.

Six floors up a woman with a streaked red face and tired eyes was standing across a courtroom from a hefty man who minutes before had been her husband. They were listening intently as the judge read the final divorce decree.

The judge explained the particulars of the separate existence they would be living from now on.

He repeated how and when the couple's three children would be shifted about and how much money would exchange hands on what dates and who would get to keep which of the possessions that had accumulated in nine years of marriage.

The man was 30. She was 28.

During the divorce proceedings the wife had charged mental cruelty and infidelity. The husband had not challenged the charges or made any of his own, but he said privately that he felt she was to blame for the breakup.

Both the man and the woman felt a vague embarrassment at airing their most personal failings in public. So the divorce had been handled with little emotion.

As the judge concluded, the man glanced at his wife. He tried to sneer but it came off instead as a look of boredom. The woman alternated between paying polite attention to the judge and searching her husband's face as if to see if he would have a last-minute change of heart.

When the court proceedings were finished, the couple stood separately in the wide hallway, each talking quietly with their respective attorneys. After a few minutes, the woman approached the man who was now her ex-husband.

"Well, good-by," she said. "I hope you'll be happy."

"I will, don't worry," he returned.

After a pause, however, he thought better of what he had said and added, "Well, I hope you're happy too. I don't know what happened, but I guess we'll both be better off."

"Sure, I agree, sure," she said, straining to smile.

With that the man turned and walked across the hallway to a bench where a young woman in a bright blue dress was waiting. They talked together in whispers for a moment and then disappeared into an elevator. The girl was smiling. The man was not.

The ex-wife watched them go and then sighed deeply, shrugged her shoulders and got onto another elevator alone.

On the main floor, the newly married couple was staring out the high glass doors at the rain with the perspective that only comes when you are young and everything is yet to happen.

"I love storms," the girl said. "Don't you?"

"Let's go then," her husband said. Grabbing her around the waist. They raced down the sidewalk for a few feet and then stopped and leaned against a pole in a tangle, oblivious to the fact they were getting drenched.

A few moments later, the divorced woman peered out the same glass doors.

"This is the lousiest weather I've ever seen in my life," she said. "But, what the hell, maybe I'll catch a cold."

She passed the young couple on the sidewalk but didn't notice them. Her head was down and she was looking for puddles.

Follow-Up

1. *The newly divorced man says to his now former wife, "I don't know what happened, but I guess we'll both be better off." They were married nine years. How could the relationship disintegrate without them knowing what happened? Would you guess that the newly divorced couple were like the newly married couple nine years ago? Offer your views on these questions.*
2. *Write about or discuss any other thought that this article evokes.*

Are Money Fights Ruining Your Marriage?

Dianne Hales

Whether couples are rich, poor or somewhere in between, whether they have two steady incomes or one that's erratic, most fight about money. And as money gets tight—which is increasingly common these days—battles over the budget increase.

"When couples are forced to set priorities, someone has to give up something—and that's when the fights begin," explains Victoria Felton-Collins, author of *Couples and Money: Why Money Interferes with Love and What to Do About It*. Once money spats flare up, they can turn ugly. "Money is a magnet that draws in all the frustrations in our lives," she observes.

It doesn't have to be this way, but you do have to delve beyond the dollars-and-cents dilemmas before you can stop the fights. Says Felton-Collins: "Money is a metaphor for power, freedom, self-esteem and love. You must understand how you and your spouse view and use money if you're going to stop fighting about it."

Consider how some real couples—who asked that their names be changed—handled these typical situations:

"WHAT AM I WORTH IF I LOSE MY JOB?"

Despite 15 years' seniority, Ned was fired when his company was sold. At first, he and his wife were thankful they had Pam's salary. But after months of fruitless job hunting, Ned started making snide remarks. "I can't spend a dime without getting her highness's approval," he complained. And Pam grew resentful. "I'm working extra hours just to pay our mortgage, utility and food bills," she said.

"When I get home at night, I'd like to feel appreciated."

Losing a job is a blow to ego as well as to income—especially for men, who define manhood in terms of money, sex and power. When Ned lost his job, he—like many men—pulled away from his family. Pam didn't know what to say to make him feel better. Ned interpreted her silence as criticism. When they started sniping at each other, both realized something was wrong.

"Men never talk about it," says Felton-Collins, "but when their wives make more money than they do,' they worry about being needed. If his family doesn't need him as a provider, a man wonders if they need him at all."

Pam finally took the initiative. "I told Ned that I felt we were both tiptoeing around on eggshells because money had become such a sensitive issue," she explains. "It took a lot of encouragement, but Ned gradually began to open up. He felt he wasn't contributing to the family anymore, so I told him all the things I'd assumed he knew—like how much we all love him, what a wonderful husband and father he is. I also described my own feelings about being the primary breadwinner. He'd thought I enjoyed having the upper hand, when I really hated it."

Pam and Ned also talked about practical matters. After losing his job, Ned stopped paying the bills. That made Pam feel that all their financial problems had been dumped on her. Once Ned resumed an active role in managing their money, both felt better. He also volunteered to help with school sports and other activities. "He saw how much the kids loved having time with him, and that made a difference too," says Pam. "And now that everything is out in the open, we all have the sense that we'll get through these tough times together."

"WHOSE MONEY IS IT ANYWAY?"

Before his marriage last year, Jake never thought twice about spending money. "Why not have fun when I'm young?" he said. Now, whenever Jake spends $50 on a night out with the guys, his wife, Lucy, gets angry. "How can you be so selfish?" she asks. "We could use that money for a down payment on a house."

"Why should you tell me how to spend my money?" Jake counters.

In more than half of all marriages today, both spouses work. Yet many enter marriage with very different notions about what's his, hers and theirs. Jake, for instance, simply assumed he could spend "his" money as he chose; Lucy thought his earnings were "theirs."

Lucy and Jake finally had an overdue talk about their goals and priorities. "We both want to buy a house before starting a family," says Jake. "To me, that's down the road a bit. But Lucy thinks we have to start saving now or we'll never make it. She spent her childhood moving from one military post to another with her dad. To her, having a house is the dream of a lifetime. When she explained that, I understood why she'd gotten so upset."

Talking, though, is just the first step. According to Alexis Mitchell, a certified financial planner and vice president of Fidelity Investments in Sacramento: "Two people have to negotiate until they reach a decision—and then make a commitment to stick to their agreement."

For Jake, the bottom line was having some money to spend as he pleased. Lucy, on the other hand, wanted a real commitment to shared goals. Their solution involved three separate bank accounts—an individual account for each, plus a joint account. Jake can spend his money without answering to Lucy. She can do the same. But both deposit 75 percent of their take-home pay into the joint account to cover expenses and start saving toward their own home.

"WHY DOES HE KEEP OVERDRAWING OUR CHECKING ACCOUNT?

Allison meticulously records every check she writes. Steve often forgets to make a deposit or record a withdrawal. When their telephone was cut off after yet another check bounced, Allison was furious. "How can you be so irresponsible?" she demanded.

"I work hard; I've got other things on my mind. Give me a break," Steve said.

Allison and Steve are a financial "odd couple," with her playing finicky Felix to his disorganized Oscar. To break out of their checkbook checkmates, they decided Allison would be responsible for the family's paperwork. All Steve had to do was put all his receipts in a shoe box. Every week Allison unfolded these crumbled papers and recorded them.

The system worked: No more checks bounced. But Steve began to wonder where the money was going. "I felt I had no control," he explained. "Whenever I asked Allison about our balance, she got defensive."

Allison explains why: "Here I was, cleaning up his chaos, and he was second-guessing me."

To stop this new round of spats, they talked about money in terms of control and security. For Allison, keeping tabs on every dime made her feel in control. Steve didn't care about every dime or dollar, but he needed a sense of the big financial picture. Both would feel more comfortable, they decided, with a weekly conference.

Allison now fills Steve in on their bank account balances every Sunday. Together they

HOW TO AVOID MONEY CONFLICTS

Many money fights can be avoided by taking these practical steps in advance:

- *Don't let a lack of information create misunderstandings.* Go over your finances together. Prepare a simple financial worth statement so you're both aware of debts, assets, investments and obligations.
- *Discuss your feelings about money.* Does having it make you feel independent, secure, successful, loved, powerful? How do you feel when you spend money on yourself or give it to others? What worries you the most?
- *Tackle one financial chore at a time.* Don't try to establish a budget and make investment decisions all at once.
- *Recognize the value of unpaid work.* A husband in school or a wife raising children at home should feel that these contributions are just as vital as a salary.
- *Set financial goals and discuss how you'll meet them.* "Management by objective is always preferable to management by accident," notes financial planner Victoria Felton-Collins.
- *Make sure each partner has money to spend without answering to the other.* Even $10 a week can ease tensions.
- *Take your time on major decisions.* "A truly wonderful opportunity," says psychotherapist Arlene Modica Matthews, "should stand up to scrutiny. Do not bend to pressure to act hastily."
- *Consider "what-if" scenarios.* What would you do if you lost your job? If a family member had enormous medical bills? If the stock market crashed? By planning ahead, you'll feel less anxious.
- *Ask each other how you'd feel if you got what you want* (more money, more spending freedom or whatever). "Most people say, 'I'd feel loved,' or 'I'd feel respected' or 'I'd feel secure,' " observes therapist Suzanne Pope. "That feeling can help pinpoint what money fights are really about."

---

decide which bills to pay. When they have extra savings, Steve, who enjoys reading the financial pages, looks into possible investments. "I do what I do best, and Steve does what he likes best," says Allison. "We work together rather than harping at each other."

"WHY SHOULD I HAVE TO BEG FOR MONEY?"

Jennie worked from the time she graduated from high school until her first child was born. Now a full-time mother of three, she feels she has to plead for money. "If I ask Greg for $20, he wants to know what I'm going to spend it on," she says. "He even checks the receipts to make sure I really did buy diapers."

Greg, a salesman whose commissions have fallen off, feels he's simply being responsible. "Jennie used to blow $20 on makeup every week," he says in self-defense. "We can't afford that kind of spending with three kids."

Babies invariably change the emotional and economic dynamics of a relationship. "A lot of working couples live like financial roommates until they have a child," notes psychologist Arlene Modica Matthews, author of *If I Think about Money So Much, Why Can't I Figure It Out?* "Parenthood makes them feel more bonded to each other."

"Couples who have been very modern and businesslike in handling money may return to old family patterns once they become parents," Mitchell observes. "The husband may have thought in terms of *his* money and *her* money. When her money stops coming in, he's still thinking it's all *his* money—and he resents spending some of it on her needs."

Mitchell urges new parents to talk about their feelings. Jennie, for example, told Greg that his failure to discuss money matters made her feel that she didn't count anymore. When she accused him of treating her "like a child," Greg remembered that his own father had handled the family finances by controlling every penny. "When I became a father, I guess I thought that was how I had to act," he admitted.

Jennie and Greg decided that both needed to keep track of their money. For three months, they recorded every dollar that came in and how it was spent. That gave them a clear idea of their cash flow. They discussed ways to supplement their income if Greg's commissions continued to drop. For example, Jennie might take care of neighborhood children. They also agreed on a weekly amount for Jennie to receive to cover household expenses.

"HOW CAN YOU TAKE SUCH RISKS WITH OUR MONEY?"

When Andy won $10 on a $2 lottery ticket, he bet on a horse and won $20. He thought his wife would be thrilled. Lisa was annoyed. "How can you gamble when we can't even afford new tires for the car?" she asked. But when Lisa suggested shifting their savings into high-yield stocks, Andy got angry. "We can't afford to play the stock market," he said. "You're the real gambler in the family."

Risks are always relative. Andy, who follows horse racing, thinks he knows a safe bet when he sees one. But he doesn't know a blue chip from a poker chip, so the stock market seems far more treacherous to him than the track. Lisa, on the other hand, works for an investment firm and sees that money put into good stocks grows a lot faster than it does in a savings account.

To stop their arguments, Andy and Lisa took the advice of experts in her firm: They discussed their financial objectives, considered various ways to reach them and tried to anticipate what could go wrong with each approach. "We realized that, in a sense, Andy was right: I *am* more of gambler," says Lisa. "He doesn't mind blowing a few bucks on a horse, but when it comes to serious money, he's very cautious."

Ultimately, they decided to diversify—to invest a limited portion of the money they're saving for their children's college education in high-yield bonds. They kept another portion in insured certificates of deposit and put the rest into mutual funds.

"Couples should realize that risk-taking doesn't have to be an all-or-nothing venture," says Mitchell. "They need to be conservative about money saved for emergencies, but should agree on a certain percentage—say 10 to 25 percent—that they'll wager for greater rewards."

"WHY CAN'T WE GET OUT OF DEBT?"

Jason and Molly aren't quite broke, but they owe thousands of dollars on their credit cards. Despite promises to stop spending, both continue to find—and charge—items they can't resist. "How could you spend so much on a tennis racquet?" Molly cries when she sees the bills. "Well, look at how much you spent on clothes!" counters Jason.

Jason and Molly are out-of-control spenders. "They're like kids in a candy store," says Mitchell, who finds that such couples often need professional help. Molly and Jason consulted a therapist with experience in solving money problems. As a first step, she advised leaving their credit cards at home.

Each calculated how much cash was needed each day and carried only that amount. "At first, I was crushed when I'd see great earrings and not be able to buy them," says Molly, "but when I went back to the store later they didn't have the same appeal. I began to see that I bought a lot of things simply to make me feel better." Jason came to a similar realization: He spent money impulsively when he felt unsure of himself. He'd buy a sports jacket, for instance, before calling on a new client.

Jason and Molly also made a list of all their assets and liabilities. They agreed to allocate $300 a month to paying off their credit cards before making any new purchases. Then they came up with alternative ways to boost their spirits: weekend drives in the country, free concerts in the park, dinners at inexpensive restaurants. "We also learned how to express our feelings directly," says Molly "Now if I get angry, I tell Jason how I feel rather than heading for the mall to shop."

"HOW CAN WE STOP FIGHTING?"

Bill and Jeanne had bickered about their budget for years, but their arguments grew more fierce after they retired. Jeanne claims that Bill turns every conversation into a money fight. "If I say it's raining, he'll say he hopes the roof doesn't leak because we can't afford to fix it when I spend so much on the grandchildren," she complains. "Money is all he thinks about." Bill's usual response: "Well, someone has to think about it."

When arguments are repetitive, more than dollars and cents is at stake. Bill was used to calling the shots in his own appliance-repair firm. To him, keeping a keen eye on finances was simply good business. After retirement, he shifted his focus from office to home—and the sudden intensity of his involvement was bewildering to Jeanne.

Underlying Bill's penny-pinching was anxiety about the future. Had he saved enough for their golden years? What if one of them developed a serious illness? What if something happened to their investments? Were they in danger of losing all they'd worked for?

Jeanne finally asked Bill why he was so concerned about every penny. When he spoke vaguely about their fixed income, she asked for details. Then, seeing Bill's anxiety, she suggested they talk to a financial adviser. At first Bill balked at revealing details of their finances to a stranger. But after meeting with the adviser, he felt less anxious.

The money fights eased for a while. But each minor crisis caused the squabbling to resume. One day Jeanne borrowed her granddaughter's tape recorder and turned it on as another battle erupted. The next day she played it back. Both had to smile as they listened to their familiar attacks and counterattacks. "Now what was that really all about?" Jeanne asked. It turned out that Bill was worried about his health, but found it easier to focus on money.

For Bill and Jeanne—as well as other couples torn by money conflicts—finding solutions isn't easy but can result in unexpected dividends. "If couples learn to deal with money, they can tackle other issues—such as success, independence, trust, commitment, power," says Rodney Shapiro, Ph.D., director of family therapy at California Pacific Medical Center in San Francisco. "Once they've worked out their money problems, they have more confidence in their problem-solving skills and more trust in each other. If they can stop fighting about money, they think they can handle anything. They may be right."

Follow-Up

1. *Select one of the situations described as causing conflict and apply it to your life. What are some possible actions that could help in this situation?*
2. *Apply one or more of the suggestions under "How to Avoid Money Conflicts" and report on the results.*
3. *Select two statements or ideas from the article and apply them to your life. Discuss your thoughts.*
4. *For a related reading, see "Personality and Money Orientations" in Section Six (A Quality Life).*

Internet Romance

Meghan Daum

One morning I logged on to my America On-line account to find a message under the heading "is this the real meghan daum?" It came from someone with the screen name PFSlider. The body of the message consisted of five sentences, entirely in lowercase letters, of perfectly turned flattery, something about PFSlider's admiration of some newspaper and magazine articles I had published over the last year and a half, something else about his resulting infatuation with me, and something about his being a sportswriter in California.

I was charmed for a moment or so, engaged for the thirty seconds it took me to read the message and fashion a reply. Though it felt strange to be in the position of confirming that I was indeed "the real meghan daum," I managed to say "Yes, it's me. Thank you for writing." I clicked the Send Now icon and shot my words into the void, where I forgot about PFSlider until the next day, when I received another message, this one labeled "eureka." "wow, it is you," he wrote, still in lowercase. He chronicled the various conditions under which he'd read my few and far between articles: a boardwalk in Laguna Beach, the spring training press room for the baseball team he covered for a Los Angeles newspaper. He confessed to having a "crazy crush" on me. He referred to me as "princess daum." He said he wanted to propose marriage or at least have lunch with me during one of his two annual trips to New York. He managed to do all of this without sounding like a schmuck. As I read the note I smiled the kind of smile one tries to suppress, the kind of smile that arises during a sappy movie one never even admits to seeing. The letter was outrageous and endear-ingly pathetic, possibly the practical joke of a friend trying to rouse me out of a temporary writer's block. But the kindness pouring forth from my computer screen was unprecedented, bizarrely exhilarating, and I logged off and thought about it for a few hours before writing back to express how flattered and touched—it was probably the first time I had ever used "touched" in earnest—I was by his message. . . .

PFSlider and I tossed a few innocuous, smart-assed notes back and forth over the week following his first message. His name was Pete. He was twenty-nine and single. I revealed very little about myself, relying instead on the ironic commentary and forced witti-cisms that are the conceit of most e-mail messages. But I quickly developed an oblique affection for PFSlider. I was excited when there was a message from him, mildly depressed when there wasn't. After a few weeks he gave me his phone number. I did not give him mine, but he looked me up anyway and called me one Friday night. I was home. I picked up the phone. His voice was jarring yet not unpleasant. He held up more than his end of the conversation for an hour. . . .

Pete, as I was forced to call him on the phone—I never could wrap my mind around his actual name, privately referring to him as PFSlider, "e-mail guy," or even "baseball boy"—began calling me two or three times a week. He asked if he could meet me in person and I said that would be okay. Christmas was a few weeks away, and he would be returning east to see his family. From there, he would take the short flight to New York and have lunch with me. "It is my off-season mission to meet you," he said. "There will probably be a snowstorm," I said. "I'll bring a team of sled dogs," he answered. . . .

Other times we would find each other logged on to America Online at the same time and type back and forth for hours. For me, this was far superior to the phone. Through typos and misspellings, he flirted maniacally. "I have an absurd crush on you," he said. "If I like you in person you must promise to marry me." I was coy and conceited, telling him to get a life, baiting him into complimenting me further, teasing him in a way I would never have dared in the real world or even on the phone. I would stay up until 3:00 A.M. typing with him, smiling at the screen, getting so giddy that I couldn't fall asleep. I was having difficulty recalling what I used to do at night. My phone was tied up for hours at a time. No one in the real world could reach me, and I didn't really care. . . .

My interaction with PFSlider was more human than much of what I experienced in the daylight realm of live beings. I was certainly putting more energy into the relationship than I had put into any before, giving him attention that was by definition undivided, relishing the safety of the distance by opting to be truthful rather than doling out the white lies that have become the staple of real life. The outside world, the place where I walked around on the concrete, avoiding people I didn't want to deal with, peppering the ground with half-truths, and applying my motto of "let the machine take it" to almost any scenario, was sliding into the periphery of my mind. I was a better person with PFSlider. I was someone I could live with.

This borrowed identity is, of course, the primary convention of Internet relationships. The false comfort of the cyberspace persona has been identified as one of the maladies of our time, another avenue for the remoteness that so famously plagues contemporary life. But the better person that I was to PFSlider was not a result of being a different person to him. It was simply that I was a desired person, the object of a blind man's gaze. I may not have known my suitor, but for the first time in my life I knew the deal. I knew when I'd hear from him and how I'd hear from him. I knew he wanted me because he said he wanted me, because the distance and facelessness and lack of gravity of it all allowed him to be sweeter to me than most real-life people had ever managed. For the first time in my life, I was involved in an actual courtship ritual. Never before had I realized how much that kind of structure was missing from my everyday life.

And so PFSlider became my everyday life. . . .

Since graduating from college, I had spent three years in a serious relationship and two years in a state of neither looking for a boyfriend nor particularly avoiding one. I had had the requisite number of false starts and five-night stands, dates that I weren't sure were dates, emphatically casual affairs that buckled under their own inertia even before dawn broke through the iron-guarded windows of stale, one-room city apartments. Even though I was heading into my late twenties I was still a child, ignorant of dance steps or health insurance, a prisoner of credit card debt and student loans and the nagging feeling that I didn't want anyone to find me until I had pulled myself into some semblance of a grownup. I was a true believer in the urban dream, in years of struggle succumbing to brilliant success, in getting a break, in making it. Like most of my friends, I was selfish by design. To want was more virtuous than to need. I wanted someone to love me, but I certainly didn't need it. I didn't want to be alone, but as long as I was I had no choice but to wear my solitude as though it were haute couture. . . .

My addiction to PFSlider's messages indicated a monstrous narcissism. But it also revealed a subtler desire that I didn't fully understand at the time. My need to experience an old-fashioned kind of courtship was stronger than I had ever imagined. . . .

For the first time in my life, I was not involved in a protracted "hang out" that would lead to a quasi-romance. I was involved in a well-defined structure, a neat little space in which we were both safe to express the panic and intrigue of our mutual affection. Our interaction was refreshingly orderly, noble in its vigor, dignified despite its shamelessness. We had an intimacy that seemed custom made for our strange, lonely times. It seemed custom made for me.

The day of our date was frigid and sunny. Pete was sitting at the bar of the restaurant when I arrived. We shook hands. For a split second he leaned toward me with his chin as if to kiss me. . . .

He talked and I heard nothing he said. He talked and talked and talked. I stared at his profile and tried to figure out if I liked him. He seemed to be saying nothing in particular, though it went on forever. Later we went to the Museum of Natural History and watched a science film about storms. We walked around looking for the dinosaurs, and he talked so much that I wanted to cry. Outside, walking along Central Park West at dusk, through the leaves, past the horse-drawn carriages and yellow cabs and splendid lights of Manhattan at Christmas, he grabbed my hand to kiss me and I didn't let him. I felt as if my brain had been stuffed with cotton. Then for some reason I invited him back to my apartment, gave him a few beers, and finally let him kiss me on the lumpy futon in my bedroom. The radiator clanked. The phone rang and the machine picked up. A car alarm blared outside. A key turned in the door as one of my roommates came home. I had no sensation at all, only the dull déjà vu of being back in some college dorm room, making out in a generic fashion on an Indian throw rug while Cat Stevens's *Greatest Hits* played on the portable stereo. I wanted Pete out of my apartment. I wanted to hand him his coat, close the door behind him, and fight the ensuing emptiness by turning on the computer and taking comfort in PFSlider.

When Pete finally did leave I sulked. The ax had fallen. He'd talked way too much. He was hyper. He hadn't let me talk, although I hadn't tried very hard. I berated myself from every angle, for not kissing him on Central Park West, for letting him kiss me at all, for not liking him, for wanting to like him more than I had wanted anything in such a long time. I was horrified by the realization that I had invested so heavily in a made-up character, a character in whose creation I'd had a greater hand than even Pete himself. How could I, a person so self-congratulatingly reasonable, have gotten sucked into a scenario that was more like a television talk show than the relatively full and sophisticated life I was so convinced I lead? How could I have received a fan letter and allowed it go this far? Then a huge bouquet of FTD flowers arrived from him. No one had ever sent me flowers before. I was sick with sadness. I hated either the world or myself, and probably both. . . .

As human beings with actual flesh and hand gestures and Gap clothing, Pete and I were utterly incompatible, but I pretended otherwise. . . .

Unlike most cyber romances, which seem to come fully equipped with the inevitable set of misrepresentations and false expectations, PFSlider and I had played it fairly straight. Neither of us had lied. We'd done the best we could. We were dead from natural causes rather than virtual ones. . . .

At least seven people confessed to me the vagaries of their own e-mail affairs. The topic arose, unprompted, over the course of normal conversation. Four of these people had gotten on planes and met their correspondents, traveling from New Haven to Baltimore, New York to Montana, Texas to Virginia, and New York to Johannesburg. These were normal people, writers and lawyers and scientists I knew from the real world. They were all smart, attractive, and more than a little sheepish about admitting just how deep they had been sucked in. Very few had met in chat rooms. Instead, the messages had started after chance meetings at parties and on planes; some, like me, had received notes in response to things they'd written on-line or elsewhere. Two of these people had fallen in love, the others chalked it up to strange, uniquely postmodern experience. . . .

If Pete and I had met at a party, we probably wouldn't have spoken to each other for more than ten minutes, and that would have made life easier but also less interesting. At the same time, it terrifies me to admit a firsthand understanding of the way the heart and the ego are snarled and entwined.

Follow-Up

1. *Describe the advantages and disadvantages of e-mail romances.*
2. *According to Daum, online encounters allow you to portray another identity, or to express an aspect of yourself that is normally hidden in face-to-face encounters. Is this true in your online encounters? What are the advantages and disadvantages of this portrayal?*
3. *E-mail exchanges cannot reveal one's non-verbal behaviors such as gestures, frowns or smirks, voice tone, eye contact, and so on. Studies show that the majority of emotional messages are conveyed through non-verbal means. Discuss the effects of the absence of non-verbal behaviors in e-mail exchanges.*
4. *Starting a relationship through e-mail exchanges often results in a flurry of intense correspondence. This raises expectations. Upon meeting your cyberpartner in person, you are disappointed. Comment on this phenomena.*
5. *The author discovered that she wanted an "old-fashioned courtship" after several exchanges with her Internet partner. Why do you think this intimacy need had gone undetected? Is this unusual or typical in our society today? Offer your thoughts.*
6. *Choose any two statements or ideas from this article and offer your commentary.*

Kinds of Friends

In her book *Necessary Losses,* Judith Viorst discusses how we form different categories of friendships. A brief description of each kind of friendship is given below:

1. *Convenience Friends*—Persons with whom we exchange small favors; a friendly, but limited, intimacy relationship.
2. *Special Interest Friends*—Persons with whom we share common interests and activities; regular involvement, but not deep intimacy.
3. *Historical Friends*—Persons who were friends in our past but who we do not see often; there may be little in common now, but there is an intimacy that derives from being able to say, "I knew you when. . . ."
4. *Crossroads Friends*—Significant friends at a special time of our lives (e.g., college, former roommate, military service); little current contact, but the specialness can be quickly regenerated if there is an interaction.
5. *Cross-Generational Friends*—The older–younger relationships that have influence and intimacy. It may be a relationship of a mentor, or a cherished non-family friendship in which the older persons are valued for their counsel and acceptance and the younger persons for their liveliness and eagerness to learn.
6. *Close Friends*—Persons who hear our deeper disclosures; those whom we can trust and with whom we can just "be."

Follow-Up

1. *Do your friends generally fall into the categories listed above? If not, what other friend categories would you add?*
2. *Viorst says we have ambivalent feelings toward close friends. There may be envy and competition, as well as affection and love. We generally are more aware of the positive feelings. Is this true for you?*
3. *How would you (or do you) feel about being classified into these categories by your friends?*
4. *Discuss and/or write about your reactions.*

Lamenting the Fading of Friendships

Mark Murrmann

People change.

I know I'm a different person, in some aspects, than I was just six months ago.

It's hard to deal with people changing, especially when those people are, or used to be, your friends.

Of my good friends in high school, I am still close with exactly none of them. Some of them I see once in a while, and we still get along well. Others I see maybe once a year, passing each other by chance on the street. We haven't got much to say, though.

Most of my old friends and I haven't really got much in common anymore. Thus, our conversations are limited to what we've been doing with our lives, what we plan on doing with our lives and what others are doing with their lives.

That is a boring, tired conversation. I may as well be talking to a stranger.

I am at fault for not seeing many of my old friends, and that makes me mad at myself. One of my best friends in high school lived one block away for the past year. I saw him only a few times—the times he came to my house.

Now that he's moved, I feel dumb for never stopping by.

SHARED PAST NOT ENOUGH

Other friends I have shut out of my life on purpose. We were once friends, and now we're not. We once had a lot in common; now we have little. All we have in common is a part of our past.

It's hard to have a relationship with someone based solely on the past. There is only so much you can reminisce over.

But I'm not going to take full blame for the friends with whom I've lost touch.

People change, but I'm not the only one.

It's sad sometimes, thinking of all the great plans we had for the future, all the "forevers, alwayses, nevers."

Then we drifted apart, for one reason or another. And now sometimes when I see an old friend approaching on the street, I almost wish I could turn invisible.

There are other times when I'd like nothing more than to call an old friend, if nothing else, just to say hello.

But I've lost contact.

Now I have more acquaintances, but fewer friends. And while sometimes I miss my old friends, my new friends are great. Really good friends are hard to come by, and it's sad that so many of mine have been swallowed by shadows.

People change, and so do I.

1. *Mark Murrmann discusses how he and his former high school friends now have little in common. Do you feel some sense of guilt when former friendships are not maintained? What seems to be the norm for changing friends? How should we act when it is time for a friendship to change?*

The Human Potential of Whip Gimby

Nels Goud

While on a picnic my seven-year-old son and I walked over to watch a couple innings of a men's baseball game. It was the end of a close game, the bases were loaded, and the pitcher was nervously pawing the dirt on the mound. The pitcher peered in toward the plate, took a quick look over at third and fired an aspirin fastball. The batter was ready and took a mighty swing and conked the catcher on the back of the head. Everyone on the field and in the stands remained frozen for a few seconds and stared. Except for the catcher. He fell forward and sprawled face down over home plate. His mask had protected his skull but the force of the blow knocked him out. The ump removed his mask and called "Time Out!" Players and coaches from both teams ran toward home plate, some sounding like medical students: "You all right Pete?" Pete slowly rolled over on his back, opened his eyes and looked for the freight train that roared onto the diamond. "Pete, you okay?" yelled the medical teammates. Pete stood up, rubbed his head and hoped it was still connected to his neck. Between home and first base a big argument was brewing. The catcher's coach was shouting at the ump "He swung! It's strike two!" The ump appeared mystified at the sense of priorities here and told the coach to shut up and walked over to the catcher. The coach marched behind the ump and kept yelling "It's a strike!" This guy wanted to win. The catcher staggered to his feet and began slowly rotating his head.

"What's the coach arguing about, Dad?" asked my son.

"Well, he is saying that the batter swung and even though he hit the catcher, it should be called a strike."

"What difference does that make?" responded my son with some anger, "The catcher's hurt!"

A single baseball play escalates into human drama. A young boy becomes puzzled by the lack of agreement on the obvious ethical choice. Once again I realize how life's fundamentals are reflected in almost any activity. All you have to do is look in a certain way. A single wild flower revealed the whole world to the philosopher Suzuki. Since it is summer, baseball seems to fit nicely as a mirror.

During my high school years I had to find the best players for my Little League team, the Decatur Tigers. The selection criteria was simple—choose the best hitters and fielders. You would have been surprised on how many good players were passed over in the general draft. This happened because human bias weaseled its way into the coaches' choices. In Decatur there was a negative image of the "farm kid." Most other coaches selected these players last, and then grudgingly. Maybe this was because most coaches were "town kids." Although I lived in town I knew many farm families through my father's work, truck farming. I also knew who could run, hit, and throw. Seven Tiger regulars were farm kids and even though these players helped win League championships for the Tigers, each year they were passed over by other coaches. It was one of the few times in my life that I applauded bias.

This farm kid prejudice brought disaster to the other teams during one particular year. The Tigers were struggling about half way through the season due to erratic pitching. My third baseman, a farm kid, happened to bring his neighbor Harmon to a practice. Harmon looked like he just finished cleaning barns. He wore baggy pants held up with suspenders, had a long-sleeved work shirt, and his head almost hidden by a floppy wide-brimmed hat. He was a quiet kid and when he did speak it was in a slow drawl. I asked Harmon to help us out by chasing down foul balls during batting practice and throw them back to me. After the fifth foul ball my catching hand was turning red from the force of his throws.

"Hey Harmon, how old are you?" I asked.

"Twelve," he quietly drawled. The upper age for Little League.

"Have you ever played baseball?"

"No."

"How would you like to play for the Tigers?"

"OK."

I walked Harmon over to the other coaches and asked if they minded if I added Harmon to my roster, he being a friend of my third baseman and having nothing to do. They looked over Harmon, barely holding back the wisecracks, and with large smiles generally said, "Go ahead, fine with me." I showed Harmon how to wind up like a pitcher. I told him to throw as hard as he could into the catcher's mitt. Harmon threw hard and straight and the Tigers won every game from there on out.

Harmon was a natural. If he were a flower, he would only have needed a couple inches of dust and an occasional sprinkle to achieve full bloom. But as most coaches know, for every Harmon there is a Whip Gimby.

If Whip was a flower, it would take daily pampering all spring on the finest soil to get his seed to break ground surface. Whip was one of those boys who, not really knowing why or questioning it, was supposed to play baseball because it seemed boys did that sort of thing in the summer. Whip appeared genuinely interested but somewhat baffled by the sport. The first practice sessions quickly revealed that he did not know how to hold a bat, what a shortstop did, or what to do if he happened to stop a ball hit at him. At ten years old his spindly frame had yet to show signs of any musculature, and hand-eye coordination was best classified in the potentials category. The regulation size baseball glove hung from his hand like a heavy saddle. There was only one position for Whip—right field. There was where he earned the nickname. He would stand motionless in right field until a ball flew by him. Tracking it down, he would stand there with a puzzled look. "Throw it to second base!" shouted the other players.

Wide-eyed, he would unfurl a long, skinny arm for a mighty heave. The ball would arch lazily for a few feet and roll to a stop, almost making it to the infield. "Arm like a whip," said the center-fielder. The name stuck. I think he liked it. He had something special— a baseball name.

Whip's first time at bat found him straddling the plate facing the pitcher head on, his hands holding the bat like it was an ax. Whip was a true coaching challenge. We straightened out his batting stance. The remaining problem was that his swing went in the same arc and speed whether the pitch was high or low, fast or slow. No amount of coaching could change this swing. It had to be a genetic fixed action pattern. Whip would make contact only if the ball happened to pass in the space of his lone swing pattern. He was just as surprised as the rest of us when this did occur.

Strangely, it was Whip Gimby who taught us a great deal about positive human character. Blessed with the aptitude of a turnip for baseball and having to prove it each practice and game, I cannot remember a single instance when he was angry, withdrawn, frustrated, or blaming someone. Whip retained an eagerness to learn and attended every practice. An infrequent catch or hitting a weak ground ball was enough to sustain him through many failures. Whip seemed to accept his limited abilities and was proud to be a Tiger. How do you not like a kid like this?

Whip became a key figure for many Tigers on learning the meaning of human respect. During the first practices Whip became the target of jokes and taunts by several good hitters. My lecturing did not seem to stop these wisecracks. It became obvious that another method had to be employed. I called it "empathy training." If a player persisted in making degrading remarks about Whip's hitting, I made sure he would not have a chance to hit the ball when his turn came to practice. For a high school pitcher, this was not hard to do; I could really bring the heat from the Little League mound. The superstars would miss every pitch and I would offer a comment or two on their pathetic hitting prowess. The wisecracking diminished to zero after one empathy session.

The real thrills in Little League baseball came from playing in actual competition. You got a chance to show your stuff in front of family and friends, match skills with opposing players, and even play with a spanking brand new baseball. And if you were on a winning team, it was all magnified. To play in a game as a Tiger you had to attend practice. The Tigers were always in contention for first place and the guys attended practice regularly in order to play. This, of course, made us a better team. The "you practice, you play" rule combined fairness with the work ethic so cherished by the culture. It also produced an ethical dilemma one season.

It was the next to the last game and the Tigers were tied for first place. The final game was against the other first-place team. A win in this game was crucial. Harmon was doing his usual job, sizzling fast balls by batters making them look for holes in their bats. But a few errors and walks and an occasional hit got them enough runs to tie us going into the last two innings. We had two more chances at bat. It was then I realized that I had not played four Tigers who had attended practice that week. No one said anything and it was common practice to stick with your best players in tight games. I was tempted. But what can you do when your players faithfully follow the practice-play rule? I sent the four out to their fielding positions. Whip loped out to right field.

An inning passes with no change in score. Harmon strikes out the side in the first half of the last inning. Our last chance at bat. Jimmy hits a double. A strike out and a ground out make it two down, but Jimmy has scampered to third. The opposing pitcher is getting tired and wild. He walks the next batter. Two on and two out. Seems like I read a similar baseball story before, but now I'm in it. Yes, it is Whip Gimby's turn at immortality. True to form, Whip doesn't realize it's his turn. "Whip!" I call, "It's your turn to hit." Whip catapults off the bench and runs to homeplate. He has forgotten his bat, and runs back to the bench. Normally a pumped up state can help a player. It's making Whip more confused. I walk over to calm him down. His eyes are wide, darting left and right.

"Should I swing?" he asks.

"Swing if it is a pitch you can hit. Do not swing if it's a bad pitch." Sound advice to a nervous batter if he knows the difference between a bad and good pitch. This is not one of Whip's strengths. "You'll do fine Whip, just watch the pitch." There is another choice. Just tell him to take all pitches because the pitcher is getting wild and there's a good chance of getting a walk. The odds for a walk are considerably higher than Whip hitting a pitch. But what does this coaching advice communicate to a young boy? I'm beginning to hate principles.

Whip swings at the first pitch and misses. The second pitch comes in head high. Whip swings about when the catcher throws it back to the pitcher. He is consistent, though. Both swings were in his fixed lone swing pattern. I can tell he is too pumped up yet. I go over to talk to him, tell him he's doing fine, and to really watch the ball before he swings. He settles back into the batter's box with his wide eyes. The pitcher winds up and a fastball streaks over the middle of the plate. Whip unleashs his only swing. POOF, he misses again. A few groans are heard. As Whip walks back to the bench I think I catch the first look of dejection I've seen on him the whole season. A couple Tigers go out and tell him that it was all right, they struck out earlier too.

The Tigers survived this game and clinched the championship in the final game. Harmon set a league strikeout record. Whip could say he was on a champion team.

If you happen to watch some baseball you might take a minute to look at the human drama out there. You might also cheer on a kid throwing aspirins or even a skinny one who swings the same way no matter if the pitch is high or low, fast or slow.

Follow-Up

1. *In almost any organized activity—sports, music groups, and so forth—there is a Whip Gimby or two. Not having the aptitude or background of more skilled peers, these persons often have other redeeming qualities that contribute to the group. Try to think of an example of this phenomenon in your life. Offer your analysis of why the less talented are, or can be, needed and valued members of a group.*
2. *The author states that "life's fundamentals are reflected in almost any activity." Discuss another life activity for which this is true, and provide examples.*
3. *Write about or discuss your views on any other aspect of this piece.*

Parents

Martin Shepard

Learning to accept your parents as people in their own right—different and distinct from you—is a task that poses difficulties for quite a large number of people. There should be nothing surprising in all of this. For we all have one very good historical reason—our childhoods.

The infant is born into a world in which he is, literally, *part* of his mother. Without her to comfort, clothe, feed and shelter him, he could not survive. During childhood our little girl and boy still depend greatly on their parents. They have not yet acquired the skills necessary to provide for and sustain themselves. This is a time one learns certain "do's" and "don'ts." You learn how to count and how to read, how to cook and how to sew, how to hammer and how to saw. And you learn *not* to swallow iodine, *not* to put a fork in the electrical outlet, and *not* to cross a street unless you look to make sure there is no traffic approaching.

Typically the child's contract with the parent is one in which he accepts the dependent role in return for the favors/protection/guidance/and support he receives from them. There are, of course, dissatisfactions. He prefers taking things out to play with more than he does putting them away. He wants to do and try things he sees grown-ups doing and resents it when they say "No." He may want to come and go more freely than they are ready to allow. And he'd rather watch television than do his homework or practice the piano.

Adolescence marks the years during which relatively accepting and "sweet" children become adults in their own right. Following the sexual maturation of puberty, adolescents typically reject the dependent contracts that as children they had with their parents. It is a period of much storm and strife, both in the inner life of the adolescents and in their relationships to their parents. Opposition/confrontation/argumentation are a natural part of the process as the adolescent seeks to break away and find his or her own adulthood. If it is accomplished smoothly, and the adolescent truly feels adult, he comes to accept his parents as he would other adults. If they share common interests and *if* the parents accept him as an adult (not only as their child), they remain close. If their interests are not similar and/or if the parents cannot transcend their *roles* as parents, there is a polite distance—as any adult would have with people who are on different wavelengths. This second alternative is a more common outcome of maturation.

What I have described thus far is "normal" maturation. Many individuals, no matter how old they are, never make it, psychologically speaking, past either childhood or adolescence when it comes to relating to their parents. Those stuck in the childhood phase remain overly docile and dependent. Those stuck in adolescence relate to their parents in a perpetually rebellious and ill-tempered way.

Given the cultural roles males and females are assigned (males presumably being "aggressive" and females "passive"), one might expect that women are more likely to become stuck in the childhood state and men in the adolescent one. And—although there are many reversals to this expectation—such is usually the case.

Louise is a good example of such a child/woman. In her childhood and adolescence, her parents were perpetually available to her.

They were quick to comfort and pamper her. They always soothed her hurts, took her side, indulged her fancies. She, in turn, pampered their egos by letting them know how exceptional they were, how they were the only people who understood her, how much wisdom and sage advice they had, and how appreciative she was.

At twenty-two she married for the first time. Her husband, Greg, was an insurance salesman and just out of college. He was a decent, responsible, upright young man, who looked forward to supporting Louise and raising a family. But it never worked out that way.

Louise was incapable of accommodating herself to the rigors of a more spartan and independent existence. She consulted her mother daily, both to ask for advice on simple housekeeping chores and for consolation over any minor inconveniences she was having with Greg. She was incapable of sticking to a budget and so, behind Greg's back, ran to her physician father for extra funds to pay her charge-account bills and indulge her passion for clothes, cars (which she insisted on changing yearly), and innumerable redecoration schemes.

When her first and only child was born, her parents hired a maid for her. And Mother came over daily for several months to help out and give advice.

After three years of marriage, Louise left Greg. Marriage didn't conform to her picture of "picket fences and lace curtains." She was interested in playing more and working less. Her parents were sympathetic. They agreed with Louise that Greg was "cheap," "selfish," and that he "always got his way." Besides which, Mother was willing to raise Louise's daughter while Louise went back to school and tried to find a new man.

Now thirty-nine years old and on her fifth husband, Louise lives in another city. But she still phones her family a few times each week.

Sam, who is twenty-eight, is the sort of person who typifies adolescent "stuckness."

For he remains continuously close to, yet antagonistic toward, his parents.

While attending a local college, he, like many other students, began smoking marijuana. Not content to do it privately, he naturally let his parents know of his activities. They were frightened, shocked, and strongly disapproving. Sam, rather than dropping the subject, continued to let them know of his usage by smoking at home. Quarrels/insults/door-slamming occurred frequently on both sides.

Dinner conversations to this day are reminiscent of the popular television series *All in the Family*—with Sam typically attacking his father's political and social points of view and Mother acting as a harassed peacemaker.

Four years ago Sam moved out of his parents' home but continued to bring home his laundry for his mother to wash. His attitude was sullen. If his mother inquired about his life he would give her flippant answers or accuse her of trying to hold on to him. Yet he made it a point to inform his parents of many of his activities that he knew they objected to—his dating a woman of another religion, his intention of quitting a promising job, his experimentation with LSD.

Every now and then he would ask his father for a loan or the use of the family car. He felt it was coming to him. On those occasions when his father refused him, he always had some unkind words for the old man.

Two years ago he married. He made it a point to tell his mother not to interfere when she offered to help care for Suzy, Sam's daughter, who was born eight months ago. But whenever Sam and his wife, Brenda, have a party to attend, Sam calls up his mother, expecting her to be always available for babysitting. When she is not, he accuses her of being a hypocrite for having offered to help out earlier.

How can you tell if you are *stuck,* in any respect, regarding your parents? One way is to see if they embarrass you. Perhaps you don't want your parents to meet your friends because you fear they will act in a way that will humiliate you; that they will treat you as their little girl or boy, correct you, or behave "coarsely" in front of your friends.

Such embarrassment is often related to your still feeling yourself a *part* of—an extension of—your parents. You fail to realize that if your parents do react absurdly, it is *they* who will be laughed at, not you. Unless, of course, you take it as personally as a thirteen-year-old who brings her first date over to the house.

Other indications of dependency are the making of routine daily or weekly telephone calls to your parents, wanting their approval constantly, or finding that there is "no other person as good, wise, and kind to me as my mother (or father)."

Signs of rebelliousness are so self-evident, emotionally, to the sufferer, that they need no further elaboration.

There is a certain validity to a child's blaming a parent when things don't work out to his satisfaction. After all, the parent *is* in charge. If a meal doesn't taste good, the child can't very well cook his own. If the family moves and the child must give up his neighborhood friends, that is the parents' responsibility, not his. *But once you pass the age of eighteen,* those conditions no longer hold true. There is no further need to depend upon your parents.

The task of both the *child-stuck* and *adolescent-stuck* person is to get *un-stuck,* by learning to do things on your own and, in doing so, becoming a more self-sufficient human being. You can't have a very good self-concept—can't very well consider yourself any person's equal—if you remain a child-at-heart in relationship to your parents. Whatever *advantages* there are in taking things from your parents by continuing the "child" or "adolescent" integrations are more than offset by the loss of basic self-esteem that results from staying in that role.

The "child" is reluctant to go *through* the adolescent, rebellious, phase. The "adolescent" is reluctant to achieve total self-sufficiency. He wants all of the advantages of both childhood *and* adulthood, but none of the disadvantages of either. "Adolescents" are too embarrassed to admit how much they still *want* their parents, and how much they might even love them.

Both groups ask for their parents' support and approval (albeit in different ways) long after they are capable of managing their own lives. Not only does this interfere with their lives in general (witness Louise and Sam), but it certainly prevents the possibility of their establishing a realistic present-day relationship with their parents.

I've talked frequently in this book* about living in the *here and now,* and how emotions, people, and relationships change. One of the things that can certainly be said of people who have trouble dealing with their parents is that they are usually reacting to *memories* of both their parents and themselves—as they all were ten, fifteen, or twenty years ago—and *not* in terms of the realities of all of them now. This is always due to the *holding back* of the maturational process.

We are left, therefore, with many adults who still *blame* their parents for the way they have treated them. As if their parents had chosen to make the child's life miserable.

Yet there are very few parents who *intentionally* act cruelly. Every set of parents, if they could choose, would elect to be the world's best parents.

Of course, lack of "intent" does not mean that parents don't occasionally act cruelly. Why shouldn't they? They are primarily *people* before they are parents. All of us are capable of cruelty. Besides, they had parents who "misunderstood" them, too. Parents, like all people, can be tight-fisted, generous, disappointing, helpful, indifferent, funny, tender, or short-tempered.

When I was twenty-five and a student in medical school, I was still reacting to my parents as an adolescent. I resented having to go visit them each week. I felt they were still try-

---

Editor's Note: Martin Shepard is referring to his book *The Do-It-Yourself Psychotherapy Book.*

ing to control me. When I was questioned by my analyst whether the situation might not be reversed—whether I might not be trying to control *them*—I realized that I made my weekly sojourns to pick up a weekly allotment that they were generous enough to offer me. And that I could possibly manage to get by with a much lower amount. And that I needn't show up weekly to "pay my dues" for their generosity—that they gave it out of kindness and not for my weekly shows of obeisance. With that realization I stopped my mechanical visits, cut down on what I was receiving and began to relate to them more adultly.

A therapist friend of mine was treating a young man who constantly fought with his mother. He wanted her approval, but she was constantly critical. Mother was an exceptionally irrational woman and never saw how much her son wanted her blessings. He, in turn, could not accept her irrationality.

My friend asked his patient the following question: "If you passed by a mental institution and saw your mother looking through the barred windows on one of the floors, and she was screaming the same things at you, as you passed by, that she now screams at you at home, would it still trouble you?"

"No," said the young man. "I'd discount it, because I'd know she was crazy."

"From now on, then, every time your mother gets on your nerves, I want you to recall that picture of her shouting from that hospital window."

His patient did just that and found his aggravation and frustration subsiding.

A device such as this is I think, a useful tool for people who find themselves continuously fighting with a non-accepting parent.

A rule to bear in mind that will help you to see your parents more realistically, is:

Grown-ups are merely children in aging skin.

When you get to feeling overwhelmed by your parents' (or parent substitutes—such as bosses or teachers) "wisdom" or resentful over their "shortcomings," try to see the child that is hiding and acting inside of them.

I have purposely avoided writing a chapter on *being a parent*—on dealing more effectively with your children—for a number of reasons. One is that there is no way to be a *parent*. You can only be *yourself*. And if you become a mentally healthy adult (as, I'm sure, all of the readers of this book are trying to become), you will do all right both as *yourself* and as a parent.

As a psychiatrist, I have seen hundreds upon hundreds of people complaining about their parents. If they were given a great deal of material advantages, they would complain that "my parents bought me things as a substitute for love." If they were given few things, the complaint was "my parents were cheapskates and didn't love me enough." If they were given a great deal of freedom by their parents, they would lament that their "parents weren't interested in me or what I did." But if they were closely supervised, it was because "my parents were too strict."

Naturally it helps to be kind, tolerant, and understanding of your children. Remembering your own childhood helps. But sometimes a spanking or some punishment may well be in order.

So there are no suggestions I have to offer you as a parent, except to bear in mind that *whatever you do, it is likely to be wrong in your child's eyes.* But when and if your child grows to maturity—if he or she doesn't get stuck in child-like or adolescent behavior—your child will come to appreciate that you did the best that you could.

And further—it is your *child's* responsibility to grow up, to mature—not yours to do it for him. Just as you must realize that you are no longer part of your parents—that things aren't *their fault*—your child has to learn the same things about you.

The exercises that follow attempt to help you continue your own maturational process vis-à-vis your parents. You may need *repeated* work on the exercises in order to abandon your unrealistic views of both yourself and your parents. For you must, eventually, learn to let go of them, give up your demands that they be different than they are, forgive them their faults (and all of the things that they "should" have done, did do, and didn't do)—and come to realize that your parents couldn't possibly have been anything other than what they were and what they are.

SHEPARD'S EXERCISES

1. Work with two empty chairs. Put your father in one and tell him all of the negative things you've held back from him—your resentments, frustrations, hatreds. Be as specific as you can. Then, switch seats, be him, and respond to "you." Say how you feel hearing all of these negative things. Keep the dialogue going by changing chairs once more and telling your father what you needed, now need, wanted, and now want from him. Have him respond by saying what he needs and wants from you (past and present). See whether or not you can achieve any greater understanding of one another's positions, as you keep the dialogue going, as opposed to finding yourselves simply *arguing*.

2. Repeat exercise 1, substituting your mother for your father.

3. Pretend you are your father and write a short composition about "The Difficulties I Had in Raising My Child."

4. Repeat exercise 3, but now write as your mother instead of your father.

5. Place your father back in the empty chair. Tell him all of the things you've appreciated or loved about him. Switch seats and, as your father, say what you *feel* about your child's telling you such nice things. Keep the dialogue going.

6. Repeat exercise 5 with your mother.

7. Be your father and tell your child all the things you've loved and appreciated about her (or him). Switch chairs, be yourself, and say how you feel about hearing these things. Be your father again and respond.

8. Repeat exercise 7 with your mother.

9. List all of the secrets concerning your private life that you would never tell your parents. Place each of your parents in an empty chair in front of you and tell each one, in turn, these secrets. Be your parents and react. Again, keep switching chairs and get a dialogue going. See whether you can move toward mutual understanding rather than conflict and confrontation.

10. If your relationship with either parent is characterized by dependent routines, daily or weekly phone calls or visits (if you are living away from home), take a month's vacation from these activities. Don't call. Don't visit. Politely tell your parents that you simply want to see what it's like to live without such regular contact with them. And stick to your word.

   If you are over twenty-one and still live with your parents spend the next month living elsewhere, giving the same reasons. Move in with a friend or series of friends, into a Y, a hotel room, with a sibling, or with a different relative. Better still, try all of these different arrangements for a few nights each so that you might see what it is like to live in different spaces.

11. If your relationship with either parent is characterized by aloofness or grumpiness, or if you have not had much contact with them in some time, see what it is like to try to get closer.

   Make a date to meet them somewhere and treat them to a dinner. Give them a small gift—a token of your "appreciation" (whether it is felt or not). Ask them details about their lives. Tell them whatever things you appreciate or like about them—and work hard at avoiding unkind words during this experience.

   A day later, write about your experience. Describe what it meant to you and what you learned from it.

   If either of your parents is dead, do the above exercise in fantasy for the one (or ones) you can't bring along in reality.

Follow-Up

1. *In what major ways are you like and unlike each of your parents (guardians)? How much choice do you have in keeping or changing these qualities?*
2. *If you are a parent of adolescent or adult children, explain why you agree or disagree with some of Shepard's ideas.*
3. *Write about and/or discuss any other main point of this article.*
4. *Attempt one or more of the exercises listed at the end of the article and report what you learned.*

Eye for Sale

Bob Greene

The advertisement appeared in the classifieds section of the June issue of the *Illinois Medical Journal.* It was listed under "For sale, lease or rent," and it was brief:

> Totally disabled veteran with four children in college wishes to negotiate sale of one left eye, hazel in color, to highest bidder. For transplant. Contact Donald K. Henry, Sr., in care of Donald K. Henry, Jr., 117 W Fifth, Peru, Indiana 46907.

A telephone call to the residence in Indiana brought Donald Henry, Jr., to the phone. He had not heard about the advertisement. It was read to him.

"Oh, my God," he said. "Donald Henry, Sr., is my father. I had no idea he'd done this. I'm a college student, and he probably used my address because he doesn't have a permanent place of his own. He does that sometimes, and then sends for his mail. He's living in a little town in Texas now."

The son said his father is severely handicapped, the result of breaking his back on two separate occasions, a deterioration of his veins and sixteen operations, including six on his brain in an effort to deaden the nerves that were causing unbearable pain in his back and legs.

"My father is only 48 years old," the son said. "Some days he can't walk at all. On those days he just lies in bed. When he can walk, it takes him ten minutes to move across a room, using a cane. He has to stay in warm climates; otherwise when it gets below 70 degrees his legs and feet turn blue. He and my mother were divorced in 1964, and now he is alone."

The son said his father did not have a telephone, but was reachable through a phone number in McAllen, Texas.

A call to the Texas number was answered by a male voice saying, "La Vista Apartments." The caller asked for Donald K. Henry, Sr.

"He's across the courtyard in his room," the voice said. "I can get him for you, but it will take him a long time to come to the phone."

Minutes passed. Then Donald Henry picked up the phone and identified himself. The caller said that it was about the advertisement in the *Illinois Medical Journal.*

"Was an offer made?" Henry asked, his voice excited.

The caller said no. The caller said he was curious about the ad. Did Mr. Henry mean to sell his eye at the time of his death?

"No, not when I'm dead," Henry said. "I'm talking about now."

But why?

"Financial reasons," Henry said.

There was a silence. Then Henry continued:

"I would like to leave something for my children. I would like to set up some sort of estate for them. I have no money. This is the only way I can think of to raise some. My eyes are the only good thing I have left."

He said he had served in the Navy during, World War II and Korea, and then had become a mortgage broker. He developed arteriosclerosis and heart disease, and despite all the operations his condition worsened.

"Because of my illnesses, I couldn't be much of a father," Henry said. "And after the divorce I didn't feel like a father at all. After my last operation I got the idea to sell one of my eyes, and I thought that if I put an advertisement in a medical journal, a doctor might see it and know of a person who needed an eye. If I can get enough money for it, then I will be able to feel that I have contributed to my children's lives."

Is he afraid of losing the eye?

"No," he said. "What the hell's one more thing?"

Did he think much about it before he decided to offer his eye for sale?

"I thought about it for a month or so," he said. "But like I told you before, I couldn't think of any other way to raise any money. I'll still have one eye left. I'm sure that my vision won't be as complete as it is now, but I'll still have one eye."

There was another silence. Then Henry spoke again:

"I was hoping that this call was news that there was a buyer."

The caller could not find any more words, but finally managed to ask Henry whether he was sure he was willing to make the sacrifice.

"I don't consider it a sacrifice," Henry said. "When it comes to your children, there is no such thing as a sacrifice. They are the most important thing in the world to me. I love them. This is the only way I have to show my love, so that they will have a little something to remember me by when I'm gone."

Follow-Up

1. In "Eye for Sale," a father wanted to sell one of his eyes so that he could establish a small estate for his children. To him it was a way of being a better father. "I will be able to feel that I have contributed to my children's lives," he said. This is an example of extreme parental sacrifice. Reflect and comment on your parents' (or guardians') sacrifices to better your life. If you are a parent, how does this need manifest itself for your children?

*Editor's Note: Selling organs in this manner is illegal.

The Missing Halloween

Nels Goud

When you are ten years old, Halloween takes a good four weeks to plan if you want to do it right. For one, you want to make sure your costume is different from the others and this requires some checking around. Then there is the challenge of planning the route. A route which hits the big givers first before they run out of the good stuff. This means several sprints from one neighborhood to the next, swooping in on the target homes, and then hustling back to get the homes you skipped. It is also crucial to play along with the crazy adults. Adults like Mr. and Mrs. Parish who dress up in monster costumes and try to scare the kids by jumping out from behind furniture, but if you scream real loud it is good for at least a Snickers bar. And when you have all the rounds made you and your friends make sure to knock on Mr. Warren's door. We know he is in there, but he will not come to the door, and one of us stands guard while the others soap a few of his windows. After all there is a "trick" in trick-or-treat. And along the way it is mandatory to hide behind a large tree until your sister and her friends come along, and then leap out in the midst of screeches which will echo the nights until December. Advanced Halloween veterans remember their sacrificing parents and share some of the booty with them—things like apples, walnuts, and other assorted items you don't like.

Everything went as planned that Halloween except that I did not get to go. A sore throat and a stiff neck kept me out of school three days before Halloween. The town Doc came over—they did that back then—and checked me over and told my folks "He has polio." I was whisked off to a big hospital in Kalamazoo and spent Halloween looking out a window at the wall of another building.

A ten-year-old does not get depressed about things like this, unlike older persons. Confused and worried, but not bummed out. For one, the pain was not too bad and everyone paid me a lot of attention. Nurses told jokes as they placed steaming hot packs on my back and legs. The doctors just asked me to do simple things like touching my toes, and when I could not do that they said it was okay anyway. My parents came by often and brought a radio, my favorite foods, and acted very normal in the way only parents can when they are afraid but cannot let their children know it. And there were cards, candy, and comic books coming in on a steady basis. In a way I became a small celebrity.

After a week or so I was taken out of isolation and placed in a large room with five other guys who had polio also. Some seemed to have it worse. Johnny had braces and could not walk so I had to drag his bed next to mine to play cards. Then there was Mike, about 6, who never had a visitor. He whined and cried a lot at night and we eventually had to tell him to shut up but he kept crying anyway.

The World Health Organization is predicting that polio will be eliminated from the Western Hemisphere. It was reading this news release that released my memories. I was one of the fortunate ones who eventually fully recovered. Johnny remained permanently impaired. I do not know what happened to the 6-year-old who cried at night. I do know that the year of the missing Halloween was the one Jonas Salk first introduced the polio vaccine. Bad timing for some of us. But Halloween and polio are only background for my real story.

Each day in the hospital I received at least two cards from classmates. There was always one card which had a puzzle and the next day would bring a card with the answer and a new puzzle. Natural fifth-graders do not send cards this reliably. But 10-year-olds in Mrs. Pollack's fifth grade class did.

Mrs. Pollack was a charter member from the traditional school of thought and looked about 90 years old. Adverbs, fractions, and proper punctuation were ecstatic expressions to Mrs. Pollack. No one dared question these life verities. Her face was stern and could contort in a way which even made Max Thundermouth cringe when he got the urge to express his inner being. Even her generous acts had a price. If your birthday fell on a schoolday, Mrs. Pollack would give the lucky student a dime and everyone would get a treat. Then the celebrant would have to walk a gauntlet of classmates for a good ol' birthday spanking and she got in the last lick for good luck. Mrs. Pollack lived in a house on a hill surrounded by trees and no one knew anything about her. I must have thought, back then, that six weeks away from Mrs. Pollack was like an excused vacation. Now I ask, "Why did my classmates send those cards to me?"

Then there was Miss G. Miss G. was our music teacher. Almost all of us liked music until she came along. Other music teachers let us sing like we were spring meadowlarks, like music was to be a joyous occasion and a celestial right of being human. But Miss G. had standards. We were to be the midwest version of the Mormon Tabernacle Choir. I was having problems with Miss G. because of my low voice, a baritone at the time. As I was a short male, Miss G. felt that I should have a higher voice and told me to sing higher. I tried but could only sing louder. I was faking, she said. We argued a lot. I received my first S– from Miss G. Miss G. even gave me an S– during the time I had polio and wasn't in school. I discovered then that teachers, too, had personalities. Some, like Miss G., were awful. Mrs. Pollack was awful tough, but not awful.

Two weeks after I returned from the hospital, I was still at home trying to regain muscle strength. My mother said I should put on my regular clothes and get into the living room.

"Why?" I asked.

"Because," she said, "there is a school bus in front of our house and your whole fifth grade class is coming to the door."

I threw off my pajamas and put on a shirt and pants and tried to run to the living room but my muscles were too weak and I fell down. I got up and made it to the couch just as Mrs. Pollack knocked on the door.

"Mrs. Goud," she asked. "Is it all right if we visit Nelson for a few minutes?"

"Of course, Mrs. Pollack," said my mother. Mrs. Pollack led the troops into the house and asked how I was doing as she gave me a small gift. All I could muster was an "Okay . . . uh . . . thank you, Mrs. Pollack."

My classmates also gave me several presents and we goofed around for a while and then they left.

Each year there are studies which try to define "the good teacher." I will now suggest they add Mrs. Pollack to the list.

Follow-Up

1. *Think of your favorite teachers from elementary school to the present. What qualities made them so special? Have you ever let them know what they meant to you? (If not, when will you?)*
2. *What effect have teachers, good and bad, had on your development?*

Think Nanny

Stephen D. Regan

Zonona was remarkable. Even her name was remarkable—Zonona. She had been named for an Indian woman who fed her grandfather's family during a terrible Iowa winter when the Sargood stores were depleted. But I couldn't pronounce it so I just called her Nanny. And she was everything a small boy could ever hope to imagine: candy provider, malt maker, bruise comforter. The aroma of her house surrounded guests with wonderful smells of warmth, kindness, and love. As I close my eyes and drift through the years I can still smell Nanny's house.

She lived but two doors away and somehow was always home when I needed her. When I burned my fingers lighting an illicit bonfire in the bushes behind the old barn, she soothed the pain. When I got my first bike, she shared my joy. When I graduated from college she was the first to acknowledge my triumph. And I wrote my dissertation with her in mind.

Nanny always listened. She always understood, when I was little and when I wasn't. And she seemed to have an amazing amount of knowledge. I once discussed at long length the pros and cons of the economic interpretations of the U.S. Constitution, and she asked profound questions and added insights I had not seen in my studies. She had never heard of Abe Maslow but had a good understanding of needs and self-concept and self-actualization though she had never been to college nor studied psychology.

One day when I was hardly ten, I went to Nanny's house and when I discovered no one was home I explored her house as if it was a treasure house filled with magnificent riches. My glance caught the mahogany and cedar cigar box she had given her husband on her first wedding anniversary. Pulling out one of the large green Cuban cigars I went to an upstairs bedroom to smoke and pretend I was grown up. By the time Nanny got home I was quite ill and as green as the cigar butt. Instead of being angry she asked me what lessons I had learned, and was satisfied when I mumbled about not taking things that belong to others and smoking cigars before I was at least fifty years old. Quietly, in a loving voice, Nanny told me that since I had learned my lesson there was no reason to tell my parents and that she had the perfect cure for my illness—a strawberry malt.

No matter how big the hurt or large the scrape, she soothed the pain with care and love. In total acceptance she listened openly and unconditionally. She shared her feelings and cared about mine. Nanny always let you know that occasionally kids did bad things but there were no bad kids. You were always safe at Nanny's house. Sometimes we talked long after my scheduled bedtime. Sometimes in silence we just sat and watched prism-made rainbows stretch across the walls. Sometimes she read poems to me or recited passages from literature.

My first book, *How big are you, baby*, had an inscription from Nanny. My collection of Robert Louis Stevenson came from her. History of war and peace and diplomacy and discovery flowed in volumes. Quietly without ever saying a word she guided my thinking and my beliefs through modeled leadership, care, love, service, loyalty, dedication, devotion, honor, and patriotism. Never a lecture was made about caring for others but her long hours at the camp for handicapped children and the veterans hospital taught powerful lessons. And regardless of planned activities or pleasures, each Memorial Day morning was spent at the cemetery remembering those who paid the full price for the liberties we prized and the rights we have maintained.

Her long, weekly letters were inspirations of gossip, profound thought, curiosity, and ideas that I looked forward to whether I was in a dorm room or barracks or my own home. And try as I might, my responses were but shadows of hers.

When I was grown up and graduated I took a job as a school counselor. Often I was confronted with adolescent burdens of such magnitude I could hardly cope myself, let alone assist my young students. Facing child abuse, incest, poverty, ignorance, and junior high school–aged pregnancy on a daily basis I floundered looking for ways to ease the suffering. In frequent desperation for just the right technique or intervention strategy that would alleviate the aches of these young people, I plowed through text books and lecture notes searching for answers. How could I help these kids? What could I do?

Books and notes were no help. Emulation of idolized professorial mentors failed. Then I thought of the one person who always eased my pain, who brought rainbows through storms. I thought of Nanny. I remembered what she so patiently taught me not through lessons or lectures but through the quiet, behavior of love. On that day I put a small hand-written sign above my worn, brown desk. It simply said THINK NANNY.

From that day on I simply did as Nanny did. I accepted kids for what they were. I listened and cared. I let kids know that occasionally bad things happen but they themselves were special and unique people with infinite capacities of goodness. Slowly, I believe, my students began to realize that though I could not eliminate their problems, my office was a special place of warmth and love. In my office everything was OK.

We buried Nanny in last November's rain beneath an old maple tree in an Iowa cemetery. Much of what I am or shall become, I owe to her. And whatever pain I have helped reduce, I reduced because of her. And when I am depressed or lonely or hurting I sit in my living room and watch Nanny's rainbows cast by her prism now in my window as they bounce off an old mahogany and cedar cigar box. And I THINK NANNY.

Follow-Up

1. *Sometimes, our role models come from unusual places. Regan's came from next door. Have you had a person similar to "Nanny" in your life?*
2. *See the Applied Activity entitled "Heroes, Heroines, and Role Models" at the end of this section to discover how much these persons have influenced your life.*

Applied Activities for Section Four

SIGNIFICANT OTHER PERCEPTION INVENTORY

Significant others are persons who influence how you perceive yourself. Some significant other categories include: family members, lovers, spouses, friends, colleagues, teachers, supervisors, mentors. Each person determines who is a significant other to them.

This activity asks your significant others to offer their perceptions of you. One of the strengths of significant others is that they can often see things we are not aware of or that we believe are hidden. They can often provide some helpful hints on how to approach life. Look at the sample Significant Other Perception Inventory at the end of this activity.

If you choose to try this activity, follow these guidelines:

1. Try to get at least seven significant other responses. This is necessary to get a minimum number of reactions for analysis and interpretation.
2. Make sure that the significant other is comfortable in filling out the inventory—this helps to attain genuine responses. Sometimes a significant other is not willing to complete the inventory for a number of reasons (it may lead to awkward conversations, they place too much pressure on themselves to please you). You may be asked to complete an inventory on them. Do *not* require the significant other to discuss their responses—only do so if they seem willing.
3. Allow sufficient time for significant others to respond to the activity (sometime these are mailed). If necessary, provide a stamped envelope addressed to you or the instructor. You can also e-mail the request.
4. Complete a Significant Other Perception Inventory on yourself from your point of view.
5. Analysis and interpretation suggestions:
   a. After all the inventories have been collected, list all responses to each item.
   b. Examine each list for patterns and common responses. Note these themes. Circle any response or theme that has impact for you in any way (positive or negative).
   c. Attempt to really "listen" to your significant others. Try not to dismiss a response if it bothers you or if you disagree with it. Be open to any message before judging or criticizing it.
   d. How did your inventory compare with those of your significant others? Which (if any) responses surprised you or were unexpected? Are there any observations that need further exploration on your part? Are any specific action steps indicated?
6. Discuss or write about what you learned.

SIGNIFICANT OTHER PERCEPTION INVENTORY

You have been selected by _____ as having an important influence on his or her life. As part of a group activity, this person has been asked to obtain *your personal perceptions* of him or her as indicated by your completion of this inventory. Your observations and comments will be valuable and appreciated. You do *not* have to sign your name to this inventory.

Your comments will *not* be used in determining any type of grade for this person or as a personal reference. Try to be as open and genuine as you can in answering each item. Also, answer according to *your* point of view, *not* according to the way you think others see this person.

You can approach the inventory in one of two ways:

1. Complete it and return it directly to the person.
2. Type your responses and do not write your name on the inventory. Send the completed form by mail to the group facilitator. (The person who asked you to complete the inventory has provided you with an addressed, stamped envelope.) The facilitator will then give your inventory to the appropriate person without revealing the source.

Directions

Keeping the aforementioned person in mind, complete each of the following unfinished sentences as honestly as you can. If you cannot think of an appropriate completion or if you choose not to complete an item, do not write anything in the blank provided.

1. *Three adjectives* (traits) that immediately come to mind when I think of this person are . . .

2. At least *three* strengths consistently manifested by this person are . . .

3. a. A potential or ability that this person possesses, but has *not* fully developed yet is . . .

   b. One way to further develop this ability would be to . . .

4. a. One obstacle (originating either from outside or from within the person) to this person's realization of full personal growth is . . .

   b. One way to overcome this obstacle would be to . . .

5. Within the next year I believe that it will be very important for this person to . . .

6. If I could give this person a gift (either tangible or intangible) that would make a difference in his or her life right now, it would be . . .

Thank you for your efforts and cooperation.

LOVE MAPS

Editor's Note: Gottman and Silver believe that emotionally intelligent couples are intimately familiar with each other's world. They remember the major events in each other's history, and keep updating this information. They call this a love map. Couples with detailed love maps are better prepared to cope with stressors and to create shared meanings.

Directions: With your intimate significant other, attempt to answer the following items about the other person. The more items answered accurately, the more extensive the love map.

1. Names of two closest friends
2. A favorite hobby or leisure activity
3. Birthplace
4. A favorite relative
5. A favorite meal
6. A current stress or challenge
7. A fear
8. An unrealized dream or aspiration
9. Favorite time for lovemaking

10. Greatest source of support (other than yourself)
11. Nature of an upcoming event and feelings about it
12. Philosophy of life/religious beliefs
13. Beliefs about money
14. Favorite musician or entertainer
15. Health or medical concerns
16. Favorite holiday and why
17. Ideal job or vacation
18. A regret or failure
19. A major accomplishment or success
20. Favorite activity together (besides sex)

Follow-Up

1. Describe what you learned from attempting this activity.

SEXUALITY QUIZ

Directions: Complete the quiz individually before checking the answers (you could also discuss your answers with a small group prior to checking the answers).

1. What is the age of first sexual intercourse for the average American?

   (a) 11–12   (b) 13–14   (c) 16–17   (d) 18–19

2. How many sex partners, on average, do American *males* report during their lifetime?

   (a) 3   (b) 6   (c) 12   (d) 19

3. How many sex partners, on average, do American *females* report during their lifetime?

   (a) 2   (b) 4   (c) 5   (d) 8

4. Which category below reports the lowest incidence of sexual intercourse?

   (a) married couples   (b) single persons   (c) unmarried couples who live together   (d) professors

5. The approximate percentage of *men* who claim to be virgins at the time of marriage (as of 1995).

   (a) 10%   (b) 20%   (c) 30%   (d) 40%

6. The approximate percentage of *women* who claim to be virgins at the time of marriage (as of 1995).

   (a) 15%   (b) 25%   (c) 35%   (d) 45%

7. Which category is most responsive to cultural shifts in sexual attitudes and practices over several decades?

   (a) unmarried females   (b) unmarried males   (c) married couples
   (d) neurotic rabbits

8. Both males and females experience a four-stage sexual response during intercourse. Out of order these stages are: resolution, plateau, excitement, and orgasm. What is the correct order?

9. Which of the following contraceptive techniques has the *lowest* failure rate (i.e., is most reliable)?

   (a) condom   (b) diaphragm with spermicide   (c) combined oral contraceptive pills   (d) spermicidal foam   (e) coitus interruptus

10. Using lubricants such as petroleum jelly enhances the effectiveness of a condom or diaphragm.

    True   False

11. Which group is statistically more likely to contract an STD (sexually transmitted disease) after a single act of intercourse with an infected person?

    Males   Females

12. The most common STD in the United States is:

    (a) gonorrhea   (b) chlamydia   (c) acquired immune deficiency syndrome   (d) syphilis   (e) genital herpes

13. A woman or teenage girl can get pregnant during her menstrual flow.

    True   False

14. Menopause causes the majority of women to lose interest in sex.

    True   False

15. Erection problems are most often started by *physical* factors.

    True   False

16. Approximately what percent of persons in their 60s are sexually active?

    (a) 15%   (b) 25%   (c) 40%   (d) 80%

17. Most women prefer a partner with a larger-than-average penis.

    True   False

18. Below are common sexual fantasies. Try to identify the top three fantasies for males and females. Place M's beside your choices for men and W's beside your choices for women.

(a) _____ having sex with a complete stranger (by choice)

(b) _____ being forced to have sex with a chosen partner

(c) _____ group sex

(d) _____ sex with a celebrity

(e) _____ sex in front of an audience

(f) _____ oral sex

(g) _____ sex with a friend's spouse

(h) _____ sex with a person of the same gender

(i) _____ watching two members of the opposite gender have sex

Answers to Sexuality Quiz

1. c

2. b

3. a

4. b

5. a

6. b

7. a.   Studies show that unmarried females are the most responsive to shifts in cultural sexual attitudes and practices.

8. Excitement, plateau, orgasm, and resolution.

9. c.   Here are the failure rates for selected contraceptive techniques:

Method	Failure Rate
Tubal sterilization	0.4%
Vasectomy	0.4%
Combined oral Pill	0.5%
Progestin-only Pill	1.0%
Condom	2.0%
Diaphragm with spermicide	2.0%
Spermicidal foam/cream	3.0–5.0%
Coitus interruptus	16%

10. False.   Lubricants erode a condom or diaphragm, allowing STD organisms to pass through.

11. Females.

12. b. Chlamydia is a bacterial disease transmitted during intercourse. It often goes unnoticed. Experts estimate that as many as 10% of sexually active women have chlamydia. It is effectively treated with antibiotics.

13. True.

14. False. Some women report a lowered sex drive, but this can be treated with hormone replacement therapy.

15. True. Physical factors include disease (e.g., diabetes), drug or alcohol abuse, and medications. Most erections problems can be successfully treated.

16. d. Additionally, approximately two out of three women and four out of five men are sexually active in their 70s.

17. False. Most surveys show that women are not as concerned with penis size as are men. Some women even consider a larger-than-average penis to be a problem.

18. The top three *male* fantasies are b, c, and i. The top three *female* sexual fantasies are a, d, and g. If you do not agree, then list your own!

References
Items 1, 9, 10, 11, 13, 14, 15, and 17 are from Reinisch, J. (1990). *The Kinsey Institute new report on sex.* New York: St. Martin's Press.
Items 2, 3, 4, 5, 6, 8, 12, and 16 are from Lefrancois, G. (1996). *The lifespan.* Belmont, CA: Wadsworth Publishing.
Item 7 is from Brehm, S. (1992). *Intimate relationships.* New York: McGraw-Hill, Inc.
Item 18 is from Walker, R. (1996). *The family guide to sex and relationships.* New York: Macmillan.

HEROES, HEROINES, AND ROLE MODELS

A person who has attained the highest human possibilities we value is our hero or heroine. These persons serve as ultimate guides and inspirations for our own strivings. Our heroes or heroines may even have a flaw or two, but this can make them even more powerful to us because we, too, have flaws. A hero/heroine has qualities that often transcend a particular discipline. One of my heroes is Maynard Ferguson, a jazz trumpeter. While he inspires my trumpet-playing, he has an enduring exuberance and commitment that I admire and that I try to emulate in my work as a professor. Our heroes and heroines provide clear standards and ways of being for our lives.

Role models demonstrate highly valued skills and personal qualities in a specific life role. More often than not, we know them. They are the people we strive to be like in our careers, as parents, or as citizens. Like heroes and heroines, role models are inspirational, but their influence may or may not extend beyond a specific role.

Our heroes/heroines and role models help define us as people and shape our values. Try the following activities to see their effects on your life:

1. Briefly list the heroes/heroines from your early childhood until now. These may have been fictional as well as real-life persons. They may have been historical figures or contemporary persons. Who inspired you in ways you admired and imitated?
2. Examine your list. What qualities do these heroes/heroines represent? How do your current heroes/heroines influence your life?
3. Imagine that one of your heroes/heroines talked with you for five minutes. What do you think they would say to you?
4. Identify some of your role models. Which of their qualities do you have? Which qualities do you need to work on?
5. Discuss and/or write about your responses and what you learned.

PERSONAL GOALS—HUMAN RELATIONSHIPS

Within the next year I will enhance the ways I relate to other persons by:

Goal 1:

Needed actions, support, and resources:

Timeline:

Progress notes (use extra page if necessary):

Goal 2:

Needed actions, support, and resources:

Timeline:

Progress notes (use extra page if necessary):

EMOTIONS AND FEELINGS

From the list below, place a check by the five feeling states that you most like to experience:

1. Excited	16. Angry
2. Afraid	17. Proud
3. Confident	18. Embarrassed
4. Ashamed	19. Brave
5. Tranquil	20. Hurt
6. Despairing	21. Marveling
7. Joyous	22. Rejected
8. Lonely	23. Trusting
9. Loving	24. Nervous
10. Jealous	25. Inspired
11. Surprised	26. Hopeless
12. Guilty	27. Spontaneous
13. Friendly	28. Resentful
14. Disgusted	29. Admiring
15. Reflective	30. Confused

Review your choices—there is a high probability that the majority are odd-numbered items. These are some of the positive emotions we experience. The even-numbered feeling states are those that most humans do not desire to experience. The listed feeling states are only a small sample of what a human is capable of experiencing. Like colors, emotions can blend to form an almost infinite range of feeling tones. For example, if you are happy, you may be either pleased, cheerful, or ecstatic. If you are angry, your range of anger can extend from annoyance to rage.

To be human means to experience a rich and complex world of emotions. Almost everyone has an approach–avoidance relationship with emotions. We welcome some emotions, resist or even deny others. We easily reveal some emotions, but we have trouble expressing others. Sometimes we even try to conceal how we feel, only to be betrayed by a tapping foot or quivering lips. Occasionally, humans use one emotion to mask another (e.g., we feel rejected but we show anger, or we feel attracted to another but we look unconcerned, aloof). We know that many of our "disliked" emotions, such as anxiety, are sending us helpful warnings, but often we don't like the message and therefore blame the messenger.

If our thoughts are like books on library shelves, then our emotions are like wildlife creatures wandering through the library—some playful and curious, some quiet and timid, some sitting sullenly in corners, and some snarling and prowling about when the lights are out.

Sometimes, to fully experience a life event, emotions are *required.* Victoria Lincoln explains why in a passage from a short story she wrote over 50 years ago in *The New Yorker* (Sept. 28, 1946):

Why are we never prepared, why do all the books and all the wisdom of our friends avail us nothing in the final event? How many deathbed scenes we have read, how many stories of young love, or marital infidelity, of cherished ambition, fulfilled or defeated. There is nothing that can happen to us that has not happened again and again, that we have not read over a thousand times, closely, carefully, accurately recorded; before we are fully launched on life, the story of the human heart has been opened for us again and again with all the patience and skill of the human mind. But the event, when it comes, is never anything like the description; it is strange, infinitely strange and new, and we stand helpless before it and realize that the words of another convey nothing, nothing.

What good are emotions? Probably the best way to answer this query is to imagine a life without them. Do you love someone and are you loved? Do you anticipate with great joy an upcoming concert or athletic event? Have you found that anxiety, guilt, anger, or envy have actually helped you to function better at times? Think of any event or time that is a milestone in your life. Would it be a milestone without emotion? "Nothing great was ever achieved without enthusiasm," said Emerson. It's the emotions that provide our lives with a sense of aliveness and mystery. Emotions alone would lead to a chaotic existence. But thoughts alone would lead to an arid, stale existence. The best balance we can hope for is a good thought propelled by sound emotion.

The articles herein address a wide variety of major emotions and feelings:

- In "What's Your Emotional IQ?" Daniel Goleman contents that emotional intelligence is a requirement for a successful life.
- Worrying and fretting are unnecessary emotions and block growth according to Wayne Dyer in "Worry."
- Overwhelming anxiety is almost always detrimental. In "The Positive Face of Anxiety," Daniel A. Sugarman and Lucy Freeman show how less intense forms of anxiety are helpful and necessary for growth.
- Five dimensions of loneliness are discussed and examined by William A. Sadler, Jr., in "The Causes of Loneliness."
- In "You Never Know," Nels Goud highlights the power of the need to belong in a story of a high school student.
- Abe Arkoff introduces a powerful and simple way to experience happiness in "Little Joys."
- "Anger" by Wayne Dyer examines some causes and practical advice in this common emotion.
- The nature and effects of "Jealousy and Envy: The Demons within Us" are examined by Jon Queijo.
- Tom Peyton reveals how he self-imposed a feeling of aloneness in "My Tyrant."
- "Sarcasm and Apathy" are the theme of an essay written by an anonymous graduate student and teacher.
- A personalized account of reacting to the death of a parent is expressed by Sanford Colley in "On the Death of a Father."
- The three phases of "Loss and Mourning" are explained by Judith Viorst.

Practical exercises involving emotions are found in both the Follow-Up questions and the Applied Activities.

What's Your Emotional I.Q.?

Daniel Goleman

It was a steamy afternoon in New York City, the kind of day that makes people sullen with discomfort. I was heading to my hotel, and as I stepped onto a bus, I was greeted by the driver, a middle-aged man with an enthusiastic smile.

"Hi! How're you doing?" he said. He greeted each rider in the same way.

As the bus crawled uptown through gridlocked traffic, the driver gave a lively commentary: there was a terrific sale at that store . . . a wonderful exhibit at this museum . . . had we heard about the movie that just opened down the block? By the time people got off, they had shaken off their sullen shells. When the driver called out, "So long, have a great day!" each of us gave a smiling response.

That memory has stayed with me for close to 20 years. I consider the bus driver a man who was truly successful at what he did.

Contrast him with Jason, a straight-A student at a Florida high school who was fixated on getting into Harvard Medical School. When a physics teacher gave Jason an 80 on a quiz, the boy believed his dream was in jeopardy. He took a butcher knife to school, and in a struggle the teacher was stabbed in the collarbone.

How could someone of obvious intelligence do something so irrational? The answer is that high I.Q. does not necessarily predict who will succeed in life. Psychologists agree that I.Q. contributes only about 20 percent of the factors that determine success. A full 80 percent comes from other factors, including what I call *emotional intelligence*.

Following are some of the major qualities that make up emotional intelligence, and how they can be developed:

1. Self-awareness. The ability to recognize a feeling as it happens is the keystone of emotional intelligence. People with greater certainty about their emotions are better pilots of their lives.

Developing self-awareness requires tuning in to what neurologist Antonio Damasio, in his book *Descartes' Error*, calls "somatic markers"—literally, gut feelings. Gut feelings can occur without a person being consciously aware of them. For example, when people who fear snakes are shown a picture of a snake, sensors on their skin will detect sweat, a sign of anxiety, even though the people say they do not feel fear. The sweat shows up even when a picture is presented so rapidly that the subject has no conscious awareness of seeing it.

Through deliberate effort we can become more aware of our gut feelings. Take someone who is annoyed by a rude encounter for hours after it occurred. He may be oblivious to his irritability and surprised when someone calls attention to it. But if he evaluates his feelings, he can change them.

Emotional self-awareness is the building block of the next fundamental of emotional intelligence: being able to shake off a bad mood.

2. Mood Management. Bad as well as good moods spice life and build character. The key is balance.

We often have little control over *when* we are swept by emotion. But we can have some say in *how long* that emotion will last. Psychologist Dianne Tice of Case Western Reserve University asked more than 400 men and women about their strategies for escaping foul moods. Her research, along with that of other psychologists, provides valuable information on how to change a bad mood.

Of all the moods that people want to escape, rage seems to be the hardest to deal with. When someone in another car cuts you off on the highway, your reflexive thought may be, *That jerk! He could have hit me! I can't let him get away with that!* The more you stew, the angrier you get. Such is the stuff of hypertension and reckless driving.

What should you do to relieve rage? One myth is that ventilating will make you feel better. In fact, researchers have found that's one of the worst strategies. Outbursts of rage pump up the brain's arousal system, leaving you more angry, not less.

A more effective technique is "reframing," which means consciously reinterpreting a situation in a more positive light. In the case of the driver who cuts you off, you might tell yourself: *Maybe he had some emergency.* This is one of the most potent ways, Tice found, to put anger to rest.

Going off alone to cool down is also an effective way to defuse anger, especially if you can't think clearly. Tice found that a large proportion of men cool down by going for a drive—a finding that inspired her to drive more defensively. A safer alternative is exercise, such as taking a long walk. Whatever you do, don't waste the time pursuing your train of angry thoughts. Your aim should be to distract yourself.

The techniques of reframing and distraction can alleviate depression and anxiety as well as anger. Add to them such relaxation techniques as deep breathing and meditation and you have an arsenal of weapons against bad moods. "Praying," Dianne Tice also says, "works for all moods."

3. Self-motivation. Positive motivation—the marshaling of feelings of enthusiasm, zeal and confidence—is paramount for achievement. Studies of Olympic athletes, world-class musicians and chess grandmasters show that their common trait is the ability to motivate themselves to pursue relentless training routines.

To motivate yourself for any achievement requires clear goals and an optimistic, can-do attitude. Psychologist Martin Seligman of the University of Pennsylvania advised the MetLife insurance company to hire a special group of job applicants who tested high on optimism, although they had failed the normal aptitude test. Compared with salesmen who passed the aptitude test but scored high in pessimism, this group made 21 percent more sales in their first year and 57 percent more in their second.

A pessimist is likely to interpret rejection as meaning *I'm a failure, I'll never make a sale.* Optimists tell themselves, *I'm using the wrong approach,* or *That customer was in a bad mood.* By blaming failure on the situation, not themselves, optimists are motivated to make that next call.

Your predisposition to a positive or negative outlook may be inborn, but with effort and practice, pessimists can learn to think more hopefully. Psychologists have documented that if you can catch negative, self-defeating thoughts as they occur, you can reframe the situation in less catastrophic terms.

4. Impulse Control. The essence of emotional self-regulation is the ability to delay impulse in the service of a goal. The importance of this trait to success was shown in an experiment begun in the 1960s by psychologist Walter Mischel at a preschool on the Stanford University campus.

Children were told that they could have a single treat, such as a marshmallow, right now. However, if they would wait while the experimenter ran an errand, they could have two marshmallows. Some preschoolers grabbed the marshmallow immediately, but others were able to wait what, for them, must have seemed an endless 20 minutes. To sustain themselves in their struggle, they covered their eyes so they wouldn't see the temptation, rested their heads on their arms, talked to themselves, sang, even tried to sleep. These plucky kids got the two-marshmallow reward.

The interesting part of this experiment came in the follow-up. The children who as four-year-olds had been able to wait for the two marshmallows were, as adolescents, still able to delay gratification in pursuing their goals. They were more socially competent and self-assertive, and better able to cope with life's frustrations. In contrast, the kids who grabbed the one marshmallow were, as adolescents, more likely to be stubborn, indecisive and stressed.

The ability to resist impulse can be developed through practice. When you're faced with an immediate temptation, remind yourself of your long-term goals—whether they be losing weight or getting a medical degree. You'll find it easier, then, to keep from settling for the single marshmallow.

5. People Skills. The capacity to know how another feels is important on the job, in romance and friendship, and in the family. We transmit and catch moods from each other on a subtle, almost imperceptible level. The way someone says thank you, for instance, can leave us feeling dismissed, patronized or genuinely appreciated. The more adroit we are at discerning the feelings behind other people's signals, the better we control the signals we send.

The importance of good interpersonal skills was demonstrated by psychologists Robert Kelley of Carnegie-Mellon University and Janet Caplan in a study at Bell Labs in Naperville, Ill. The labs are staffed by engineers and scientists who are all at the apex of academic I.Q. tests. But some still emerged as stars, while others languished.

What accounted for the difference? The standout performers had a network with a wide range of people. When a non-star encountered a technical problem, Kelley observed, "he called various technical gurus and then waited, wasting time while his calls went unreturned. Star performers rarely faced such situations because they built reliable networks *before* they needed them. So when the stars called someone, they almost always got a faster answer."

No matter what their I.Q., once again it was emotional intelligence that separated the stars from the average performers.

Follow-Up

1. *Rate yourself, or have someone you know well rate you, on the five major qualities of emotional intelligence.*

    1 = Very low   2 = Low   3 = Average
    4 = High   5 = Exceptionally high

1. Self-awareness	1	2	3	4	5
2. Mood management	1	2	3	4	5
3. Self-motivation	1	2	3	4	5
4. Impulse control	1	2	3	4	5
5. People skills	1	2	3	4	5

2. *Choose one or more of the five factors of emotional intelligence to further develop in yourself and report your actions.*

3. *Observe persons who are very skillful in one or more of the five areas of emotional intelligence and report what you learned.*
4. *One of the more powerful techniques for managing moods is* reframing—*how to reinterpret a situation. Try this idea in your life and report on the results.*
5. *Discuss or write about your reactions to Goleman's contention "that I.Q. contributes only about 20 percent of the factors that determine success."*

Worry

Wayne Dyer

THE PSYCHOLOGICAL PAYOFFS FOR CHOOSING WORRY

• Worry is a present-moment activity. Thus, by using your current life being immobilized over a future time in your life, you are able to escape the now and whatever it is in the now that threatens you. For example, I spent the summer of 1974 in Karamursel, Turkey, teaching and writing a book on counseling. My seven-year-old daughter was back in the United States with her mother. While I love writing, I also find it an intensely lonely, difficult chore which requires a great deal of self-discipline. I would sit down at my typewriter with paper in place and the margins set, and all of a sudden my thoughts would be back on little Tracy Lynn. What if she rides her bicycle into the street and doesn't look? I hope she's being watched at the swimming pool, because she has a tendency to be careless. Before I knew it, an hour had elapsed, and I had spent it worrying. This was all in vain of course. But, was it? As long as I could use up my present moments worrying I didn't have to struggle with the difficulty of writing. A terrific payoff indeed.

• You can avoid having to take risks by using your worry as the reason for immobility. How could you possibly act if you are preoccupied with your present-moment worry? "I can't do a thing, I'm just too worried about ——." This is a common lament, and one with a payoff that keeps you standing still and avoiding the risk of action.

• You can label yourself as a *caring person* by worrying. Worry proves that you are a good parent, good spouse or good whatever. A handsome dividend, although lacking in logical healthy thinking.

• Worry is a handy justification for certain self-defeating behavior. If you're overweight, you undoubtedly eat more when you worry, hence you have a sensational reason for hanging on to the worry behavior. Similarly, you find yourself smoking more in worrisome situations, and can use the worry to avoid giving up smoking. This same neurotic reward system applies to areas including marriage, money, health and the like. The worry helps you to avoid changing. It is easier to worry about chest pains than to take the risk of finding out the truth, and then have to deal forthrightly with yourself.

• Your worry keeps you from living. A worrier sits around and thinks about things, while a doer must be up and about. Worry is a clever device to keep you inactive, and clearly it is easier, if less rewarding, to worry, than to be an active, involved person.

• Worry can bring ulcers, hypertension, cramps, tension headaches, backaches and the like. While these may not seem to be payoffs, they do result in considerable attention from others and justify much self-pity as well, and some people would rather be pitied than fulfilled.

Now that you understand the psychological support system for your worry, you can begin to devise some strategic efforts for getting rid of the troublesome worry bugs that breed in this erroneous zone.

SOME STRATEGIES FOR ELIMINATING WORRY

• Begin to view your present moments as times to live, rather than to obsess about the future. When you catch yourself worrying, ask yourself, "What am I avoiding now by using up this moment with worry?" Then begin to attack whatever it is you're avoiding. The best antidote to worry is action. A client of mine, formerly prone to worry, told me of a recent triumph over it. At a vacation resort he wandered into the sauna one afternoon. There he met a man who couldn't take a holiday from his worries. The other man elaborated all of the things my client should be worrying about. He mentioned the stock market, but said not to worry about short-range fluctuations. In six months there would be a virtual collapse, and that was the thing to really worry about. My client made sure of all the things he should worry about, and then left. He played a one-hour game of tennis, enjoyed a touch football game with some young children, participated with his wife in a Ping-Pong match which they thoroughly enjoyed, and finally, some three hours later, returned for a shower/sauna. His new friend was still there worrying, and began once again to chronicle more things to worry about. Meantime, my client had spent his present moments excitedly alive, while the other man had consumed his in worry. And neither man's behavior had any effect on the stock market.

• Recognize the preposterousness of worry. Ask yourself over and over, "Is there anything that will ever change as a result of my worrying about it?"

• Give yourself shorter and shorter periods of "worry-time." Designate ten minutes in the morning and afternoon as your worry segments. Use these periods to fret about every potential disaster you can get into the time slot. Then, using your ability to control your own thoughts, postpone any further worry until your next designated "worry-time." You'll soon see the folly of using any time in this wasteful fashion, and will eventually eliminate your worry zone completely.

• Make a worry list of everything you worried about yesterday, last week and even last year. See if any of your worry did anything productive for you. Assess also how many of the things you worried about ever materialized at all. You'll soon see that the worry is really a doubly wasteful activity. It does nothing to alter the future. And the projected catastrophe often turns out to be minor, or even a blessing when it arrives.

• *Just Worry!* See if it is something that you can demonstrate when you are tempted to worry. That is, stop and turn to someone and say, "Watch me—I'm about to worry." They'll be confounded since you probably won't even know how to demonstrate the thing you do so well, so often.

• Ask yourself this worry-eradicating question, "What's the worst thing that could happen to me (or them) and what is the likelihood of it occurring?" You'll discover the absurdity of worry in this way.

• Deliberately choose to act in some manner that is in direct conflict with your usual areas of worry. If you compulsively save for the future, always worried about having enough money for another day, begin to use your money today. Be like the rich uncle who put in his will, "Being of sound mind, I spent all my money while I was alive."

• Begin to face the fears you possess with productive thought and behavior. A friend of mine recently spent a week on an island off the coast of Connecticut. The woman enjoys taking long walks, and soon discovered that the island was populated by many dogs who were allowed to run wild. She decided to fight her fear and worry that they might somehow bite her or even tear her limb from limb—the ultimate calamity. She carried a rock in her hand (insurance) and decided to show no sign of fear as the dogs approached. She even refused to slow down when the dogs growled and came running toward her. As the dogs charged forward and encountered someone who refused to back down, they gave up and ran away. While I am not advocating dangerous behavior, I do believe that an effective challenge to a fear or worry is the most productive way to eradicate it from your life.

These are some techniques for eliminating worry in your life. But the most effective weapon you have for wiping out worry is your own determination to banish this neurotic behavior from your life.

Follow-Up

1. *Which of the psychological payoffs of worrying most apply to you? Discuss your answer.*
2. *Attempt one or more strategies for eliminating worry and report on the outcomes.*
3. *Select two statements or ideas from this article and offer your interpretations.*
4. *For further information, see Wayne Dyer's* Your Erroneous Zones.

The Positive Face of Anxiety

Daniel A. Sugarman
and Lucy Freeman

Anxiety is the most painful of all emotions, and many people will do anything to avoid direct confrontation with it. Like a child terrified of going to the dentist, they permit anxiety to fester and cause psychic decay. They refuse to submit to the direct confrontation which removes the decay and the chronic pain. Some use so much energy defending themselves against anxiety that there is little left for the enjoyment of living.

We are learning that it is not anxiety itself, but the way we handle anxiety, that makes the difference between emotional sickness and health. A refusal to acknowledge the anxiety within us prevents the possibility of greater personality growth.

The widespread use of tranquilizers has helped—and hindered. On one hand, millions have obtained sufficient relief from anxiety to cope with daily difficulties; but the indiscriminate use of these powerful medications has prevented many from coming to terms with their conflicts. If they were just a little more desperate, they might seek psychological help and get at the source of the anxiety.

THE GIFT OF ANXIETY

In our hedonistic society, it is difficult for many to believe that anything which stings a bit can be of value. Nevertheless, in spite of our love of the sun, rainy days are important in the total scheme of things. Without any anxiety, we would become like vegetables, unable to sense the passing danger that threatens us from every side. The hyper-vigilance anxiety brings makes it easier for us to detect danger and take appropriate measures against it.

One mother described to me how, in putting her eight-month-old baby to bed one night, she felt suddenly anxious about his health. It seemed he did not look healthy, as though he were coming down with a cold; nor did she like the way he sounded when he cried. With these thoughts in mind, when she went to bed, she had difficulty sleeping. About two in the morning, she became aware of wheezing noises from the child's bedroom. Dashing to his side, she found him in the midst of a severe attack of the croup. Hardly breathing, the child was rushed to the emergency room of a hospital where his life was saved. In this case, as in others, without anxiety on the part of the mother, there might have been a tragedy.

A patient of mine, made anxious one evening by a television program warning against breast cancer, decided to examine her breasts. To her horror, she noted a small lump. Prompt biopsy, performed forty-eight hours later, revealed the lump to be malignant. Although she lost a breast, she is now, five years later, very much alive and well. Without her anxiety, the outcome probably would have been different.

Too often we are ashamed to admit anxiety. Nourished by an emotional diet of heroes, we inflict unreasonable expectations upon ourselves. A deer or rabbit, unencumbered by the pretense of courage, will take to its heels at the first sign of danger and, by doing so, ensure its survival.

Anxiety is the force behind much learning. A student under the pressure of a final examination in physics may be motivated to pick up the book, burn the midnight oil, and cram. As a result, he may find that, not only has he passed the test, but learned a bit of physics. His more carefree classmate, not anxious enough to study, may find his academic career prematurely terminated as a result of flunking the exam.

Anxiety may also prepare us for a stressful future situation. A man who has to give an important speech can be goaded by anxiety to rehearse not only his speech but the fear he may feel on the podium. As he faces this fear in anticipation of the event, there is a better chance that on the day of the speech he will be less afraid.

THE PRICE OF GROWTH

As we move through life, the stability of our personality is not always the same. There are times our defenses work well and life proceeds with little anxiety; but there are other times when defenses fail and we feel less stable or more anxious. Sometimes we experience anxiety when underlying growth is taking place. There has been little awareness that hardly any personality growth occurs without some anxiety.

Many positive steps in our life are accompanied by anxiety. Each time we extend ourselves further, accept new responsibility, or affirm our independence, we may also feel a measure of anxiety.

Once while traveling on a train in September, I sat next to a young girl who, pale and tense, sat with her teeth clenched, obviously very anxious. We began to talk; she told me she was on her way to college and that this was the first time she had ever been away from her family. As she spoke of leaving home, she plainly revealed both the anxiety she felt and her determination to become independent.

She described how she had always been overprotected by her mother and three older brothers and said that although it was hard for her to do, she had decided it would be the best thing for her to go to college in a distant city.

After she got off at her destination, I thought about her and the fact that she would have been relatively free of anxiety had she decided to remain at home. She was not going to let a little anxiety stop her from developing into an independent young woman. Some others, afraid of the anxiety of separation, have remained home, tied to mother and hearth forever.

Observation of children shows that they will attack again and again a fear situation until it no longer causes anxiety. Once they have mastered it, they are ready to move on to the next fearful situation. Almost every sign of growth and independence contains some seeds of anxiety. The first day at kindergarten, the first night of sleeping at a friend's house, the first time on a bicycle—all produce anxiety. The child who has learned early not to shrink in the face of anxiety, but to move through it, will have that sense of increasing mastery which sets the foundation for a healthy personality.

THE WILLINGNESS TO BE HUMAN

To some extent I have stressed the anxiety that results from conflict and from crisis. There is, however, the anxiety that comes from being alive, for, to be human is to be finite and limited, and to be finite and limited is to be anxious.

In some dark, deep recess of our minds, in spite of the din of music and noise and friends and work and travel and sports and food, we never lose the awareness that some day we will die. When we feel alive, we are using our full potential and the thought of death drifts into the shadows.

The knowledge of our finiteness can help us to savor the moments we live, to help us use our limited time in a useful, enjoyable manner. That knowledge can also help keep us appropriately humble in the face of the forces of nature, can make us give pause and consider our little vanities. The knowledge that we are temporary visitors on this planet can put petty quarrels into proper perspective. Temporary frustrations can be seen as part of reality. We can live more in the present and stop pursuing a vain, relentless search for security. Once we accept a certain basic anxiety, we can begin to live more fully.

The willingness to recognize the reality of anxiety indicates an ability to recognize all of reality. Most of us are all too eager to deny that we are anxious. When we do, we gain momentary relief, but pay a high price. We keep out of touch with our real feelings. Our chances of facing our conflicts and easing our anxiety are lessened. We find that we are more alienated than ever, both from our feelings and other people.

If one is able to acknowledge anxiety and battle it, healing forces are frequently set in motion. Dr. Paul Tillich once spoke of the necessity of having the "courage to be," which includes the acceptance and facing of anxiety.

Paradoxically, true courage seems to begin with the admission of anxiety, just as the possibility of true living begins when we do not deny the possibility of death.

If someone looks on anxiety as an enemy, a "disease," the therapeutic way is likely to be rougher and longer. But if he views anxiety as an opportunity to look within, as a mandate for further development, not only will the psychic way be easier, but his anxiety will also lessen that more swiftly. Anxiety is a feeling to become aware of, to be faced, to be understood, and then, almost automatically, it is present only when we realistically need it.

Follow-Up

1. *Respond to the authors' argument that anxiety is a gift. Provide examples from your life.*
2. *How has anxiety presented itself during periods in your life? Discuss the ways you handled it.*
3. *The authors propose that by accepting and trying to understand anxiety, we can learn what is needed and the anxiety will decrease. Explain an instance where this has happened to you, or possibly apply this idea to your current situation.*
4. *Choose any other idea from the article to write about or discuss.*

The Causes of Loneliness

William A. Sadler, Jr.

About a year ago, I had an interview with a reporter that illustrates one of the paradoxes associated with loneliness. She called to ask about my work on the subject, hoping to get help with an article. After giving her some information, I suggested she get in touch with the department of urban studies at a university in the city where she worked. I felt certain that its in-depth, long-range study of a large urban area would yield some insights into loneliness that would be relevant to her article and her newspaper's readers.

Several weeks later, the reporter called back to say that she had been turned away at the university. She was told by the department's assistant director that loneliness was not a social problem worth studying, that no data on loneliness were available, and that none was expected from their study program. Yet during the reporter's visits to mental health clinics and counselors in that area she was told that breakdowns, divorces, alcohol and drug addiction, and suicide were markedly increasing, and that problems such as these were related to chronic loneliness.

That's the paradox. Loneliness is so often dismissed by experts studying modern life, while at the same time it is reported to be an increasingly significant problem in individual and social being.

How can we account for the fact that loneliness, which I find to be a serious problem for many persons in modern America, is virtually ignored by the social sciences? I think there are two basic reasons. The first is theoretical. Until recently we lacked the clear concepts that would allow investigators and counselors to define loneliness and to understand it in a re-liable way. The second reason is personal and has to do with the general attitude of the public toward loneliness, which sees it merely as a symptom of a weak character. The result is that one tends to downplay the impact it has in one's life, or even to deny that it has any significance at all. A common response given to persons who admit being lonely is: "Well, what's wrong with you? You don't need to be lonely. Go out and get busy. Join a club. Do something." Frequently through workshops, interviews, and articles I have found the response to be even more negative than this.

Investigations done in the last few years have permitted us to be more precise in defining loneliness. The conceptual understanding of loneliness, which will be presented in this article, shows why the accusatory response misses the mark. Many people in our society are lonely, not because of personality defects, but because there are factors "out there" that cause them to be lonely. Hopefully, this attitude will do more than resolve the paradox. It will help us all understand loneliness more intelligently and sympathetically, and provide a few realistic ideas about how to cope with it productively.

What is meant by *loneliness?* People use the term in different ways. Often loneliness is confused with merely being alone or with isolation. Your own experience should tell you that these are not identical. You can be alone and not lonely. People locked in solitary confinement do not always experience loneliness, at least not to any severe degree. To concentrate on isolation as much as social science has done when it has tried to get at loneliness is to miss the obvious. Some of the most painful, lonely feelings arise in the midst of a relationship or a group. Dr. Carl Jung suggested that "loneliness does not come from having no people about one, but from holding certain views that others find inadmissible." Adolescents, for example, frequently complain of the loneliness they experience in their homes, when they sense a generation gap. Adults they love simply do not understand them.

For this reason I suggest that loneliness is not just a physical condition. It is primarily an *experience.* Furthermore, it is probably unique to mankind. In his study on "the biology of loneliness" the late Dr. Ralph Audy Ph.D., M.D., of the U.C.L.A. Medical Center in San Francisco came to the conclusion that although there are analogies to it in the animal world, only human beings really know loneliness. Animals certainly manifest discomfort from prolonged separation. Ethologists and animal psychologists suggest that there is a basic animal need for attachment and that problems arise when that need is frustrated. It seems likely that humans have a similar need. But the kind of loneliness that I think is particularly troublesome in modern society is more complicated than mere frustration of this need for attachment.

In studying countless expressions of loneliness, both of modern Americans and from other times and places, I have found some common elements. The first and most outstanding feature of loneliness is a painful feeling, sometimes experienced as a sharp ache, as in moments of grief or separation; but it can also be a dull lingering form of stress that seems to tear a person down. Sometimes lonely feelings produce the "blues" of depression; but again, there is a difference between loneliness and depression. In the latter case, when a person is really "feeling down," he does not want to do anything. Depression corrodes motivational resources. Loneliness, by contrast, has a driving power. It sets people in motion—to go out, turn on TV, write a letter, make a phone call, or even get married.

There is another important aspect to this feeling. It is a significant signal coming from within ourselves that something is missing from our lives. Isolation does not imply any special type of awareness; loneliness does. A chief element of loneliness is a painful feeling that tells us something unpleasantly important about ourselves. All types of loneliness that I have studied have this element of painful self-awareness.

Loneliness also speaks of relationship, or rather, the absence or weakness of relationship. There are many different forms of relationship that can produce loneliness. One can be lonely for another person, a group, a home, a homeland, a tradition, a type of activity, and even a sense of meaning, or God.

A notable factor in much modern American loneliness is the quality of surprise. Loneliness so often strikes us unexpectedly. If you plan a trip by yourself, you prepare for lonely moments along the way. When they occur, you can handle them. When loneliness happens where you least expect it, such as in the home, at work, or among friends, it has a tremendous impact. We often do not know how to cope. It can make us confused, distraught, depressed, frightened, and even outraged.

Loneliness that frustrates our expectations is particularly hard to manage. It is this kind that so frequently disturbs people today. In nomadic and hunting societies persons were reared to expect long periods of aloneness. Facing loneliness was once a mark of manhood in American civilization. In an earlier era, Americans were reared to face life on their own in the struggle to achieve success through work. In that sense, being alone was part of the definition of successful living.

In this century the emphasis has been different. "Making it" has come to include "getting along with others." Learning to "fit in" is stressed at home, in school, in churches, and even in sports. Growing up in America often means developing expectations of involvement, popularity, and numerous attachments.

Today, as we tend to evaluate our personal success in terms of being liked, loneliness strikes with a force that is hard to handle. It suggests failure or at least a frightening vulnerability.

One reason loneliness hangs on is because people are either not fully aware of it or not prepared for it. They push it out of their consciousness. They try to find some remedy in drugs, in "busyness," in overly dependent relationships, or by increasing their memberships. I am convinced that much of the fear associated with loneliness, as well as many behavioral problems that arise from too much of it, are unnecessary. We will continue to misunderstand the pain and the problem associated with loneliness until we recognize how complex its multiple causes or sources can be.

I have chosen to refer to these different sources and types of loneliness in terms of *dimensions*. After studying a variety of expressions of lonely people in different contexts, I now classify these expressions according to the object that a person feels is missing or from which he or she feels separated. The dimension aspect refers to the area of relationship a person perceives to be the source of his suffering. There seem to be *five* fairly distinct dimensions. I have labeled them: *interpersonal, social, cultural, cosmic,* and *psychological.* The term dimension suggests that the loneliness has a particular source and also constitutes a distinct type. However, there are few pure types. Sometimes people may experience several of these dimensions at once, often without being fully aware of it. More importantly, they indicate the extent of distress that lonely people may experience. For example, when individuals experience loneliness in four or five dimensions simultaneously and over a long period of time, they can find the stress intolerable and eventually break down.

Of the five the *interpersonal dimension* is generally the most familiar type. In this situation one person misses another. Often it is most intense when a very special person is missed. For example, one English study done by the Women's Group on Public Welfare, a social action organization, suggested that in this context the worst loneliness is a communication gap, such as one preceding the dissolution of a marriage:

"Perhaps there is no greater loneliness than that suffered when a marriage breaks down, particularly in a situation where partnership has so far foundered that communications between the two have become impossible," the study stated. "The divorced and widowed are often more lonely than those who have never been married. This deeper loneliness could be due not only to the loss of a close companion but also where, having married young they have never learned to live with or face up to loneliness in earlier life."

The *social dimension* of loneliness is another familiar type. Here the individual feels cut off from a group that he or she considers important. Here it is a social relationship rather than an interpersonal one that is felt to be ruptured or lacking. Terms such as *ostracism, exile, rejection, blackballed, fired, discrimination,* and *expelled,* to mention only a few, resonate with the sense of this particular kind of loneliness. Often one gets an important sense of self-worth through membership and participation in a particular social environment. Once that membership is denied and participation is no longer possible, a person feels not just cut off but lacking in self-esteem. Not surprisingly a person who feels this social isolation often develops a low self-image and feels impotent to change this unsatisfactory relationship. Literature of minority groups, deviants, and more recently both the youth and the elderly is filled with lamentation and outrage at this kind of loneliness that is unwittingly imposed by society.

When these two forms of loneliness occur in the same individual simultaneously over a prolonged period of time, the result can be unfortunate in growth as well as behavior. Dr. Gisela Konopka, professor of social work at the University of Minnesota, found, for example, that complex, chronic loneliness was a primary factor contributing to the delinquency of adolescent girls. They were unwanted at home, often had no close friends, and were rejected at school and by clubs. Without any meaningful social role in which to demonstrate their worth and have it approved, as well as being without intimate communication, they acted out their feelings of lonely worthlessness in destructive acts of crime. The same applies to boys. The black Puerto Rican author, Piri Thomas, in his autobiography *Down These Mean Streets,* traces back the violent behavior, which led to his imprisonment, to an agonizing loneliness that stemmed from two sources: a lack of communication in his family, and ostracism by a white society because of his dark skin.

Retired persons may also experience an unexpected frustration associated with job severance. These people feel cut off, not merely from work, but from a network of relationships that had provided them with companionship and meaningful support. Housewives, too, have complained of similar combinations of lonely feelings, especially after several moves which leave them cut off from old friends, neighborhoods, and favorite groups.

My own research suggests that there may be a connection between rage and unmitigated complex loneliness. I have found that as you press people with questions on their loneliness they get very violent. In one group I had there was a divorced woman who felt extremely hostile toward her husband. She had lost her father at an early age and looked to her husband as a kind of father figure. He was a failure in every conceivable way and as a result she had bottled up this frustrated rage toward him. One day I threw a pillow down on the floor and said "There's your husband. Do to it what you would do to him." She killed him. Stomped him to death.

I believe that further investigation will bear out this tentative conclusion: very lonely people, who get angry rather than get depressed, will be prone to express their lonely frustration in destructive ways. I do not think it is mere coincidence that we are witnessing an unequalled rise in violence at the same time loneliness is so pervasive and intense. Personal accounts like that of Piri Thomas and studies of the Watts riots have shown that loneliness can be linked with violence when it is combined with a deep sense of frustration, especially in the economic and political realms.

The *cultural dimension* of loneliness refers to an experience some people have who feel themselves separated from a traditional system of meanings and a way of life. Immigrants and people who are continually mobile often experience this in the form of homesickness. People in America can sense this kind of loneliness if they feel the American heritage to be disintegrating. The term alienation may point to this form of loneliness, when it refers to a particular perception. Alienated people often feel that they are strangers in their own land. Members of American minority groups are particularly prone to this kind of loneliness. Even with close family relations they sometimes suffer from lingering loneliness, of being unable to identify with the American cultural heritage.

The feelings linked with cultural dislocation and culture shock likewise indicate a distinct form of loneliness, a sense of being uprooted and out of place. The nostalgia for those "good old days" when there was predictable order and cohesiveness also suggests this form of loneliness. In some cases loneliness may merely be a part of alienation; but in others, where there is a definite awareness of being separated from a meaningful tradition, I think the term loneliness is more accurate.

The *cosmic dimension* of loneliness may take a variety of forms, but essentially it refers to an experience in which a person feels out of touch with an ultimate source of life and meaning. Often it takes a religious form. Religious persons sometimes lament a felt absence of God. The Bible is filled with expressions of lonely persons longing for God. Much contemporary religion also answers to this need of loneliness, promising people a sense of presence and communion in their condition of existential estrangement or loneliness.

In workshops I have had persons express this cosmic loneliness in various ways. One middle-aged man confessed that a constant source of frustration came in the form of "missing God." Earlier he had been a strong believer, but now was an agnostic. He missed the sense of relatedness his youthful faith had given him. Religious persons who have been divorced have found themselves excluded from their religious community and they too have felt the anguish of this kind of loneliness. Some people have expressed a cosmic loneliness in their perception of the apparent absurdity of life. Erich Fromm suggested in *Escape from Freedom* that the experience of being morally and cosmically lonely is characteristic of persons who have realized the implications of autonomy in the modern world. Flight into conformity, becoming overly dependent on others, obsessive concern with others, a compulsive drive for achievement and recognition are some of the unproductive attempts of people to escape this dimension of loneliness.

The *psychological dimension* refers both to the experience a person has of being separate from himself as well as to the personal impact of the other four causes. A student who was in one of my courses made an observation that I have found many respond to: "I am loneliest when I am out of touch with myself." William James and C. J. Jung suggested the experience of a divided self is the root of modern man's search for a deeply personal religion or self-actualization or both. Much success of the Human Potential movement is related to the resolving of loneliness within one's self as well as that which comes from the lack of any intimate relationships with others. The perception of one's self as divided is a distinct form of "suffering self-recognition of separateness."

Here again one usually stumbles into this perception unawares so that this loneliness is aggravated by a clash of expectations.

The psychological dimension indicates a distinctly internal source of loneliness, whereas the other four dimensions specifically refer to external sources. Some aspects of loneliness can be traced to personality features that possibly stand in the way of self-actualization. Shyness, fear of loving and being loved, self-pity, and the development of a schizoid personality are examples of traits that can contribute to loneliness. But one point I emphasize as a sociologist is that *personal troubles often come from outside*, even though the individual experiences them as very private and intimately his own. This sociological analysis helps to get us beyond a narrow psychological and everyday notion that somehow an individual is at fault when he is feeling lonely. On the contrary, if an individual has lost a parent, a friend, or child in death, has moved from home, has changed or lost his job, is rejected by his group, and has lost his religious faith, is confused by his ambiguous American heritage, and does not feel deep, abiding loneliness, then I suspect that something drastic is lacking within him. Much loneliness that I have examined is a normal response to breaks in an individual's important relationships.

In all five dimensions there is the element of a suffering self-recognition of separateness from something, though each general type can be distinguished from the others. In each situation there are different kinds of relationships lacking. Consequently, there are different needs to be met. Recognizing specific needs proper to different dimensions is extremely important when someone is trying to cope with loneliness. For example, a person who sorely misses a special other person will not have the need satisfied by joining a group. Yet in spite of an impressive history of failure, we continue to encourage widows to compensate by joining organizations. That is, we tell

"HIDEWAYS"

1

IF I SHUT THE DOOR TO
MY HOUSE, YOU CAN'T
COME INSIDE...

2

& EVERYTHING'S FINE
BECAUSE I DON'T
THINK ABOUT YOU....

3

EXCEPT SOMETIMES &
THOSE TIMES I LOCK
MYSELF IN MY ROOM...

4

BECAUSE NOTHING THERE
REMINDS ME
OF YOU...

5

BUT SOMETIMES SOMETHING
DOES & I HIDE IN A
BOX THE TV CAME IN...

6

& THAT KEEPS
YOU AWAY
FROM ME....

7

MOST OF THE TIME... BUT
WHEN IT DOESN'T, I CRAWL
INTO A SHOE BOX
I KEEP IN THE TV BOX....

8

WHERE NOTHING YOU
DID OR SAID
CAN REACH ME..

9

EXCEPT SOMETIMES SO
THEN I CLIMB INTO
A PRESCRIPTION BOTTLE
INSIDE THE SHOE BOX...

10

& IT
HIDES ME FROM
YOU...

11

& IF IT DOESN'T, I ROLL
UP INTO A BALL
BECAUSE I DON'T HAVE
ANYTHING SMALLER TO GET INTO...

12

I WISH I HAD
A THIMBLE...

tom McCain

"Hideways" by tom mcCain. Copyright © 1996.

them to look to the social dimension to satisfy an interpersonal need. We offer hand-holding to members of minority groups who suffer from a sense of exclusion, instead of creating a place for them to experience participation. Many attempts to cope with loneliness are unsuccessful because the need of a particular type of loneliness has not been met. The conventional wisdom that recommends lonely people keep busy does not confront the problem of loneliness. It dodges it and instead applies compulsive activity like a narcotic. I have been told by countless widows that they have tried this formula only to find that they return home to an empty house exhausted and all the more vulnerable to the painful void of their lives.

If we recognize loneliness as a significant form of self-perception, consider its context, and identify the dimensions involved, then we will be better prepared to face it realistically and positively. We need to get away from the simplistic notion that for loneliness "all you need is love." Love is often not enough. Social action is sometimes necessary and individual preparation for loneliness is essential.

If more than just an interpersonal dimension is present, then a more complex form of response will be needed. For example, persons suffering from both interpersonal and social loneliness are more prone to low self-esteem. The latter can jeopardize close, interpersonal relationships and discourage persons from taking an active role in a group. Meaningful participation in a group and developing some social role of importance can help combat the troubles stemming from the societal dimension of loneliness. It also can improve self-esteem, and prepare a person to become more ready for mature friendships and love.

If we are to meet the needs of lonely people effectively, we must get at the sources of their loneliness. Too often we treat loneliness merely as a symptom; that's one reason it keeps recurring. To confront loneliness in the modern world, our response will have to be a multi-level one. This concept of the five dimensions of loneliness can be helpful to social scientists, counselors, and anyone in detecting intelligently the types of loneliness we may encounter in the course of our lives. It also suggests the various sources from which it arises, and the multi-dimensional approach needed to cope adequately with the complex problem of loneliness.

Follow-Up

1. *Sadler describes five distinct dimensions of loneliness: interpersonal, social, cultural, cosmic, and psychological. Explain how you have experienced each of these dimensions, or as many as you can; how you handled the particular type of loneliness; and its consequences for you.*
2. *Sadler states that loneliness often strikes us unexpectedly. Not being prepared for it, we become confused, frightened, depressed, or find ways to avoid it. Discuss or write about your reactions to his argument.*
3. *Choose any other aspect of this article and write about or discuss your response.*
4. *Sadler says that each kind of loneliness requires a different intervention. Apply this idea and offer your opinion.*

You Never Know

Nels Goud

There are times when someone does something so totally unexpected, so outside of what you thought possible, that there is no choice but to change the way you think. Here's one such instance.

During my senior year in high school there was a freshman I'll call Joanie. Today Joanie would be placed in a class for the mildly mentally handicapped. But my school had no special education program, so Joanie was put in general curriculum classes where she performed poorly but was passed anyway. Beside her limited intellectual capacity, Joanie was saddled with other qualities that placed her near the bottom of the prevailing status scales. Her face was pocked with pimples and her tongue protruded slightly. She spoke with a lisp. Joanie had a very out-of-date, drab, and baggy wardrobe. She had a strong body odor. Her long, loping strides seemed out of place on her plump, short frame. It was a common sight to see guys following directly behind her mocking her gait. A newcomer, Joanie was cast into high school society with no friends and seemingly no social skills to find any.

Soon Joanie became a laughing stock and scapegoat for the insecure members of the school culture. Strangely it did not affect her behavior. She remained very friendly and smiled a lot. Joanie had one organizing force in her life—to be liked. She would do almost anything to get someone to notice or talk to her. It did not make any difference if the attention was respectful or derogatory. She seemed to exist to belong to someone, something, anything.

Joanie often asked "Do you like me?" This would usually happen after someone told her that "Larry" liked her. She would then seek out Larry and ask him "Do you like me?" Larry, of course, would loudly protest in the midst of a chorus of guffaws and taunts of his buddies. Joanie would just stand there and smile, not completely aware of what was going on, but hanging on to the chance that maybe this time it was true. Besides, it was a human connection.

If students treated Joanie with civility, they did so at a price. They would have a shadow for days that made it impossible for them to have a normal social life. These students soon learned to escape physically or adopt techniques of polite disregard. Then Joanie would hang around the outside of a group—a human satellite.

It was a big deal in those days to attend dances following football games. Everyone was into human connections at these events. There seemed to be a ritual. For the first half hour or so the guys would be slouched against one wall of the gym trying to look "cool" but afraid to dance. The girls would be dancing with each other, or gathered in small groups occasionally stealing glances at some "cool" guy across the floor. It was the slow ballad that awakened a few slouchers to saunter across the floor to ask a girl to dance. Then the other girls grabbed a few wall-huggers. Soon the floor was back-to-back with young adolescents discovering all sorts of human connections. All except Joanie. Surprisingly, she attended these dances knowing she would be isolated for the whole evening. Joanie would stand in the corner alone and stare into the mass of swaying couples. After a couple hours her parents would arrive to take her home.

At one of these dances one of those moments occurred when you know there is hope for the species—all because of a classmate of mine named Lance. Lance was an athlete, very good looking, a senior, and he drove a new white convertible. In addition, he dated girls from out of town (a *big* status point). Lance was a popular guy—so popular that he could go over and ask a girl, any girl, to dance during the first dance of the night. I wasn't jealous at all. I had a better baseball batting average than he, and besides, I could slouch better.

About an hour into the dance Lance was dancing about his 50th dance and, naturally, with the best looking junior girl in the whole world. The song ended and the next song was Elvis's "Love Me Tender." This ballad even brought *me* out of my slouch, and I went over to ask the new clarinetist to dance. I happened to notice that Lance walked over to Joanie's corner. He asked her to dance. She didn't know how to dance, but this did not matter to Lance. He swept her into his arms and led her through the best fox-trot I've ever seen.

Joanie shadowed Lance for at least a week after the dance. He just politely acknowledged her presence and went his way. No one ribbed Lance. They were too astounded, or afraid of getting knots pounded on their heads. Some of us even learned something.

I saw Lance at a high school reunion fifteen years later and told him of my observations. He had forgotten it. He mentioned that Joanie had since married and was living on the edge of town. Joanie finally belonged.

Follow-Up

1. *A strongly felt need to belong can often make individuals act in unexpected ways. Describe how you have experienced this phenomenon.*
2. *In the story Lance showed compassion when no one else did. Have you witnessed or been part of similar acts? If so, describe one and explain how it affected you afterwards.*
3. *Respond to any other aspect of the article.*

Little Joys

Abe Arkoff

When Salman Rushdie was sentenced to death by the Ayatollah Khomeini for writing "The Satanic Verses," he went into hiding. Reminiscing about the life he left behind, he said, "What I miss is ordinary life: walking down the street, browsing in a bookshop, going to a grocery store, going to a movie. I've always been a big movie addict, and I haven't been in a cinema for a year."

"I haven't driven a car for a year," Rushdie continued. "I really love driving, and suddenly I have to sit in the back seat all the time. What I miss is just that, these tiny little things."

The value of little things was what playwright Thornton Wilder had in mind when he wrote *Our Town,* which proved to be his most famous work. The play was, he said, "an attempt to find a value above all price for the smallest events in our daily life." In this simple but moving drama, he eloquently shows what is extraordinary about the most ordinary and commonplace.

In *Our Town,* Emily, who has died in early adulthood, finds she can return to relive a day of her life. When she returns to relive her twelfth birthday, she finds her experience—from the vantage point of death—too poignant and in too great a contrast to the living who move matter-of-factly through the day. Overcome, she returns to death saying:

> Good-by, good-by, world. Good-by Grover's Corners . . . Mama and Papa. Good-by to clocks ticking . . . and Mama's sunflowers. And food and coffee. And new-ironed dresses and hot baths . . . and sleeping and waking up. Oh, earth you're too wonderful for anybody to realize you . . . Do any human beings realize life while they live it?—every, every minute?

My favorite essay on joy is a brief paper by Hermann Hesse. Although written almost 100 years ago, it sounds remarkably up-to-date as it laments the speed of "modern life," with the feverish pursuit of entertainment and ironically less and less joy. Hesse reminds the reader of the little joys available in daily rounds if one will only take a moment for them. He concludes his essay, "It is the small joys first of all that are granted to us for recreation, for daily relief and disburdenment, not the great ones."

Some recent research suggests that Hesse's advice is good psychology. Seek out as many as possible of the small joys each day. Studying both college-age and older persons, Professor Ed Diener of the University of Illinois has found that it is frequent little joys rather than an occasional big joy that make for a general sense of well-being. While less intense positive emotions are common, intense positive emotions are infrequent; furthermore, such intense events are often purchased at the price of past unhappy events and can serve to diminish the sensation of future positive events. Diener found happiness to be associated with those persons who frequently experience positive emotions rather than those whose positive experiences are intense. Thus, Diener and Hesse agree that the key to well-being is to fill one's days with little joys.

More evidence concerning the limited value of big joy was found by a research team who compared the levels of happiness in 22 major lottery winners with the levels of a control group similar in other respects. Each group indicated how happy they were at present, had been earlier (for the winners, before winning, for the controls, 6 months earlier), and expected to be in a couple of years. Significant differences between winners and controls in previous, present, or anticipated levels of happiness: none.

Even more striking results were found when both groups were asked how pleasant they currently found seven activities: eating breakfast, reading a magazine, watching television, talking with a friend, hearing a funny joke, getting a compliment, and buying clothes. Compared to controls, the winners found significantly less pleasure in these activities. Although the emotional big high of winning had not brought a significant, lasting increase in happiness, seemingly, by comparison, everyday little highs had paled.

The Chinese philosopher Lin Yutang passionately described the little pleasures that made his own life joyful. Indeed there were many, and in his enthusiasm, he gave a number of them first place. For example, he wrote, "If there is a greater happiness than lying in the sun, I'd like to be told." But then he noted, "If a man will be sensible and . . . count on his fingers how many things give him enjoyment, invariably he will find food is the first one." Still, later, seemingly to settle the matter, he set down the final truth: "If one's bowels move, one is happy, and if they don't move one is unhappy. That is all there is to it."

There is much in our day we think of as routine that could become little joys if approached in another way. Rushdie noted that he missed things he once thought completely unimportant—even chores—such as shopping for groceries. What once were tasks now were seen as privileges.

George Leonard recommends the Zen strategy of finding joy in the commonplace. What this requires is not a change of activity but rather a change of attitude. Leonard writes, "You might think that the value of Zen practice lies in the unwavering apprehension of the present moment while sitting motionless. But a visit to a Zen retreat quickly reveals that potentially, *everything* is meditation—

building a stone wall, eating, walking from one place to another, sweeping a hallway."

Psychologist Frank Dougherty has made an important distinction between the pursuit of relief and the pursuit of delight. Some of us who (perhaps without knowing it) have spent our lives pursuing relief, wonder why we never feel delight, but no amount of relief can produce delight. People whose minds are set on relief work to make sure that everything is taken care of and under control. There will be time for delight, they think, when things settle down, but of course, things never do.

To pursue delight requires a different mindset, and we can pursue delight even though everything isn't in order. We don't let the work waiting on Monday morning interfere with our enjoyment of the picnic this lovely Sunday afternoon.

Sir Alexander Korda recalled talking with Winston Churchill during the war when some bad news arrived. Churchill glanced at his watch and announced he was due back at 10 Downing Street. "It will all look different after a good lunch, a cigar, and a nap," he said. "Besides, Marshall Stalin has sent us some excellent caviar by courier, and it would be a shame not to enjoy it."

Often, the event that produces relief for one person delivers delight to another who approaches it in a very different way. In this connection, one of my students recalled a backpack trip he had been on with a group of others. Each day, the same person was first to reach their destination. One evening, the group was sharing the memories of the day's beautiful vistas, and this person finally spoke and said, "I guess all I really saw today was the top of my shoes."

Years ago, Sol Gordon wrote a brief set of instructions on how to be happy in an unhappy world. It was simply "to be able to enjoy at least the number of things equal to our age." Gordon was 51 years old at the time, and he wrote out the 51 things he enjoyed. The list included bittersweet stories and chocolate, uninterrupted classical music, reading slowly the good novelists, being warm and intimate with people he really cared about, and fantasizing that one of his still unpublished books was number one or number two on the *New York Times* best-sellers list.

Following Gordon's advice, my students and I make up our own lists of little joys when we are on the topic of happiness. I have found that just making up a list and sharing it with others makes one feel good.

As director of a freshman seminar program and coordinator of a program for older persons, I have taught some of the youngest and oldest students on my campus. The older students seem to compose their long lists of joys as easily as the youngest students do their much shorter ones.

My oldest student (and the one most full of fun and joy) was 91 years old when she made out her list and had no trouble in arriving at 91 items. Now 95, she is recovering from open-heart surgery and writes that she is enjoying in anticipation her next trip to Hawaii.*

After my students compose their little joy lists, I ask them to go back and put a star or asterisk by each item they have actually enjoyed in the past 30 days. What good is something

*Since I wrote this, she has made the trip to Hawaii, and we celebrated her 96th birthday together; she is as full of fun and joy as ever.

that can bring joy if one doesn't take time to enjoy it? I enjoy reading my students' lists as much as my own. Most of the items cost very little or nothing at all. One of the most common items, of course, is chocolate. It appears on Sol Gordon's list and, I confess, my own. However, other common items are calorie-free, such as music, reading, nature, movies, a favorite TV program or comic strip.

The most uncommon joy producer that I have seen on any list is "Standing in the barn loft—after feeding hay to about 100 cattle—and listening to them crunch or munch the hay." It was on the list of one of my older students—a 64-year-old man from Tennessee. His whole list was quite special and not only because it didn't mention chocolate even once. Other items on his list included giving a flower to a lovely lady and watching her eyes light up; sitting on the patio and watching the fields and valleys and mountains change with the shadows as the sun moves across the sky; looking at—and feeling proud of—the many afghans and quilts his mother made and gave to him; driving a good, responsive car on a curvy mountain road; and after a hard, tiring day outside, a drink of good straight sour mash whiskey, mixed with a little 7-Up and cranberry juice.

Make up your list of little joys today, and make sure that in 30 days, each has a star by it.

Follow-Up

1. *Make a list of all the things you are able to deeply enjoy, and include as many items as you are years old. Put a star or asterisk in front of each item you have actually enjoyed in the past 30 days. Then write an account of your thoughts and feelings as you worked on and read over your list.*
2. *Live an ordinary day as you usually would, except be especially aware of everything in the day that brings you joy. Before you go to sleep, write an account of this experience.*
3. *Live an ordinary day as you usually would, except make the most of each joyful moment or each opportunity for one. Before you go to sleep, write an account of this experience.*
4. *How much is your life a pursuit of relief, and how much a pursuit of delight? Discuss this aspect of your life.*

Anger

Wayne Dyer

SOME COMMON CAUSES OF ANGER

You can see anger in operation all the time. Examples of people experiencing varying degrees of immobility, from mild upset to blind rage, are everywhere. It is the cancer, albeit a learned one, that permeates human interactions. Below are some of the more common instances in which people choose anger.

• Anger in the automobile. Drivers scream at other motorists for virtually everything. Pulse-racing behavior results when someone else is going too slow, too fast, doesn't signal, signals improperly, changes lanes or any number of mistakes. As a driver, you may experience a great deal of anger and emotional immobility because of the things you tell yourself about the ways others should be driving. Similarly, traffic jams are key signals for attacks of anger and hostility. Drivers yell at passengers and swear at the cause of the delay. All this behavior is the result of a single thought, "This shouldn't be happening, and because it is, I'm going to be upset and help others to choose unhappiness as well."

• Anger in competitive games. Bridge, tennis, pinochle, poker and a variety of other games are excellent anger inducers. People get angry at partners or opponents for not doing it right or for infractions of the rules. They may throw things like a tennis racket because they made an error. While stomping and throwing equipment are healthier than hitting or screaming at others, they are still barriers to present-moment fulfillment.

• Anger at the out of place. Many people feel rage at an individual or event which they consider out of place. For example, a driver in traffic may decide the cyclist or pedestrian shouldn't be there and try to drive him off the road. This kind of anger can be extremely dangerous. Many so-called accidents are actually the result of just such incidents in which uncontrolled rage has serious results.

• Anger about taxes. No amount of anger will ever change the tax laws of our country, but people rage just the same because taxes aren't what they would like them to be.

• Anger over the tardiness of others. If you expect others to function on your timetable, you will choose anger when they do not and justify your immobilization with, "I have a right to be angry. He kept me waiting half an hour."

• Anger at the disorganization or sloppiness of others. Despite the fact that your rage will probably encourage others to continue to behave in the same manner, you may persist in choosing anger.

• Anger at inanimate objects. If you hit your shin bone or hammer your thumb, reacting with a scream can be therapeutic, but feeling real rage and doing something about it such as driving your fist through a wall is not only futile, but painful as well.

• Anger over the loss of objects. No amount of rage will turn up a lost key or wallet and will probably prevent you from launching an effective search.

• Anger over world events beyond your control. You may not approve of politics, foreign relations, or the economy, but your anger and subsequent immobilization aren't going to change anything.

THE MANY FACES OF ANGER

Now that we've seen some of the occasions on which you might choose anger, let's look at some forms anger takes.

"Anger" by tom mcCain. Copyright © 1996.

- Being verbally abusive or ridiculing a spouse, children, or loved ones, or friends.
- Physical violence—hitting, kicking, slamming—objects or people. Carried to extremes, this behavior leads to crimes of violence which are almost always committed under the influence of immobilizing anger. Murder and assaults don't occur unless emotions are out of control and anger has led to temporary insanity. Believing that anger is normal or subscribing to the psychological schools that encourage you to get in touch with your anger and let it out can be potentially dangerous. Similarly, television, movies and books which popularize anger and violence and present them as normal undermine both the individual and society.
- Saying things like, "He infuriates me," or "You really aggravate me." In these cases you are choosing to let someone else's behavior make you unhappy.
- Using phrases like, "kill him," "clobber them," or "destroy the opposition." You may think they're only expressions, but they encourage anger and violence and make it acceptable even in friendly competition.
- Temper tantrums. Not only is this a common expression of anger, it frequently serves to get the tantrum thrower exactly what he wants.

- Sarcasm, ridicule and the silent treatment. These expressions of anger can be just as damaging as physical violence.

THE REWARD SYSTEM THAT YOU'VE CONSTRUCTED FOR CHOOSING ANGER

Getting a grip on lengthening your fuse will most effectively start with some insight into the reasons for using it in the first place. Here are some of the psychological motives for keeping that fuse as short as it is.

- Whenever you find it difficult to handle yourself, feel frustrated or defeated, you can use anger to direct the responsibility for how you feel to the person or event itself, rather than taking charge of your own feelings.
- You can use your anger to manipulate those who fear you. This is particularly effective in getting those who are younger, or physically or psychologically smaller, in line.
- Anger draws attention and thus you can feel important and powerful.
- Anger is a handy excuse. You can go insane—temporarily—and then excuse yourself by saying, "I couldn't help myself." Thus you can exonerate your behavior with out-of-control logic.

• You can get your way because others would rather placate you than have to put up with the angry exhibition.

• If you are afraid of intimacy or love, you can get angry over something, and thus avoid the risky business of sharing yourself affectionately.

• You can manipulate others with guilt by having them wonder "Where did I go wrong to make him so angry?" When they feel guilty, you are powerful.

• You can break down communication in which you feel threatened because someone else is more skillful. You simply use anger to avoid the risk of looking bad.

• You don't have to work on yourself when you are angry. Therefore you can use up your present moments in the easy business of being fierce and avoid doing whatever it might take to improve yourself. Thus you can use anger to take the heat off yourself.

• You can indulge in self-pity after you've had an attack of anger and feel sorry for yourself because nobody understands you.

• You can avoid thinking clearly, simply by getting angry. Everyone knows that you can't think straight at these times, so why not haul out the old anger when you want to avoid any of the hard straight-thinking.

• You can excuse losing or poor performance with a simple fit of temper. Maybe you can even get others to stop winning, because they fear your anger so much.

• You can excuse anger by saying you need it to help you carry out some task, but in fact anger is immobilizing and never improves performance.

• By saying it's human to be angry, you have a ready justification for yourself. "I'm human, and that's what humans do."

SOME DESIGNS FOR REPLACING ANGER

Anger can be eliminated. It will require a great deal of new thinking and it can be done only one present moment at a time. When confronted with people or events which provoke you to choose anger, become aware of what you are telling yourself, and then work at new sentences which will create new feelings and more productive behavior. Here are some specific strategies for attacking anger.

• First and most important, get in touch with your thoughts at the time of your anger, and remind yourself that you don't have to think that way, simply because you've always done so in the past. Awareness is paramount.

• Try postponing anger. If you typically react with anger in a particular circumstance, postpone the anger for fifteen seconds, and then explode in your typical fashion. Next try thirty seconds, and keep lengthening the intervals. Once you begin to see that you can put anger off, you'll have learned control. Postponing is control, and with lots of practice, you'll eventually eliminate it totally.

• When trying to use anger constructively to teach a child something, try faking the anger. Raise your voice and look stern, but don't experience all of the physical and psychological pain that goes with anger.

• Don't try to delude yourself into believing that you enjoy something that you find distasteful. You can dislike something and still not have to be angry about it.

• Remind yourself at the moment of anger that everyone has a right to be what he chooses and that your demanding that anyone be different will simply prolong your anger. Work at allowing others to choose just as you insist on your own right to do the same.

• Ask someone that you trust to help. Have them tell you when they see your anger, either verbally or with an agreed signal. When you get the signal, think about what you're doing and then try the postponing strategy.

• Keep an anger journal, and record the exact time, place and incident in which you chose to be angry. Be religious about the entries, force yourself to record all angry behavior. You'll soon find, if you are persistent, that the very act of having to write the incident down will persuade you to choose anger less often.

• Announce after you have had an angry outburst that you've just slipped and that one of your goals is to think differently so that you don't experience this anger. The verbal announcement will put you in touch with what you've done, and will demonstrate that you are truly working on yourself.

• Try being physically close to someone that you love at the moment of your anger. One way to neutralize your hostility is to hold hands, despite your inclination not to, and keep holding hands until you've expressed how you feel and dissipated your anger.

• Talk with those who are the most frequent recipients of your anger at a time when you are not angry. Share with each other the most anger-provoking activities in the other, and devise a way of communicating your feelings without debilitating anger. Perhaps a written note, or a messenger, or a cooling-off walk can be mutually agreed upon, so that you don't continue abusing each other with senseless anger. After several cooling-off walks, you'll begin to see the folly of striking out.

• Defuse your anger for the first few seconds by labeling how you feel, and how you believe your partner feels as well. The first ten seconds are the most crucial. Once you've passed these, your anger will often have subsided.

• Keep in mind all the things you believe will be met with disapproval by fifty percent of the folks, fifty percent of the time. Once you expect others to disagree, you will not choose to feel angry. Instead, you'll say to yourself that the world is straight since people aren't agreeing with everything I say, think, feel and do.

• Keep in mind that while the expression of anger is a healthy alternative to storing it up, not having it at all is the healthiest choice of all. Once you stop viewing anger as natural or only human, you'll have an internal rationale for going to work at eliminating it.

• Get rid of the expectations you have for others. When the expectations go away, so will the anger.

• Remind yourself that children will always be active and loud and getting angry about it won't do any good. While you can help children to make constructive choices in other areas, you will never be able to alter their basic nature.

• Love yourself. If you do, you won't ever burden yourself with that self-destructive anger.

• In a traffic jam, time yourself. See how long you can go without exploding. Work at the control aspect. Instead of hollering at a passenger, ask him a civil question. Use the time creatively to write a letter, or a song, or to devise ways out of the traffic jam, or relive the most exciting sexual experience of your life, or better yet, plan to improve on it.

• Instead of being an emotional slave to every frustrating circumstance, use the situation as a challenge to change it, and you'll have no present moment time for the anger.

Anger gets in the way. It is good for nothing. Like all erroneous zones, anger is a means of using things outside yourself to explain how you feel. Forget others. Make your own choices—and don't let them be angry ones.

Follow-Up

1. *Discuss your most common causes of anger, the faces your anger shows, and the rewards for being angry as described by Dyer.*
2. *Select two strategies for replacing anger and try them out. Report your results.*
3. *Choose any two statements or ideas in this article and offer your commentary.*
4. *For further information, see Wayne Dyer's* Your Erroneous Zones.
5. *See also the Anger Management Applied Activity.*

Jealousy and Envy

The Demons within Us

Jon Queijo

Rick and Liz seemed to have a wonderful marriage; they did everything together. This changed suddenly, however, when Liz's ex-boyfriend began working at her law firm. Besieged by insecurity, Rick began calling Liz's office at odd hours and at night questioned her suspiciously. In a coup de grace, he burst in on her during a business luncheon and falsely accused her of having an affair.

Ann worked extremely hard to achieve success as a real estate agent. Her satisfaction turned sour, however, when a new agent was hired who managed to work less, yet made more sales. Ann hid her dislike of the new agent by offering to take her phone messages while she was out. When Ann began making more sales than her rival, no one made the connection between this turn of events and Ann's tendency to "accidentally" forget to deliver certain phone messages.

The jealous rage of a lover. The shameful actions of envy. Despite our better intentions, most of us feel these emotions dozens of times in our lifetimes. Pulling us apart from lovers, friends, family members, co-workers and even perfect strangers, jealousy and envy can devastate our lives and cause effects ranging from sadness, anger and depression, to estrangement, abuse and even violence.

Although we see jealousy and envy arise in numerous situations, their basic definitions are fairly simple: jealousy is "the fear of losing a relationship" (romantic, parental, sibling, friendship); and envy is "the longing for something someone else has" (wealth, possessions, beauty, talent, position).

Probably the most practical understanding of jealousy and envy, however, emerges from the work of social psychologists—researchers who look at the way people react to each other and society. To them, jealousy and envy arise when the right mix of internal *and* external ingredients are present in society.

"I tend to look at jealousy and envy in terms of motivation and self-esteem," explains Peter Salovey, a social psychologist at Yale University. "It's the interaction between what's important to you and what's happening in the environment. The common denominator is this threat to something that's very important to the person—something that defines self-worth."

Richard Smith, a social psychologist at Boston University who has conducted several studies on jealousy and envy, emphasizes external factors, such as how society affects our view of ourselves. "My perspective is from social comparisons," he explains, "which says we have no objective opinion for evaluating our abilities, so we look at others."

Smith, like Salovey, also stresses internal factors—the role of self-esteem, for example—in determining whether we will feel jealous or envious in any given situation. "People who are dissatisfied with themselves are primed for having other people's talents and possessions impinge on them," Smith points out. "If, on the other hand, you're satisfied with yourself, then what other people have or do won't unduly raise your expectations for yourself, and you should be less likely to feel envy."

Embarrassed by his display of jealousy, Rick apologizes to Liz and they discuss the problem. Soon they realize that while Rick loves Liz and fears losing her, something else is at work here. Because Liz's ex-boyfriend is a lawyer, he possesses skills Rick does not. While Rick is proud of his ability as a store manager, he fears Liz's ex-boyfriend could lure her away with other skills.

Feeling guilty about her actions, Ann calls a friend for support. Ann knows she feels inadequate because the new agent is succeeding in a career that is very important to her, but that doesn't explain everything; others have done better whom Ann has not envied. Then it occurs to her: What bothers her is the way *the woman was bettering Ann. She was more outgoing and self-confident—two skills about which Ann has always felt insecure.*

As Rick and Ann's situations illustrate, if someone is unsure about an ability—such as Rick and his law knowledge or Ann and her communication skills—then a social situation can bring out that insecurity. "In envy," notes Salovey, "the threat may come from someone else's possessions or attributes. In jealousy the situation is the same, except that the other person's possessions or attributes cause you to fear losing the relationship. Either way, somebody else threatens your self-esteem."

Dave and Marcia had been dating for a year when Marcia decided she wanted to see other men. Dave was devastated—not only because he cared for her, but because he was older and feared his age was working against him. One evening he bumped into Marcia, arm-in-arm with another man. As Dave talked to the couple, sarcasm led to verbal abuse, until finally Dave took a swing at Marcia's date— a man at least 10 years his junior.

In case you haven't guessed, Dave wanted back more than his relationship with Marcia; he also wanted the return of his youth. He was feeling a painful mixture of jealousy *and* envy. Explains Salovey, "The same feelings emerge when your relationship is threatened by some- one else as when you'd like something that person has. I think one reason is that in most romantic situations, envy plays a role. You're jealous because you're going to lose the relationship, but you're also envious because there is something the other person has that allows him to be attractive to the person you care about."

As illustrated here and isolated in a survey Salovey and Yale associate Judith Rodin conducted with *Psychology Today* readers, there are three major coping strategies: *Self-reliance*, in which a person does not give into the emotion, but continues to pursue the goals in the relationship; *Selective ignoring*, or simply ignoring the things that cause the jealousy or envy; and *Self-bolstering*, or concentrating on positive traits about yourself.

Surprisingly, "We found that the first two coping strategies are very effective in helping a person not feel jealousy," reports Salovey. "We thought that self-bolstering would also be good, since if something that's important to you is threatened, then maybe you should think of things in which you do well."

Although self-bolstering was not helpful in preventing jealousy, "Once you were *already* jealous, it was the only thing that kept you from becoming depressed and angry," notes Salovey. "So the first two keep jealousy in check, but if jealousy does emerge, self-bolstering keeps jealousy from its worst effects."

In the same study, Salovey and Rodin also uncovered some interesting data about how men and women experience jealousy and envy. "Men tend to be more envious in situations involving wealth and fame, and women more so in beauty and friendship," reports Salovey, but he emphasizes, "I should put that finding in context. We looked at a lot of variables and very rarely found differences. Men and women were very similar on nearly everything you could measure except that one difference."

Jealousy and envy can have an unpleasant knack of cropping up between the people who

COMPARING OURSELVES TO OTHERS

In Sickness and in Health

Envy, according to Richard Smith, arises when we compare ourselves to others and can't cope with what we see. Indeed, he believes that the way in which we cope with "social comparisons" plays an important role in our physical as well as mental health.

Smith theorizes that we use one of four "comparison styles" to cope with social differences. Two of these styles are "constructive" to well-being, while two are "destructive." "It's a difficult problem to tackle," says Smith, "but we're trying to measure these styles and see if they predict a person's general satisfaction with life or ability to cope with illness." For example, he notes, "There's considerable evidence" that one way people cope with serious illness is by focusing on others who are not doing as well.

Smith has arranged the four comparison styles in a matrix, with the descriptions in each box referring to the characteristics of that style. "*Upward*-Constructive," for example, represents those who compare themselves to others who are better off, and use it as a healthy stimulus. In this category, "You don't feel hostile to others who are better," says Smith, "because you hope to be like them. It suggests that upward comparisons are not necessarily bad."

"*Upward*-Destructive," however, shows how comparing yourself to those doing better can be unhealthy. Envy, resentment, Type A behavior and poor health all fit into this category. Smith points to a study that looked at personalities of people who had heart attacks, "and the only dimension that predicted heart disease was this jealousy-suspicion trait."

What Smith calls "*Downward*-Constructive," refers to people who compare themselves to those worse off, and use it to feel better about themselves. Such people, says Smith, "realize that others aren't doing so well and how lucky they are. There's some solid evidence in the health literature showing the value of that kind of comparison."

Finally, "*Downward*-Destructive," describes those who get pleasure out of comparing themselves to others who are worse off. "I'd call the effect 'schadenfreude,' or joy at the suffering of others," says Smith. "It's akin to sadism and it's probably not conducive to health."

"What's interesting about all four comparison styles," notes Smith, "is that they don't necessarily have any relation to reality. They reflect what people construe and focus on." While Smith stresses, "This is all speculative," he adds that "my feeling is that 'Upward-Destructive' explains people's hostility in terms of their social comparison context. It shows why their relation to people doing better leads to envy and why they'd feel hostile to begin with."

—J. Q.

RANKING JEALOUSY AND ENVY

What situations are most likely to evoke feelings of jealousy and envy? In a study published in the Journal of Personality and Social Psychology, Peter Salovey and Judith Rodin asked subjects to rank 53 situations according to the degree of emotion each would evoke. Below are 25 of those situations, listed in decreasing order, that received the highest "jealousy/envy" ratings:

1. You find out your lover is having an affair.
2. Someone goes out with a person you like.
3. Someone gets a job that you want.
4. Someone seems to be getting closer to a person to whom you are attracted.
5. Your lover tells you how sexy his/her old girl/boyfriend was.
6. Your boyfriend or girlfriend visits the person he or she used to date.
7. You do the same work as someone else and get paid less than he or she.
8. Someone is more talented than you.
9. Your boyfriend or girlfriend would rather be with his/her friends than with you.
10. You are alone while others are having fun.
11. Your boyfriend or girlfriend wants to date other people.
12. Someone is able to express himself or herself better than you.
13. Someone else has something you wanted and could have had but don't.
14. Someone else gets credit for what you've done.
15. Someone is more intelligent than you.
16. Someone appears to have everything.
17. Your steady date has lunch with an attractive person of the opposite sex.
18. Someone is more outgoing and self-confident than you.
19. Someone buys something you wanted but couldn't afford.
20. You have to work while your roommate is out partying.
21. An opposite-sex friend gives another friend a compliment, but not you.
22. Someone has more free time than you.
23. You hear that an old lover of yours has found a new lover.
24. Someone seems more self-fulfilled than you.
25. You listen to someone tell a story about things he did without you.

—J. Q.

care most about each other. Our first reaction is often to blame the other person—my *wife* is the one who is lunching with her ex-boyfriend; my *co-worker* is undeservedly making more sales; why should my *brother* have a happy family *and* a big house? Part of our blame is understandable: life *is* unfair; society and circumstance *do* create differences between us beyond our control.

Nevertheless, the bottom line is not how we view other people, but how we view ourselves. When jealousy or envy become overwhelming, it is as much from passing judgment on ourselves as on others. That's when we owe it to everyone to talk it out, change what needs to be changed and—perhaps most importantly—accept ourselves for what we are.

Follow-Up

1. *Queijo writes that jealousy and envy are most likely to happen whenever individuals are vulnerable and insecure about a specific aspect of their lives. Is this true in your experience?*
2. *Coping strategies for jealousy and envy are: (1) self-reliance, (2) selective ignoring, and (3) self-bolstering. Apply them to prevent or ease jealousy or envy in your current situation, if applicable.*
3. *Analyze your "social comparison styles" according to the explanations given in the boxed section entitled "Comparing Ourselves to Others: In Sickness and in Health." Are you satisfied with your current styles?*
4. *After reading the boxed section entitled "Ranking Jealousy and Envy," circle the three statements that would most likely cause you high levels of jealousy or envy. Discuss or write about your reactions to these three selections.*
5. *Choose any other idea in the article to write about or discuss.*

My Tyrant

Tom Peyton

In 1776 a handful of hardy and determined souls decided to leave the tyranny of the English government. Their purpose was to find the freedom to live a life they chose, instead of one chosen for them. They sought independence. This past Fourth of July, I discovered the tyrant of my own mind.

I wandered downtown through the crowds of people and watched happy couples embracing. I observed families celebrating together and kids running through the blocked-off city streets. There were smiling faces everywhere—except for mine. The tyrant in my mind spoke: You are alone, Tom. Totally alone. You are all by yourself. Incomplete without a partner, without a spouse. The rest of society is complete. Look at how happy everyone is—it's because they have someone. You, Tom, have no one. The voice beat at my heart and soul. My shoulders tightened and my mood darkened; my body started to feel very tired. My thoughts turned to the incompleteness of the moment and my own incompleteness. My head lowered, heavy with thought. My eyes focused on the blades of grass in front of me, and my thoughts turned to my divorce.

HOPING FOR WHOLENESS

Since my divorce, I have spent more than a year waiting to feel whole again. Waiting for the tyrant in my mind to ease. Waiting for the voice of guilt and shame to quiet. Waiting for something or someone to still the abusive chatter that swirls in your head when you think you have created a situation so ugly, so hideous that you must keep it to yourself. It is a lonely feeling to carry this weight of guilt and shame. This weight is of my own creation, I thought. The guilt is my guilt, and the shame of failure is my shame. I am the one giving it the power to ruin my day. I am the one letting it destroy my mental health. I should be the one to get myself out of this insane dialogue with myself. But I could not. I was trapped, and I surrendered to the rambling in my head. At that moment a drop of rain landed on my forehead, then another and another. In the middle of my self-absorption, it was raining. Perfect, I thought. Perfect?

I looked up and noticed that the sun was still shining. I gazed to the left and saw a beautiful rainbow arching across the sky. A smile crept onto my face.

"Guilt Trip" by tom mcCain. Copyright © 1996.

For a moment, the tyrant stopped. My brain grew quiet, and the only thing that existed was the rainbow. At that moment, my past was in the past, and my future was too far away to see. At that moment, I was completely present with myself. I was no longer searching for my feeling of completeness—I was experiencing it. I was with myself, not by myself.

In the chaos of thousands of people, I understood that I had never been alone. That for 30 years, I have lived this drama we call life, feeling as if I needed someone in my life to feel complete. And for the entire time, that someone was me. I laughed at the irony of it, then felt the sadness of the illusion. To expect someone else to make you whole is a path of misery and depression.

I wrote this very personal column for my own healing. I decided to share it because I know there are people in this world who have the same illusion—that they are alone. I hope, for a moment today, that they understand that they are with themselves, and it's a great place to be. I understand, too, that I will slip and falter along this path of self-acceptance. But, for the rest of the evening, I quietly celebrated with myself. A celebration of independence from the tyranny of my own mind. Freedom on the Fourth of July.

Follow-Up

1. *What is your response to these statements?*
   - *"I have lived this drama we call life, feeling as if I needed someone in my life to feel complete. And for the entire time, that someone was me."*
   - *"You are alone, Tom. Totally alone. . . . The rest of society is complete. Look at how happy everyone is—it's because they have someone. You, Tom, have no one."*
2. *Do you have an inner tyrant at times? How does it influence how you see yourself?*

Sarcasm and Apathy

When I was young, *Leave It To Beaver* and *Father Knows Best* were topics of household conversations. There was a lot of admiration for straightforward, innocent, polite people. Sarcasm wasn't something people carried like a badge. Although I have no desire to go back to that era and to give up some of the freedoms we have now, I find myself wishing we could do without some of the sarcasm we have developed. Sometimes the sarcasm that has become such a living, breathing part of our daily lives drives me up the wall.

I grew up on a farm in rural Indiana. For years I actually believed that people could talk to each other without "put-downs." This isn't to say that we never gave opinions—Farmers and small town people can be very frank. But when we talked it was from the heart. Possibly our hearts didn't have so many dark spots. Possibly we were more naive.

By the time I reached high school, the sarcastic revolution had started. Our class had the proud distinction of being the first senior class in the town's history to be released a week earlier than every other grade because of the apathy of the entire senior class. For four years it wasn't "cool" to answer questions in class. It wasn't "cool" to get involved. The administration had an assembly for the senior class to tell us that, after four years of struggling to try and please us and being met with apathy, at last they were tired. They wanted us out.

Eventually I moved to the city and though I had maintained my non-sarcastic attitude, I couldn't keep it forever. One day I was with my sister and she commented on how sarcastic I had become. She was right. I spent a week trying to keep from saying anything sarcastic. Oh, it was tough. I told my son how proud I was of him for doing a chore. He was so confused, he actually asked me if I meant it. Amazingly, though, trying not to be sarcastic has rewards. I felt more real. I felt as if I wasn't trying to cover up my real feelings as much. As a result I was much more relaxed that week. Sometimes, on days when I am in a particularly sarcastic mood, I go to bed wishing that the children were still awake so that I could hold them. On those days I wonder if they know how much I love them. During the week that I was trying not to be sarcastic, I didn't have those down feelings. I went to sleep feeling that my day had been fulfilling.

In my graduate education class I interacted with two other teachers. I noticed the amount of their sarcasm. We all find sarcasm funny so we encourage it, but it was odd to me that these teachers acted in ways that my teachers hated so much in the class of 1970. "Do we have to do this?" "How much of this do we have to do?" "I don't want to do this." I couldn't help wondering how much sarcasm and apathy they tolerated from their students.

One night in class I sat between these two teachers. We had seen the *Griffin and Phoenix* movie, and they were talking about the movie's "over-kill." After several sarcastic comments, one of them turned to me and asked me what I thought. I feigned that I had been too tired to listen to their conversation. The second woman generously filled me in and I replied, "It was pretty sappy." I couldn't believe myself! I thought about the movie all the way home. In fact, I *cried* about the movie—remembering how some people find living harder than dying. So why did I say that? Probably for the same reason that the woman who had a whole notebook full of writing for one of her papers had said that she hadn't started her papers. It isn't "cool" to be non-sarcastic or non-apathetic.

There is probably a good chance that half of the time people are being sarcastic or apathetic it isn't genuine. Some people probably aren't even comfortable being that way.

Comedy clubs, friends, books, and all types of resources help us to develop the idea that sarcasm and apathy should be associated with things that are fun. Sarcasm and apathy are more than just a form of humor—they are becoming a way of life.

Leave It To Beaver has been replaced by Bart Simpson. Bart Simpson is more than a sarcastic underachiever. Bart Simpson is proud to be called that.

—A graduate student and teacher

Follow-Up

1. *The author says that she felt more real when not being sarcastic. Do you agree with this idea?*
2. *Describe the source and effects of any sarcasm and/or apathy in your life.*

On the Death of a Father

Sanford Colley

Wednesday April 29, 1992

My father died last night.

For nearly 2 hours I stood at his bedside, held his hand, and watched the digital readout on a heart machine register an increasingly weaker pulse, slower heart rate, and lower blood pressure. Finally, all three blinked zero.

The ventilator was the only intrusion into what was otherwise a peaceful death. It continued to pump air into his lifeless body in a grotesque parody of breathing. When it was over, my sister asked, "May we turn that damned machine off now?"

Dad, a retired minister, was 85, and he had been in declining health for several years. Dylan Thomas would have been proud of him. He did not go gentle into that good night. A few weeks ago I pushed him in a wheel chair through the halls of a retirement center that had been his home for several months. "Look at all these old people," he snorted. "They're pitiful . . . just pitiful." I did not have the heart to point out the obvious; most were more ambulatory than he.

Two days ago, the morning started like a number of others during the last few months. There was an early morning call from the retirement home, "Your father has fallen again . . . we don't know how serious, but he does appear to be in some pain . . . we've sent for an ambulance . . . you should meet us in the emergency room."

I canceled meetings, rearranged classes, called on wonderfully supportive faculty colleagues to cover appointments, and left a long list of things to do with an accommodating and understanding secretary. X-rays revealed that his hip was broken. The options were to remove the hip joint completely and confine him to a wheelchair or to replace the joint and hope he might regain some of his ability to walk. Although surgery was risky because of his weak heart, the physician recommended joint replacement and surgery was scheduled for the next morning.

I arrived at the hospital in time to see him before the operation. The wait during surgery was long—much longer than my sisters and I had been led to expect. The young surgeon finally came out wearing a thin smile that masked his concern. (Was it only last week I warned my counseling students to never assume a smile means all is well?) He told us that during the operation Dad had gone into cardiac arrest. They had him stabilized, but the next few hours would be critical. At first, Dad improved, then he weakened, and finally, his physician told us, "he's not going to make it."

My two sisters and I stayed with Dad in the intensive care cubicle. His eyes were half closed, but once he shifted his gaze to mine and for a long time we looked at each other intently. I tried desperately to read what was in that gaze. Was it fear? Resignation? Love? Whatever he felt at that moment, I *know* he was aware his three children were there with him.

Dad seemed to sense that his life was nearly over. Last week he told me his days were numbered and asked about his will. I assured him everything was in order. The surgeon seemed to be quite moved when he told us of a comment Dad made to the anesthetist just before surgery. "I'm going to have a heart attack," he said. Those were his last words.

When the ventilator was turned off, I embraced my sisters, and we wept. The last time I cried aloud was 3 years ago when Dad was staying at our home. About 3:00 in the morning I had gotten out of bed and spent nearly an hour struggling to help him to the bathroom. He could hardly stand, much less walk, and he was dead weight in my arms. When I finally returned to bed, exhausted, I saw a guide to the Appalachian Trail (AT) on my bedside table. Dad had always talked about wanting to hike the AT, and I had the guide out because we had talked about spending a couple of days on an accessible part of the trail. That night I knew that he would never realize his dream, and I wept because he *could* have done it when he was in better health had he only chosen to do so. I did a hundred miles on the AT just prior to the American Association of Counseling and Development convention in Baltimore, and realized that I was doing it partly for me and partly for him.

A major concern was how my mother would respond to news of the death. She was in reasonably good physical health, but has experienced a significant reduction in her mental functioning as a result of Alzheimer's disease. She lives in a nursing home, seems to be content and happy, and recognizes members of the family, but she is usually unable to structure her thoughts well enough to form a complete sentence.

I decided it would be best to be direct and unambiguous, so I told her in simple language about the fall, the surgery, and the heart attack. "He's dead, Mom," I concluded, my heart aching.

For a fleeting moment, she seemed to understand. "Oh no," she responded, her eyes filling with tears, an incredibly pained look on her face. Then, almost immediately, she relaxed, her dementia seemingly insulating her from intense grief.

She glanced around the room and pointed to an old tennis shoe in her closet. The mate to it had been lost several weeks earlier. "It's gone, but that one is still there." I was stunned. A shoe with a lost mate; the most gifted and creative writers on our faculty would have been hard pressed to come up with a more striking metaphor for the loss of a spouse. Her thoughts confused and scrambled, Mom had seized that image. Perhaps she had understood.

Friday, May 1, 1992

We buried Dad today.

I woke up early this morning and ran—14 long, leisurely, lung-clearing miles. Halfway through I stopped to watch a hazy sunrise over the Tennessee River. I absorbed the beauty and remembered the fishing trips Dad and I took there when I was a boy. I reflected on his active life, my love for him, and how terribly unhappy he had been confined to the retirement home. When I resumed running, I had acknowledged a feeling of relief that I had not wanted to admit before. I was at peace.

The love and concern we felt at the funeral home last night and at the funeral today was a moving experience. I was overwhelmed that university colleagues would drive so far to express their support. Many individuals spoke of how effectively Dad had ministered to them in their times of grief. One young woman told me of seeing him go by her home every morning during his daily walk to the coffee shop.

"I'll never forget that funny old crooked walking cane he used," she said. "He told me once he wanted to be buried with it."

"I'll tell you a secret," I whispered, "It's with him in the casket."

Sunday, June 21, 1992

Father's Day. My first in 53 years without Dad. It has been nearly 2 months since his death, and the wrenching pangs of grief I experienced initially have started to subside. The healing is not complete, but it has started.

Going through Dad's library has been interesting. I found first editions of Rollo May's 1939 *The Art of Counseling* and Carl Rogers's 1942 *Counseling and Psychotherapy*. A real treasure was an 1892 copy of William James's *Principles of Psychology*, the very first book ever published (initially in 1890) with "psychology" in the title.

Although nothing more than coincidental, I was deeply moved by a book of daily devotionals over 20 years old. I started to chuck it because there were no notations or anything else of apparent value, only a single rusty gem clip on a page with the corner turned down. It marked the devotion for April 28.

That was the date of his death.

Follow-Up

1. *If one or both of your parents have died, compare your initial reactions to those of the author.*
2. *If one or both of your parents are alive, what are some things you'd like them to experience, with or without you, before they die? When will these happen?*
3. *If you are a parent, what are some things you can do* now *with your child (children) that won't be realistic years from now? When will you do these things?*
4. *Discuss or write about any other point in this article.*

Loss and Mourning

Judith Viorst

We are separate people constrained by the forbidden and the impossible, fashioning our highly imperfect connections. We live by losing and leaving and letting go. And sooner or later, with more or less pain, we all must come to know that loss is indeed "a lifelong human condition."

Mourning is the process of adapting to the losses of our life.

Freud (1920/1953) said that mourning is an extremely slow, inner process of letting go. He is talking, as I will be here, about the mourning we do at the death of people we love. But we may mourn in a similar fashion the end of a marriage, the coming apart of a special friendship, the losses of what we'd once had . . . been . . . hoped might be. For, as we shall see, there is an end, an end to much that we have loved. But there can be an end to mourning, too.

How we mourn and how, or if, our mourning is going to end, will depend on what we perceive our losses to be, will depend on our age and their age, will depend on how ready all of us were, will depend on the way they succumbed to mortality, will depend on our inner strengths and our outer supports, and will surely depend on our prior history—on our history with the people who died and our own separate history of love and loss. Nevertheless, there does seem to be a typical pattern to normal adult mourning, despite individual idiosyncrasies. And it seems generally agreed that we pass through changing, though overlapping, phases of mourning and that after about a year, sometimes less but often far longer indeed, we "complete" a major part of the mourning process.

Now many of us find it difficult to hear about phases of mourning without bristling, without the sense that some Julia Child of sorrow is trying to provide us with a step-by-step recipe for the perfect grief. But if we can hear about phases not as something that we—or others—*must* go through, but as something that may illuminate what we—or others—have gone or are going through, perhaps we can come to understand why "sorrow . . . turns out to be not a state but a process."

And the first phase of this process, whether the loss has been anticipated or not, is "shock, numbness and a sense of disbelief." This can't be happening! No, it cannot be! Perhaps we will weep and wail; perhaps we will sit there silently; perhaps waves of grief will alternate with periods of stunned incomprehension. Our shock may be mild if we've lived long and hard with the dead's impending death. Our shock may be less (let's face it) than our relief. But the fact that someone we love no longer exists in time and space is not yet entirely real, is beyond our belief.

Mark Twain, whose daughter Susy—"our wonder and our worship"—died suddenly at the age of twenty-four, writes in his autobiography of that initial state of benumbed disbelief.

> It is one of the mysteries of our nature that a man, all unprepared, can receive a thunderstroke like that and live. There is but one reasonable explanation of it. The intellect is stunned by the shock and but groping gathers the meaning of the words. The power to realize their full import is mercifully wanting. The mind has a dumb sense of vast loss—that is all. It will take mind and memory months and possibly years to gather the details and thus learn and know the whole extent of the loss.

Although an expected death will usually stun us less than one we are unprepared for, although with a fatal illness our major shock may come when that illness is diagnosed and although in the time preceding the death we may sometimes engage in "anticipatory mourning," we will initially find it difficult—despite such preparation—to assimilate the death of a person we love. Death is one of those facts of life we acknowledge more with our brain than we do with our heart. And often, although our intellect acknowledges the loss, the rest of us will be trying hard to deny it.

Some disbelief, some denial, may continue well beyond the initial shock. Indeed, it may take the entire mourning process to make of the impossible—death—a reality.

After the first phase of mourning, which is relatively short, we move to a longer phase of intense psychic pain. Of weeping and lamentation. Of emotional swings and physical complaints. Of lethargy, hyperactivity, regression (to a needier, "Help me!" stage). Of separation anxiety and helpless hopeless despair. And of anger too.

Annie, age twenty-nine when her husband and daughter were killed by a truck, recalls how angry she was, "how I hated the world. I hated that man in the truck. I hated all trucks. I hated God for making them. I hated everyone, even John [her four-year-old son] sometimes because I had to stay alive for him and if he hadn't been there I could have died too. . . ."

We are angry at the doctors for not saving them. We are angry at God for taking them away. Like Job . . . we are angry at our comforters—what right have they to say that time will heal, God is good, it is all for the best, we'll get over it?

There are those who insist that anger—toward others, and also toward the dead—is invariably a part of the mourning process.

Indeed, a great deal of the anger that we focus on those around us is the anger we feel, but won't let ourselves feel, toward the dead. Sometimes, however, we do express it directly. "God damn you! God damn you for dying on me!" a widow recalls having said to her dead husband's picture. Like her, we love the dead,

we miss and need and pine for our dead, but we also are angry at them for having abandoned us.

We are angry at, hate, the dead the way an infant hates the mommy who goes away. And like that infant we fear that it is our anger, our hatred, our badness that drove them away. We have guilt about our bad feelings and we also may have great guilt for what we have done—and what we didn't do.

Guilty feelings too—irrational guilt and justified guilt—are very often a part of the mourning process.

For the ambivalence that is present in even our deepest love relationships tainted our love for the dead while they were alive. We saw them as less than perfect and we loved them less than perfectly; we may even have fleetingly wished that they would die. But now that they are dead we are ashamed of our negative feelings and we start berating ourselves for being so bad: "I should have been kinder." "I should have been more understanding." "I should have been more grateful for what I had." "I should have tried to call my mother more often." "I should have gone down to Florida to visit my dad." "He always wanted a dog, but I would never let him have one, and now it's too late."

Of course there are times when we ought to feel guilt for the way that we treated the dead, appropriate guilt for harm done, unmet needs. But even when we loved them very, very well indeed, we still may find grounds for self-recrimination.

We feel guilt about our failures toward someone we love when he or she dies. We feel guilt about our negative feelings, too. And what we may do to defend against, or alleviate, our guilt is to loudly insist that the person who died was perfect. Idealization—"My wife was a saint," "My father was wiser than Solomon"—allows us to keep our thoughts pure and to keep guilt at bay. It is also a way of repaying the dead, of making restitution, for all of the bad we have done—or imagined we've done—to them.

Canonizing—idealizing—the dead is frequently a part of the mourning process.

Discussing idealization in her excellent book *The Anatomy of Bereavement*, psychiatrist Beverley Raphael gives us Jack, a forty-nine-year-old widower who described his dead wife Mabel in terms of unremitting adulation. She was, he declared, "the greatest little woman ever . . . the best cook, the best wife in the world. She did everything for me."

Anger, guilt, idealization—and attempts at reparation—seem to suggest that we do in fact know the dead died. Yet alternately, or even simultaneously, their death may still continue to be denied. John Bowlby, in his book *Loss*, describes this paradox:

"On the one hand is belief that death has occurred with the pain and hopeless yearning that that entails. On the other is disbelief that it has occurred, accompanied both by hope that all may yet be well and by an urge to search for and to recover the lost person." A child whose mother leaves him will deny the departure, will search for her, Bowlby says. It is in a similar spirit that we—as left, bereft adults—search for our dead.

This searching may express itself unconsciously—as restless random activity. But some of us consciously seek the dead as well. Beth looks for her husband by going again and again to all of the places they'd gone to together. Jeffrey stands in the closet among the clothes his wife used to wear, smelling her smell.

Searching for the dead we sometimes even summon them up: We "hear" their step in the driveway, their key in the lock. We "see" them on the street and eagerly follow them for a block; they turn and we confront . . . a stranger's face. Some of us may bring our dead back to life with hallucinations. Many of us bring our dead back to life in our dreams.

In this acute phase of grief some of us will mourn quietly, some vocally—though it isn't our style to rend garments and tear our hair. But in our own different ways we will have to pass through the terror and tears, the anger and guilt, the anxiety and despair. And in our own different ways, having managed somehow to work our way through our confrontations with unacceptable losses, we can begin to come to the end of mourning.

Starting with shock and making our way through this phase of acute psychic pain, we move toward what is called the "completion" of mourning. And although there still will be times when we weep for, long for, miss our dead, completion means some important degree of recovery and acceptance and adaptation.

We recover our stability, our energy, our hopefulness, our capacity to enjoy and invest in life.

We accept, despite dreams and fantasies, that the dead will not return to us in this life.

We adapt, with enormous difficulty, to the altered circumstances of our life, modifying—in order to survive—our behavior, our expectations, our self-definitions. Psychoanalyst George Pollock, who has written extensively on the subject of mourning, has called the mourning process "one of the more universal forms of adaptation and growth . . ." Successful mourning, he argues, is far more than making the best of a bad situation. Mourning, he says, can lead to creative change.

But he and his colleagues warn us that mourning is rarely a straightforward, linear process. Going through stages of grief, Pastan says, is like climbing a circular staircase—and like learning to climb it "after the amputation." In his record of mourning following the death of his cherished wife, C. S. Lewis uses identical imagery:

> How often—will it be for always?—how often will the vast emptiness astonish me like a complete novelty and make me say, "I never realized my loss till this moment"? The same leg is cut off time after time. The first plunge of the knife into the flesh is felt again and again.

And even when, eventually, we accept and adapt and recover, we may suffer from "anniversary reactions"—recurrently mourning our dead, with feelings of pining and sadness and loneliness and despair, on the day in the calendar year that marks their birth or their death or some special shared occasion. But in spite of setbacks, recurrences and the sense that our sorrow keeps doubling back on itself, there is an end to mourning, to even the seemingly most inconsolable mourning. . . .

It is by internalizing the dead, by making them part of our inner world, that we can at last complete the mourning process.

Remember that, as children, we could let our mother go, or leave our mother, by establishing a permanent mother within us. In a similar way we internalize—we take into ourselves—the people we have loved and lost to death. The "loved object is not gone," psychoanalyst Karl Abraham writes, "for now I carry it within myself. . . ." And while surely he overstates—the touch is gone, the laugh is gone, the promise and possibilities are gone, the sharing of music and bread and bed is gone, the comforting joy-giving flesh-and-blood presence is gone—it is true nonetheless that by making the dead a part of our inner world, we will in some important ways never lose them.

So perhaps the only choice we have is to choose what to do with our dead: To die when they die. To live crippled. Or to forge, out of pain and memory, new adaptations. Through mourning we acknowledge that pain, feel that pain, live past it. Through mourning we let the dead go and take them in. Through mourning we come to accept the difficult changes that loss must bring—and then we begin to come to the end of mourning.

References

Abraham, K. (1927). *Selected papers of Karl Abraham.* New York: Basic Books, Inc.

Bowlby, J. (1980). *Loss.* New York: Basic Books, Inc.

Clemens, S. (1959). *The autobiography of Mark Twain.* New York: Harper.

Freud, S. (1920/1953). *The interpretation of dreams* (Standard edition, Vols 4 and 5). James Strachey (Ed.). London: The Hogarth Press.

Osterweis, M., Solomon, F., and Green, M. (Eds.). (1984). *Bereavement: Reactions, consequences, and care.* Washington, DC: National Academy Press.

Lewis, C. S. (1963). *A grief observed.* New York: Bantam Books.

Raphael, B. (1983). *The anatomy of bereavement.* New York: Basic Books, Inc.

Follow-Up

1. *Viorst discusses the characteristics of three phases of mourning: shock, intense psychic pain (anger, guilt, idealization, etc.), and completion. Discuss the validity of these phases from your experience with loss.*
2. *Select two ideas from this article and offer your commentary.*
3. *In other sections of her work, Viorst discusses how mourning may not come to an end. Some people engage in chronic mourning, which takes the form of continual grief or its opposite, denial of grief. Because chronic grief may lead to deep disruptions in regular living, professional help is usually advised. For further information see Viorst's book,* Necessary Losses.

Applied Activities for Section Five

WELL-BEING GAUGE

Cars have oil and heat gauges to indicate fluid levels. A quick glance warns us of possible malfunctioning. While we do not come equipped with a well-being gauge, we can develop one. With this gauge one can spot danger signs in mental and physical functioning.

Directions:
1. A model of the Well-Being Gauge is provided. This chart has two dimensions: degree of health and stress (healthy, mild stress, moderate stress, severe stress), and five categories of well-being (physical, emotional, interpersonal, intellectual, miscellaneous).
2. Construct your individualized Well-Being Gauge (enlarge the blank copy provided). Some guidelines:
   a. List *at least* two examples each for the physical, emotional, interpersonal, intellectual, and miscellaneous categories. Then describe how they change according to whether you feel healthy, mildly stressed, moderately stressed, or severely stressed. Note that your examples may be different than those of the model.
   b. The miscellaneous category can include areas such as money management, music preferences, entertainment choices, free time activities, driving attitudes, dreams or fantasies, etc.
   c. Consider asking others who know you for some examples.

Follow-Up

1. Place an asterisk by your sure-fire indicators of well-being. These are the ones to check out on a weekly basis.
2. Pay particular attention if you reach the moderate stress level. This is when you must try to change how you are living—now—or you will fall into the danger zone.
3. Try to determine the conditions associated with each level of health or stress. What is causing these shifts?
4. Discuss or write about your learnings from this activity.

Model—Well-Being Gauge

Health/ Stress States	Physical	Emotional	Interpersonal	Intellectual	Miscellaneous
Healthy	1. Can fall asleep and wake up with no problems 2. Look in mirror and like what I see 3. Spend a half an hour in morning for makeup 4. Feel good; a lot of energy	1. Feel I am happier and more adjusted than most people 2. Look to future (20 years or more) with expectation and anticipation 3. Participate in church service once a week and feel close to God	1. Enjoy interacting with other people, esp. meeting new people with varied interests 2. Feel I have many friends 3. Feel my marriage is better than most 4. Two parties a week, one in our home 5. Write letters; call friends to talk	1. Tackle problems as they arise 2. Complete tasks ahead of deadlines with some creativity 3. Think of new ways to approach problems, lectures, classes 4. Look for PBS programs of interest; watch local and national news daily 5. Read newspaper daily; read news magazine weekly as well as a women's magazine and journals	1. Feel financially stable; money spent on well-thought gifts* 2. Salary is satisfactory 3. Plan meals weeks in advance; bake bread; cook from scratch 4. Able to tolerate rush hour traffic — part of life
Mild Stress	1. Can fall asleep readily, but have a difficult time waking up in the morning 2. Look in the mirror and add "things I need to improve" to my list according to what I see 3. Spend a half an hour in morning for makeup 4. Feel good; have adequate energy	1. Feel I am as happy and adjusted as most people 2. Look to future (one year) with mixed anticipation and anxiety 3. Attend church once a week and participate as I feel I should	1. Enjoy people, but prefer ones I know, and those with similar interests 2. Feel I have a few good friends 3. Feel marriage is average 4. Do not write letters, but look forward to receiving them	1. Tackle problems as they arise 2. Complete tasks ahead of deadlines as required 3. Utilize previously tested methods for problem-solving, classes, and lectures 4. Watch local and national news, some commercial television 5. Read newspaper daily, but not magazines	1. Financially stable, adequate possessions, seriously consider necessity of gift giving* 2. Salary is inadequate 3. Plan meals weeks in advance but do not bake 4. Rush hour stressful, no one else knows how to drive

*This one turned out to be the guaranteed, sure-fire, always accurate indicator of my states of stress.

Model—Well-Being Gauge

Health/ Stress States	Physical	Emotional	Interpersonal	Intellectual	Miscellaneous
Moderate Stress	1. Fall asleep after half an hour; wake up often during the night, but able to get up in the morning 2. Look in mirror with disgust and despair 3. Put makeup on in the car on the way to work 4. Frequent headaches and stomach aches; loss of energy	1. Feel I am not as happy and adjusted as others 2. Look to short term future (one year) with much anxiety and apprehension 3. Attend church because if I don't things could get worse 4. Think others should take time to help me	1. Interact with people who can help me, do something for me 2. Wonder why I don't have many friends 3. Feel my marriage is poor 4. No social activities; spend time alone with husband 5. Phone calls and letters from friends are bothersome; feel guilty	1. Procrastinate, but meet deadline dates 2. Complete required work, race to meet requirements and deadline dates 3. Avoid thinking of problems, classes 4. Watch only national news on television 5. Only first page of newspaper read	1. Financially insecure; money for rent and food only; do not buy gifts or contribute any money* 2. Salary is inadequate for the work I do 3. Plan meals day by day; must make frequent trips to store 4. Rush hour tolerable; leave work earlier and get home later
Severe Stress	1. Hour or more to fall asleep, wake up after a few hours and cannot return to sleep 2. Avoid mirrors 3. No makeup 4. Frequent headaches, stomachaches, tired, feel I must have cancer 4. Feel good; have adequate energy	1. Consider counseling or suicide 2. Focus on past bad experiences only 3. Don't attend church because I don't have time 4. Resent others for not helping me or taking time to	1. Do not interact with anyone 2. No one to turn to; no friends 3. Feel I should not be married 4. Spend time alone; no social interaction at all 5. Do not answer phone or open mail	1. Procrastinate and do not meet deadlines 2. Unable to adequately complete required work 3. Try to find someone else to take some of my work load 4. Do not watch TV 5. Do not read newspaper	1. Feel I cannot even afford food; considering going to lower-rent housing* 2. Think about part-time job to supplement income 3. Eat out 4. Leave work an hour late to avoid rush hour

Model—Well-Being Gauge

Health/ Stress States	Physical	Emotional	Interpersonal	Intellectual	Miscellaneous
Healthy					
Mild Stress					
Moderate Stress					
Severe Stress					

EMOTIONAL CHARADES

This activity provides experiences in both emotional and nonverbal expression. For best results, have the instructor prepare the emotion cards (described below). Do *not* look at the list prior to the activity.

1. Participants should divide into groups of 4–6 members (both genders if possible).
2. Place the emotion cards face down in the middle of the group.
3. Each member selects a card, reads it silently, and then places it face down.
4. Each member has a maximum of 2 minutes to nonverbally act out the emotion on the card. Only body language is permitted by the sender. The other group members are to identify the emotion expressed. If the emotion is *not* correctly identified within 2 minutes, go to the next person.
5. Complete this procedure until all the cards are correctly identified. To prepare the emotion cards, write the following emotional states on 3 × 5 separate index cards:

Sorry/remorseful	Embarrassed
Afraid	Withdrawn
Encouraging/supportive	Hesitant/unsure
Bored/apathetic	Disappointed/let down
Arrogant/superior	Angry/hostile
Dominant/showing power, authority	Wonder/amazed
Playful/spontaneous	Eager/enthusiastic
Proud/confident	Content/at ease/relaxed
Friendly/warm	Anxious/nervous
Puzzled/baffled	Romantically interested

Follow-Up

1. Which body parts dominated in expressing emotions? Why were some emotions easier to express than others? What were the effects of this activity on how you worked as a group?
2. Discuss your experience with the whole class.
3. Write a reaction paper on your observations.

EMOTIONS AND PERCEPTION

To demonstrate the power of emotions in your life, try the following activity.

1. Choose a common situation in your life (job, college class, driving, free time, interacting with others).
2. Observe and summarize your perceptions of this situation under different emotional states. (Choose at least two of these emotional states.)

Situation: _____

Emotion	Perceptions
Happy	
Angry	
Depressed	
Confused	
Anxious	
Confident	

3. Is your emotional state a main factor in how you interpret any given external event? If yes, what are some applications of this finding?
4. Discuss or write about your thoughts on this subject.

LISTENING TO EMOTIONS

With positive emotions like joy and wonder, we usually let them be and do not try to change them. With negative emotions, however, there is a tendency to try to avoid or to change them. Few people enjoy feeling anxious, guilty, or inadequate. Even these negative emotions have their gifts for us. In a sense, they are a special kind of teacher. For example, anxiety can teach us that we need to prepare for whatever we are afraid of facing; anxiety can show us how to be more alert; anxiety tells us that we are alive. Envy can teach us how we judge our own self-worth. Certain kinds of guilt can be helpful in maintaining a life of integrity.

Instead of avoiding or trying to escape negative emotions, it is often helpful to first reflect on what they mean. Reflection enables us to accept and not to deny the teaching power of negative emotions. This does not mean that you have to "like" them. There are several ways to listen to negative emotions as if they were teachers:

1. Ask yourself what is this emotion attempting to tell me? What is this emotion warning me of in this situation?
2. With a person you trust, share your negative emotion and discuss what it could be trying to "teach you."

3. Write a brief letter to your emotion asking why it is there. Have the emotion write back to you. You will have the opportunity to see the emotion's point of view if you do the latter.
4. Thomas Moore's *Care of the Soul* (1992) discusses how emotions can be teachers.

HOW DO YOU FEEL?

It is helpful to recognize your individual style of experiencing emotions. One of the best ways is to write about how each emotion affects you. Below are some excerpts concerning this technique as taken from John Wood's *How Do You Feel?* (1974).

Hope   I am beginning to see some light at the end of the tunnel. . . . Good things can happen, whereas before they have been living under a cloud of "No," powerless and trapped. . . . It is moving from a negative, nothing, zero point of view into some sort of potentiality, a letting in of the good possibilities.

Guilt   Feeling guilty is a diminishing, belittling, unworthy kind of feeling for me that always makes me think less of myself. Somehow I am smaller and the rest of the world is bigger than me, looking down on me. . . . My guilt is essentially feeling bad about myself because of some offense—real or imagined—that I have committed.

Accepted   When I feel accepted, it feels like an emotional sauna. It feels good, warm; it makes me relax. . . . The tension of how I'm going over with others seems to disappear. I think about the difference between being accepted and being liked. Acceptance is bigger than liked; it takes in being liked and disliked. . . . And it takes in more than being tolerated too.

Lonely   I usually know when I'm lonely when I find myself doing a lot of things to take up time, scheduling myself very tightly, filling up time with more than one thing. Like I'm washing dishes, listening to the record player, and watching TV. . . . I go into a lot of fantasies too. . . . It's very hard for me to say that I'm lonely. I tend to let it out in other ways; I tend to get angry, say hurtful things. It seems like the world is against me. . . . Sometimes I can make myself lonely by cutting off those very things I want, by withholding, withdrawing. When I can say "I am lonely" and fully accept it, then I can go about finding out what some of my lonely needs are and try and take care of those.

Follow-Up

1. Select one or more emotions (they may or may not be the same as above) and write a paragraph describing how it exhibits itself in you.

2. Discuss your emotion descriptions in a small group.
3. Gather examples of emotion descriptions from novels, movies, and conversations.
4. Write a reaction paper on what you learned from one or more of these activities.

NONVERBAL OBSERVATIONS

1. While watching a dramatic TV or talk show, turn off the sound and focus on the participants' body language (particularly the face and gestures). Try to guess what emotional states are being expressed. Occasionally turn on the sound to check out your hunches. For more accuracy, record the show on a VCR.
2. Observe your own ways of expressing various emotions. Some major nonverbal methods include: facial expressions, eye contact, vocal speed/volume/inflection, body positioning and distance, gestures, use of environmental objects (e.g., where you sit). Consider having someone who knows you well offer their observations on how you express various emotions. If you find that you are not expressing a certain emotion as well as you would like, experiment with your nonverbal methods.
3. Discuss or write about what you learned from any of these activities.

ANGER MANAGEMENT

Anger can be a natural emotional response in the following life situations: physical or emotional hurt, blocked needs, unmet expectations, guilt, loss, helplessness, threats, unfulfilled goals/dreams, injustice. Below are constructive and nonconstructive ways to handle anger. Mark the ones that are your typical anger responses.

Constructive Responses

___ Knowing that anger is a natural human feeling and that *you determine* whether to express it.

___ *Delay* any decision or action until your strong anger has subsided.

___ Using *diversion* techniques: Take a deep breath (or even ten) and exhale slowly; count to ten slowly or count slowly backward from fifty; take a walk; engage in physical exercise; tackle a mundane task like laundry or mow a lawn; listen to or play music.

___ Appropriate *venting:* Talk it out with an understanding friend or colleague; howl at the moon; cry it out; write about it.

___ Engage in an *incompatible behavior:* Laughter (see a funny movie or TV show, romp with a pet, have fun with a friend); relaxation activities (neck or back rub, a hot bath, view something beautiful); do something you like to do that requires full absorption.

___ You can say "Yes" to the question: Is your anger in *proportion* to whatever caused it?

___ Ask and honestly answer: "How much of my life energy is worth being spent in anger at this person or situation?"

___ Start *problem-solving* strategies if warranted. These could include: Understanding the underlying causes of your anger; seeing other points of view; initiating constructive, confrontational conversation with the other party after your anger's intensity has lessened; arranging a group meeting to resolve the issue (if it is a problem important to the group); possibly getting a third party to mediate a dispute.

___ Use the anger as a *positive energy source* and motivation.

___ Seek qualified guidance if the anger persists in ways that negatively affect your life.

___ *Observe* and learn how others handle similar anger situations in constructive ways. Also consider talking with them about their approaches.

Nonconstructive Reactions

___ *Aggression:* Physical attack, ridicule, hostile silence. Aggressive responses almost always evoke strong negative responses in others that add to the problem. Aggressors may even be negatively affected by realizing that their anger increases and/or feelings of guilt result from the aggressive acts.

___ *Displacement:* Taking out your anger on someone who is not the source of the anger (e.g., yelling at someone at home for a problem at work or school).

___ *Denial:* Refusing to acknowledge the feeling of anger. If suppressed for a long period, the angry feeling may result in resentment, volatile explosive acts or words, or depression.

___ Inappropriate *blaming:* Individuals unfairly blame someone or something else for whatever is causing the anger, or they unfairly blame themselves when the cause is truly elsewhere.

___ *Disproportional* anger expression: Individuals respond with either excessive anger intensity or duration to whatever caused the anger. Also, it means that appropriate anger has not been expressed.

Follow-Up

1. Keep an anger journal. Record the incident, place and time of any anger experience. Do this for at least 1–2 weeks. Examine your responses using the above guidelines.
2. Add one or more constructive anger management techniques to your repertoire. Decrease or eliminate nonconstructive reactions.
3. Ask people who know you well to describe their perception of your anger management skills. (And don't become angry!)
4. Discuss and/or write about what you've learned about anger management.

PERSONAL GOALS—EMOTIONS & FEELINGS

Within the next year I will attempt to more fully understand my emotions and feelings by:

Goal 1:

Needed actions, support, and resources:

Timeline:

Progress notes (use extra page if necessary):

Goal 2:

Needed actions, support, and resources:

Timeline:

Progress notes (use extra page if necessary):

SECTION
SIX

A QUALITY LIFE

I f asked what it is we want most from life, most of us shuffle our feet and mumble some words about happiness, fulfillment, or meaning. Whatever "it" is, we feel empty if we do not have it, and if we do have it, the meaning has great difficulty working its way out of our mouths. Many of our best writers have attempted to explain what people want from life. See if you can find an answer close to yours in the following attempts:

The only ones among you who will be truly happy are those who will have sought and found how to serve.

—Albert Schweitzer

How simple and frugal a thing is happiness: a glass of wine, a roasted chestnut, a wretched little brazier, the sound of the sea.

—Nikos Kazantzakis

One should not search for an abstract meaning of life. . . . Life can be made meaningful in a threefold way: first, through what we give to life . . . second, by what we take from the world . . . third, through the stand we take toward a fate we no longer can change. . . .

—Viktor Frankl

This is the true joy in life—being used for a purpose recognized by yourself as a mighty one; being thoroughly worn out before you are thrown on the scrap heap; being a force of nature instead of a feverish, selfish little clod of ailments and grievances complaining that the world will not devote itself to making you happy.

—George Bernard Shaw

He who dies with the most toys wins.
                                                    —Contemporary slogan

*Look at every path closely and deliberately. . . . Does this path have a heart?
If it does, the path is good; if it doesn't, it is of no use.*
                                                    —Carlos Castaneda

*If you have the guts to follow the risk . . . if one follows what I call one's
"bliss"—the thing that really gets you deep in the gut and that you feel is
your life—doors will open up . . . if you follow your bliss, you'll have your
bliss, whether you have money or not.*
                                                    —Joseph Campbell

*You must want to be first-class . . . meaning the best, the very best you are
capable of becoming. If you deliberately plan to be less than you are
capable of being, then I warn you that you'll be deeply unhappy for the
rest of your life. You will be evading your own capacities, your own
possibilities.*
                                                    —Abraham Maslow

*Something has to matter. Otherwise, a person's life will be miserable and
empty. Am I the last one to figure that out? The what that matters is
unimportant—God, Coke-bottle collecting, track and field—all are equally
useful in staving off the uselessness. For my stepfather, Don, bowling
matters. Napoleon wanted to conquer Russia. Lana Sue's mom thinks the
quality of her life is directly dependent on the meat prices at Kroger's. Career
and love life may be a little trite, but they seem to work as well as anything.*

*To someone on the outside, your basis may look like a joke, but if you
know it's important, really know and go on knowing, you'll never fall into
despair.*
                                                    —Tim Sandlin

*All the life you have or ever will have is today, tonight, tomorrow, today,
tonight, tomorrow, over and over again . . . and so you had better take what
time there is and be very thankful for it.*
                                                    —Ernest Hemingway

We need others. We need others to love and we need to be loved by them.
                                                    —Leo Buscaglia

*To live in love is life's greatest challenge. It requires more subtlety,
flexibility, sensitivity, understanding, acceptance, tolerance, knowledge and
strength than any other human endeavor.*
                                                    —Leo Buscaglia

*When you feel safe enough to try something which requires a risk, it'll
probably be too late.*
                                                    —N. H. Goud

*Sometimes we feel that we have paid too high a price for our comfort; that
the network of relationships and names which we have become does not
leave us room to breathe. The limits which define us for others then seem*

like prisons. And we suspect, momentarily, that we live in exile from the best part of ourselves.

—Paul Zweig

The human being needs a framework of values, a philosophy of life, a religion or religion-surrogate to live by and understand by, in about the same sense that he needs sunlight, calcium or love.

—Abraham Maslow

Life streamed through him in splendid flood, glad and rampant, until it seemed it would burst him asunder in sheer ecstasy and pour forth generously over the world. The proper function of a man is to live, not to exist. . . .

—Jack London

Every single man is a new thing in the world, and is called upon to fulfill his particularity in this world. Every man's foremost task is the actualization of his unique, unprecedented and never recurring potentialities, and not the repetition of something that another, and be it even the greatest, has already achieved.

—Martin Buber

It's not the critic who counts. . . . The credit belongs to the man who is actually in the arena. . . . And, who, while daring greatly, spends himself in a worthy cause so that his place may never be among those cold and timid souls who have known neither victory nor defeat.

—Theodore Roosevelt

The cost of a thing is the amount of what I call life which is required to be exchanged for it, immediately or in the long run.

—Henry Thoreau

Experience is, for me, the highest authority. . . . No other person's ideas, and none of my own ideas, are as authoritative as my experience. It is to experience that I must return again and again, to discover a closer approximation to truth . . .

—Carl Rogers

Follow-Up

Perhaps some of these passages speak to what you value in life. At this time in your life, which three passages would rank the highest? If none of the above quotes reveal your highest values at this time, add your own. With classmates or with those close to you, share and discuss these top three passages and their meanings.

Unlike the previous sections, you are urged to complete one or more of these Applied Activities *prior* to reading the articles: The Someday List, Talking To Wise Persons, Evolution of A Person #2. By doing so, you should get some ideas on what a quality life means to you. The readings for this section suggest several ideas and strategies for living a quality life:

- Multi-tasking and fast-forward versus slowing down and focusing are themes in Nels Goud's "Having the Time of Your Life."
- Several ideas on the concept of time as it affects living are cited in "Time Quotes."
- Carin Rubenstein and Phillip Shaver explain how "Active Solitude" is important for a balanced life.
- When it comes to money, are you a hunter, a gatherer, or a splurger? These and other money themes are described by Robert Sullivan in "Personality and Money Orientations."
- The classic O. Henry short story, "The Last Leaf," explores the idea of the will to live.
- Learning about ourselves by listening and observing in natural surroundings is the theme of Nelson Goud's "Teachers in the Forest."
- How contact with nature enhances human life is the theme of "Nature Quotes."
- How we view death is related to how we live now according to the authors of two articles: "The Dying-Readiness/Freedom-to-Live Test" by Abe Arkoff, and "Personality Death Awareness (PDA)" by J. William Worden and William Proctor.
- What if one could manufacture happiness? This idea is elaborated by the award-winning author, Ray Bradbury, in "The Happiness Machine."
- How our quality of life is influenced by the computer culture is the theme written by one of our foremost computer wizards, Clifford Stoll, in "Silicon Snake Oil."
- James Fearing provides a checklist for computer addiction in "Ten Symptoms of Computer Addiction."
- Pianist and author Michael Jones ends this section—and the book—with a lyrical essay on discovering our inner essence in "Who Will Play Your Music?"

Having the Time of Your Life

Nels Goud

Driving to work I found myself switching music stations whenever a commercial or lousy song came on, going over a couple of lesson plans, giving my opinion on the gene pools of a few fellow drivers, gazing at the bare limbs of some maple trees for signs of spring buds, and chomping down an apple.

During one 15-minute interval at a faculty meeting I sat next to a colleague who was writing a letter, eating lunch, jotting down dates in a daily planner, looking up and nodding at a point made, making notes on a student's paper, asking a question, and probably wondering why I was observing all of this.

These are examples of "multi-tasking," the simultaneous performance of multiple activities. Some of our more revered persons were multi-taskers. Burns (1993) describes a scene of a typical work day in 1621 of the artist Peter Paul Rubens who was simultaneously painting, dictating a letter, having a book read to him, and coherently carrying on a conversation. Rubens was a master multi-tasker. Burns describes the Busy/Body Syndrome, which is characterized by an intense drive to jam the most activities possible into a single time frame. Underlying this drive is the belief that one of life's most valued commodities, time, is becoming increasingly scarce. Stephan Rechtschaffen (1993) asks people "Do you feel that you have enough time in your daily life?" If you are like 90% of his sample, you would not have the time to answer him. You have what is called time poverty.

We not only do many things at once, but we like to do things quickly. Social observer Je-remy Rifkin (1987) describes the American cultural pace under one word, speed. "We are a nation in love with speed. We drive fast, eat fast, make love fast. We are obsessed with breaking records and shortening time spans. We digest our life, condense our experiences, and compress our thoughts . . . we are convinced that speed reflects alertness, power, and success" (pp. 58–59). It is like living a life on fast-forward.

Our quality of living is greatly influenced by how we choose to perceive and use time. One choice is the fast-forward, multi-tasking philosophy. But if it is *your only* choice for how to use time, then you will have restricted life options and, probably, a lower quality of life.

What's so bad about a fast-forward, multi-tasking approach to life? We get more things done—besides, sometimes there appears to be no other feasible way. In some instances this answer would be right. In other instances this approach works against us. We must be able to distinguish between these instances and employ different time-use strategies.

THE TEMPO OF LIFE EXPERIENCES

Every life experience expresses itself in a particular tempo. If the experience is to be fully understood, one must be in step with this tempo. Enjoying baseball, for example, requires a different mental tempo than enjoying basketball—as does reading Hemingway versus TV channel surfing. Each experience has its preferred and characteristic pace.

The fast-forward, multi-tasking time strategy is in synch with life experiences which call for instantaneous, multiple responses. Some examples are: a waiter at a popular restaurant during peak times; any first-grade teacher with 25 first graders with the energy of caffeine-crazed gerbils; a stockbroker; a wedding consultant handling details one week prior to the wedding; a customer service clerk of a busy department store during the holidays. You can probably think of many others. These activities favor a state of heightened arousal, of adrenaline-pumping intensity, of eyes that can dart like those of a cobra surrounded by hungry mongooses.

The fast-forward, multi-tasking strategy is completely out of synch with other life experiences. One of my students wanted a book to help her from always feeling overwhelmed and harried by work, school, and family demands. I recommended Anne Morrow Lindbergh's book *Gift from the Sea*. Here was a small book on this very topic that discussed how to center instead of fragment your life. She returned the book the very next class. I asked her if it hadn't been right for her. "Oh it was easy to read," she replied. "I finished reading it in under two hours." After a brief discussion it became apparent that she could not change how she approached life tasks. To complete this reading quickly took precedent over everything else, including her main reason for wanting the book. We then talked about that.

Maybe you are a fast-forward reader and have already finished this article. How did it end? Here is a question for you: How many animals of each species did Moses take on the Ark? Now that is an odd query at this state of the article. But maybe, just maybe it might slow down any fast-forwarders. The answer, incidentally, is none. It was Noah who built the Ark, not Moses. Ah, a trick question you say. How can it be when it is sitting right there on the page? It is how you approach the question that counts. A fast-forwarding glance at this question will most likely trigger the number two.

Here are some life events which cannot be fully experienced using a fast-forward, multi-tasking strategy: eating good food; dancing to a ballad with someone special; watching clouds while lounging on the grass; meditating or praying; showing a person that you are really listening to him or her; viewing an art exhibit; rock climbing; holding a newborn infant; watching the sun set over the ocean. Can you think of some others?

HAVING A CHOICE

To be able to adapt your tempo to different kinds of life experiences is essential for a balanced life. In short, we must be able to choose the most appropriate time strategies. Modern life seems to encourage the fast-forward, multi-tasking time strategy over others. It is the norm to say "I'm so busy" and expect it from others. The busyness syndrome often becomes habitual. Worse, it may eventually control you. Let's say, for example, that you finally have time for a leisurely lunch with a friend. One time choice is to fully absorb yourself into the conversation and the food. Another choice, often when we do not want it, is having the lunch and simultaneously planning your afternoon schedule, gazing around the room, glancing at the TV above your friend, and looking at your watch every ten minutes. Here we have the mismatch between a time strategy and the natural tempo of an experience—and we may even know it but can't stop it. Our internal engine is stuck on full throttle even when we're idling.

For many, the fast-forward, multi-tasking time approach has become a habitual reflex. Life becomes a giant *Things To Do* list with the goal of crossing off an event as quickly as possible and going on to the next. We are in a hurry to get somewhere, but we never arrive. The fast-forward, multi-tasking life is one where each moment is completed and then erased. This produces gaping holes in one's life memory bank. Rechtschaffen (1993) says it this way: "By cramming each moment so full of events, we leave ourselves no time to actually experience them in any meaningful way . . . the past is, in effect, absent from our lives."

Just having had an experience does not mean you will remember it. Without time to savor it, to talk about it, to recall the major aspects and the nuances—without this kind of processing, the experience becomes a memory trace. I have toured Japan twice with a music group within a three-year period. I can remember one tour in vivid detail. The other is basically a blur, except for a grueling 14-hour train ride standing up. What was the difference? Was it too much Japanese beer on the forgotten tour? No, I actually had more on the remembered tour. The tour that I remember in detail was one where I kept a journal and took many photos; where musicians and singers talked about their daily experiences with each other; where I discussed the trip often with friends upon my return.

It takes time to remember.

One final clue to whether you are in control of time-use strategies. Think of a situation where you have no immediate demands, no expected tasks. Down time. For a fast-forward, multi-tasking person this situation produces anxiety. Instead of enjoying this time with a slower tempo activity, this person is likely to crowd out the anxiety by engaging in a flurry of tasks. Even leisure is pursued with the same relentless intensity. Viktor Frankl, the founder of Logotherapy, calls this the "Sunday neurosis."

The eventual consequences for most people who live full-time in the fast-forward, multi-tasking mode are physical and emotional exhaustion and/or breakdowns. It may take a while for some, even years, but usually there are heavy costs. Some seek help or develop new time strategies when they cannot satisfactorily answer this question for themselves—"What is the purpose of living this way?" Or, "I accomplish a lot—so why do I feel deep down that something fundamental is missing?"

Throughout it has been emphasized that a quality life requires the ability to adapt to the different tempos of life experiences. We must be able to control these time-use strategies instead of being controlled. The fast-forward, multi-tasking time philosophy strategy is appropriate for some experiences and ill advised for others. It also has a tendency to crowd out and take over all other time-use strategies. In the next section, some ideas on how to implement alternative time-use strategies are presented.

SIMPLIFYING LIFE

Even in 1850 Henry Thoreau was criticizing the hurriedness of people—"Why should we live with such hurry and waste of life? We are determined to be starved before we are hungry. . . . Simplify, simplify . . . I say, let your affairs be as two or three, and not a hundred or a thousand" (in Krutch, 1962, pp. 128, 173). Well, you may comment, this would be easy for him to say, since all he had to do was wander around the woods and look at a pond. That's what old philosophers do. But Thoreau was about 30 when he wrote these remarks and he lived only two years at Walden Pond.

It is possible to simplify. Two primary time strategies do this: one is to focus, and the other is to slow down. Focusing means to devote your attention and energies to one thing at a time. The phrase that helps me is "Be where you are." The key is to bring your body and mind into the present moment. Do not let yourself wander off into past or future time zones. Be where you are. If you are talking with someone you value, be right there with him or her and show it. For a start, try focusing on a mundane chore; if you are grocery shopping, just do that, be *there*.

Here is a very simple but powerful way to focus, but few can do this the first few times (this is a gentle challenge). The task: Get comfortable and if possible, close your eyes. Take a deep breath and slowly exhale. Do this naturally for 10 breaths. Just observe your breathing. If at any time you become distracted and lose count, start over.

How did it go? This breathing focus activity not only is helpful in learning to "be where you are," but is an excellent relaxation and centering experience. Choosing one focusing activity each day will enable you to add this time-use strategy to your repertoire.

SLOWING DOWN

I Need to Stop So I Can Get Somewhere
Countering the fast-forward time strategy means to let up on the accelerator when appropriate. Focusing is often helpful in adjusting your speed. Here are some other ideas for slowing down:

- Apply the concept of *savoring* to selected life activities. While normally referring to taste, savoring can be generalized to other domains also. It is the gradual experiencing of an event. Gulping is the opposite of savoring. You gulp Big Macs and savor fine wine. You gulp administrative memos and savor a well-written letter or essay. You gulp local news and savor the stories of a friend or family member. See other examples at the end of the section entitled "The Tempo of Life Experiences."

- Be aware of (and beware) the *paradox* of *time-saving technology*. Electronic communication devices like E-mail, fax, Internet, and voice-mail allow us to send and receive more messages in a shorter period than any time in our history. The drawback is that speed has greatly increased the number of messages we receive, consequently creating more demands on our time than ever before. Try to be selective as to

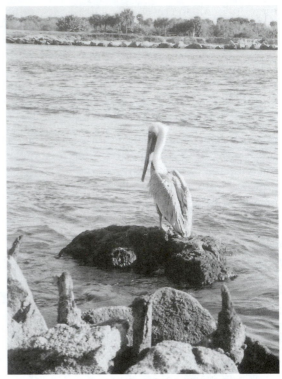

"Waiting"

He seemed to have a routine. Fly around the Sebastian Inlet of Florida for a bit, then light on a rock. A rock which had all the appearances of good fishing. And so it was. He would sit there very quietly and very relaxed, but alert. A fish of his liking would swim by and be chosen for a mid-afternoon snack. Sometimes the pelican would let a fish swim by untouched. He was in no hurry. The pelican knew that if he waited, whatever he needed would come along.

Sometimes we need to let life come to us.

which messages really require your quality efforts.
- Let experiences reveal themselves *to you* without imposing your needs and expectations on them first. One of my true life joys is to listen to the jazz trumpeter Maynard Ferguson. If he comes to town, I'm there (even my students call me to let me know, in case I missed the notice). I can remember waiting during a con-

cert with great anticipation for his band to play a certain number that had just appeared on his latest album. Maynard calls out the number. The band roared as usual and Maynard was doing things that all the rest of us trumpeters can do only in dreams. But I was somewhat disappointed. The live version did not sound like the recorded one. I wanted to hear it played like the one on the album. I had fallen into the trap I am writing about. I refused to "let" Maynard play how he felt that night, with that song, at that moment. He did not fit my preconceived expectation. Once I realized this, I could kick back and really get into whatever he and his band were doing that night. I sometimes find myself falling into this trap in meeting friends, or visiting favorite places expecting them to be exactly like they were when . . . , and on it goes until I remember to let others or even nature reveal themselves as they truly are at that moment. So, even if you know how your friend's or parent's story will end, let them finish it, not you. It might be the telling that is important, not that you know the ending.

Solomon observed that there is a time to be born and a time to die. There is a time between also. We have choices how we conduct ourselves in this interval called life. One of these choices is to enjoy and find meaning in the journey itself. We can take our time.

References

Burns, L. (1993). *Busy bodies.* New York: W. W. Norton & Co.

Krutch, J. (1962). *Thoreau: Walden and other writings.* New York: Bantam Books.

Rechtschaffen, S. (1993). Time-Shifting: Slowing down to live longer. *Psychology Today,* November/December, 32–36.

Rifkin, J. (1987). *Time wars.* New York: Henry Holt and Co.

Follow-Up

1. *Goud claims that a fragmented hurriedness is a norm for many in modern times and is used even when not appropriate. Write about or discuss your reactions to this statement based on personal experiences.*

2. *A main idea in the article is that every life experience expresses itself in a particular tempo. Provide some examples of this from your life and describe what happens when you are in synch or out of synch with these tempos.*

3. *The author states that unless we try to remember and communicate major experiences, they become blanks in our memories. Describe a time or two when this has happened to you.*

4. *Attempt the focusing and slowing-down ideas mentioned at the end of the article and report the results.*

5. *Select any other ideas from the article and report your reactions.*

Time Quotes

What is the best use of my time right now?

—Alan Lakein

Nibblers—People are so busy in modern times that the most common length of vacations is 3–5 days (the Travel Industry Association of America calls them "vacation nibblers").

We're constantly doing things faster and saving time. But what are we saving it for? The more things or activities we acquire with our efficiency, our productivity and or time management, . . . the less time we have to savor them.

—David Rohn

Time you enjoy wasting is not wasted time.

—Abraham Maslow

Never attempt to teach a pig to sing; it wastes your time and annoys the pig.
—Robert Heinlein

The high value put upon every minute of time, the idea of hurry-hurry as the most important objective of living, is unquestionably the most dangerous enemy of joy.

—Hermann Hesse

Sunday night anxiety is a real phenomenon, a recognition on Sunday night that the week is going to reappear. . . . Come Sunday night, thoughts about the work week start to intrude, and anxieties of life build . . . there's stuff not done last Friday that's due Monday . . .

—John Herman

Always doing many things quickly means neglecting those things that take time—contemplations, creating, savoring, loving, totally being there for someone.

—N. H. Goud

I am one of a growing number of students who are completing college in three years instead of four—cramming credits in the summer. We're living life on fast-forward without a pause button. . . . I am a member of a generation that is very concerned with saving time but often unaware of why we're doing it.

—Amy Wu

We seem to have lost the knack for dialing down life's speed when a day or weekend or season—summer comes to mind—calls for it. Leisure is eluding us.

—Bob Condor

Time shifting—The key is to step back from the edge, learn to get involved in the process rather than constantly longing for the end result. This does not mean giving up our goal-oriented lives—simply modifying them, finding a balance between our productive and our emotional selves . . . Whatever the activity, slow down, do just one thing, do it well, and allow yourself the sense of accomplishment . . .

—Stephan Rechtschaffen

We yearn for acceleration . . . the feeling of speed . . . the brain-fluid high we miss only when it's gone. Speed is a drug. . . . We want to be velocitized.

—Mark Kingwell

In a fast-paced world we put more energy into arrivals and departures than the experience itself.

—Jay Walljasper

A balanced life—with intervals of creative frenzy giving way to relaxed tranquility—is what people crave.

—Jay Walljasper

Time Sickness—a condition when one is obsessed with the notion that time is getting away, that there isn't enough of it, and that you must pedal faster and faster to keep up. The trouble is the body has limits that it imposes on us.

—Larry Dossey

A man is walking down the street. At a certain moment, he tries to recall something, but the recollection escapes him. Automatically, he slows down. Meanwhile, a person who wants to forget a disagreeable incident he has just lived through starts unconsciously to speed up his pace. There is a secret bond between slowness and memory, between speed and forgetting.

—Milan Kundera

To finish the moment, to find the journey's end in every step of the road, to live the greatest number of good hours, is wisdom.

—Ralph Waldo Emerson

Follow-Up

1. *Select two of these quotes and discuss how they apply to your life now.*

Active Solitude

*Carin Rubenstein
and Phillip Shaver*

For some people, being alone automatically implies loneliness; for them, the word *solitude* evokes images of isolation, panic, fear, inability to concentrate, numbness, or boredom. For others—poets and artists, for example—solitude carries almost the opposite meaning: bliss, relaxation, personal integration, a feeling of warm connectedness with the world and other people, creativity, and reflection. What are the differences between these people—or between times in the life of a particular person when one rather than another reaction predominates?

The difference is partly one of perspective. Sometimes, because of past or recent experiences, we conceive of aloneness as being cut off, bereft, alienated from others, the way a child feels after being sent to his or her room for punishment. (As the poet Coleridge put it in "The Rime of the Ancient Mariner": "Alone, alone, all, all alone, / Alone on a wide wide sea! / And never a saint took pity on / My soul in agony.") In this state of mind, we feel a keen sense of loss and powerlessness—loss of other people's approval and company, and powerlessness to do anything about it. The loss calls attention to deficiencies in ourselves; we are "bad," unworthy of love, deserving of rejection, vulnerable and helpless. In this state, self-esteem is diminished; we become frightened and defensive. We can't relax or be creative.

In contrast, the orientation we call active solitude emphasizes the positive side of being alone. In solitude, you are together with yourself, physically but not psychologically cut off from other people; free to explore thoughts and feelings without regard for anyone else's immediate reactions. You can hear your own mental voice and react to your own subtle desires and moods. Oddly enough, the result is often a deeper affection for other people. One of our respondents in Billings, Montana, wrote us, for example, that she spends ten days in total solitude each year—causing rumors among her neighbors that her marriage is on the rocks. Leaving husband, children, dog, and three canaries back home, she retreats to a mountain cabin by herself—to think, read, and write. "I have a ball—no obligations and no distractions. No radio, no TV, no screaming kids or pesky husband. For ten days I have just me. I love being away from it all for those days. Funny thing is though, I appreciate them a whole lot more when I get back—a year's worth of appreciation builds up in just ten days."

One of the people we interviewed told us: "Odd as it sounds, I'm more able to be by myself when I feel most in tune with my lover. It's easier to concentrate on work, to be creative. I know when we're apart that we'll soon be together, that she's there if I need her. And we're more valuable to ourselves and get along better when we've spent time alone."

Although the words "alone" and "lonely" come from the same middle English root—meaning "all one" (or only one)—they are not psychological synonyms. Many people—for example, those trapped in unhappy marriages or forced to live with relatives who "don't understand"—are much lonelier living with others than are the hundreds of thousands who live alone but have close ties with friends and family. It's clearly possible to be lonely without being alone and alone without being lonely.

Many people find that the first few minutes or hours of solitude are unsettling. While working individually on this book, for example, having set aside time for reflection and writing, we often spent the first half hour (at least) with unnecessary phone calls, irrelevant reading, and distracting, time-wasting trips to the bathroom or refrigerator. The urge to avoid self-confrontation, to escape the feeling of aloneness that solitary thought requires, is powerful indeed. In the first few moments of solitude, many people make a hasty decision to go shopping or turn on the television set, and they immediately lose the opportunity for creativity and self-renewal. If this pattern becomes habitual, their sense of identity and personal strength is eroded and they become chronically afraid of solitude.

The writings of religious hermits throughout history reveal that they too suffered an initial period of doubt, agitation, and panic when they first got out into the wilderness by themselves. Most of them, however, like most of us in our successful attempts at creative solitude, waited out this temporary anxiety and found themselves moved and enriched by the rewards of solitude.

In extreme forms, solitude has often been used in *rites de passage* to transform boys into men. In many primitive societies, pubertal boys were sent off into the forest, jungle, or plains, and ordered to remain alone for periods ranging from overnight to several months. The boys were thought to die a symbolic death and become transformed: when they returned to the world of the living as men, their boyhood ignorance and dependence were gone forever. If this sounds barbaric, consider that Outward Bound, a popular American recreation group for men and women of all ages, requires its participants to take solo wilderness trips; the experience of solitary survival is assumed to foster independence and self-sufficiency.

Some researchers have tested the idea that solitude can be strengthening. During the sixties and seventies, John Lilly experimented with "restricted environmental stimulation" by placing people in immersion tanks full of warm salt water, asking them to remain inside for hours, even days, at a time. Psychologist Peter Suedfeld claimed more recently that REST, or *Restricted Environmental Stimulation Therapy*, calms mental patients, helps overweight people lose weight, smokers quit smoking, alcoholics reduce their drinking, and stutterers speak more clearly. REST simply places patients in dark, sound-proof rooms for about eight hours without radios, books, or other diversions.

Strangely enough, meditation and reflection—although usually solitary activities—are almost the opposite of what we normally think of as self-consciousness or self-preoccupation. When properly pursued, they aren't at all narcissistic. When we are self-conscious in the usual sense (anxious or embarrassed), the self that occupies our attention is, meditation experts say, a figment of our social imagination; it is the self of the adolescent conformist wondering nervously if he is accepted by the group. Surprisingly, when we are alone and allow ourselves to pass through the initial period of agitated discomfort, this social pseudo-self eventually evaporates, revealing a more relaxed and substantial self underneath. This genuine self needs no outside approval and is not simply a social creation. People who make contact with this deeper self find that their subsequent social relations are less superficial, less greedy, less tense. They have less need to defend their everyday social selves, their social masks.

Our first piece of advice, then: *When you are alone, give solitude a chance. Don't run away at the first sign of anxiety, and don't imagine yourself abandoned, cut off, or rejected.* Think of yourself *as with yourself, not without* someone else. Allow yourself to relax, listen to music that suits your feelings, work on something that you've been neglecting, write to a friend or for yourself in a journal, or just lie back and be at peace. If you are religious, your solitude may take the form of conversations with God or meditation on religious ideas. Whatever the content of your solitude, if you allow the first burst of anxiety to fade, you will open a door to many rewarding hours: of quiet prayer or contemplation; full enjoyment of music, sketching, or painting; total involvement in a novel or book of poetry; recording your own thoughts, feelings, songs, or poems. This solitude is a far cry from loneliness.

If you think about this, you can begin to see why active solitude and intimacy are related. In solitude, we experience our most genuine needs, perceptions, and feelings. We listen to our deepest selves. Intimacy involves the disclosure of this deeper self to trusted friends or lovers, and really listening, in turn, to their needs, thoughts, and feelings. In other words, in solitude we are intimate with ourselves in a way that enhances our intimacy with other people.

If you find that you can't be comfortable with yourself, you are probably a dissatisfying friend and lover as well. Perhaps you fear there is really nothing very interesting about you; your value is assured only when you are with and approved by someone else. This idea was taken to a supernatural extreme by Henry James, in a story called "The Private Life." Lord Mellifont completely vanishes when he is left alone. "He's there from the moment he knows someone else is." Mellifont is "so essentially, so conspicuously and uniformly the public character" that he is simply "all public" and has "no corresponding private life." Discovering this horrible fact, the narrator of the story feels great sympathy for Mellifont. "I had secretly pitied him for the perfection of his performance, had wondered what blank face such a mask had to cover, what was left to him for the immitigable hours in which a man sits down with himself, or, more serious still, with that intenser self his lawful wife."

We know from our research that adults who have suffered painful losses or rejections in the past are more likely to feel this way and to panic when they are alone; we also know that such people tend to have self-esteem problems. But as long as they cling desperately to others rather than confronting and overcoming their fears and feelings of inadequacy, they are unlikely to become confident and independent. For these people, spending time alone is an essential part of overcoming loneliness.

We don't want to oversell solitude. In fact, for some people solitude replaces normal social life, causing them to become self-contained, fussy, and rigid. Psychiatrist George Vaillant described such a man, in his late forties at the time they talked: "During college he had dealt with his very real fear of people by being a solitary drinker. He enjoyed listening to the radio by himself and found math and philosophy his most interesting courses. Although afraid to go out with girls, he was very particular about his appearance. . . . Thirty years later, [he] was less interested in clothes, but had become terribly preoccupied with keeping fit. He admitted that in his life 'things had taken the place of people' and that he loved to retreat into the 'peace and quiet of a weekend alone.' Approaching old age with no family of his own, he daydreamed of leaving his rare book collection to a favorite young cousin; but he had made only a small effort to get to know this cousin personally." Vaillant went on: "Not only had he never married, but he never admitted to being in love. Unduly shy with women in adolescence, at forty-seven [he] was still put off by 'eager women' and still found 'sex distasteful and frightening.' He had gone through life without close friends of any kind, male or female, and . . . still found it difficult to say good-bye to his mother."

How can you tell if solitude is leading you toward or away from other people? In general, if you find yourself soothed and strengthened by solitude, more *aware of your love for other people*, and less frightened or angry in your dealings with them, then solitude is a healthy part of your social balance. If you find, on the other hand, that you use solitude as a chronic escape from other people, and if people generally seem to you to be scary, selfish, cruel, or too messy, then you are retreating into a shell of solitude. We say this not because we wish to impose some superficial standard of sociability on everyone, but because studies like Vaillant's indicate that long-term defensive withdrawal from other people leads to unhappiness, alcohol and [other] drug abuse, underachievement, and vulnerability to illness.

Practice active solitude, then, *but not to the detriment of intimacy, friendship, or community.* Let active solitude be the ground from which your feelings of intimacy and community grow.

Follow-Up

1. *Write about or discuss your views of one or more of these statements:*
   - *It is clearly possible to be lonely without being alone and alone without being lonely.*
   - *The urge to avoid self-confrontation, to escape the feeling or aloneness that solitary thought requires, is powerful.*
   - *If you find that you can't be comfortable with yourself, you are probably a dissatisfying friend and lover as well.*
2. *The authors warn that solitude can become a vice in the form of chronic escape from other people. Write or discuss your reactions to this idea.*
3. *Attempt one or more periods of active solitude. If you are not used to being alone, start with a period of two hours. Gradually increase the duration of your solitude. Take note of any resistance in the form of doubt, anxiety, or "antsiness." For some interesting insights, try a 24-hour "solo," where you spend a full day and night away from normal activities and distractions. Report your reactions and what you learned from any of these activities.*
4. *For further reading on this topic see Anne Morrow Lindbergh's* Gift from the Sea *and* The Stations of Solitude *by Alice Koller.*

Personality and Money Orientations

Robert Sullivan

Complete this quiz before reading further.

MONEY ORIENTATION QUIZ

A. I'd rather be safe than sorry in my investment decisions 0

    I believe in taking financial risks to get ahead 1

    If you answered 1, then you are a hunter.

    If you answered 0, then go to question B.

B. When it comes to money, a person has to look out for himself first 0

    Even with financial matters, it is important to think of others before yourself 1

    If 0, continue to question C.

    If 1, skip to question G.

C. Wealth makes a person more attractive. (1 = *disagree completely*; 7 = *agree completely*)

    1   **2**   **3**   **4**   **5**   **6**   **7**

    If you answered 1, 2, 3, 4, or 5, continue to question D.

    If you answered 6 or 7, then you are a striver.

D. I most enjoy buying luxury items 0

    I most enjoy buying things that are practical and sensible 1

    If you answered 0, then you are a splurger.

    If you answered 1, skip to question E.

E. With money, I feel it is more important to plan for the future than to enjoy what I have now. (1 = *disagree completely*; 7 = *agree completely*)

    1   **2**   **3**   **4**   **5**   **6**   **7**

    If you answered 1, 2, or 3, then you are a nester.

    If you answered 4, continue to question F.

    If you answered 5, 6, or 7, then you are a gatherer.

F. How to do you feel about assessing your options when it comes to buying life insurance?

1. Quite competent
2. Somewhat competent
3. Uncertain
4. At a loss

If you answered 1, 2, or 3, then you are a gatherer.

If you answered 4, then you are a nester.

G. My top priority is to get ahead financially. (1 = *disagree completely*; 7 = *agree completely*).

| 1 | 2 | 3 | 4 | 5 | 6 | 7 |

If you answered 1 or 2, then you are an idealist.

If you answered 3 or 4, then continue to question H.

If you answered 5, 6, or 7, then you are a protector.

H. How do you feel about assessing your options when choosing a sound investment?

1. Quite competent
2. Somewhat competent
3. Uncertain
4. At a loss

If you answered 1 or 2, then you are a protector.

If you answered 3 or 4, then you are an idealist.

The following are descriptions of seven money orientations. See if your quiz score matches the description of your orientation. Keep in mind that not all characteristics may fit, but the overall picture should be relatively accurate.

Hunter: 13% of the population; have the highest average income; aggressive and eager to make, spend, and invest money; money means happiness, achievement, power; feels competent in money management skills; willing to risk; can tend toward extravagance.

Gatherer: 19% of the population; conservative attitude toward money matters (hold tight to what you earn, take low risks in investing); money means security; high competence in money management and high spending discipline; often seen as miserly; can be overly cautious in money matters.

Protector: 16% of the population; providing for others is the primary value of money (others take precedence regarding expenditures); have the second highest incomes of all types; adverse to money risk-taking; financial success is *not* a measure of self-worth.

Splurger: 14% of the population; money is a means to consumption; more indulgent than practical in money expenditures; wants to go "first class" concerning clothing, dining, travel, etc; tend to make low risk investments; may purchase items even if they cannot be afforded.

Striver: 13% of the population; money is the controlling force of their life; money success is due to luck or who you know; has the lowest average income of all the types; most do *not* feel competent in money management skills; money is equated with power and happiness; tend to be jealous of those with more money.

Nester: 14% of the population; wants just enough to get by; has low emotional attachment to money; money is not equated with status, worth or happiness; have minimal money management skills; most likely of all groups to quit jobs if winning a large lottery.

Idealist: 10% of the population; least materialistic of all types; has second lowest average income; money is seen as one of life's necessities but not related to happiness or self-worth; close to Nesters with the difference being that Idealists are more generous with their money if they have it; most likely group to have term life insurance and savings accounts but few investments; generally indifferent to money.

Editor's Note: For a more complete description of these money types, see "Americans and Their Money" by Robert Sullivan. *Worth*, June 1994.

Follow-Up

1. *Explain why you agree or disagree with your quiz score and/or orientation description. You may have characteristics of more than one orientation; however, there should be a dominant one.*
2. *Consider having a significant other or two rate you according to the money orientation descriptions. See if they agree with your self-scoring. Discuss your learnings.*
3. *Have you always tended to have your current money orientation or has it changed over the years? Discuss your answer.*
4. *How would you describe your parents' (guardians') money orientations? How have these influenced your orientation?*
5. *If you are married or in an intimate relationship, what is your partner's money orientation and its compatibility with yours? Discuss your answer.*
6. *If you are dissatisfied with your money orientation, consider talking with others with differing orientations and discuss your learnings.*
7. *See Section Four, "Human Relationships," for a related article by Dianne Hales.*
8. *Describe how your money orientation influences your well-being, relationships, and growth.*

The Last Leaf

O. Henry

In a little district west of Washington Square the streets have run crazy and broken themselves into small strips called "places." These "places" make strange angles and curves. One street crosses itself a time or two. An artist once discovered a valuable possibility in this street. Suppose a collector with a bill for paints, paper and canvas should, in traversing this route, suddenly meet himself coming back, without a cent having been paid on account!

So, to quaint old Greenwich Village the art people soon came prowling, hunting for north windows and eighteenth-century gables and Dutch attics and low rents. Then they imported some pewter mugs and a chafing dish or two from Sixth avenue, and become a "colony."

At the top of a squatty, three-story brick Sue and Johnsy had their studio. "Johnsy" was familiar for Joanna. One was from Maine; the other from California. They had met at the table d'hote of an Eighth street "Delmonico's," and found their tastes in art, chicory salad and bishop sleeves so congenial that the joint studio resulted.

That was in May. In November a cold, unseen stranger, whom the doctors called Pneumonia, stalked about the colony, touching one here and there with his icy finger. Over on the east side this ravager strode boldly, smiting his victims by scores, but his feet trod slowly through the maze of the narrow and moss-grown "places."

Mr. Pneumonia was not what you would call a chivalric old gentleman. A mite of a little woman with blood thinned by California zephyrs was hardly fair game for the red-fisted, short-breathed old duffer. But Johnsy he smote; and she lay, scarcely moving, on her painted iron bedstead, looking through the small Dutch window-panes at the blank side of the next brick house.

One morning the busy doctor invited Sue into the hallway with a shaggy, gray eyebrow.

"She has one chance in—let us say, ten," he said, as he shook down the mercury in his clinical thermometer. "And that chance is for her to want to live. This way people have of lining-up on the side of the undertaker makes the entire pharmacopeia look silly. Your little lady has made up her mind that she's not going to get well. Has she anything on her mind?"

"She—she wanted to paint the Bay of Naples some day," said Sue.

"Paint?—bosh! Has she anything on her mind worth thinking about twice—a man, for instance?"

"A man?" said Sue, with a jewsharp twang in her voice. "Is a man worth—but, no, doctor; there is nothing of the kind."

"Well, it is the weakness, then," said the doctor. "I will do all that science, so far as it may filter through my efforts, can accomplish. But whenever my patient begins to count the carriages in her funeral procession I subtract 50 per cent from the curative power of medicines. If you will get her to ask one question about the new winter styles in cloak sleeves I will promise you a one-in-five chance for her, instead of one in ten."

After the doctor had gone Sue went into the workroom and cried a Japanese napkin to a pulp. Then she swaggered into Johnsy's room with her drawing board, whistling ragtime.

Johnsy lay, scarcely making a ripple under the bedclothes, with her face toward the window. Sue stopped whistling, thinking she was asleep.

She arranged her board and began a pen-and-ink drawing to illustrate a magazine story. Young artists must pave their way to Art by drawing pictures for magazine stories that young authors write to pave their way to Literature.

As Sue was sketching a pair of elegant horseshow riding trousers and a monocle on the figure of the hero, an Idaho cowboy, she heard a low sound, several times repeated. She went quickly to the bedside.

Johnsy's eyes were open wide. She was looking out the window and counting—counting backward.

"Twelve," she said, and a little later "eleven;" and then "ten," and "nine;" and then "eight" and "seven" almost together.

Sue looked solicitously out of the window. What was there to count? There was only a bare, dreary yard to be seen, and the blank side of the brick house forty feet away. An old, old ivy vine, gnarled and decayed at the roots, climbed half way up the brick wall. The cold breath of autumn had stricken its leaves from the vine until its skeleton branches clung, almost bare, to the crumbling bricks.

"What is it, dear?" asked Sue.

"Six," said Johnsy, in almost a whisper. "They're falling faster now. Three days ago there were almost a hundred. It made my head ache to count them. But now it's easy. There goes another one. There are only five left now."

"Five what, dear? Tell your Sudie."

"Leaves. On the ivy vine. When the last one falls I must go, too. I've known that for three days. Didn't the doctor tell you?"

"Oh, I never heard of such nonsense," complained Sue, with magnificent scorn. "What have old ivy leaves to do with your getting well? And you used to love that vine so, you naughty girl. Don't be a goosey. Why, the doctor told me this morning that your chances for getting well real soon were—let's see exactly what he said—he said the chances were ten to one! Why, that's almost as good a chance as we have in New York when we ride on the street cars or walk past a new building. Try to take some broth now, and let Sudie go back to her drawing, so she can sell the editor man with it, and buy port wine for her sick child, and pork chops for her greedy self."

"You needn't get any more wine," said Johnsy, keeping her eyes fixed out the window. "There goes another. No, I don't want any broth. That leaves just four. I want to see the last one fall before it gets dark. Then I'll go, too."

"Johnsy, dear," said Sue, bending over her, "will you promise me to keep your eyes closed, and not look out the window until I am done working? I must hand those drawings in by to-morrow. I need the light, or I would draw the shade down."

"Couldn't you draw in the other room?" asked Johnsy, coldly.

"I'd rather be here by you," said Sue. "Besides, I don't want you to keep looking at those silly ivy leaves."

"Tell me as soon as you have finished," said Johnsy, closing her eyes, and lying white and still as a fallen statue, "because I want to see the last one fall. I'm tired of waiting. I'm tired of thinking. I want to turn loose my hold on everything, and go sailing down, down, just like one of those poor, tired leaves."

"Try to sleep," said Sue. "I must call Behrman up to be my model for the old hermit miner. I'll not be gone a minute. Don't try to move 'till I come back."

Old Behrman was a painter who lived on the ground floor beneath them. He was past sixty and had a Michael Angelo's Moses beard curling down from the head of a satyr along the body of an imp. Behrman was a failure in art. Forty years he had wielded the brush without getting near enough to touch the hem of his Mistress's robe. He had been always about to paint a masterpiece, but had never yet begun it. For several years he had painted nothing except now and then a daub in the line of commerce or advertising. He earned a little by serving as a model to those young artists in the colony who could not pay the price of a professional. He drank gin to excess, and still talked of his coming masterpiece. For the rest he was a fierce little old man, who scoffed terribly at softness in any one, and who regarded himself as especial mastiff-in-waiting to protect the two young artists in the studio above.

Sue found Behrman smelling strongly of juniper berries in his dimly lighted den below. In one corner was a blank canvas on an easel that had been waiting there for twenty-five years to receive the first line of the masterpiece. She told him of Johnsy's fancy, and how she feared she would, indeed, light and fragile as a leaf herself, float away when her slight hold upon the world grew weaker.

Old Behrman, with his red eyes plainly streaming, shouted his contempt and derision for such idiotic imaginings.

"Vass!" he cried. "Is dere people in de world mit der foolishness to die because leafs dey drop off from a confounded vine? I haf not heard of such a thing. No, I will not bose as a model for your fool hermit-dunderhead. Vy do you allow dot silly pusiness to come in der prain of her? Ach, dot poor leetle Miss Johnsy."

"She is very ill and weak," said Sue, "and the fever has left her mind morbid and full of strange fancies. Very well, Mr. Behrman, if you do not care to pose for me, you needn't. But I think you are a horrid old—old flibbertigibbet."

"You are just like a woman!" yelled Behrman. "Who said I vill not bose? Go on. I come mit you. For half an hour I haf peen trying to say dot I am ready to bose. Gott! dis is not any blace in which one so schones at Miss Yohnsy shall lie sick. Some day I vill baint a masterpiece, and ve shall all go away. Gott! yes."

Johnsy was sleeping when they went upstairs. Sue pulled the shade down to the window-sill, and motioned Behrman into the other room. In there they peered out the window fearfully at the ivy vine. Then they looked at each other for a moment without speaking. A persistent, cold rain was falling, mingled with snow. Behrman, in his old blue shirt, took his seat as the hermit-miner on an upturned kettle for a rock.

When Sue awoke from an hour's sleep the next morning she found Johnsy with dull, wide-open eyes staring at the drawn green shade.

"Pull it up; I want to see," she ordered, in a whisper.

Wearily she obeyed.

But, lo! after the beating rain and fierce gusts of wind that had endured through the livelong night, there yet stood out against the brick wall one ivy leaf. It was the last on the vine. Still dark green near its stem, but with its serrated edges tinted with the yellow of dissolution and decay, it hung bravely from a branch some twenty feet above the ground.

"It is the last one," said Johnsy. "I thought it would surely fall during the night. I heard the wind. It will fall to-day, and I shall die at the same time."

"Dear, dear!" said Sue, leaning her worn face down to the pillow, "think of me, if you won't think of yourself. What would I do?"

But Johnsy did not answer. The lonesomest thing in all the world is a soul when it is making ready to go on its mysterious, far journey. The fancy seemed to possess her more strongly as one by one the ties that bound her to friendship and to earth were loosed.

The day wore away, and even through the twilight they could see the lone ivy leaf clinging to its stem against the wall. And then, with the coming of the night the north wind was again loosed, while the rain still beat against the windows and pattered down from the low Dutch eaves.

When it was light enough Johnsy, the merciless, commanded that the shade be raised.

The ivy leaf was still there.

Johnsy lay for a long time looking at it. And then she called to Sue, who was stirring her chicken broth over the gas stove.

"I've been a bad girl, Sudie," said Johnsy. "Something has made that last leaf stay there to show me how wicked I was. It is a sin to want to die. You may bring me a little broth now, and some milk with a little port in it, and—no; bring me a hand-mirror first; and then pack some pillows about me, and I will sit up and watch you cook."

An hour later she said:

"Sudie, some day I hope to paint the Bay of Naples."

The doctor came in the afternoon, and Sue had an excuse to go into the hallway as he left.

"Even chances," said the doctor, taking Sue's thin, shaking hand in his. "With good nursing you'll win. And now I must see another case I have downstairs. Behrman, his name is—some kind of an artist, I believe. Pneumonia, too. He is an old, weak man, and the attack is acute. There is no hope for him; but he goes to the hospital to-day to be made more comfortable."

The next day the doctor said to Sue: "She's out of danger. You've won. Nutrition and care now—that's all."

And that afternoon Sue came to the bed where Johnsy lay, contentedly knitting a very blue and very useless woollen shoulder scarf, and put one arm around her, pillows and all.

"I have something to tell you, white mouse," she said. "Mr. Behrman died of pneumonia to-day in the hospital. He was ill only two days. The janitor found him on the morning of the first day in his room downstairs helpless with pain. His shoes and clothing were wet through and icy cold. They couldn't

"Ode to the Last Leaf"

There it stands alone. The last leaf of autumn. At the top of a branch of a young broadleaf oak, it is hanging on for a while longer than the others. Maybe it likes the view. It does not seem to mind that its edges are frayed and that you can even see through it. But soon it will join its comrades below. Below, where it will add a little color to the ground. Then slowly, very slowly, get smaller until it becomes part of the soil. It will not be forgotten. In the spring the bare oak branch will gather sustenance from the soil. It will sprout buds and then leaves—leaves which exist because of the last leaf of autumn.

You will leave a legacy. What will it be?

imagine where he had been on such a dreadful night. And then they found a lantern, still lighted, and a ladder that had been dragged from its place, and some scattered brushes, and a palette with green and yellow colors mixed on it, and—look out the window, dear, at the last ivy leaf on the wall. Didn't you wonder why it never fluttered or moved when the wind blew? Ah, darling, it's Behrman's masterpiece—he painted it there the night that the last leaf fell."

Follow-Up

1. *One's "will to live" is often connected to a commitment to something larger than oneself (another person, group, vocation, incompleted work). Johnsy had lost this connection. What in your life gives you this sense of being involved*

in something larger than yourself? How do you function when this connection is weak?

2. *Johnsy believed that when the last leaf fell she would die. Reflect on a time when you let something or someone determine your life direction versus you taking the initiative. Would you characterize yourself as primarily outer-directed or inner-directed concerning major life decisions? Explain your answer.*

3. *Behrman, the old painter, can easily be negatively rubricized (see "Rubricizing," Section Two). Think of a time when you negatively rubricized someone who eventually turned out to be a good guy. Discuss this idea.*

4. *Select a statement or idea from this story and offer your commentary.*

Teachers in the Forest

Nelson Goud

Coming upon my first forest Titan I stopped, stared, and whispered something like "ZZANG!" The Titan, a giant sequoia, appeared to materialize from a secluded space in the forest. It was so colossal that "tree" did not seem to be a proper designation. Its cinnamon hued trunk, as wide as a two-car garage, rose to a point beyond which I could see. Nature writer Barry Lopez bows to wildlife and landscape features. He considers them to be part of his moral universe and a bow is a way of acknowledging a spiritual connection. I agree with Lopez's sentiment, but how do you bow to a tree hundreds of feet above you?

It was mid-October and I was prowling the Giant Forest region of the Sequoia National Park. This is the home of the largest concentration of the sequoias, scientifically known as Sequoia-dendron giganteum. Sequoias grow only on the western slope of California's Sierra-Nevada mountains at about 6,500 feet elevation. I went there to experience directly these trees that have fascinated me from afar. Little did I know that I was also to be a student. Below are a few of the learnings encountered from my Titan teachers.

1. *The sequoia challenges one's concept of the possibilities of growth.* The massiveness of a sequoia stuns a first time beholder. Up close a mature sequoia will require all of your peripheral vision, and the ability to bend your back like a Slinky to even approach seeing its summit. For example, the General Sherman sequoia qualifies as the world's largest living thing. It is approximately 275 feet high, has a 37-foot base diameter, and weighs about 2.5 million pounds. For a comparison, a good sized maple or oak tree will be about 90 feet tall and 5–7 feet

in diameter. Earth's heaviest animal, the blue whale, weighs in at 300,000 pounds, eight times lighter than General Sherman. General Sherman is 2,600 years old. This sequoia was middle-aged when Shakespeare was writing, and nearly 2,400 years old when Thomas Jefferson was writing the Declaration of Independence. And it is not the oldest sequoia. Astoundingly, the life force in the General Sherman sequoia is as potent as a young twig; it adds new wood equivalent to a 60 foot oak each year. The sequoia had no qualms about realizing its potential; its essence is the process of growth and has been since a seedling.

2. *Balanced growth is valued by the sequoia.* To remain standing as it ascends toward the clouds, the sequoia relies on an intricate system of equalizing forces. Its root system may extend for an acre but it is very shallow, rarely more than five feet deep. The trunk is straight and the sequoia's mammoth branches cluster at the upper third of the trunk and act as counterbalances. The sequoia demonstrates the wisdom of a life with balance.

3. *Sequoias beckon you to come to your senses.* If you hike the trails away from the tourist stops, you will encounter sequoias that have existed for thousands of years. Some sequoias stand with other trees—white pine, red fir, incense cedar, and often surrounded by braken fern. In sequoia groves there is little other vegetation, and the ground cover is a deep needle layer that has a spongy feel as you walk over it. Small, dark cones lie scattered on the needles. If you are lucky, one of these forest Titans will invite you to take a break there. The first thing you notice is the sequoia's bark. Furrows

crease into the bark and some have so much depth that it is possible to cushion a daypack in them. The bark can be as much as 30 inches deep. Its color is a reddish-brown except for black scars from hundreds of years of battling forest fires. Sequoias are among the most fire resistant organisms on earth. The surface of the bark is soft and crumbly to the touch; the wood underneath is hard but brittle. (This, thankfully, made sequoias somewhat undesirable in pre-national park years to harvest, although some were used for things like fencing, toothpicks, and even a dance floor).

It is cloudy and a mist winds its way through the grove simultaneously darkening and magnifying the sequoias. When the clouds depart, openings in the canopy allow streaks of sunlight to fuse with the sequoia bark, which now radiates a cinnamon tinge. You are not just looking at trees and the sun and shadows this October, but watching what it has been like for a couple thousand years in this same place. You are observing time as well as space. The only new object is you.

A distinct scent from a controlled burning pierces the giant sequoia grove and if you hang around these Titans for a couple days, this scent seems to go with you. The bottom of my hiking shoes and a couple of sequoia cones have retained this scent and when I need to remember how it was in the grove, I smell them. Unlike the smell of a campfire or fireplace, the sequoia grove scent is a burned muskiness. It is tempting to call it a primordial smell, but this would be a bit difficult to verify. You could possibly come close to the smell if you burned some dry mushrooms, bark, and pine needles in an earthen pit—and then kept re-burning them for a couple hundred years. The sequoia tree itself does not have this pungent aroma (you can smell the remnant of fire on the charred trunk segments). Other trees in the area have treats for the olfactory devotees and among the suggested actions is to whiff the bark of an incense cedar.

On the back trails there is little sound. Any noise becomes exaggerated in these environs. Cones falling through branches sound like baseballs cracking against bats and when one hits the ground it resounds with a concussive Whump! Scampering squirrels and chipmunks may have you twitching the first few instances, especially when you have just finished reading about what to do if a bear or cougar is encountered on a trail. But the most enticing sound comes from another wild creature. If you shaped a piece of the darkest night into a bird, you would create a raven. Slightly larger than a crow, ravens call to each other in the empty groves. Unlike the higher pitched caw-caw of the crow, the raven's call is a series of low, reverberating croaks. The raven's sound is closer to a big frog than a crow. The raven calls were initially intrusive. Then I eventually realized that this sound is natural to the grove. But the sound that endeared me to the raven was its flight. I have never heard a bird fly. When a raven flies directly overhead you hear a soft WHOOSH-WHOOSH from its wings. Each time this happened I would look up and smile. Barry Lopez would bow. Once a flock of over 80 ravens flew overhead and the dozens of whispering WHOOSH-WHOOSH sounds made me feel like I was beneath scores of silent helicopters with feathered blades.

A large part of what many value most in life is best experienced directly—love, beauty, music, nature, our bodies. Modern living emphasizes indirect modes of knowing and interacting with the world: electronic communications, virtual realities, and working with abstractions. The sequoias remind us that we are sensory beings too, and that direct experience is necessary for a full, balanced life.

4. *When the sounds of the grove vanish, there is total silence.* The silence deepens into stillness. No sound, no motion—quietude. The sequoias stand in the thick hush that now dwells in the grove. "It is stillness and yet it echoes," says Ira Progoff (1992).

For some, silence is to be avoided; it makes us feel lonely and makes us turn inward and we may not like what we find there. Or silence is a reminder of nothingness, death. One then turns to noises that mask the silence. Listen about you at any moment of the day. Sounds. Many sounds. Some are nice sounds, but there are many intruding annoyances.

Where can one go to find silence, or at least relative quiet on a consistent basis? The news had a feature about a man who was attempting to get federal protection in each state for one simple thing: "one square inch of silence." In most states this would mean protecting many miles of landscape to attain the one square inch of silence. We may not find that perfect space of silence, but we do need something close to it. It is silence that can create something from nothing. Only in stillness can one hear the faint voices from our deepest sources. And consider the power of the pause, that quiet interval between notes of music or in conversation. Finally, as Thoreau (1854/1962) tells us, "there are many fine things which we cannot say if we have to shout."

5. *There is a connectedness among living things.* Experiencing the stillness of a sequoia grove is disorienting for a few moments. Watching the silent harmony of everything in the grove and how natural the stillness is for them marks you as an outsider. If you sit quietly for awhile this strangeness dissolves. Sitting in stillness *with* the Titans will eventually yield a sense of acceptance—that it is all right for you to be there, too. More moments pass in the stillness and you begin to be aware of another change. Time suspends itself so that there is only this moment, and the moment extends into infinity. The boundaries between you and the things in the grove become less distinct. You share a common identity somehow—a merge at a deeper level.

Others have commented on this common identity among humans and nature. In 1836, Emerson (1926/1951) wrote that "the greatest delight which the fields and woods minister is the suggestion of a mystical relation between man and the vegetable." Thomas Moore (1992), a Jungian therapist and former monk,

claims that "when we disallow soul to the simple things around us, we lose that important source of soul for ourselves. Concretely, a tree can tell us much . . . in the way it presents itself as an individual. But in this expression of itself, it is also showing us the secrets of our own souls, for there is no absolute separation between the world's soul and our own." Nikos Kazantzakis's Zorba asks "Can you make it out, boss? It's beyond me. Everything seems to have a soul—wood, stones, the wine we drink and the earth we tread on. Everything, boss, absolutely everything!" (Kazantzakis, 1952)

Even biology hints at this fundamental linkage between living things. Carl Sagan (1980) states that "at the very heart of life of Earth—the proteins that control cell chemistry, and the nucleic acids that carry the hereditary instructions—we find these molecules to be essentially identical in all plants and animals. An oak tree and I are made of the same stuff. If you go far enough back, we have a common ancestor." You, the raven, and the giant sequoia have identical genetic building blocks—the variations come in the coding. One song, many instruments.

6. *Living with paradox.* This lesson begins with one of the Titan's smallest forest companions, the chickaree (Douglass squirrel). Larger than a chipmunk but smaller than a squirrel, the perky chickaree is two million pounds lighter than the giant sequoia. But many Titans exist because of this furry Lilliputian. This is because chickarees get hungry. Chickarees cannot resist a tasty sequoia cone. Whether snatching one from the ground or from a sequoia branch, the chickaree holds the ends of the cone between its paws and spins it while munching the outer layers—somewhat like a kid eating a buttery ear of corn at a state fair. The seeds from the sequoia cone are released and scattered by the chickaree's snacking. The cones contain about 200 seeds and one sequoia tree will produce about 2,000 cones. The sequoia seed itself is unexpectedly tiny. I just

placed one on the word *seed* and it covered only the first three letters. Paradox. The giant sequoia exists because of small things.

Paradox occurs in other dimensions of the Titan's existence. Very few giant sequoias are destroyed by fire. Hundreds of years of fires have left scorch marks on the sequoia trunks—some are blackened gouges over a foot deep and 10 feet long. Still, the Titan will not burn for long. Sequoias have built in fire departments. Tannins, the chemicals which turn the bark a cinnamon brown, are potent fire retardants. The tannins also repel insects and fungus growth. By withstanding fire, the sequoia benefits from its after effects. Forest fires prepare mineral-rich seedbeds; they open holes in the canopy allowing more sunlight to reach the soil; fires reduce competition from less fire resistant plants. Fires dry sequoia cones, which makes them open and disperse their seeds. The Titan instructs us how to make a potentially destructive force into an ally.

7. *Aging.* No giant sequoia dies from aging. As mentioned earlier, the sequoia's life force is as vigorous at 2,000 years old as it was as a sprig of 200. But sequoias do die. A small percentage are destroyed by natural disasters, and some were destroyed in the 1800s by lumbermen. But no sequoia has ever been confirmed of dying of old age. The main cause of death is by toppling. The root system that is essential to the sequoia's balance may be undercut by natural or human-made soil erosion. It may take a few hundred years, but without its counter-balancing roots a sequoia will fall, usually without notice. The sequoia teaches how to die: grow until you topple.

8. *Wonder.* Sequoias emanate a sense of silent dominion. Their immensity and mysteriousness cause one, says John Steinbeck (1963) "to go under a spell." Some ask, what is the purpose of a sequoia anyway? It is a query that the Titans do not address. The sequoias are content to *be.* In *Apology To Wonder* (1969), Sam Keen

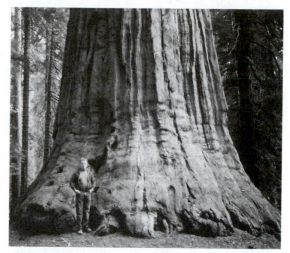

"Sequoia"

contends that the primal source of all wonder is the jarring realization that something actually exists in the first place. It could, in short, not exist. The sequoias being here is a triumph over nonbeing or nothingness. It is, continues Keen, a cause for "rejoicing in the presence of things rather than going beyond them." Similarly, *you* are here. But why you? One man produces billions of sperm in a lifetime and one woman produces several hundred ovum. You began by the joining of just one of these sperm and ovum. If another sperm swimming right next to yours had been a jot quicker, you would not be here and someone else would be. Your existence, too, is a case for wonder.

And so ended my seminar with the sequoias. I had confirmed Thoreau's conclusion that "we need the tonic of wildness" and to be "refreshed by the sight of inexhaustible vigor, vast and titanic features . . . We need to witness our own limits transgressed, and some life pasturing freely where we never wander" (Thoreau, 1854/1962).

You do not have to go among the sequoias to learn some life lessons. The idea is to find a place where wonder dwells and drop in for a spell.

References

Emerson, R. (1926/1951). *Emerson's essays.* I. Edman (Ed.). New York: Perennial Library.

Kazantzakis, N. (1952). *Zorba the Greek.* New York: Simon and Schuster.

Keen, S. (1969). *Apology for wonder.* New York: Harper & Row.

Moore, T. (1992). *Care of the soul.* New York: Harper Perennial.

Progoff, I. (1992). *At a journal workshop.* New York: Jeremy P. Tarcher/Perigee.

Sagan, C. (1980). *Cosmos.* New York: Random House.

Steinbeck, J. (1963). *Travels with Charley.* New York: Bantam.

Thoreau, H. (1854/1962). *Thoreau: Walden and other Writings.* J. W. Krutch (Ed.). New York: Bantam Books, Inc.

Follow-Up

1. *Select two statements from this article and offer your commentary.*
2. *Describe how two of the lessons mentioned in this article have relevance in your life.*
3. *Goud claims that much of what we value most in life is experienced directly instead of indirectly. Explain if this is true for you. Why or why not?*
4. *Explain how you relate to silence. Is it needed, as the author claims, to hear our deeper voices? Comment on this question.*
5. *The author describes how the sequoia turns a destructive force (fire) into a constructive one. Describe how you have turned a crisis, problem, or adversarial situation into a positive stance.*

Nature Quotes

How long has it been since you were intoxicated by the fresh smells of a forest after a gentle spring rain? When were you last lullabyed by the whispering of pines? You are human. It is your right to experience these things often.

—Whit Bronaugh

Going to the mountains is going home; wildness is necessity; mountain parks and reservations are useful not only as fountains of timber and irrigating rivers, but as fountains of life.

—John Muir

The best remedy for those who are afraid, lonely, or unhappy is to go outside, where they can be alone with the heavens and nature. Only then does one feel that all is as it should be. Nature brings solace to all troubles.

—Anne Frank

Biofilia—The tendency for humans to feel an affinity and awe for living things. . . . When we destroy the natural world we court spiritual disaster.

—E. O. Wilson

In reality we are an integral part of what we call nature, the dynamic principle that holds the world of the living together. Nature is an organizing presence, the deepest dimension of the universe.

—Thomas Berry

We can never have enough of Nature. We must be refreshed by the sight of inexhaustible vigor, vast and titanic features, the seacoast with its wrecks, the wilderness with its living and its decaying trees, the thunder cloud, and the rain which lasts three weeks and produces freshets. We need to witness our own limits transgressed, and some life pasturing freely where we never wander.

—Henry Thoreau

To see the sun rise or go down every day, so to relate ourselves to a universal fact, would preserve us sane forever.

—Henry Thoreau

At the gates of the forest, the surprised man of the world is forced to leave his city estimates of great and small, wise and foolish.

—Ralph Waldo Emerson

To the attentive eye, each moment of the year has its own beauty, and in the same field, it beholds, every hour, a picture which was never seen before, and which shall never be seen again.

—Ralph Waldo Emerson

Any fool can destroy trees. They cannot defend themselves or run away.
　　　　　　　　　　　　　　　　　　　　　　　　　　—John Muir

None of Nature's landscapes are ugly so long as they are wild.
　　　　　　　　　　　　　　　　　　　　　　　　　　—John Muir

The fields would be very silent if no birds sang there except those who sang best.
　　　　　　　　　　　　　　　　　　　　　　　　　　—Audubon

A degree or two temperature change = a shift of winds = effects the weather on the other side of the mountain.
　　　　　　　　　　　　　　　　　　　　　　　　　　—Gwen Frostic

A little bird sings from a tree top—a lovely sound—it will not last—but other birds will sing—the music goes on.
　　　　　　　　　　　　　　　　　　　　　　　　　　—Gwen Frostic

Man feels himself isolated in the cosmos, because he is no longer involved in nature. . . . His contact with nature has gone, and with it has gone the profound emotional energy that this symbolic connection supplied.
　　　　　　　　　　　　　　　　　　　　　　　　　　—Carl Jung

Follow-Up

1. *Explain how contact with nature influences your life.*
2. *Describe two of your favorite experiences in nature.*

The Dying-Readiness/ Freedom-to-Live Test

Abe Arkoff

My work has led me to believe that those of us who ready ourselves to die also free ourselves to lead our lives more fully than ever before. Typically, in my workshops on dying readiness, I administer my "Dying-Readiness/Freedom-to-Live" Test. I give it item by item, discussing each item as I go, so that the participants may have some basis for their answers.

The 10 items of the test are presented in the material that follows, and each item is briefly delineated. You are invited to take the test now. After you have read each item and delineation, answer by drawing a circle around "Yes" or "No" as is appropriate in your own case. If your answer isn't clearly yes or no, circle the question mark.

Yes ? No   1. I have allowed myself to think deeply about death and my own death and to experience the feelings that this engenders.

Yes ? No   2. I have made out a will.

Why don't people make out wills? One important reason is that a will is associated with the idea of our death. . . . Thoughts of our mortality can be anxiety-provoking and whatever provokes anxiety may be pushed aside or avoided.

Some of us find it comforting to assume a kind of immortality for ourselves—or at least a nonmortality—and this is inconsistent with making out a will. Somerset Maugham once wrote that if one were small, one might hope to be overlooked by death. For some, making out a will is like registering to die and signing

a will is like signing a death certificate or, at least, a promissory note. By not making out a will or not signing it, we feel we haven't put ourselves in jeopardy.

A second reason for not completing a will is that we assume this is something that can be delayed. Because we don't expect to die soon (if at all), why bother now? We can take care of this when we're old and gray.

A third reason for not making out a will is the assumption that one is not leaving much of value. (But if you die a "wrongful death," you may be worth a lot more dead than alive—and who gets it?) A fourth reason is the wishful thought that somehow things will work out all right and that those who should inherit will inherit; because making out a will is an expense and bother, why not just hope for the best?

It seems a bit curious that folks who care for their loved ones and who also care about their own hard-earned or carefully acquired possessions would leave both in limbo upon death. Making out a will shows that you care. It also shows that you weren't afraid to face your own demise. It's an important step in getting your house in order. Before proceeding further, answer Item 2 by circling one of its three alternatives.

Yes ? No   3. I have made known my choice between having and not having my life extended through artificial or heroic measures in the event that there is no reasonable expectation of my recovery from physical or mental disability. (Or I have made out a living will or executed a durable power of attorney.)

Competent adults have the right to refuse life-sustaining treatment, but what happens if one becomes incompetent to make one's wishes known? In this litigious age, physicians run into few problems if they continue to treat a patient, but there can be considerable danger in stopping treatment. In the absence of specific instructions, it is unlikely that life-support systems would be withdrawn and much less likely in the case of a relatively young patient.

A *living will* (not to be confused with a living trust) is a written, signed, witnessed, and possibly notarized declaration that specifies your wishes concerning the use of life-sustaining procedures in your own case if you become terminally ill and incompetent. A *durable power of attorney for health care* is a written, signed, witnessed, and possibly notarized document in which you (the principal) give another (the agent) the legal authority to make health-care decisions on your behalf if you become terminally ill and incompetent. Because some living wills also provide for a health proxy who, in effect, can serve as an agent, and some durable powers of attorney also specify your health-care wishes, there can be a great deal of overlap in these two approaches. State laws vary, so it is important that a local attorney or some other knowledgeable authority be consulted for assistance as you weigh your options and devise your own plan.

Yes ? No 4. I have planned my own funeral or planned to dispense with a funeral and have made these plans known.

Yes ? No 5. I have chosen and made known a plan for the disposal of my body after death.

Although we don't plan our entrance into this world, we have an opportunity to plan our departure. In our plans, we will want to consider our own wishes and also the needs of our survivors and what would be helpful and convenient for them.

In our final planning, we also help those we leave behind in two ways: (1) We remove the necessity of decision making just at the time when our survivors might be least able to make decisions, guess at what we would have wanted, or resolve differences among themselves. (2) We may ameliorate a common tendency of bereaved persons to overspend on funeral arrangements.

Yes ? No 6. I have made out a survivor's guide.

Survivor's guides take various forms. A typical guide contains the information relative to your death certificate and obituary, desired funeral arrangements, will, safety deposit box, insurance, social security benefits, pensions, annuities, checking accounts, property, and other financial assets and liabilities.

Yes ? No 7. I have made my relationships with "significant others" current by "clearing the past."

We want, of course, to be treated fairly. We want our world to be just. We want what is due to us. We want to get as good as we give. We want others to treat us as nicely as we treat them and to pay us back for all we've done for them.

Alas, our world is not always just and the people in it who are most important to us—our "significant others"—are not always fair. When we are treated unfairly, unjustly, we may build up a good deal of anger and resentment. The raw deals, the things that others did to us and shouldn't have, the things they didn't do, but should have—these things may fester in our minds and memories.

It is important to distinguish between two kinds of wrongs. There are the wrongs to work on and the wrongs to let go of. It takes some wisdom to know the difference.

Some of us become resentment collectors. We are unable to forgive or forget the wrongs done to us. This kind of collecting accomplishes nothing and can become self-destructive. Our resentment consumes energy and keeps us stuck in the past. Like other persistent negative emotions, resentment can have corresponding physiological reactions that wear down the body and make us ill.

Why do we sometimes choose the heavy burden of resentment rather than the liberation that comes with forgiving? What do we get out of it?

Some persons don't forgive because they confuse forgiveness with condonation. They think that to forgive is to condone or overlook or even give approval to a wrong. By being unforgiving they continue to bear witness to the wrong. They keep the offender on the hook (and perhaps themselves as well). But to forgive does not require one to overlook or approve a wrong. Forgiveness notes there is something to be forgiven and also something to be gained by letting go and moving along.

Yes ? No 8. I keep my relationships with "significant others" current by manifesting my love.

It will be helpful to run a check on yourself now. In the space below make a list of all the people in your life whom you love (names, initials, or symbols will do). Then cross out every one to whom you haven't manifested your love in the past half year. (My dictionary says that *to manifest* means to make clearly apparent to sight or understanding; obvious. So just knowing they know that you love them doesn't qualify.)

<u>Persons Whom I Love</u>

Yes ? No 9. I have learned to die my "little deaths" in preparation for my "big death."

Plato, on his death bed, gave this advice to a visiting friend: "Practice dying." Life gives us plenty of opportunity for this practice because life is filled with a number of little deaths. These are the times when we lose not life but something very important to it. Perhaps someone dear to us dies or we are permanently disabled or we lose a relationship or position of many years or we suffer a great financial reversal or we come to the realization that something we have dreamed of and hoped for will never come to pass.

What little deaths have you suffered? And how have you managed them? What have you learned? Have you learned to accept the reality of your losses? Can you allow yourself to feel the pain of your griefs? Are you able to accommodate your deprivation? Have you invested your emotional energy anew?

Yes ? No 10. I make it a point to appreciate and deeply enjoy the "little joys" of life.

None of us—whether seriously ill or seemingly hale—can count on endless tomorrows. Our lives could end at any moment. Are we fully living our lives; or are we saving our lives to be lived at a later date?

If we don't think of ourselves as mortal, if it's inconceivable to us that we will ever die, then we have forever. What's one day, if we have forever? We can throw it away. What's a little joy, if we have forever? We can keep pursuing big joys, whatever they may be.

One unfortunate notion of life is that it is a staircase. We climb up step by step, and when we get to the top we can be happy. If we are not happy at the top, maybe it isn't the top—maybe it's just a landing—so we need to resume climbing until we get to some place where happiness is.

Hermann Hesse (1988) wrote of the little joys available to us as we make our daily rounds. These are small things to which we may pay little notice but which can give us some moments of delight if we give them their due. A flower, a stretch of sky, a piece of fruit, children's laughter. His advice was that we seek out each day as many as possible of these small joys. He wrote, "It is the small joys first of all that are granted us for recreation, for daily relief and disburdenment, not the great ones."

Take a moment to recall the little joys you have delighted in today. How about yesterday? What about the day before? Do the memories of little joys come easily to mind, or are you drawing a blank? What about your life as a whole? Are you waiting for some Big Joy to make it all worthwhile? Think about this, and answer Item 10 before you go on.

Take a few moments to review your responses to all 10 items of the test. In your own estimation (there is no exact passing score), do your responses indicate you are ready to die? If so, congratulations because then your house is in order, and you are free to live. If your answers indicate you have more work to do, get busy and do it—not for death's sake but for life's sake.

References

Hesse, H. (1988). On little joys. In A. Arkoff (Ed.), *Psychology and personal growth* (3rd ed, pp. 270–271). Boston: Allyn and Bacon.

Kalish, R. A. (1985). *Death, grief, and caring relationships* (2nd ed.). Monterey, CA: Brooks/Cole.

Keleman, S. (1974). *Living your dying.* New York: Random House/Bookworks.

McCabe, C. (1975, September 16). Love untold. *San Francisco Chronicle.*

Perlin, S. (1982). Death visualization: A teaching and learning device. *Death Education,* 6, pp. 294–298.

Follow-Up

1. *Is your Personal Death Awareness (PDA) at an optimal level? How does your personal awareness of death affect the way you live your life?*
2. *Have you made out a will? Why or why not? Concerning personal items or property with sentimental value or special meaning, who would you like to inherit these items in the event of your death? Why them? Have you ensured that this will be so? Concerning damages that might be paid your estate be-*

cause of your "wrongful death" (for example, through accident), who would you like to inherit this money? Why them? Have you ensured that this will be so?

3. *Are there any conditions under which you would consider measures to prolong or shorten your life if you were terminally ill or irreversibly comatose? What have you done to ensure that your wishes in this regard are respected?*

4. *What plans for funeral or memorial services or for the disposal of your body after death do you prefer? Why? What have you done to ensure that your wishes in this regard are respected?*

5. *Have you made your relationships with "significant others" current by "clearing the past"? If so, give your proof. If not, why not?*

6. *Do you keep your relationships with "significant others" current by manifesting your love? If so, give your proof. If not, why not?*

7. *How have you dealt with a little death or some great loss in your life? What did you learn from this experience?*

8. *Do you make it a point to appreciate and deeply enjoy the little joys of life? If so, give your proof. If not, why not?*

Personal Death Awareness (PDA)

J. William Worden and William Proctor

Personal Death Awareness Index

Low	Low Moderate	High Moderate	High

Your Personal Death Awareness is a fluctuating phenomenon, moving up and down daily. Some days, you'll be more aware of your own limited life span, and other days you may act and think as though you're going to live forever.

Most of us usually register quite low on the awareness index because we tend to shy away from thoughts of our own death. Consciously or subconsciously, we deny that someday our lives must end. The more intense our denial, the lower our PDA.

I am purposely asking you to raise your Personal Death Awareness so that you can begin to perceive an entire range of choices about your life and death that you might not have been aware of before.

Just as there are extremes of introversion and extroversion, there are extremes of Personal Death Awareness. You may have willingly experienced only one polarity—the low side of the awareness index. Any high death awareness you've experienced was probably associated with something very unpleasant, such as the death of a friend or loved one, and that makes you resist increasing your death awareness. But I've often found that if a person *willingly* increases his own Personal Death Awareness and looks his mortality squarely in the face, he seldom prefers to return to his previous state of unawareness.

SELECTED PDA EXERCISES

1. Draw a line of any length, a straight one with a beginning and an end.
    Consider this line to be your total life span. Place a slash mark at any point along the line where you think you are today in your life's chronology. Now, complete the following sentences by filling in the blanks:

    I expect to live until age _____

    I am currently age _____

When you compare your present age with the age at which you expect to die, how much of your life do you find you've already lived? A third, a half, two-thirds, or more? Now look back at the line with the slash mark. How does your estimate of the time you have left to live on the life-span line compare with your numerical estimate?

Many people who have done this exercise have found that they placed the slash mark at an earlier age than their written guess. When you see your life starkly depicted on a line in front of you, like a racetrack or a road map, the tendency is to give yourself more time to live than you know you probably have.

How did it feel to commit yourself to a definite life span? Some people worry that they may jinx themselves by doing this. Old superstitions rise up and haunt them. Does this concern you?

2. Take a few minutes to compose your own obituary-eulogy. No, don't close the book yet! Many of my students who have taken the time for this exercise have been impressed with its value, especially with the way it makes death personal for them. You can use your own format or the one suggested below. If you use the one below, take your time and fill in the blanks thoughtfully.

OBITUARY-EULOGY

_____ died today at the age of _____. A native of _____, he/she died _____.

He/she is best remembered for _____

_____

_____

_____.

He/she is survived by _____

_____

_____.

Details of the funeral and the burial are as follows: _____

_____

_____

_____.

What was it like for you to compose your own obituary? Did you feel anxious or upset? Did any of the questions make you think about things you had refused or neglected to think about before? Look back at some of the first exercises you did in this chapter. Did you increase or decrease your estimates of your life span in your obituary?

How did you see yourself dying? Was it a so-called "natural" death, a terminal illness, or a quick, violent death, as in an accident or homicide? Perhaps you chose a self-inflicted death like suicide?

Some people find how they want to be remembered a particularly hard question, so they insert something funny. Humor can eliminate the sting, the uncomfortable feelings invoked by a serious issue.

In writing your own obituary one of the most difficult details is listing survivors. It's fairly easy for most people to conceive of living longer than their parents and not living as long as their children. But when it comes to surviving brothers and sisters, that's a much harder matter. Who among your siblings still living do you expect to die before you? Who will outlive you? If you are married, do you anticipate outliving your spouse?

An awareness of your own mortality can also help you live a more effective life in the here and now:

- You can deal with feelings and not have to hide them.
- You can identify what it is specifically about dying that is causing you anxiety. Once you've pinpointed the cause, you can proceed to do something about it.
- You can take more advantage of opportunities which happen your way. A healthy Personal Death Awareness will prevent you from postponing until tomorrow tasks which can *only* be done today. Tomorrow may be too late.

If you remember that you and your loved ones won't live forever, you can have more significant, less superficial, personal relationships. But if you postpone expressing appreciation and love, death may intervene to make your temporary delay a permanent thing. Or if you harbor long-standing grudges, the grave may prevent them from being resolved. In psycho-therapy sessions, I often have to work with people who have profound resentments which they never expressed to their parents. The parents are now dead, but the resentments linger on and have to be worked out in therapy.

I think psychologist Rollo May understood the place of death in life when he wrote, "The confronting of death gives the most positive reality to life itself. It makes the individual existence real, absolute, and concrete. Death is the one fact of my life which is not relative but absolute, and my awareness of this gives my existence and what I do each hour an absolute quality."

People often ask me if working with the dying is a depressing experience. It can be a *sad* experience, especially with a person to whom I am particularly close. But on the positive side, working with the dying has increased my awareness of the brevity of life and the importance of living my life now and not postponing things until tomorrow.

As you allow yourself to experience a healthy increase in your own Personal Death Awareness, you too may find yourself reaching out for life with a new healthy zest.

Follow-Up

1. *Discuss your learnings from one or more of the PDA exercises explained by Worden and Proctor.*
2. *Discuss the way in which the subject of death was (is) dealt with in your family. Do you find that this is how you want to remain, or do you want to change certain aspects?*
3. *Explain why you agree or disagree with the thesis that increasing your PDA is helpful.*
4. *See Abe Arkoff's article "The Dying-Readiness/Freedom-to-Live Test" in this section. Also, see the "Evolution of a Person #2" Applied Activity at the end of this section.*

The Happiness Machine

Ray Bradbury

On Sunday morning Leo Auffmann moved slowly through his garage, expecting some wood, a curl of wire, a hammer or wrench to leap up crying, "Start here!" But nothing leaped, nothing cried for a beginning.

Should a Happiness Machine, he wondered, be something you can carry in your pocket?

Or, he went on, should it be something that carries you in *its* pocket?

"One thing I absolutely *know,*" he said aloud. "It should be *bright!*"

He set a can of orange paint in the center of the workbench, picked up a dictionary, and wandered into the house.

"Lena?" He glanced at the dictionary. "Are you 'pleased, contented, joyful, delighted'? Do you feel 'Lucky, fortunate'? Are things 'clever and fitting,' 'successful and suitable' for you?"

Lena stopped slicing vegetables and closed her eyes. "Read me the list again, please," she said.

He shut the book.

"What have I done, you got to stop and think an hour before you can tell me? All I ask is a simple yes or no! You're *not* contented, delighted, joyful?"

"Cows are contented, babies and old people in second childhood are delighted, God help them," she said. "As for 'joyful,' Leo? Look how I laugh scrubbing out the sink . . ."

He peered closely at her and his face relaxed. "Lena, it's true. A man doesn't appreciate. Next month, maybe, we'll get away."

"*I'm* not complaining!" she cried. "*I'm* not the one comes in with a list saying, 'Stick out your tongue.' Leo, do you ask what makes your heart beat all night? No! Next will you

ask, What's marriage? Who knows, Leo? Don't ask. A man who thinks like that, how it runs, how things work, falls off the trapeze in the circus, chokes wondering how the muscles work in the throat. Eat, sleep, breathe, Leo, and stop staring at me like I'm something new in the house!"

Lena Auffmann froze. She sniffed the air.

"Oh, my God, look what you done!"

She yanked the oven door open. A great cloud of smoke poured through the kitchen.

"Happiness!" she wailed. "And for the first time in six months we have a fight! Happiness, and for the first time in twenty years it's not bread, it's charcoal for supper!"

When the smoke cleared, Leo Auffmann was gone.

The fearful clangor, the collision of man and inspiration, the flinging about of metal, lumber, hammer, nails, T square, screwdriver, continued for many days. On occasion, defeated, Leo Auffmann loitered out through the streets, nervous, apprehensive, jerking his head at the slightest sound of distant laughter, listened to children's jokes, watching what made them smile. At night he sat on neighbors' crowded porches, listening to the old folks weigh and balance life, and at each explosion of merriment Leo Auffmann quickened like a general who has seen the forces of darkness routed and whose strategy has been reaffirmed. On his way home he felt triumphant until he was in his garage with the dead tools and the inanimate lumber. Then his bright face fell away in a pale funk, and to cover his sense of failure he banged and crashed the parts of his machine about as if they really did make sense. At last it began to shape itself and at the end of the ten days and nights, trembling with fatigue, self-dedicated, half starved, fumbling and looking as if he had been riven by lightning, Leo Auffmann wandered into his house.

The children, who had been screaming horribly at each other, fell silent, as if the Red Death had entered at the chiming of the clock.

"The Happiness Machine," husked Leo Auffmann, "is ready."

"Leo Auffmann," said his wife, "has lost fifteen pounds. He hasn't talked to his children in two weeks, they are nervous, they fight, listen! His wife is nervous, she's gained ten pounds, she'll need new clothes, look! Sure—the machine is ready. But happy? Who can say? Leo, leave off with the clock you're building. You'll never find a cuckoo big enough to go in it! Man was not made to tamper with such things. It's not against God, no, but it sure looks like it's against Leo Auffmann. Another week of this and we'll bury him in his machine!"

But Leo Auffmann was too busy noticing that the room was falling swiftly up.

How interesting, he thought, lying on the floor.

Darkness closed in a great wink on him as someone screamed something about that Happiness Machine, three times.

The first thing he noticed the next morning was dozens of birds fluttering around in the air stirring up ripples like colored stones thrown into an incredibly clear stream, gonging the tin roof of the garage softly.

A pack of multibred dogs pawfooted one by one into the yard to peer and whine gently through the garage door; four boys, two girls, and some men hesitated in the driveway and then edged along under the cherry trees.

Leo Auffmann, listening, knew what it was that had reached out and called them all into the yard.

The sound of the Happiness Machine.

It was the sort of sound that might be heard coming from a giant's kitchen on a summer day. There were all finds of hummings, low and high, steady and then changing. Incredible foods were being baked there by a host of whirring golden bees as big as teacups. The giantess herself, humming contentedly under her breath, might glide to the door, as vast as all summer, her face a huge peach-colored moon gazing calmly out upon smiling dogs, corn-haired boys and flour-haired old men.

"Wait," said Leo Auffmann out loud. "I didn't turn the machine on this morning! Saul!"

Saul standing in the yard below, looked up.

"Saul, did you turn it on?"

"You told me to warm it up half an hour ago!"

"All right, Saul, I forgot. I'm not awake." He fell back in bed.

His wife, bringing his breakfast up, paused by the window, looking down at the garage.

"Tell me," she said quietly. "If that machine is like you say, has it got an answer to making babies in it somewhere? Can that machine make seventy-year-old people twenty? Also, how does death look when you hide in there with all that happiness?"

"Hide!"

"If you died from overwork, what should I do today, climb in that big box down there and be happy? Also tell me, Leo, how is our life? You know how our house is. Seven in the morning, breakfast, the kids; all of you gone by eight-thirty and it's just me and washing and me and cooking and socks to be darned, weeds to be dug, or I run to the store or polish silver. Who's complaining? I'm just reminding you how the house is put together, Leo, what's in it! So now answer: How do you get all those things I said in one machine?"

"That's not how it's built!"

"I'm sorry. I got no time to look, then."

And she kissed his cheek and went from the room and he lay smelling the wind that blew from the hidden machine below, rich with the odor of those roasted chestnuts that sold in the autumn streets of a Paris he had never known. . . .

A cat moved unseen among the hypnotized dogs and boys to purr against the garage door, in the sound of snow-waves crumbling down a faraway and rhythmically breathing shore.

Tomorrow, thought Leo Auffmann, we'll try the machine, all of us, together.

Late that night he awoke and knew something had wakened him. Far away in another room he heard someone crying.

"Saul?" he whispered, getting out of bed.

In his room Saul wept, his head buried in his pillow. "No . . . no . . ." he sobbed. "Over . . . over . . ."

"Saul, you had a nightmare? Tell me about it, son."

But the boy only wept.

And sitting there on the boy's bed, Leo Auffmann suddenly thought to look out the window. Below, the garage doors stood open.

He felt the hairs rise along the back of his neck.

When Saul slept again, uneasily, whimpering, his father went downstairs and out to the garage where, not breathing, he put his hand out.

In the cool night the Happiness Machine's metal was too hot to touch.

So, he thought, Saul was here tonight.

Why? Was Saul unhappy, in need of the machine? No, happy, but wanting to hold onto happiness always. Could you blame a boy wise enough to know his position who tried to keep it that way? No! And yet . . .

Above, quite suddenly, something white was exhaled from Saul's window. Leo Auffmann's heart thundered. Then he realized the window curtain had blown out into the open night. But it had seemed as intimate and shimmering a thing as a boy's soul escaping his room. And Leo Auffmann had flung up his hands as if to thwart it, push it back into the sleeping house.

Cold, shivering, he moved back into the house and up to Saul's room where he seized the blowing curtain in and locked the window tight so the pale thing could not escape again. Then he sat on the bed and put his hand on Saul's back.

"*A Tale of Two Cities?* Mine. *The Old Curiosity Shop?* Ha, that's Leo Auffmann's all right! *Great Expectations?* That *used* to be mine. But let *Great Expectations* be his, now!"

"What's this?" asked Leo Auffmann, entering.

"This," said his wife, "is sorting out the community property! When a father scares his son at night it's time to chop everything in half! Out of the way, Mr. Bleak House, Old Curiosity Shop. In all these books, no mad scientist lives like Leo Auffmann, none!"

"You're leaving, and you haven't even tried the machine!" he protested. "Try it on, you'll unpack, you'll stay!"

"*Tom Swift and His Electric Annihilator*—whose is that?" she asked. "Must I *guess?*"

Snorting, she gave *Tom Swift* to Leo Auffmann.

Very late in the day all the books, dishes, clothes, linens had been stacked one here, one there, four here, four there, ten here, ten there. Lena Auffmann, dizzy with counting, had to sit down. "All right," she gasped. "Before I go, Leo, prove you don't give nightmares to innocent sons!"

Silently Leo Auffmann led his wife into the twilight. She stood before the eight-foot-tall, orange-colored box.

"That's *happiness?*" she said. "Which button do I press to be overjoyed, grateful, contented, and much-obliged?"

The children had gathered now.

"Mama," said Saul, "don't!"

"I got to know what I'm yelling about, Saul." She got in the machine, sat down, and looked out at her husband, shaking her head. "It's not me needs this, it's you, a nervous wreck, shouting."

"Please," he said, "you'll see!"

He shut the door.

"Press the button!" he shouted in at his unseen wife.

There was a click. The machine shivered quietly, like a huge dog dreaming in its sleep.

"Papa!" said Saul, worried.

"Listen!" said Leo Auffmann.

At first there was nothing but the tremor of the machine's own secretly moving cogs and wheels.

"Is Mama all right?" asked Naomi.

"All right, she's fine! There, now . . . there!"

And inside the machine Lena Auffmann could be heard saying, "Oh!" and then again, "Ah!" in a startled voice. "Look at that!" said his hidden wife. "Paris!" and later, "London! There goes Rome! The Pyramids! The Sphinx!"

"The Sphinx, you hear, children?" Leo Auffmann whispered and laughed.

"Perfume!" cried Lena Auffmann, surprised.

Somewhere a phonograph played "The Blue Danube" faintly.

"Music! I'm dancing!"

"Only *thinks* she's dancing," the father confided to the world.

"Amazing!" said the unseen woman.

Leo Auffmann blushed. "What an understanding wife."

And then inside the Happiness Machine, Lena Auffmann began to weep.

The inventor's smile faded.

"She's crying," said Naomi.

"She can't be!"

"She is," said Saul.

"She simply can't be crying!" Leo Auffmann, blinking, pressed his ear to the machine. "But . . . yes . . . like a baby . . ."

He could only open the door.

"Wait." There his wife sat, tears rolling down her cheeks. "Let me finish." She cried some more.

Leo Auffmann turned off the machine, stunned.

"Oh, it's the saddest thing in the world!" she wailed. "I feel awful, terrible." She

climbed out through the door. "First, there was Paris . . ."

"What's wrong with Paris?"

"I never even *thought* of being in Paris in my life. But now you got me thinking: Paris! So suddenly I want to be in Paris and now I'm not!"

"It's almost as good, this machine."

"No. Sitting in there, I knew. I thought, it's not real!"

"Stop crying, Mama."

She looked at him with great dark wet eyes. "You had me dancing. We haven't danced in twenty years."

"I'll take you dancing tomorrow night!"

"No, no! It's not important, it *shouldn't* be important. But your machine says it's important! So I believe! It'll be all right, Leo, after I cry some more."

"What else?"

"What else? The machine says, 'You're young.' I'm not. It lies, that Sadness Machine!"

"Sad in what way?"

His wife was quieter now. "Leo, the mistake you made is you forgot some hour, some day, we all got to climb out of that thing and go back to dirty dishes and the beds not made. While you're in that thing, sure, a sunset lasts forever almost, the air smells good, the temperature is fine. All the things you want to last, last. But outside, the children wait on lunch, the clothes need buttons. And then let's be frank, Leo, how long can you *look* at a sunset? Who *wants* a sunset to last? Who wants perfect temperature? Who wants air smelling good always? So after awhile, who would notice? Better, for a minute or two, a sunset. After that, let's have something else. People are like that, Leo. How could you forget?"

"Did I?"

"Sunsets we always liked because they only happen once and go away."

"But Lena, that's sad."

"No, if the sunset stayed and we got bored, that would be a real sadness. So two things you did you should never have. You made quick things go slow and stay around. You brought things faraway to our backyard where they don't belong, where they just tell you, 'No, you'll never travel, Lena Auffmann, Paris you'll never see! Rome you'll *never* visit.' But I *always* knew that, so why tell me? Better to forget and make do, Leo, make do, eh?"

Leo Auffmann leaned against the machine for support. He snatched his burned hand away, surprised.

"So now what, Lena?" he said.

"It's not for me to say. I know only so long as this thing is here I'll want to come out, or Saul will want to come out like he did last night, and against our judgment sit in it and look at all those places so far away and every time we will cry and be no fit family for you."

"I don't understand," he said, "how I could be so wrong. Just let me check to see what you say is true." He sat down inside the machine. "You won't go away?"

His wife nodded. "We'll wait, Leo."

He shut the door. In the warm darkness he hesitated, pressed the button, and was just relaxing back in color and music, when he heard someone screaming.

"Fire, Papa! The machine's on fire!"

Someone hammered the door. He leaped up, bumped his head, and fell as the door gave way and the boys dragged him out. Behind him he heard a muffled explosion. The entire family was running now. Leo Auffmann turned and gasped, "Saul, call the fire department!"

Lena Auffmann caught Saul as he ran. "Saul," she said. "Wait."

There was a gush of flame, another muffled explosion. When the machine was burning very well indeed, Lena Auffmann nodded.

"All right, Saul," she said. "Run call the fire department."

Everybody who was anybody came to the fire. There was Grandpa Spaulding and Douglas and Tom and most of the boarders and some of the old men from across the ravine and all the children from six blocks around. And Leo Auffmann's children stood out front, proud of how fine the flames looked jumping from the garage roof.

Grandfather Spaulding studied the smoke ball in the sky and said, quietly, "Leo, was that it? Your Happiness Machine?"

"Some year," said Leo Auffmann, "I'll figure it and tell you."

Lena Auffmann, standing in the dark now, watched as the firemen ran in and out of the yard; the garage, roaring, settled upon itself.

"Leo," she said, "it won't take a year to figure. Look around. Think. Keep quiet a little bit. Then come tell me. I'll be in the house, putting books back on shelves, and clothes back in closets, fixing supper, supper's late, look how dark. Come, children, help Mama."

When the firemen and the neighbors were gone, Leo Auffmann was left with Grandfather Spaulding and Douglas and Tom, brooding over the smoldering ruin. He stirred his foot in the wet ashes and slowly said what he had to say.

"The first thing you learn in life is you're a fool. The last thing you learn in life is you're the same fool. In one hour, I've done a lot of thinking. I thought, Leo Auffmann is blind! . . . You want to see the *real* Happiness Machine? The one they patented a couple thousand years ago, it still runs, not good all the time, no! but it runs. It's been here all along."

"But the fire—" said Douglas.

"Sure, the fire, the garage! But like Lena said, it don't take a year to figure; what burned in the garage don't count!"

They followed him up the front-porch steps.

"Here," whispered Leo Auffmann, "the front window. Quiet, and you'll see it."

Hesitantly, Grandfather, Douglas, and Tom peered through the large windowpane.

And there, in small warm pools of lamplight, you could see what Leo Auffmann wanted you to see. There sat Saul and Marshall, playing chess at the coffee table. In the dining room Rebecca was laying out the silver. Naomi was cutting paper-doll dresses. Ruth was painting water colors. Joseph was running his electric train. Through the kitchen door, Lena Auffmann was sliding a pot roast from the steaming oven. Every hand, every head, every mouth made a big or little motion. You could hear their faraway voices under glass. You could hear someone singing in a high sweet voice. You could smell bread baking, too, and you knew it was real bread that would soon be covered with real butter. Everything was there and it was working.

Grandfather, Douglas, and Tom turned to look at Leo Auffmann, who gazed serenely through the window, the pink light on his cheeks.

"Sure," he murmured. "There it is." And he watched with now-gentle sorrow and now-quick delight, and at last quiet acceptance as all the bits and pieces of this house mixed, stirred, settled, poised, and ran steadily again. "The Happiness Machine," he said. "The Happiness Machine."

A moment later he was gone.

Inside, Grandfather, Douglas, and Tom saw him tinkering, make a minor adjustment here, eliminate friction there, busy among all those warm, wonderful, infinitely delicate, forever mysterious, and ever-moving parts.

Then smiling, they went down the steps into the fresh summer night.

Follow-Up

1. *Written over 40 years ago, Bradbury's* The Happiness Machine *foreshadows contemporary virtual reality technology. Many thinkers have warned if you "seek happiness for its own sake, you will not find it" (Tyron Edwards). Have your attempts to directly find happiness also been unsuccessful? Try to find the underlying reasons for when you feel happiness, and why.*

2. *Leo Auffmann was driven to build his machine even though it created large problems between him and those closest to him. Have you ever been so driven that similar results occurred? If yes, describe the reasons why, the effects, and whether you will do that again.*

3. *The story implies that happiness is meant to be shortlived, that permanently happy conditions would eventually get boring, and that one's Happiness Machine is essentially where you are and those most important to you. Write about or discuss your reactions to these points.*

4. *Select any other aspect of the story to write about or discuss.*

Silicon Snake Oil

Clifford Stoll

Me, an Internet addict? Hey—I'm leading a full life, with family, friends, and a job. Computers are a sideline, not my life.

Jupiter is rising in the east, looking down on the Connecticut farm where I'm vacationing. On one side, a forest; on the other, a cornfield. Three guys are talking about the Knicks in the next room; in the kitchen, several women are buttering popcorn. One of them just called my name. But I don't care.

Fingers on the keyboard, I'm bathed in the cold glow of my cathode-ray cube, answering e-mail. While one guy's checking the sky through binoculars, and another's stuffing himself with popcorn, I'm tapping out a letter to a stranger across the continent. My attention's directed to the Internet.

Tonight, twenty letters want replies, three people have invited me to chat over the network, there's a dozen newsgroups to read, and a volley of files to download. How can I keep up?

I see my reflection in the screen and a chill runs down my spine. Even on vacation, I can't escape the computer networks.

I take a deep breath and pull the plug.

For fifteen years, I've been online, watching as thousands of computers joined hands to form a ubiquitous global network. At first, the nascent Arpanet seemed like an academic toy, a novelty to connect inanimate computers across the continent. Later, this plaything began supplying electronic mail and an occasional data file from other astronomers.

As the Arpanet grew into the Internet, I began to depend on e-mail to keep up with colleagues and friends. The Usenet brought news from around the continent. It became a whole new way to communicate.

Then, in 1986, while managing a computer system in Berkeley, I stumbled on a group of hackers breaking into computers. No ordinary cyberpunks, these: they sold their discoveries to the Soviet KGB.

It took a year to chase them down. During that time, I realized that our networks aren't simple connections of cables and computers; they're cooperative communities.

Since then, the Internet has become a most inviting and intriguing neighborhood. E-mail and chat lines keep me in touch with friends around the world; data transfers let me exchange information with colleagues. I join in discussions over the Usenet, posting queries and answering questions. One click of the mouse and I can read the daily news or a monthly report. At once it's fun and challenging.

But what a price! Simply keeping track of this electronic neighborhood takes a couple of hours every night. I find myself pawing through Internet archives or searching for novelties over the World Wide Web. I spend still more time downloading files and following newsgroups. Bit by bit, my days dribble away, trickling out my modem.

But for all this communication, little of the information is genuinely useful. The computer gets my full attention, yet either because of content or format, the network doesn't seem to satisfy.

I can't turn my back on the network. Or can I? Right now, I'm scratching my head, wondering.

Perhaps our networked world isn't a universal doorway to freedom. Might it be a distraction from reality? An ostrich hole to divert our attention and resources from social problems? A misuse of technology that encourages passive rather than active participation? I'm starting to ask questions like this, and I'm not the first.

And so I'm writing this free-form meditation out of a sense of perplexity. Computers themselves don't bother me, it's the culture in which they're enshrined.

What follows, I suppose, shows my increasing ambivalence toward this most trendy community. As the networks evolve, so do opinions toward them, and my divergent feelings bring out conflicting points of view. In advance, I apologize to those who expect a consistent position from me. I'm still rearranging my mental furniture.

I suspect I'll disappoint science-fiction romantics as well. Nobody can offer utopia-on-a-stick, the glowing virtual community that enhances our world through discovery and close ties while transcending the coarseness of human nature.

Oh, I care about what happens to our networked neighborhood. However, I care more about—and am affected more by—what's happening in our larger society. So do parents, professors, teachers, librarians, and, yes, even politicians.

When I put on my cone-shaped thinking cap, I wonder what I would have said fifty years ago, when the interstate highway system was first proposed. Plenty of people favored it: truckers, farmers, and shippers wanted to break the railroad monopoly. Political subdivisions, car makers, and construction unions knew it would generate money. Politicians from every state felt highways were universally good things.

Who spoke out against the superhighway system? I don't remember anyone saying, "Hey, these beltways will destroy our cities. They'll pave over pristine lands and give us hour-long commutes. They'll change our society from one of neighborhoods to that of suburbs."

In advance, then, here are my strong reservations about the wave of computer networks.

They isolate us from one another and cheapen the meaning of actual experience. They work against literacy and creativity. They will undercut our schools and libraries.

Forgive me. I don't want to pontificate. But I do want people to think about the decisions they're making. It'd be fun to write about the wonderful times I've had online and the terrific people I've met through my modem, but here I'm waving a flag. A yellow flag that says, "You're entering a nonexistent universe. Consider the consequences."

It's an unreal universe, a soluble tissue of nothingness. While the Internet beckons brightly, seductively flashing an icon of knowledge-as-power, this nonplace lures us to surrender our time on earth. A poor substitute it is, this virtual reality where frustration is legion and where—in the holy names of Education and Progress—important aspects of human interactions are relentlessly devalued.

End of philippic. I don't mean to lay down an unwelcome mat. Nor do I feel that I'm entitled to technogoodies and others aren't. Quite the contrary: I look forward to the time when our Internet reaches into every town and trailer park. But the medium is being oversold, our expectations have become bloated, and there's damned little critical discussion of the implications of an online world.

The popular mythos tells us that networks are powerful, global, fast, and inexpensive. It's the place to meet friends and carry on business. There, you'll find entertainment, expertise, and education. In short, it's important to be online.

It ain't necessarily so.

Our networks can be frustrating, expensive, unreliable connections that get in the way of useful work. It is an overpromoted, hollow world, devoid of warmth and human kindness.

The heavily promoted information infrastructure addresses few social needs or business concerns. At the same time, it directly threatens precious parts of our society, including schools, libraries, institutions.

No birds sing.

For all the promises of virtual communities, it's more important to live a real life in a real neighborhood.

I began this meditation with a perplexed ambivalence toward computers, networks, and the culture that enshrines them.

At first, I wanted to think about technical issues. But I found myself returning to the same themes: real life and authentic experience mean much more than anything the modem can deliver. The culture of information isn't knowledge. Electronic networks erode important parts of our community.

Computer networks, like cars and televisions, confer a most seductive freedom, the "freedom to." As I step back from the insistent messages beckoning from across my computer, I'm beginning to wonder about a different kind of freedom—call it a "freedom from."

Certainly, few will toss out their computers or back away from their keyboards. Our networks are far too useful, and there's so much available over the modem.

Oh?

It's late on an October evening in Oakland; I smell popcorn in the kitchen.

I'm done meditating.

Follow-Up

1. *Stoll is one of the most famous and skilled computer experts in the United States. He now sees the computer and Internet as both a help and a hindrance. Choose one or more of these statements and offer your views:*
   - *Real life and authentic experience mean much more than anything the modem can deliver.*
   - *Simply keeping track of this electronic neighborhood takes a couple of hours every night.*
   - *Perhaps our networked world isn't a universal doorway to freedom. Might it be a distraction from reality? A diversion from social problems? A misuse . . . that encourages passive rather than active participation?*
2. *How does the "electronic neighborhood" influence (positively and negatively) the way you live?*

Ten Symptoms
of Computer Addiction

James Fearing

1. A demonstrated "loss of control" when trying to stop or limit the amount of time on the computer. (Breaking promises to self or others. Promising to quit or cut down and not being able to do so.)
2. Being dishonest or minimizing the extent of the time you stay on the computer, or covering up or being dishonest about what activities you participate in when on the computer.
3. Negative consequences experienced by the computer user or his/her friends or family as a direct result of time or activities spent on the computer.
4. Participation in high risk or normally unacceptable behaviors when using the computer. Compromising your morals and values based on the opportunity to remain anonymous and protected on the computer. (A good test for this is to ask yourself if your spouse, partner, or family would approve of what you were doing on the computer.)
5. An overdeveloped sense of importance for the computer in your life. Defending your right to use the computer as much as desired, regardless of the fact that people in your life are feeling left out and neglected. (Denial of the problem and justification; not being able to hear or feel what the other people are saying regarding your computer behavior.)
6. Mixed feelings of euphoria (a "rush"), combined with feelings of guilt, brought on by either the inordinate amount of time spent on the computer or the abnormal behavior acted out while using the computer.
7. Feelings of depression or anxiety when something or someone shortens your time or interrupts your plans to use the computer.
8. Preoccupation with the computer and computer activities when you are not using the computer. (Thinking about the computer and its activities when doing something else; i.e., having a family dinner, working on project deadline, etc.)
9. Finding yourself using the computer at times when you are feeling uncomfortable, irritated, or sad about something happening in your life. (Feeling uncomfortable in your relationship, so you will self-medicate and "hide out" on the computer.) Using time on the computer to become externally focused as a way to avoid facing what is

happening in your life and avoid feeling the appropriate feelings inside yourself (self-medicating).

10. Experiencing financial concerns or problems in your life as a result of money being spent on computer hardware, computer on-line charges, or any other costs associated with computers.

After honestly answering, if you said yes to one question you *may* have a problem with computer addiction. If you said yes to two questions, there is a *good chance you do* have a problem with computer addiction. If you answered yes to three or more, you are demonstrating a pattern of behavior which would suggest that *you are addicted to your computer* and/or the activities you participate in when you are using it. If you are experiencing problems in this area of your life, it is important for you to contact a psychotherapist in your area who has experience in working with addictive behaviors. A safe place to start would be to have an assessment done to help you and your therapist gain insight into what's happening in this area of your life. Based on this evaluation, the appropriate plan can be formulated for help in your specific situation.

Editor's Note: For further information on this topic, visit http://www.uslink/ -ncis/ or email the author: ncis@uslink.net

Who Will Play Your Music?

Michael Jones

Although I spent long periods of time playing my own music, I was uncomfortable performing for others, with the exception of close friends. Instead, I did covers of other people's music and relied upon these arrangements when I played in public.

It was one of these arrangements I was exploring while sitting at a piano in a hotel lobby one quiet evening. I had been at the hotel for several days, leading a management seminar. We had given ourselves the night off. Now, I sat for a time, lost in my musings. The building around me appeared to be so quiet and empty that I even felt free to let some of my own music weave in and out of these musical conversations.

It wasn't *that* empty, however. Soon an old man walked unsteadily out of the nearby lounge and plopped himself into a big easy chair beside the piano. There, he slowly sipped his wine and watched me play. I felt distracted and uneasy, trapped on the bench, where any moment he might request one of his favorite tunes, one I most likely did not know how to play.

"What's that?" he asked when I was done.

"Oh, a little bit of 'Moon River,'" I replied.

"Yeah, I recognized that," he said. "But there was something else before it, what was that?"

"That was some of my own music," I replied. "I don't have a name for it yet."

"You should," he said. "It deserves one." He looked thoughtful for a moment, then he said, "Your music is beautiful, but you're wasting your time with that other stuff."

His comment dropped into my lap so quickly I wasn't sure I fully understood what I'd just heard.

"What do you mean?" I asked.

"It's *your* music that brought me out here."

"But . . ." I said, cutting him off. "It's the other music that people want to hear."

"Not when they hear this," he replied. "Please, play some more." Then he closed his eyes and sat back in his chair.

When I am being deeply heard, playing my music feels less like a performance and more like an intimate act of love. I become more conscious of being carried along by a current of feelings, and following these feelings becomes more important than holding to the accuracy of the notes. Perhaps it is when we are in the company of another, particularly one whose appreciation for our work knows no bounds, that this love is most likely to be found.

When I finished playing, he and I sat together quietly for a long time. Slowly, he opened his eyes and sipped again from his glass.

"What are you doing with your music?" he asked.

"Nothing," I said. "It's just something I do for myself."

"Is that *all?*" he replied, surprised by my words.

Then I explained briefly what had brought me to the hotel.

"But how many others can do this consulting work?" he asked.

'Oh, perhaps twenty or thirty," I said, adding quickly, "but I don't want to give it up; my mission through this work is to change the world."

"I'm sure it is," he said. He seemed unmoved by the forced conviction of my words. Then he set his wineglass down on the table and looked directly at me.

"But who will play your music if you don't do it yourself?"

"It's nothing special," I protested.

"No," he agreed. "But it's you, and the world will be poorer without it."

I was about to offer other excuses when, with fire in his eyes and a voice sober and clear, he said, "This is your gift—don't waste it."

With that, he stood up, steadied himself by resting his hand on my shoulder for a moment, raised his glass in a silent toast, and then weaved slowly back to the lounge.

I sat frozen on the bench. Who will play my music? I asked myself over and over again. An hour or so passed, but I was still in shock. In his memoirs, Chilean poet Pablo Neruda speaks of how people who have lived unfulfilling lives sometimes complain that no one gave them any advice. No one warned them in advance that they were off course. But this was no longer true for me—I had just been warned.

Later, I went in search of this man, to insist that he tell me more. But he was gone, and a part of me suspected that perhaps he had never been there. If I had not heard his advice on the bench that evening, something else might have happened—a dream, perhaps, or an accident—to get my attention. For some people, it is the ending of a relationship or the onset of an unexpected illness—something comes along that brings our lives up short. What we had always thought secure suddenly becomes finite. In that moment, the larger universe, of which we have always been a part but often ignored, has our full attention. Its presence can be as dramatic and frightening as a raging storm at sea or as gentle as the intimate act of kissing the princess awake. It knows how to find the weak point, the undefended part where we are most likely to yield. This one wake-up call is enough to set us on a path. Following this path as it spirals inward and outward, and honoring it, even though the purpose of it and the final re-

sult may remain unclear, becomes our new work. "The truth dazzles gradually," as Emily Dickinson says, "or else the world would go blind."

Often, I imagined that my true vocation was to be a painter, or a poet, or something else equally remote or extraordinary. When friends asked about the music, I was emphatic in my reply. "No," I would say. "This is something *special*." But there is no mystery to the work that is ours to do. Although it may appear to be some attribute situated in the heavens somewhere, it is often found in the familiar and ordinary and located close at hand. Indeed, it is the idea that it should be special and extraordinary, that it is something out there—remote, elusive, and difficult to do—that throws us off track.

What is ours to do comes so easily, because from the very beginning it has always been there. It may not necessarily be a special talent like writing or music; it may instead be a quality of caring that we offer, a capacity for listening deeply to others, or simply the wonder and beauty we bring to the world through how we give our attention to a piece of music, a flower, or a tree. Our purpose is to give ourselves to the world around us—including people, musical instruments, trees, and words—and through the attention we bring to them help them blaze to life. When we offer ourselves to the world, the world gives itself back to us. In the words of D. H. Lawrence, "Life rushes in."

What is it that we desire to do that brings an increase to life? This often offers a clue as to where our gifts are to be found. Beneath the long list of things we *must* do is a deeper purpose, one that involves being present with ourselves and, in so doing, bringing some aspect of the world to life. But we cannot do it alone, for the recognition of who we truly are is most often found through the other. "The mystery of creation was always between two," Laurens van der Post writes, "in an awareness that there was always both a 'thou' and an 'I.'"

We all need at least one other person to recognize this spark in ourselves, to make us the one we were meant to be. For me, it was that man in the lobby of the hotel.

Who is it that offers the act of confirmation in your life, the one willing to hold the match to light the fire to set your gift to the world ablaze? And who, or what, does your gift serve? As Laurens van der Post says, "most of us indeed have become distorted into knowing only the 'I' of ourselves and not the 'thou.'" Yet, once ignited, the flame that burns within us does so with such intensity that we would go blind if we looked upon ourselves directly. Our "thou" is seen through the actions of others in relation to us; they are the moons that reflect back to us the intensity of our sun.

When I said yes to that moment, I was re-learning how to say yes to the pleasure I knew the music would bring. But I was also opening myself to the fulfillment of larger intentions, ones that were not entirely my own. I trembled at the thought. Sometimes others have already tried to set our lives ablaze, and we have not accepted the match. We know that once the genie is out of the bottle, our lives will never be quite the same. There is burning that takes place, burning that has the power to transform to ashes old, limiting beliefs and everything else that we hold to be true. Nothing is exempt; everything may change, including even the smallest of acts.

I could neither push forward nor go back. When we reach this step in our creative life, we are often asked to go beyond our skills, to do the opposite of what has gone before. If we have been unfocused, it's time to focus; if we have been driven, as I had been from time to time, it's time for space. Nourish the longing, Kabir says to us, for it is the intensity of the longing that does all the work.

Yet we cannot be casual about this step, either. To turn our attention from our longing, even for a moment, may be one moment too long.

How many of us have turned away from living an imaginative life? How many of us would rather sacrifice ourselves to the security of institutional life than engage with the volatility of a soulful one? What is it that so often compels us to turn away from our longing rather than into it? Perhaps the dream seems so distant from the reality we live with day to day that we simply don't know where to begin or how to find a convenient time to start. There is also an awkwardness in our initial attempts to put ourselves into our art. We can feel unsure and self-conscious—quick to judge our progress and ready to admit defeat in the presence of those who say what we are doing is silly or frivolous, or through the constant pesterings of our own self-doubt.

When we take these first tender and delicate steps into our own imaginative life, we often need a bold and fiery image, one large

"Trumpet"

and intense enough to make it a part of ourselves until our own small, gentle fire is strong enough to burn on its own.

The encounter with the old man had encouraged my return to music, but it offered something more. Being at the piano had opened a pathway in which I could feel once again the tenderness that lay deep within my heart. And as my heart opened, it, in turn, offered an invitation to a wedding—a marriage between the ambitions of my intellect and the yearning for a deeper truth that was emerging within my soul. I was learning to love the other half of my self.

Could I, like Beethoven, hold a vision large enough to fill the entire span of my life? Could I say yes to it all despite the setbacks and confusion and self-doubt? Could I not only accept but embrace the uncertainty, not only tolerate but engage the ambiguity? Could I step forward and meet the suffering, the bliss, and the frustration? Could I willingly receive the future with a humble and prayerful acceptance and say, as philosopher Rudolph Steiner once said, that "whatever the next hour or day may bring, I cannot change it by fear or anxiety, for it is not yet known"? The terrors I feel may simply be shadow images from a more limiting past, not predictors of times to come.

When I left consulting to begin sitting at the piano again, I believed that I played poorly. And I had little experience with writing when I later took time from music to begin working on this book. Perhaps this is what life asks of us—to step faithfully into that very place in our lives where we can no longer fall back on our cleverness or wits. To serve the impulse to create is to accept that it may ask everything from us and offer little assurance in return. Moses guided his people into the Red Sea on faith; they were apparently up to their necks before the sea finally parted. Perhaps it is only when we have emptied ourselves of all guarantees that life finds us.

As I experienced their joining together, I was saddened by the years that had been lost, the times I had willfully struggled to try to get everything right when I didn't know what right was. They were times of planting seeds and then impatiently digging them up to see if they had grown, of trying to figure out what others wanted from me instead of asking what I most wanted for myself, of feeling the fear of not knowing where this was all going to lead, of believing that I needed to rely upon the individualistic and achieving parts of my nature to do all of the work, because I did not believe in asking for help.

Learning to trust that these terrifying leaps of faith are in fact *of* life and not *against* it came slowly for me. And I am grateful now for knowing that perhaps it is when we feel truly lost, groping our way somewhere between the in breath and the out breath that the gods are most near.

How do we discover in words the same depth of truth and inspiration that flows from our hands when we paint or our dancing when our feet touch the floor? Is it possible to suspend our schedules and routines to experiment with the deeper insights that can emerge when we are free to bring our different voices forward without fear of embarrassment or concern? Can we share our most deeply held beliefs with the possibility that behind them lies an even greater truth, one which, once revealed, might allow us to live in a more imaginative and peaceful world?

When I set aside my consulting practice to return to music, I could not foresee where it would lead. But over time, the painful uncertainties have evolved into a wonderful dance that elegantly weaves together all of the various significant but seemingly separate strands of my life. Finding the marriage between my intellect and my soul could not have been planned, at least not by me. It would have been too complex and perhaps too terrifying for my strategic mind to grasp. But perhaps, just as Wagner spoke of Beethoven's spontaneous and deeply felt performances as being "child's play" for him, creating our lives so that they are a reflection of what we love is child's play for the heart.

So now when I join these groups, I don't bring charts and theories and projectors as I did before. Instead, I simply bring myself and a nine-foot-six-inch concert grand. And as we form into a circle, I'm careful to save a place beside the piano for the old man from the lobby of the hotel.

Editor's Note: Michael Jones, pianist and composer, is a founding artist of Narada Productions and has released ten recordings. He is also an organizational consultant with DIA Logos in Cambridge, MA.

Follow-Up

1. *Choose one or more of these statements and apply them to your life:*
   - *There is no mystery to the work that is ours to do . . . because from the very beginning it has always been there.*
   - *Our purpose is to give ourselves to the world around us—including people, musical instruments, trees, and words. . . . When we offer ourselves to the world, the world gives itself back to us. . . . What is it that we desire to do that brings an increase to life?*
   - *Perhaps this is what life asks of us—to step faithfully into that very place in our lives where we can no longer fall back on our cleverness or wits. . . . Perhaps it is only when we have emptied ourselves of all guarantees that life finds us.*
2. *Jones states that we all need at least one other person to recognize our gifts, our life work. Comment on this idea and explain if it is true for your life.*
3. *Select any other idea(s) from the article and write about and/or discuss your reactions.*
4. *Who will play your music?*

Applied Activities for Section Six

THE SOMEDAY LIST

Between now and your death there are (and will be) many things you hope to experience and accomplish. Listing some of these often reveals some themes that can be helpful as you seek to understand your life. Below is a technique for finding these themes:

1. List at least twenty things you would like to experience or accomplish before you die that you have not started or completed at this time. Note that an accomplishment is a goal-oriented effort while an experience refers to just being there (letting something happen). Here are a few examples to clarify the difference:

   Accomplishments—earning a degree, writing an article/book, mastering a skill, building something, changing a habit.

   Experiences—attending a concert or art exhibit, having a child or grandchild, feeling inner harmony, standing on a mountain top, riding in a hot air balloon.

   It may be difficult to complete this list at one sitting. Do as many as you can in a free-associating manner. No one will see your list. Include "unrealistic" items as well as expected ones. Include fantasies and dreams. Leave this task for awhile or even a few days and go back to it. Try to list items from several categories of life.

2. Analysis and interpretation suggestions:
   (a) Identify common themes (patterns or clusters) among your listed items. For example, you may have a few items with the theme of physical challenge and excitement, or creativity, or family/interpersonal relationships, or professional goals, or inner states of being, and so on. In a list of twenty-five items, there are usually four or five themes. Some individual items may fit under more than one theme. Once you have identified the themes, label them.
   (b) Think of your themes as *unmet needs* that are present *now* (instead of the future). Do you think this list would be the same as one written five years ago? Why or why not?
   (c) When will you begin to do these things on your list? Some will, realistically, have to be started later. Others, though, can be started now. Beware of the "wait-until" illusion. People keep putting off desired life actions until certain conditions occur—but they may never occur just by waiting. The most common wait-until conditions are time and money. "I'll be able to X when I finish school." Five years later: "When I don't have so many demands at work," or "When the kids are grown." This can continue until

the wait-until becomes a wish-I-had . . . ," or "if-only. . . ." If an item has existed for a few years, it probably falls under the wait-until illusion.

Consider items with short time frames. Physical challenges such as high-level athletics or performance dancing have short lifespans. Many items are very difficult to do with family responsibilities. In short, pay close attention to valuable experiences that have small windows of opportunity.

(d) *Activate your themes* in some manner. Remember that the themes act as unmet needs that call for some attention. Choose one or two themes that seem to shout the loudest. If the actual items under the theme are not truly feasible, think of a substitute activity that fulfills the spirit of this theme. For example, if you cannot begin a book, start a chapter or even a short story. If you cannot travel to Europe with a loved one for two months now, plan a nice escape weekend in a location you both like. Any theme can be activated by creating similar, substitute activities.

(e) Try at least one activity per theme over the next month.

3. Discuss your Things To Do list and themes in small groups and/or with the whole class. Write about your themes, possible wait-until traps, and your attempts to activate the themes.

For further reading on this activity and additional ideas, see *Strategies for Experiential Learning: Book Two* (1981) by Louis Thayer (Ed.), published by LT Resources, 8594 Sleepy Hollow Dr., Saline, MI 48176.

TALKING TO WISE PERSONS

A wise person has deep knowledge and understanding and is capable of profound insight and judgment. A wise person may or may not be a highly educated person in the traditional sense. A wise person is one from whom we seek some guidance that will aid us in moments when wisdom is needed. There are many ways in which we can hear from those who are wise. One of these ways is described below. All that is required is a willingness to hear what these wise persons have to say to you.

1. Think of three persons who have the qualities of wise persons as described above. You may have known them as a grandparent, aunt, parent, teacher, neighbor, or mentor. Or, they may be known indirectly to you as a philosopher, religious leader, writer, or historical figure. Somehow these persons connect with you on a deep, inner level. Name these three wise persons:

_____ , _____ , _____

2. Select one of these wise persons with whom you would like to talk at this time. This wise person would be able to offer answers for a current decision, dilemma, or just life in general.

3. Recall the qualities of this person whom you respect so much. Try to remember a couple of instances when he or she was helpful to you in the past. Sense his/her presence with you now.

4. On a sheet of paper start a dialogue by first greeting this wise person and stating why you are requesting guidance. Continue the dialogue with the wise person's imagined response. Continue your conversation in a natural manner. Do not force any words. Let the conversation flow in the manner you think it actually would with this person. You may reach a natural stopping point. If this happens, stop the conversation and pick it up at a later time.

5. If desired, complete steps 2–4 with other wise persons in your life.

6. Follow-up ideas: What ideas or actions resulted from your dialogue(s) with this wise person? Can you now contact this wise person more readily?

This idea is an adaptation of a technique from *A Journal Workshop* by Ira Progoff (1992), Jeremy Tarcher/Perigee Books.

EVOLUTION OF A PERSON #2

1. *Lifeline* (from now to death). List the events you *expect* and *want* to occur during the rest of your life. Try to estimate your age at each event (including your death). Consider the following major events: career/education changes; marriage/family plans; loss of significant others; lessening mental/physical powers; places you want to visit; special goals or dreams.

2. Follow-up questions: What are the one or two things that stand out to you on your projected lifeline? Which part of your life has the most incomplete predictions and what do you think this means? How does your estimate of your age at death influence how you are living now and in the near future?

3. Consider completing this activity during some time of "active solitude" (see the article entitled "Active Solitude" in this section).

4. Discuss or write a reaction paper on what you've learned from this activity.

PERSONAL GOAL—A QUALITY LIFE

Within the next year I will enrich the quality of my life by:

Goal 1:

Needed actions, support, and resources:

Timeline:

Progress notes (use extra page if necessary):

Goal 2:

Needed actions, support, and resources:

Timeline:

Progress notes (use extra page if necessary):

Epilogue

Healthy growth means living in a stream of change. We are continually modifying and discarding ways of being. Sometimes we determine when and how we will change, sometimes not. What was fitting in one era of our lives may not be in the next. Even Thoreau ended his experiment at Walden Pond: "I left the woods for as good a reason as I went there. Perhaps it seemed to me that I had several more lives to live, and could not spare any more time for that one" (Thoreau, 1854/1962, p. 343).

We face our time to leave the woods when current ways of being no longer provide the needed stimulus for growth. Courage must be summoned for the challenge of re-inventing ourselves. The alternative is sameness and stagnation. If you peer deeply, the way will eventually reveal itself. Like a distant star, the light may be faint but its source is strong. A glimmer is all you need. You may discover, like Thoreau, that "if one advances in the direction of his dreams, and endeavors to live the life which he has imagined, he will meet with a success unexpected" (Thoreau, 1854/1962, p. 343).*

---

*Thoreau, H. (1854/1962). *Thoreau: Walden and other writings,* J. W. Krutch, Ed. New York: Bantam Books, Inc.